Arcadia for All

The Legacy of a Makeshift Landscape

Arcadia for All
The Legacy of a Makeshift Landscape

Dennis Hardy
and Colin Ward

Photography by Dot Davies

Five Leaves

www.fiveleaves.co.uk

Arcadia for All
Dennis Hardy and Colin Ward

This edition published in 2004
by Five Leaves Publications,
PO Box 81, Nottingham NG5 4ER
info@fiveleaves.co.uk, www.fiveleaves.co.uk

First published by Mansell in 1984

ISBN: 0 907123 59 7

Five Leaves acknowledges financial support from
Arts Council England

Typeset by Four Sheets Design and Print
Printed in Great Britain

Contents

Foreword to the new edition

Since this book first appeared from the publisher Mansell, and rapidly became out of print, we have been grateful to Ann Rudkin of Alexandrine Press, who originally commissioned the book, for her efforts to find a publisher for a new edition, and we are indebted to Ross Bradshaw of Five Leaves Publications for taking on this role.

The climate of town and country planning as a public activity has changed since this book was published, but the issues involved have not. We were fortunate in appearing with our notebooks in time to gather the reflections of the first generation of 'plotlanders'. Their closest equivalent in contemporary Britain has been the New Age settlers, seeking a place where they could live on their own terms while consuming far fewer resources and making very small demands on the environment.

The argument has been expressed very effectively in Simon Fairlie's book *Low Impact Development: Planning and People in a Sustainable Countryside* (Oxford: Jon Carpenter, 1996) and in a subsequent series of publications drawing upon Chapter 7 of the Rio Declaration of the governments of the major nations in 1992 (Chapter 7, Flaxdrayton Farm, South Petherton, Somerset TA13).

Agenda 21 of that Declaration, agreed by the British government of the day, urged that "all governments should, as appropriate, support the shelter efforts of the urban and rural poor by adopting and/or adapting existing codes and regulations to facilitate their access to land finance and low cost building materials."

This was the claim of the low-income re-populators of rural England, at a time when a dozen official reports were seeking to remedy the rural depopulation of the early twentieth century. A hundred years later, a combination of market forces and the assumptions of the administrators of planning legislation, coupled with the end of local authority rentable housing and with the growth of what is known as the NIMBY factor ('Not in *my* backyard'), have ensured that incoming low-income people are successfully excluded from rural England.

In compiling this book we confined our surveys to the south-east of England and the London hinterland, but the plotland phenomenon was not confined to this region. Every industrial conurbation in Britain once had these escape routes to the country, river or sea. For the West Midlands there was the Severn Valley or North Wales, for Glasgow there was the Ayrshire coast and even the banks of Loch Lomond. Serving the towns and cities of the West Riding there was the Yorkshire coast and the Humber estuary, and for those of Tyneside and Tees-side the coasts of Northumberland and Durham.

It is as though a proportion of the population felt obliged to follow an ancient human custom in seeking out some place, however hard to find, where people could build for themselves. We have not yet seen studies of the plotland hinterland of other urban regions, but there have been a number of detailed studies of some of the areas described in this book.

For example, there is a range of well-illustrated local histories, published by Phillimore of Chichester, including *Basildon Plotlands* by Deanna Walker (2001); *Canvey Island* by Geoff Sarsby (1992); and *Peacehaven: A Pictorial History* (1993) by Bob Poplett, who was a valuable contributor to our own research. The plotlands have also provided the background to at least one novel, Derek Beaven's *If the Invader Comes* (Fourth Estate, 2001) and to a 1997 BBC drama series produced by Louis Marks and written by Jeremy Brock under the title *Plotlands*. Sad to say, the remaining plotland sites that are most frequently in the news today are those where that land was originally leasehold rather than freehold, and where an incoming landlord has been determined to find a more profitable use of the site.

We are grateful to a long series of wellwishers of this book.

Preface

In the first half of the twentieth century a unique landscape emerged along the coast, on the riverside and in the countryside, more reminiscent of the American frontier than of a traditionally well-ordered English landscape. It was a makeshift world of shacks and shanties, scattered unevenly in plots of varying size and shape, with unmade roads and little in the way of services.

To the local authorities (who dubbed this type of landscape the 'plotlands') it was something of a nightmare, an anarchic rural slum, always one step ahead of evolving but still inadequate environmental controls. Places like Jaywick Sands, Canvey Island and Peacehaven became bywords for the desecration of the countryside.

But to the plotlanders themselves, Arcadia was born. In a converted bus or railway carriage, perhaps, and at a cost of only a few pounds ordinary city-dwellers discovered not only fresh air and tranquillity but, most prized of all, a sense of freedom. Revisiting the plotlands has enabled us to record how these settlers themselves valued what others frequently maligned. With the benefit of hindsight, we have also been able to reflect on some of the wider issues raised, and case studies are used to illustrate the extent and variety of the plotland experience.

In confrontations that ensued, between custodians of the environment and these new Arcadians, questions arise that are no less important today than they were at the time. Can private property of this sort really offer a route to freedom? What is a proper balance between public control and individual initiative? Should the role of planning be 'draconian action' or 'benign neglect'? Is there room today for this kind of self-help in creating one's own housing and living environment?

Comparisons are made with similar developments in other parts of the world in the United States, elsewhere in Europe and in Third World countries. Parallels are also drawn with contemporary initiatives, and the scope for new experiments is examined. To the extent that the English plotlands were part of a wider trend, are there lessons for housing and planning today?

Early twentieth-century plotlands have now all but disappeared, but the legacy of this strange landscape is still with us in a variety of ways.

Acknowledgments

We gratefully acknowledge support for this research, in the form of a two-year project grant from the then Social Science Research Council. The research was based at Middlesex Polytechnic (now Middlesex University), and we wish to record our gratitude for the institutional support that has been generously provided.

At a personal level, Dot Davies has taken on the photographic work in the project, and her professional skill and enthusiasm have been greatly appreciated. Likewise, our thanks to Alison Shepherd for handling the map collection and cartographic work; and to other colleagues for their warm support and practical help in a variety of ways. We are also grateful to Marian Sheppard for her expert typing of a lengthy manuscript.

Elsewhere our research has gained from the invaluable assistance of numerous contacts. Examining a theme like the plotlands, on the margins of the accepted history of housing, planning, conservation and the dreams of ordinary people leads us into aspects of unrecorded history where everyone's recollections are important and are a key to other sources. Some of our informants, both plotlanders and local government officers, asked that their contribution should not be recorded, but we are indebted to a great variety of people who have provided anything from a comprehensive local history to an individual nugget of information. Among people with a general view of the plotland phenomenon we must thank Martin Gaskell, Anthony King, Tom Clarke and John Noble, and we have a particular debt to students at every level who have examined one aspect or another of plotlands. Their work is acknowledged in the source notes.

For information about particular places, we are especially grateful in the case of Rye Bay to Miss Pat Green, Mr J.H. Daniels, Mrs Pauline Miles and officers of Rother District Council; for Peacehaven to Bob Poplett and to staff at the Peacehaven Library in the Meridian Centre; for Shoreham Beach to Dr Peter Brandon; and for the Selsey Peninsula to Robert Hamlin. On the East Coast, for telling us about Jaywick Sands, we wish to thank Percy Harding, Mrs Elizabeth Moorcroft, Mrs Ivy Robinson and staff at Clacton County Library; for Canvey Island we are grateful to Fred McCave, Sir Bernard Braine and Stephen Ralph; and for the Isle of Sheppey to Professor Ray Pahl and Claire Wallace. Elsewhere, our thanks to Andrew Day, Mark Gimson, Mr A. Selby and to Mrs Wood of the East Hampshire Planning Department for information on inland sites in Kent and Surrey; to Mr N. Timpson of Wycombe District Council Planning Department and members of the Thameside Residents Association on the Thames Valley; to Mr Cadman of the Isle of Wight Planning Department on Cranmore; to Mrs Doreen Biggs and to Mrs Joyce Bellamy and colleagues at the Greater London Council on Havering Park; to past and present officers of the Essex County Council Planning Department, Rochford and Basildon District Councils, Basildon Development Corporation and to the Essex County Record Office, and to Mrs Elizabeth Granger, Maurice Warrington, Betty Watts, Brian Cumbers, Mr L.W. Ramuz and John Whittam on South-East Essex; and to John Fisher and Terry Philpot on South Woodham Ferrers.

Our interpretation of current American developments has been supported by the British Academy which made this part of our research possible. In turn, we are indebted to Professor Roger Barnett at the University of the Pacific, Stockton, and Professor James Vance at the University of California, Berkeley for personal interviews and help with site visits. We also benefited from conversations with colleagues at the Departments of Urban and Regional Planning and of Geography at Florida State University, Tallahassee, and the Department of City and Regional Planning at the University of California, Berkeley.

Finally, we are greatly indebted to our editors, Ann Rudkin, the late Professor Gordon Cherry and Professor Anthony Sutcliffe for their kind encouragement coupled with constructive criticism and comments.

In the end, of course, not everyone will agree with all that is written, and any errors and omissions are ours.

Chapter 1

Property and Freedom

Grant me, indulgent Heaven! a rural seat
Rather contemptible than great

(Nahum Tate, 'The Choice', in Sir Francis Meynell, *Memorable Poetry*, 1965)

Traditional concentrations of cities and urban life gave way in the early twentieth century to a new landscape of dispersal. Rings of low-density houses with gardens encircled the closely-packed streets of earlier years; images of green replaced a backcloth of relentless grey. Popular, if illusory, dreams of country cottages and a lost rural order underpinned a modern taste for villas in their grounds, twelve to an acre.

For holidays as well as homes, towns reached ever further into the countryside, a fragile countryside already in the throes of change. Demands for green field sites, fresh air and a sight of the sea seemed insatiable. Even the new suburbanites, themselves refugees from the city, joined the seasonal exodus for weekend breaks and holidays. Sylvan retreats, romantic river valleys, gentle hills and vantage points but, most of all, the evocative features of a varied coastline lured more and more away from the towns to a lost Arcadia.

England was suddenly a smaller place. Beyond the suburbs, themselves a product of people moving out, the new ways were soon to make their mark. Roadhouses along the arterials, teahouses perched on clifftops, riverside hotels, petrol pumps in picturesque villages, advertisements painted on cottage roofs and walls, charabancs and caravans all bore witness to a process of dispersal.

It was as part and parcel of this new landscape, alongside more conventional developments, that a curious makeshift world emerged. Defying even the minimal building codes of the day, a motley of makeshift structures, often on the most unlikely sites, carried dispersal to its very limits.

What was it about these settlements that made them so unconventional, and where were they? Were they peculiar to their time, or did they have roots in earlier periods? Why was it that they flourished when they did, and how far were they a part of broader processes? And,

1

as an instance of small-scale property ownership, how can they be interpreted in terms of conflicting views on property and freedom?

MAKESHIFT LANDSCAPES

My little plot I have not forgot
It is mine I am sure, but I am so poor
That I cannot afford to build a door

(From a poetry competition in *Peacehaven Post*, Vol. 1, No. 2, 1921)

If there is a single key to the appearance and location of this makeshift world, it is that of 'marginality'. Frequently such developments were to be found on marginal land, neglected by commercial builders or spurned by farmers suffering hard times in the face of overseas competition. Sites liable to flood, steep slopes, shingle ridges and wind-swept sand-dunes, heavy clays or dry chalky uplands all offered a place in the sun for the enterprising, if not the rich.

Invariably it was a landscape put together on the cheap, a manifestation by poor people of the fashionable trend for a place in the country. Plots of land were bought cheaply and sometimes, through squatting, acquired at no cost at all. And the varied structures they accommodated were more a product of necessity than of a conscious sense of Arcadian design. In a period when the idea of a 'property-owning democracy' gained political credence, this makeshift process opened the way for more people to own their own property than would otherwise have been the case.

Although essentially a landscape of the poor this very fact, in turn, attracted to such areas its own 'Bohemian' clientele. Actors and actresses, artists and writers, stars of music halls and early films enjoyed and, in turn, contributed to the libertarian atmosphere of such places. In some cases, too, the simple life and ethnic architecture won the hearts of businessmen and their families, who could well have afforded a more conventional bungalow or villa.

Quite apart from localised examples of a conscious Bohemian influence, other factors — a pressing need for economy, the direct involvement of unskilled builders, and the challenge of marginal sites — combined to produce a brand of architecture that was, to say the least, unique. It was invariably a world of single-storey houses, simply built and often using wood, though never refusing whatever material (corrugated iron, asbestos, pre-cast concrete and bricks) lay at hand. Some could have taken their place alongside more conventional bungalows but others, a colourful kaleidoscope of shacks and shanties, were a world apart.

Conversions were widespread, demonstrating considerable invention and yielding economy as a reward. Of these, redundant railway carriages proved especially popular. In the inter-war years there were few parts of

2

East Bognor Regis: converted railway carriages

the country where railway companies were not shedding out-dated stock, and the sturdy construction of Victorian carriages made them an ideal choice. As little as £15 could secure, delivered to your own site, a ready-made retreat with character that grew with the years. Sometimes the railway companies themselves retained ownership of their stock — converting corridor carriages into camping coaches. In 1939 the four main companies owned more than four hundred of these, scattered in sidings in various parts of the country [1].

Other than railway carriages, old bus bodies, vans, trams and even a disbanded aircraft fuselage provided a basis for on-site conversion. Garden sheds also found a new lease of life, while in one case a small colony of 'mud huts' was built along a railway embankment. Another popular source was that of surplus army huts from the First World War. In the development of new smallholdings, this proved to be as attractive to official bodies as to private individuals. The Board of Agriculture, for instance, saw in surplus army huts a cheap way to settle returning soldiers on the land:

> We estimate that if the material were placed at the disposal of the Board, it would be possible to remove, re-erect and convert a hut into a cottage with three bedrooms, at a total cost, including water supply and drainage, of £125, and that such a cottage if properly maintained would last for thirty years at least.
>
> A detached cottage with similar accommodation, but built of brick or stone, would probably cost £250 at the present time [2].

What made this makeshift landscape distinctive, though, was not simply the unusual architecture of individual buildings but equally their haphazard distribution. It is the overall layout with land subdivided into plots of varying size which endowed these areas with the term

3

'plotlands'. Sometimes a patchy distribution resulted when not all the plots were taken up; or sometimes individual cases of squatting varied the pattern. In other cases holdings were enlarged through the purchase of adjoining plots. Perhaps here and there enclosures were 'protected' by a fading notice declaring that the land was private, but often unused plots were left unattended or taken over for rough grazing. A landscape of scattered and irregular development, the plotlands stood in contrast to the predictability of well-ordered suburban estates that were built at the same time.

No less distinctive in the early plotlands was the lack of any overall planning and provision of services. Land was subdivided to enable the quickest and cheapest means of disposal, and the results showed little regard for amenity or for convenient access. Indeed, it was not uncommon to have to cross another plot to reach one's own. Roads were little more than lines on a map, and remained unmade for many years — rutted in the summer months, and waterlogged in winter. A mains water supply, sewerage system, electricity and other services passed the plotlands by. Likewise, shops, schools and other facilities which one would expect in a small community were few and far between. With their unfinished appearance and lack of amenities the plotlands were in some ways akin to frontier settlements in the New World.

Most of the plotlands were developed in the first half of the twentieth century, some before 1914 but the majority in the inter-war period. Though many have survived since then, their continuing formation came to an abrupt end with the introduction of effective planning legislation in 1947. With localised exceptions they never really constituted a large proportion of early twentieth-century development. Yet they were quite widely dispersed and attracted a degree of public concern that far exceeded what one might have expected in terms of their limited acreage. Few parts of the country escaped at the least isolated examples of shacks and rough conversions though larger concentrations of plotland development were more restricted [3].

Undoubtedly many were close to home, offering an easy escape from the city. So much the better if this proximity could be combined with a special landscape feature such as a lake, some hills, a river or woodland. In the days before green-belt restrictions there was little to check the proliferation of makeshift huts and shacks in prime sites. As the largest centre of population, London generated the greatest concentrations of plotland development, scattered here and there throughout the home counties.

The banks of the Thames and Lea were always popular with Londoners, in spite of perennial flooding and waterlogged conditions. Little chalets were built on vacant sites that others had spurned because of their marginal setting. No less popular were the drier slopes of the North Downs, with clusters of huts wherever opportunities arose along the entire length of the chalky ridge. Unlike the conspicuous presence of weekenders in the Chilterns to the northwest of London, many of these clusters were tucked away in the woodland that characterises the area. Writing in the late-1930s, S.B. Mais deplored the fact that:

4

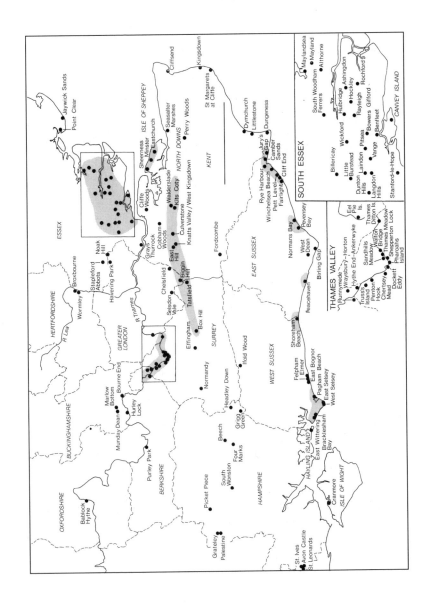

Jaywick Sands
Point Clear

ESSEX

Wormley
Broxbourne
Stapleford Abbots
Havering Park
Noak Hill

HERTFORDSHIRE

R Lea

Cliffe Woods
Cobham Woods
Grays Thurrock

Sheerness
Minster
Eastchurch

ISLE OF SHEPPEY

Wadesslade
Kitts Coty
Culverstone
Knatts Valley / West Kingsdown

NORTH DOWNS

Seasalter Marshes
Perry Woods

Cliffsend

Kingsdown

St Margarets at Cliffe

KENT

Dymchurch
Littlestone
Dungeness

Jury's Gap
Camber Sands
Cliff End
Farleigh
Pett Level
Winchelsea Beach
Rye Harbour

Fordcombe

EAST SUSSEX

Normans Bay
Pevensey Bay
West Dean
Birling Gap

Peacehaven

SURREY

East Hill
Biggin Hill
Tatsfield
Chelsfield
Selsdon Vale
Effingham
Box Hill

GREATER LONDON

R Thames

Normandy
Headley Down
Itold Wood

Shoreham Beach

WEST SUSSEX

Felpham
Elmer
East Bognor
Pagham Beach
East Selsey
West Selsey

Marlow Bottom
Munday Dean
Hurley Lock
Bourne End

BUCKINGHAMSHIRE

Purley Park

Beech
Grigg Green

South Wonston
Four Marks

Picket Piece

BERKSHIRE

Bablock Hythe

OXFORDSHIRE

Grateley
Palestine

HAMPSHIRE

HAYLING ISLAND
East Wittering
Bracklesham Bay

Cranmore

ISLE OF WIGHT

St Ives
Avon Castle
St Leonards

SOUTH ESSEX

Maylandsea
Mayland
Althorne
South Woodham Ferrers
Hulbridge
Ashingdon
Hockley
Rochford
Rayleigh
Bowers Gifford
Benfleet
Vange
Wickford
Pitsea
Laindon
Dunton Hills
Langdon Hills
Billericay
Little Burstead
Stanford-le-Hope

CANVEY ISLAND

THAMES VALLEY

Runnymede
Wraysbury
Horton
Hythe End
Ankerwyke
Sandhills Meadow
Truss's Island
Penton Hook
Chertsey Mead
Dockett Eddy
Eel Pie Is.
Thames Ditton Is.
Walton Bridge
Thames Meadow
Shepperton Lock
Pharoahs Island

the whole side of the Chiltern escarpment that leads down to Aston Rowant is now honeycombed with hideous shacks thrown haphazard like splodges of mud against a hillside once covered with trees. The hut-dwellers both get the view and spoil it [4].

City-dwellers elsewhere found their own distinctive retreats. Mancunians escaped to the Pennine fringes, to places like Marple and Mottram. Elsewhere river valleys were a source of attraction. Huts took their place at various points along the River Severn, within reach of the industrial towns of the West Midlands. Complete with examples of bus body conversions as many as 200 survive today in the Bridgnorth area, with further clusters in north Worcestershire. Dating from the 1920s, a smaller concentration can be found on the River Dee, some ten miles upstream from Chester. The River Wye also proved to be a popular choice — especially what others regarded as 'those unsightly booths that ring the Wye bank at Tintern' [5].

Sometimes Arcadia took the form of a lakeland setting, albeit perhaps a stretch of water resulting from subsidence, like Winsford Lower Flash in Cheshire. Pickmere is another Cheshire example, while further south in North Staffordshire timber and asbestos retreats lined the western shore of Rudyard Reservoir. In contrast, others sought relief from urban life in the shade and security of a nearby woodland. East Midlanders made for Charnwood Forest; with more localised examples elsewhere, like Hardwick Wood and Sutton Spring Wood near Chesterfield, or the Middlesbrough venue of Holmhouse Wood near Aislaby.

In contrast to places within easy reach, when it came to the coast distance was rarely an obstacle; sites beyond reach for a weekend visit were no less attractive as seasonal retreats. Right round the coast, as Dr J.A. Steers (who surveyed its entire length) observed, 'there are many instances of these hideous settlements' [6].

Sometimes these 'hideous settlements' amounted to little more than a small group of huts, though these were seen to be 'often as disfiguring as a large mass' [7]. The example of a cluster of makeshift structures on a remote stretch of Lancashire coastline near Cockersand Abbey was a case in point. Other examples included the string of huts, mixed with older fishermen's homes, along the Dungeness peninsula in Kent, and a variety of sites in South-West England.

In the wake of the Steers survey, regional civil servants took a closer look at the South West [8]. They confirmed that its greater distance from major population centres had not saved it from a widespread incidence of holiday huts and motley encampments. Tumbledown shacks on tumbledown cliffs, or railway carriages perched cheekily on sand dunes; from Severn Beach on the north coast, through Redcliffe Bay, Croyde and Hayle Towan; and then along the south coast to include Whitsand Bay, Exmouth and Beer, sizeable clusters were noted.

It was the larger colonies along the South and East Coast, though, which attracted greater attention. Aesthetes deplored them, but

Londoners loved the self-made resorts along the South Coast. Shoreham Beach, Peacehaven and Camber Sands were sizeable settlements in their own right that all grew rapidly from the early years of the twentieth century. Obsolete rolling stock, London trams and omnibuses faced seawards, alongside more conventional wood, brick and asbestos bungalows.

Likewise the open aspect of the East Coast eased the way for numerous examples of individual opportunism — enormously popular for cheap and healthy holidays, but consistently deplored for their impact on the scenery. In his survey Steers found much of which to complain on the East Coast:

> Amongst the worst is Flamborough Head where a whole town of hutments has completely ruined the scenery of that fine chalk headland... Miles of the Lincolnshire and Norfolk coasts are disfigured by long lines of jerry-built wooden erections, and parts of Essex are notorious for it [9].

With Jaywick Sands and Canvey Island, not to mention the smaller groupings around its estuaries, Essex was indeed 'notorious for it'. This notoriety, however, had a totally different meaning for the East Londoners who came to experience Arcadia than it did for the coastline surveyors and officials of the day.

As well as holiday settlements there are also interesting examples of plotlands designed for permanent occupation. These include schemes where farms were sold speculatively in plots of an acre or more for smallholdings, as at Cranmore on the Isle of Wight or St Leonards in Dorset. Typically though, the unrealistic expectations of speculators led to a mixed landscape of vacant plots, rough grazing, the odd workshop here and there, storage yards, and boarding kennels, interspersed with an occasional agricultural smallholding for which the original scheme was intended.

The largest instance of what soon emerged as a permanent plotland settlement is that of Laindon-Pitsea in South Essex. Scattered apparently at random on the heavy Essex clay, self-built cottages on plots of varying size coalesced to form what was described by officials as a vast rural slum [10]. But for those who lived there, in spite of conditions which evoked this description, the little plots offered a refuge from the slums of London (and, later, from the risk of air raids in the Second World War). To the plotlanders from the metropolis, enjoying fresh air and a little land, there could be no such thing as a 'rural slum'.

In the North-East of England permanent plotlands might mean, yet again, something different — in this case associated with coal-mining and the practice of assigning colliery houses for miners and their families. A miner who was sacked could also be expected to be evicted from the company's housing. Stories are told of how families then moved into the 'crees', cabins or huts which they had built in allotment gardens which they rented for 2s 6d a year from the local authority. In one area in the 1930s, thirty-two families were living on the allotments in Horden, while others were reduced to living in caves along the beach between Easington Colliery and Blackhall. One observer recalls an instance when a single family was evicted three times in two days when a miner was sacked from one pit, was taken on at another belonging to the same company, sacked again when this was discovered, and sacked from a third when his dismissal from the other two became known. His unfortunate family shunted its belongings on a handcart from one village to another, ending in the allotment gardens. Boys who lost their jobs at the mines would be obliged to leave their parental colliery-owned home, and move into a hut on the allotments, returning at weekends for a bath. One family at Horden Colliery, resigned to living on the allotments, bought with their savings a hut from the mail-order firm of J. Thorn, and contrived a kitchen and other amenities [11].

The story of permanent plotlands is certainly not always associated with hardship. Quite commonly, modest ventures designed for weekends and holidays in the 1920s and 1930s have evolved over the years into expensive and sought-after properties. With services now laid on, their choice sites overlooking the sea or commanding a fine countryside view have become highly marketable assets far removed from their original simplicity. In fact, it is this trend from temporary to permanent occupation which accounts for one of the most striking changes in the plotland landscape since the years of its inception.

Relatively few of the original makeshift structures remain in the present landscape. Perhaps surprisingly, in spite of all the rhetoric and the advent of a comprehensive planning system, their disappearance has only, in a limited number of cases, been the result of a deliberate clearance policy. In some cases, time has taken its toll; flimsy properties have decayed, or plot-owners have disappeared without trace. More commonly, though, the process has been one of market evolution — 'traded-up' over the years to replace one landscape with another. It has become a landscape of *nouveau* house-styles and outward signs of wealth, consciously rejecting its humble and even illegitimate past. Yet with its irregular layouts and conspicuous locations, not to mention the persistence of an odd shack, such areas never entirely throw off their makeshift ancestry.

QUEST FOR ARCADIA

The makeshift landscape of the early twentieth century was very much a product of its age — with new social opportunities to weigh against new demands on the environment. And yet, at the same time, there are elements in the new scene with roots running deeper into a history of popular movements. Two traditions, in particular, can be discerned — the one, 'pastoralism', with its call back to an image of lost rural bliss and to an affinity with Nature; the other, 'agrarianism', with its ideal of peasant proprietorship and of reclaiming land which had been wrongly appropriated in times past. Though diverse in origin, the two traditions can be seen to coalesce in twentieth-century plotlands.

8

'SWEET ARCADY'

In pastoralism is an image of a purer way of life rooted in a past, more natural setting. It is a fantasy of gentle scenery, of mellow farms and villages and of beautiful people filled with love; it is a world of perfection and harmony, of the Garden of Eden before the Fall. Poets, painters, musicians and writers enriched and varied the image over centuries.

When Sir Philip Sidney wrote of Arcadia in the sixteenth century he revived the Greek tradition of such a place:

> Arcadia among all the Provinces of Greece was ever held in singular reputation, partly for the sweetness of the air and other natural benefits; but principally for the moderate and well-tempered minds of the people following the course of Nature... [12].

Through subsequent use the term 'Arcadia' has come to mean 'an idealised region or scene of simple pleasure, rustic innocence and uninterrupted quiet... a rural paradise' [13].

For some this rural paradise was centred on villages and village life; it was this, for instance, that was immortalised in Oliver Goldsmith's 'Deserted Village' in 1769. Others looked more to natural beauty and to the fullness of the countryside; as in Abraham Cowley's 'The Wish':

> Oh Fields! Oh Woods! when, when shall I be made The Happy Tenant of your shade? [14].

With the advance of science, nature lost some of the mystique and superstition surrounding it. In place of fear and detachment it became something to admire and discover. By the eighteenth century, landscape architects had joined the ranks of 'pastoralists', creating and exploiting natural scenery in pursuance of extravagant backcloths for new country houses. Aristocrats were amongst the first to find enjoyment in a way of life shared between town and country, a form of existence which others of lesser means later tried to emulate. It was an attempt such as this which William Howitt observed in Nottingham in the 1830s — a landscape in which ordinary townsfolk had secured a modest place in the country:

> There are on the outskirts of Nottingham upwards of 5,000 gardens, the bulk of which are occupied by the working class... These lie on various sides of the town, in expanses of many acres in a place, and many of them as much as a mile and a half distant from the centre of the town... The advantage of these gardens to the working-class of a great manufacturing town is beyond calculation... [15].

9

As forerunners of a plotland type of development, the landscape is distinguished by a wide variety of summer-houses, greatly appreciated by Howitt:

Every garden has its summer-house; and these are of all scales and grades, from the erection of a few tub staves, with an attempt to train a pumpkin or a wild-hop over it, to substantial brick houses with glass windows, good cellars for a deposit of choice wines, a kitchen and all necessary apparatus, and a good pump to supply them with water. Many are very picturesque rustic huts, built with great taste, and hidden by tall hedges in a perfect little paradise of lawn and shrubbery — most delightful spots to go and read in with a pleasant party of friends. Some of these places which belong to the substantial tradespeople have cost their occupiers from one to five hundred pounds, and the pleasure they take in them may thence be imagined; but many of the mechanics have very excellent summer-houses, and there they delight to go and smoke a solitary pipe, as they look over the smiling face of their garden, or take a quiet stroll amongst their flowers; or to take a pipe with a friend; or to spend a Sunday afternoon, or a summer evening, with their families [16].

In Nottingham as, no doubt, elsewhere, industrialisation only served to heighten the attraction of a world now seemingly lost for ever. Earlier in the nineteenth century, Shelley, Coleridge, Southey and Wordsworth were amongst those who idealised nature against a growing backcloth of towns and factories. And some years later the pre-Raphaelites in their various ways sought to depict the essence and truth of nature.

Romanticism opened up two routes. The one was of sentimentality and nostalgia; Victorian profiles of rose-covered country cottages and ruddy-faced yeomanry. The other was a synthesis of intellect and emotion, of rationality and imagination; Thoreau's contemplation of his experience in a log cabin by a lake, or the writings of William Morris. Each had its own following, and each contributed to a consensus of powerful emotions that country life was better than town life, a feeling that grew stronger as the century progressed.

This idealisation of the country was strengthened by political writers, like Morris, Kropotkin and Tolstoy, portraying a new form of society without cities. And an interest, if not a total commitment in 'Back to nature', showed itself in natural history societies, in organised rambles and cycling excursions from the towns, and in a variety of practical schemes for decentralised settlements (amongst which Ebenezer Howard's for garden cities attracted most attention). Journals circulated to teach their readers about the morality of a simpler, more natural life:

To know that every May-time the hawthorn whitens for us, and the blackbird whistles, and the king-cups fill the meadows with their golden glory, and we poor prisoners drag our weary eyesight up and down the length of smoky bricks or desolate stucco and lose it all, because we or someone else cannot do without silk dresses, diamond rings and hot-house fruits! What wickedness it is when one comes to think of it! [17].

By the turn of the century those ordinary folk who sought to leave the city, if only for the weekend, were already bound up in a long and powerful tradition of 'anti-urbanism'. Love of the countryside and scorn for the towns had become a cultural trait, touching the very heart of unspoken consciousness and desires. For those who acted on impulse, it mattered not whether this idealisation of the countryside was born of dreams or reality. What mattered was the attraction of an image, powerful enough to lure townsfolk to their tiny plots in woodland and marsh, on gentle southern hills or quiet river valleys. In all innocence thousands followed a path charted by poets and others for centuries past.

'LAND FOR THE PEOPLE'

No less deep-rooted than pastoralism is a parallel tradition of agrarianism. Unique in Europe, the English peasant was not, as a rule, a landowner. That this was so contributed to a long-standing sense of grievance, surfacing from time to time in outright attempts to reclaim the few acres which individual farm labourers believed were rightly theirs. The injustice of the massive land reallocation following the Norman Conquest was never forgotten, though it was the tangible evidence of a long process of 'enclosures' which served periodically to fuel the fires of discontent. Even into the nineteenth century common rights were usurped, and historic smallholdings and cottagers' farms disappeared.

'Agrarianism' amounted to repeated attempts to retrieve the situation and to 'resettle' a dispossessed peasantry. Mediaeval peasant revolts, the Diggers and others in the seventeenth century, the Chartist land campaign in the 1840s, and various land movements in the late nineteenth century all reflected the endurance of this basic impulse. The goal of a peasant proprietorship was seldom far down on a radical political agenda; a few acres of land retained a powerful lure.

What was it that drove people, time and again, to claim a few acres of land as their right? Undoubtedly, as those who achieved their goal found, wealth and an easy life were never amongst the rewards. Instead, what stands out is a sense of seeing justice done — of getting back that to which everyone has a right; and a belief that owning one's plot of land would secure independence and freedom. Added to these objectives, later in the nineteenth century, Robert Blatchford and others stressed the healthy life, in contrast to the debilitating conditions in towns.

Irrationally, perhaps, but understandably, the modern plotlanders themselves drew on these historic reasons for settlement. Far removed

11

though they were from the situation which gave rise to early agrarianism, there were still grounds for echoing the original claims. Their little plots — rarely of a size that could enable economic subsistence — were still to many a living symbol of freedom and independence.

Moreover the process of acquiring modern plots bears more than a passing resemblance to 'rural squatting', the means by which many staked a claim to land in times past [18]. Squatting dates back as long as the process of land settlement itself, and most cultures have a traditional belief in 'squatters' rights' whether these are recognised by statute or not.

Not only throughout Britain, but in many parts of Europe and in the New World, it was widely accepted that if a person succeeded in erecting a dwelling on common or waste land between sunset and sunrise and lighting a fire in it he could not lawfully be dispossessed. There are innumerable variants on this formula and on the definition of the amount of land that might be enclosed. There is also a variety of beliefs as to the period of time — six months, a-year and-a-day, thirty years — in which property might be occupied unchallenged to gain title. In statutory English law no squatter obtains a good title until he has retained against the assumed owner of the property open and peaceful possession for twelve years. The very use of the phrase 'a good title' implies the acceptance of the view taken for granted by Gerrard Winstanley in the seventeenth century that the very myth of freehold ownership implied some royal 'true owner' granting these freeholds, and that this royal personage might be (as he was in 1649) dispossessed of this ultimate ownership.

Many of the squatter houses of the sixteenth to eighteenth centuries can still be recognised. In some counties they are built close by the roadside and parallel to it, in others they are irregularly scattered around the village green or randomly distributed on it. Hoskins records that:

> Manor court rolls all over England and Wales contain numerous references to these squatters on the wastes in the seventeenth and eighteenth centuries. Frequently they were people who had been squeezed out of the lowland villages where no more land was available. Hence in a county like Northamptonshire we find that the so-called 'forest villages' in the seventeenth century were on an average half as populous again as the non-forest villages, because they had attracted so many of the rural poor who found the various common rights in the forests sufficient to give them a precarious living [19].

An Act was passed in the reign of Elizabeth I 'against the erecting and maintaining of cottages' with the aim of 'avoiding of the great inconveniences which are found to grow by the creating... of great numbers and multitudes of cottages' [20]. The Act was really directed against the poor, though in Dorothy George's account, it

12

allowed cottages for the impotent poor to be built on the village waste, with the consent of the lord of the manor and the parish officers. Other cottages might be licensed by the justices in Quarter Sessions, and much of the business of the Sessions in the seventeenth century was taken up by the pressing question of cottages, with ordering their demolition or sanctioning their erection, always as a measure connected with poor relief and the parish poor [21].

In 1662, after the restoration of the monarchy, a further law, the Act of Settlement, restricted the movement of those who were not freeholders or who could not afford a rent of £10 a year. Between these two pieces of legislation directed against 'cottagers and paupers' — in other words against squatters — there occurred the most famous of what we would now call 'ideologically inspired squats', that of Winstanley and the Diggers at Walton-on-Thames in Surrey in 1649. Setting the background for the Diggers' movement, Christopher Hill remarks that:

> the Midlands rising of 1607, in which we first come across the names Levellers and Diggers, was caused by enclosure... Just as the breakdown of the authority of the state church in the 1640s allowed underground sects to surface, so the breakdown of secular authority released a series of riots against enclosure all over the country [22].

He cites the conclusion of a contemporary historian that:

> the whole Digger movement can be plausibly regarded as the culmination of a century of unauthorised encroachments upon the forests and wastes by squatters and local commoners, pushed on by land shortage and pressure of population [23].

In the eighteenth and nineteenth centuries, the possession in this way of small plots of land was by no means so widespread or such an obvious threat to the authorities as at the time of the Diggers. For one thing, the possibilities diminished with the enclosure of common and waste land in this period. Even so, the practice undoubtedly persisted, often in the form of simple cottages erected on roadside verges or odd patches of unenclosed ground. As late as the 1820s, turf huts of squatters were to be found on waste land quite close to London. In Surrey, for instance [24], there is evidence that the practice posed sufficient of a problem at the end of the century to merit special legislation.

Other examples of squatting in London's countryside can be found, and not always on land that would be categorised as 'marginal'. A Victorian historian of Windsor Castle says that at one time 'paupers had squatted in many of the towers' [25], and in the early nineteenth century Ann Hicks, an apple woman, annexed a portion of Hyde Park

13

at the east end of the Serpentine. Her shanty, known as the White Cottage, grew in stages until finally it was removed by the authorities [26]. Another squatter who gradually increased her holding was Mrs Kit Nash, who at the turn of the century had a cottage between Harmer Green and Burnham Green in Hertfordshire. Katherine Lloyd writes:

> Year by year she extended the boundaries of her plot by trimming the bramble hedges always from the inside, allowing them to spread and flourish on the outside. There was a complaint, but she dealt with that by brandishing a pitchfork... She had only a squatter's title to the land, but after her death this was legally registered in her name by the local authority, and it was sold so that they could recover the money which she owed them [27].

As another instance in Southern England, the New Forest was one of those marginal districts where squatting was extensive, and the author of an old guide-book explains:

> Long years ago... if a hut could be raised and a hearth made, so that the fire could be alight before the Crown authorities came upon the scene, the hut and so much land as could be fenced in became freehold property in perpetuity... As the authorities became more vigilant, the following slow and stealthy method was resorted to, which often escaped observation. The inside of the hedge was cut, and the briars and stuff thrown outside. These shot out and formed a sort of rolling fence, and so the would-be squatters kept trimming the inside and adding to the outside. Another method was to put a fence round, and grow a hedge gradually outside the fence. Then the fence was moved to the outside of the hedge [28].

This writer admired the self-sufficiency, prosperity and independence of the New Forest squatters and their 'singular combination of reticence and self-possession, with good humour and friendliness' [29]. With the exception, perhaps, of prosperity, it is the type of judgement which modern plotlanders might also attract.

Accounts of the twentieth-century plotlands are in fact laced with stories, rumour and fact, of plots that have been 'illegally' acquired through squatting. Disputed strips of coast-line, hidden pockets of woodland, the odd patch by a river, and frequently plots long abandoned or which have never been occupied by their original owners all bear witness to this type of story. Though rumour and fact are often difficult to extricate, an association of plotlands with squatting is not surprising. What it amounts to, very often, is an attempt by people with marginal incomes to secure a small plot of marginal land. Squatting becomes, as it did at various times in the past, a product of the 'marginality' of the process. People attracted by the idea of a place

14

out of town, yet denied the economic means to follow the conventional route of paying market prices and dealing with professional traders in land, will look for cheaper alternatives. And these will inevitably be found not on high value land but in areas neglected because they flood, or yield a poor crop, or have long been in disputed ownership. It is to such areas of opportunity that common people, of necessity, have turned in the past — the twentieth-century plotlands simply adding a new chapter to a long history of popular possession of land.

HOMES, HOLDINGS AND HOLIDAYS

So an impulse for acquiring small plots of land out of town existed well before the twentieth century. But until then it remained essentially a latent force, with nothing like the scale of dispersal that followed. In its new form the incidence of scattered plots with makeshift retreats is concentrated within a fifty-year period from around 1890 to the end of the 1930s, with a peak of activity between 1919 and 1939. Circumstances were particularly conducive to plotland development in that period.

More than a hundred years of industrial capitalism had seen many changes, including a significant shift of power away from the old landowning class and towards the new masters of industry. Reflecting this shift, towns gained in influence at the expense of the countryside. One dominant class changed places with another — aristocratic landowners lost ground to industrialists — but in terms of a more general distribution of property throughout society little changed. For industrial labourers and their families inhabiting what were, arguably, the world's richest cities, their share of this new-found wealth was unimpressive. They owned neither the full fruits of their own labour, nor in most cases their own home; capital might amount to paltry savings in a Friendly Society, and possessions would be few and of little worth. Within a system ostensibly wedded to private property, the majority of the population saw that which was justly theirs appropriated by a dominant class. The ownership of property remained grossly uneven in its distribution.

In time, however, as a direct outcome of continuing capitalist development, some changes in property ownership became inevitable. In essence, the very system which created an industrial working class (and which, through sustained economic growth, increased the power and potential of that class) was forced in various ways to make some concessions in the form of a more equal distribution of wealth. These concessions, underwritten by a steadily growing surplus of capital accumulated since the early days of industrialisation, are not to be exaggerated. They were in no sense of a magnitude to threaten the viability of the system as a whole and, indeed, simply helped to guarantee its survival. The relative balance of wealth changed little in this period with enormous inequities persisting but, in absolute terms, new material opportunities opened up for a greater number of people;

15

those who had simply produced now became consumers as well. Not least of these opportunities was an increasing use of land, hitherto beyond reach, for housing, recreation and even (with the breaking-up of traditional estates) for small-scale farming.

Making comparable, albeit larger, demands on land was a growing and assertive middle class. With new recruits to the ranks, especially as a result of a substantial growth in professional and service occupations in the twentieth century, the demand for material symbols of their position was greatly increased. A survey in 1938-39 showed that 64 per cent of those earning above £250 annually (a rough measure of the middle-class income threshold) were either buying or owned their own homes [30] — and most of these would have been in what T.S. Eliot described as 'the land of lobelias and tennis flannels' [31]. With a much higher proportion of disposable income than working-class families it was these same people who led the field for the cheap and popular cars on the market, for weekend excursions into the countryside, and holidays in villas by the sea.

The early twentieth century, particularly the 1920s and 1930s, saw radical changes in the ownership and use of land beyond the traditional urban centres. It saw the outward sprawl of towns and cities, consuming acres of open land in a compelling quest for more spacious housing; it saw the fragmentation of agricultural estates and the sale of smaller farms which had been used as farmland for centuries; and, finally, it saw an unprecedented search for quiet beauty spots, country lanes, hilltops with views, woodlands and rivers and, most of all, for a stake along a diminishing natural coastline.

There were, then, three great waves of demand which swept out into the countryside in this period changing, in turn, patterns.of housing, farming and recreation. And the argument will be pursued that the makeshift world of the plotlands was no more or less than the outwash of these three waves. The incidence of plotlands, for all their differences in appearance, was 'a product of the same general processes that transformed the use of land in more conventional ways. They were 'down-market' manifestations of more extravagant dreams to own and enjoy land for housing, farming and recreation, but they were still very much a part of the same 'genre'.

'A HOME OF YOUR OWN'

And the leader looks at last toward the people,
People asking for a home, a plot of earth... [32].

Owning a home of one's own is largely a characteristic of the twentieth century. As a result of the particular process of housebuilding and wage structures of nineteenth-century industrialisation, it was common practice for most people to rent rather than own their accommodation. Even by 1914, only about 10 per cent of all dwellings were owner-occupied. The big change came in the twenty years or so after the First

World War so that, by 1939, this proportion of owner-occupation had increased to 31 per cent of all dwellings [33].

Ironically some of the first examples of post-1918 'home ownership' were in the form of plotland development. A dire shortage of housing after the war encouraged many to take matters into their own hands. Numerous army huts and other obsolete war materials led to a variety of temporary shanties (some of which proved to be less temporary than expected). A newspaper report of 1922 described the makeshift home of an ex-soldier living with his wife and four children under a patchwork shack of tarpaulins, old army groundsheets and bits of tin and canvas. 'If they'd told me in France that I should come back to this I wouldn't have believed it. Sometimes I wished to God the Germans had knocked me out' [34]. Elsewhere, 'many respectable families went to live in... army huts, wooden and metal, roughly adapted to civil life, and even in old railway carriages, and converted coal barges and lighters' [35].

But these were exceptions, unrecorded in the figure of three million new private houses built in the inter-war period. Peak years were between 1934 and 1939, with as many as 290,000 houses added to the stock in 1935 alone. The new houses were unevenly distributed throughout the country, with a distinct concentration in London and the South-East. Most dramatic was the outward accretion of the conurbation itself, growing in population by two million between 1918 and 1939 but expanding its area fivefold. And along the coast, unconfined to the towns and older resorts, new housing followed the line of the sea wherever it could, consuming former beauty-spots and transforming fragile skylines.

Significantly, the pattern of these changes in the cult of home ownership is reflected to a close degree in the incidence of plotlands. In terms of timing, private house-building occurred at little more than a trickle before 1914, before peaking in the 1920s and, more especially, the 1930s. Likewise, in terms of distribution, most new housing is concentrated in countryside around the cities and along the coast. To explain the plotlands it seems reasonable to look first at those forces which accounted for the growth of home ownership in general.

Explanations for the growth of home ownership vary less in identifying the various factors involved than in the relative importance given to them. It is obvious, for instance, that the dispersal effects of electricity and new forms of transport played their part in suburbanisation, but these technological factors were hardly, in themselves, a reason for what occurred. Likewise, one can point to a steady increase in legislation from the first public health acts, through to measures to control rent at the time of the First World War, all of which contrived to reduce the profitability of the landlord who built and rented houses to tenants. There was, too, the rise of the building societies as a major source of housing finance and, in the 1930s, contributing through advertisements to the general idea of home ownership as a good and desirable goal. The ethic of home ownership was supported, no less, by successive governments as an antidote to political extremism and, in the Smilesian tradition, as an incentive to thrift and responsible citizenry. Moreover, a continuing rise in real incomes not only encouraged a corresponding rise in expectations, but also provided a limited means to meet these in the form of better housing. And then, especially in the 1930s, there were the favourable economic circumstances of low-cost land and building materials, coupled with low interest rates (4½ per cent in 1934) for borrowers.

For reasons such as these, then, the way was open for a massive extension of home ownership. And, yet, in purely economic terms, the whole process was still for a restricted market. In spite of falling house prices in the 1930s (half the houses built in 1939 were sold for less than £600, compared with one-third at that price or less in 1931 [36]) and in spite of new arrangements between building societies, insurance companies and builders to bring down the initial payment on new properties to only 5 per cent, a home of one's own was still beyond the reach of most people. Office workers, teachers, shopkeepers and better-paid industrial workers in regular employment joined the ranks of the property-owners, but many more were excluded. Even by 1939 only about 18 per cent of working-class families were owner-occupiers (compared with the national figure of 31 per cent) [37]. For some of this latter group, the new local authority housing of the 1920s provided an acceptable alternative.

Sandwiched between the two, however, between the artisans of the council estates and the petty bourgeoisie of suburbia were many others, swayed by the arguments for home ownership yet without the economic means to enter the main race. It was from would-be property owners such as these that many of the plotlanders came to make their own distinctive bid for a house and some land. A little cottage in the Essex plotlands painstakingly built with materials carried on bus and bicycle from East London on days off work, and aptly named 'Perserverance' (sic), typifies the immense sacrifice needed to achieve what became almost a mystical objective of acquiring a home of one's own.

'THREE ACRES AND A COW'

Though on nothing like the same scale as suburbanisation, the fragmentation of agricultural land into smallholdings was of more than localised importance. The process began in the 1870s, with the competitive effects of cheaper food imports; and problems for the large landowner were exacerbated in the early twentieth century by higher levels of taxation and death duties [38]. In the face of cheap imports of grain and refrigerated meat, F.M.L. Thompson describes the dramatic change in the rural landscape over a period of forty years at the end of the nineteenth century:

> The English countryside has probably never looked more prosperous than it did in the 1860s. The farming landscape was neat and trim, businesslike and well cared for... The countryside has seldom looked more dejected than at the turn of the present

18

century; neglected and overgrown hedges, weed-infested meadows and pastures, decaying thatch, dilapidated buildings, untidy farmyards; everywhere examples of lack of attention, misfortune, or despair could be seen... [39].

Farmers who were owner-occupiers were often obliged to sell their property at throw-away prices, or have it done for them by their receivers in bankruptcy. Land speculators were often the only people with any interest in purchasing, and many a plotland was a product of this type of enterprise. A second reason for the disposal of large holdings was the culmination of political controversies over land ownership, which in the nineteenth century had begun 'as an attack upon political privilege — and ended as a demand for wholesale dispossession and redistribution' [40]. Effective legislation, early in the century, followed by the deaths of so many sons and heirs of landowning families in the First World War, put land on the market which had been held by the same families for centuries:

This legislative process culminated in Lloyd George's famous 1908 Budget with its Increment Value Duty and Undeveloped Land Duty which aimed at breaking up once and for all the 'land monopoly'. It is plausible to regard Lloyd George's measures as having been decisive. They produced a trickle of land sales between 1910 and 1914 which became a deluge once the First World War was completed. In four years between 1918 and 1922 England, in the words of a famous *Times* leader of the day, 'changed hands'. One quarter of the area of England was bought and sold in this hectic period of transaction, a disposal of land which was unprecedented since the dissolution of the monasteries in the sixteenth century [41].

Coincident with the availability of farmland was a movement to convert at least some of this into smallholdings. The idea was popularised (amongst others by the 'Allotments and Small Holdings Association') in the slogan of 'three acres and a cow'. It was argued that small plots of land had the dual attraction of stemming the flow of labourers into the towns and even of reversing the flow with a new policy of settlement in the countryside. It was this dual aim that the Liberal Party advocated in the 1885 Election, and which remained on the political agenda for some years to come:

Besides the creation of smallholdings, local authorities should have compulsory powers to purchase land... for the purpose of garden and field allotments to be let at fair rents to all labourers who might desire them, plots up to one acre of arable and three or four acres of pasture [42].

This was far from being a reactionary dream of the political right, desirous to turn back the clock to an imagined harmonious world of

19

toiling peasants and benevolent squires. Liberal campaigners, who sought to re-establish or promote smallholdings as a solution to both rural and urban unemployment, were joined by radical trade unionists like Tom Mann and Ben Tillett. Widely-sold socialist books of the 1890s, like William Morris's *News from Nowhere*, Peter Kropotkin's *Fields, Factories and Workshops* or Robert Blatchford's *Merrie England* (which sold a million copies in a few years), predicted a new accommodation of urban and rural life. Ebenezer Howard, in his book *Tomorrow: a Peaceful Path to Real Reform* (subsequently and repeatedly reprinted as *Garden Cities of Tomorrow*) hoped 'to win Tory and Anarchist, single-taxer and socialist, individualist and collectivist, over to his experiment' [43]. While garden cities were few and belated, the impact of all this literature persuaded many that the marriage of all that was best in town and country was feasible.

Quite apart from popular reforming propaganda, there was the compelling cult of 'the simple life'. Thoreau's *Walden*, scarcely noticed in America when it appeared decades earlier, found a new appeal in England at the turn of the century. When W.B. Yeats wrote his poem about the small cabin he would build and the nine bean-rows he would plant on the lake isle of Innisfree, he was inspired, not by any acquaintance with life in the west of Ireland, but by buying in Fleet Street a copy of Henry S. Salt's edition of Thoreau's book.

Those who had never been obliged to live it became attracted by 'the simple life'.

> Bound up with the strong impulse, to reshape accepted attitudes to politics, religion, labour, education, sex, aesthetics, food, drink, dress, and all the other institutions ripe for reformation, has almost always been the idea of escaping: abandoning the city, symbol of oppression, to try the simpler, freer, more creative country life [44].

In response to these various pressures for land settlement, new legislation resulted in the county council provision of smallholdings, often in the form of planned estates with new model cottages on each holding. About 30,000 families were settled in this way as a result of the 1908 Small Holdings Act. The fashion for smallholdings also encouraged private speculators to try their hand; in these cases there was less overall control, and individual plot-owners designed their own homes and used their land as they wished. Some early instances of this are to be found — at Cranmore, for instance, on the Isle of Wight; to the north of the main development at Peacehaven; and on the edge of the New Forest at St Leonards and St Ives — all in their way evolving into classic plotland landscapes.

The period immediately after 1918 was one of extensive smallholding formation. Sixteen thousand were created at that time, and 24,000 ex-servicemen settled on them. The Board of Agriculture and Fisheries produced a booklet *Land Settlement in the Mother Country*, and took every advantage to argue the case for smallholdings:

They will be of great value to the Nation as a whole, and to the agricultural community in particular. They will afford a valuable source of additional labour in agricultural districts; they will help to meet the serious shortage of rural cottages; and they will be the best means of enabling men without much previous experience or capital to begin in a small way with the least possible risk of failure. Such holdings will also be the best means of providing for partially disabled men who require an open-air life and who, with the help of their families, can supplement from the produce of their holdings their pensions and any wages they can earn [45].

Even though by 1926 about a quarter of these post-1918 smallholders had left (the majority finding them uneconomic), as a form of land occupation their effects on the landscape were not inconsiderable. Moreover, there was always the prospect of more to come. Ramsay MacDonald was talking at the time of colonising the countryside with one million 'allotment holders'. Thomas Sharp, ever watchful for signs of individuality, was amongst the first to warn of their collective impact on the landscape:

The excellent smallholdings idea was put into practice; and each smallholder must live separately on his holding. So identical detached or semi-detached villa-cottages sprang up at identical distances along the roadsides. So the poultry-farmer patterned his fields with scores of new and elaborate woooden chicken-houses till they looked like allotment gardens, and the pig-breeder did likewise with his new and elaborate piggeries with like effect [46].

The massive sales of land after 1918 were largely to tenant farmers and to building developers. Encouraged by high prices for farm products during and immediately after the First World War, many tenant farmers seized what seemed at the time to be an unprecedented opportunity to join the ranks of the land-owners. As a result, owner-occupation of farmland increased dramatically, from 11 per cent in 1918 to 36 per cent in 1928. Yet, as events in the 1930s proved, these new owners were especially vulnerable to a fresh wave of falling prices, with the result that many were amongst the first to sell to builders and housing speculators.

Against a background of declining farm fortunes and a rush to sell land, values plummeted, but this time there were few prospective buyers waiting to start a new farm. That which could not be sold for development was often left in a state of semi-use. Signs of waste and neglect — broken fences, coarse weed-colonised pastures, waterlogged fields, and sale notices — became a familiar feature in large tracts of countryside. It was land such as this, by-passed by the main builders, which was now open to what in more prosperous days would have been dismissed as uneconomic bids for occupation. In these times, bankrupt farmers were often only too willing to accept.

21

These were ideal conditions for plotland formation, and nowhere illustrates this better than South Essex. With a glut of land for building, and any number of marginal plots (away from a railway line, with no services, and on heavy, waterlogged ground, and selling for as little as £3 for a plot), the way was open for people who at other times would have stood no chance of buying their own acre of England. All manner of simple homes took shape, along with chicken huts, pig-sties and tumble-down stables. If it was not exactly Jesse Collings's utopian vision of 'three acres and a cow' it was, at least, probably a great deal better than a crowded tenement in London's East End.

'WEEKENDERS AND OTHERS'

In addition to this fixed population that drifted out of the towns to live 'in the country', motor transport created a liquid, fluctuating, weekend and fine evening population that moved over all parts of the country and that had to be catered for, man and machine, by refreshment places, garages, petrol filling stations, telephone boxes and other accommodations. This weekend and fine evening population represented a great purchasing public. So the shopkeepers and manufacturers followed it out into the country and touted for its custom through hoardings and advertisement signs [47].

This was how Thomas Sharp saw the recreational exodus from the towns in the 1930s [48]. At that time what caught his eye more than anything else was the impact of the car on a fragile countryside; by 1931 a million private cars were on the road. Austin Sevens and Morris Minors sold for little more than £100, and along with other popular models opened new horizons for the townsfolk in search of a break from city life:

Every weekend a holiday. Where shall it be this week? Through highways to old world towns and villages or byways to the woods and fields; a quick straight run to the silvery sea or a dawdle amid hills and dales? Each weekend a new scene — a new delight [49].

Before the car it was the train which served the same purpose. From the middle of the previous century railway excursions carried industrial workers away from the smoky towns, if only for a day. Seaside resorts grew to cater for the new demands, and each of the conurbations had its favoured destinations. Forty-eight seaside resorts were listed in the 1871 Census Report, including Southend, Brighton and Margate for Londoners, Scarborough for the West Riding, and Blackpool for the Lancashire towns. By 1901 another eighteen towns had been added to the list.

The railways maintained their importance in the early twentieth century, particularly with the growth of annual holidays to supplement the summer Sunday traffic. With an increasing number entitled to a week's annual paid holiday (from one and a half million in the 1920s to eleven million in 1939) families flocked to the prospering resorts and holiday camps by the sea. In 1937, it was estimated that fifteen million people took a holiday of a week or more. Towards the end of the 1930s the railways were carrying twenty million more passengers in August than in May or October. Charabancs competed for the new traffic, luring holidaymakers with the advertisement slogan 'make your journey part of your holiday', as well as carrying reputedly raucous parties bound for the seaside and hitherto peaceful beauty spots. For shorter journeys into the countryside the means of transport was more varied. In addition to the train, charabanc and motor car, bicycles and motorcycles were enormously popular; until about 1924 the number of motor-cyclists still exceeded the number of motorists, and in 1931 there were ten times as many bicycles as cars.

Cyclists and hikers in company, day excursionists,
Refugees from cursed towns and devastated areas:
Know you seek a new world, a saviour to establish
Long-lost kinship and restore the blood's fulfilment [50].

Relief from town life was nothing new, but always in the past it had been the prerogative of the rich. Thomas Cook's cheap rail outings to the Great Exhibition in 1851 symbolised the start of a new era of mass recreation. Victorian working families enjoyed the novel, though still very limited, opportunities, to experience coast and country. So too did the Edwardians, extending the scope of leisure until the outbreak of war in 1914 called a halt to that. But past patterns were renewed and then diversified with a vengeance from 1918, and the first summer after war ended saw an irresistible pressure to escape; it was the dawn of a twenty-year period that has itself been termed 'the long weekend' [51].

In August came the great holiday scramble. Thousands of people set off for the sea on their first holiday for five years. The seaside towns were overwhelmed. Fifty thousand people went to Yarmouth from London alone. Clacton received thirty-five thousand more people than it could accommodate. Sofas in living rooms and temporary beds in bathrooms were snapped up. Blackpool had more than three hundred thousand people [52].

Mass use of coast and country was a product of the twentieth century. Since the Industrial Revolution, long hours of work had been regarded as part and parcel of the new system, and time spent away from the workplace offered few options other than to recuperate and 're-create'. The dominant cycle was that of work, and successive campaigns to reduce the total number of working hours failed to change the qualitative balance between work and leisure. Gradually more leisure time was achieved, and Anthony King has shown how the use of the term 'week-end' had become commonplace by 1900. But time spent at leisure was still in its way shaped by capitalist requirements no less than time spent at work.

23

True it was that new frontiers were opened for a workforce that, for generations, had been denied this facility. Contact was made with nature, as thousands explored the countryside for the first time, and sea air was enthusiastically inhaled as the perfect antidote to the commonplace scourge of tuberculosis. Undoubtedly more than simply fun for those involved, it offered a dramatic release from urban factories and tightly-packed dwellings.

Yet it was also limited in scope — short-term in its occurrence and no more than compensatory in effect. The urban regime continued unabated, and on Monday mornings nothing had changed:

> August is nearly over, the people
> Back from holiday are tanned
> With blistered thumbs and a wallet of snaps and a little
> 'Joie de vivre' which is contraband...
> Now the till and typewriter call the fingers
> The workman gathers his tools
> For the eight-hour day .. [53].

Moreover, in the way of any capitalist activity, the pattern of leisure activities was stratified. For the wealthy, holidays abroad were possible, cars were privately-owned, and family villas by the sea a growing fashion. In contrast, for working people leisure meant little in the way of private ownership, trips were generally by public transport and accommodation (where this was enjoyed at all) was rented. And for a vast number the promises of leisure were still illusory. The minimum cost of a week's holiday for a family with two children was about £10 (including home rent) — still too high for many to contemplate. By the end of the 1930s only one-third of those who earned less than £4 a week took a week's holiday [54].

The idea of a mass exodus to coast and countryside was numerically true but, in relative terms, it was far from universal. A widespread demand was latent but, for economic reasons, could not be fully met through commercial agencies. It was from this pool of the economically disadvantaged, sharing the desires of the period for holidays and outings but unable to buy a villa or stay in a boarding house, that many of the plotlanders emerged to find their own distinctive outlets. Shacks by the sea, makeshift huts on a weekend smallholding, or riverside cabins were, in many cases, no more or less than a downmarket response to more general demands for leisure space.

PLOTS OF FREEDOM

Whether for homes, holdings or holidays, plotlands emerged because people wanted property. The lure of even a tiny plot of land was compelling. And though dreams of a place of one's own were nothing new, the time was now right: a period which combined favourable economic circumstances with an absence of effective land-use controls.

Patterns of ownership were transformed and, though just a part of this general process, plotlands always remained distinctive as a form of small-scale property ownership in its own right. In fact, by its very nature as a homespun, makeshift setting for 'rugged individualism', plotlands are in some ways an exemplar of more general trends. Owning a place of one's own acquired the appeal of a panacea, a way to cure all known afflictions. For the plot-owner, it was a promise of freedom, of independence and an opportunity to assert one's individuality. There was status to be won, security and a chance of financial returns. In contact with the land, souls would be purified, bodies rejuvenated and family life cemented. And all, perhaps, for the cost of an ex-army hut or redundant railway carriage.

But what did it all mean? Rhetoric can obscure no less than it reveals; catchphrases like 'freedom' and 'individualism' are emotive, yet also ambiguous. It is easy to draw a picture of creative individuals, each in their little plot, fulfilling an historic dream — a tranquil landscape with smoke curling from chimneys. But was it really like that? Freedom for one can also mean deprivation for another, just as individualism can equally well stand for competition, one against another. Property, small-scale no less than large, is an intensely moral issue. Many years earlier Maria Edgeworth expressed a popular and enduring sentiment, 'Well! Some people talk of morality, and some of religion, but give me a snug little property' [55]. The sentiment was, no doubt, echoed in countless decisions in the early twentieth century, yet it was as erroneous then as when first uttered. Plotlanders were not discarding morality, but were embracing it, they were inescapably part of a 'property ethic' no less distinctive in its own way than their unique plotland landscape.

So what was this ethic, and what did the plots stand for? Were the plotlands a supreme triumph of bourgeois mentality; an unequivocal expression of liberal individualism? Or were they the fulfilment of a free-flowing current of English revolt; an attempt to adapt a deep-rooted ideal of peasant proprietorship to the particular conditions of the twentieth century?

'JOINING THE PROPERTY BANDWAGON'

One view of the plotlands is that they represent no more than a colourful, but in other ways conventional, contribution to an emergent ideal of a 'property-owning democracy' [56]. For all their eccentricities they were the product of the same forces of material consumption and political conformity as those that stimulated more general property changes. Claims that ownership of a plot was a means to achieve freedom rest on a liberal concept of property. Vigorous assertions of private property and self-help inherent in the plotlands are not inconsistent with a long history of liberal individualism — from its early exponents at the end of the eighteenth century right through to early twentieth-century advocates of more widespread property ownership.

Initially, classical liberal theorists sought ways to explain and encourage new social relationships that were essential to the emergence of capitalism. Traditional beliefs in property and personal opportunities for betterment, which rested on an unyielding social hierarchy, were inadequate in an age of change. In forging new ideas the essence of liberal thought was that of creating freedom to develop, at both a personal and an institutional level.

This search for freedom is explicit in the delineation of new property relationships, and sets the pattern for society as a whole. From the time of John Locke in the seventeenth century, private property is wrenched away from traditionalists, who had defended a hierarchy of ownership on divine grounds, and is recast in — theoretically at least — a more egalitarian mould. Private property becomes a natural right and far from ascribing the existing order to a divine source it is 'God who hath given the world to men in common' [57]. People are also endowed with the faculty of reason to make good use of what had been given to them, so it was expected that no one would take more than they could manage.

The notion of private property that emerges is one that is based on Locke's basic assumption that one's own person is property. If this is the case, it follows that one's own labour is no less a form of property, and that the application of this labour to what has been given to all (and is, therefore, in its natural state 'common') is a means of converting common stock into private property.

> Whatsoever, then, he removes out of the state that Nature hath provided and left it in, he hath mixed his labour with it, and joined to it something that is his own, and thereby makes it his property [58].

So private property is a natural right, and its achievement becomes a means to achieve one's natural liberty. The only rules essential to the preservation of freedom are that one must not transgress the rights of others, nor others the boundaries of what is yours.

Subsequent theorists like Hume and Rousseau based their arguments on the belief that private property was a social rather than a natural right. But they, too, reserved for it a central place in their visions of a free society. Even in the mid-nineteenth century, in the face of alternative views as to what might constitute a free society, J.S. Mill takes on the role of Devil's advocate in examining the case against private property but, to the relief of all liberals, concludes in its lasting favour.

No less than private property, liberalism has looked to a theory of self-help to support its view of progress. The rise of capitalism is dependent not only on the removal of feudal institutions but, in turn, on the emergence of a new ethic that is wedded to the idea of free development. In the late eighteenth century, for instance, Adam Smith crystallises the view that economic prosperity would best come about if governments did as little as possible and, instead, allowed individual vigour and enterprise to proceed unhindered.

Well into the following century Samuel Smiles reinforced Smith's belief in self-help with an impressive mixture of case history and exhortation to pursue this well-tried principle:

The spirit of self-help is the root of all genuine growth in the individual; and, exhibited in the lives of many, it constitutes the true source of national vigour and strength [59].

Though critics of liberalism were also gathering strength, individual enterprise was still, in the latter half of the nineteenth century, very much alive and well. The ethic of what has been termed 'possessive individualism' remained a powerful force for development, and a rationale for all types of individual enterprise.

Extended and modified in the twentieth century this rationale has served to underwrite a host of new developments, not least of all a dramatic increase in private property. And, to apply the argument to a specific case it might well be argued that key liberal beliefs in private property and self-help are writ large in the jealously-defended holdings and makeshift buildings of plotlands. The very landscape of scattered plots, and a rhetoric proclaiming new freedom can, in one sense, be seen to epitomise a basic spirit of liberal endeavour; a world of enterprising individuals, replacing external restrictions and established privilege with their own brand of personal freedom and development.

'TOWARDS A NEW LIFE'

An alternative view can equally well see in the plotlands an expression of revolt against the inequities of urban-based capitalism, and a preference for political and geographical dispersal. From this standpoint, the association of plot-ownership with freedom rests less on the material fact of ownership as an end in itself, and more on opportunities to create a small world of one's own choosing. The plotlands become less an example of joining what was still generally a middle-class model of property ownership, and more a way of rejecting urban society as it had then emerged. What was sought, perhaps, was an opportunity to achieve, not individualism in the liberal sense of one person matched against another, but one's own wholeness.

Attention has already been drawn to the long tradition of ideas and social movements in which a notion of improvement is couched in these terms. Echoes, for instance, of Gerrard Winstanley, exhorting common people to reclaim the land that was rightly theirs; of William Godwin, charting an anarchist course in the very years that liberalism was making greatest headway in a different direction; and of Pierre-Joseph Proudhon, whose model of peasant proprietorship rekindled the hopes of those who saw a future in limited property ownership. Few consciously linked the acquisition of property with these broader political arguments, but for those who even unknowingly strayed into a world of plots new possibilities opened up. If not on the front line in the assault on alienation, at least the perspective was clear. In a variety of ways a better life could be forged.

For one thing, possession of land acquired new meaning not as a source of material wealth, but as a symbolic break with landlords and authority. It is a Proudhonian sense of possession, holding just enough property for one's own needs the sense of property as 'freedom' rather than 'theft'. Unless used as smallholdings most of the plots were small, and of little capital value. The inclusion of a house on these plots was of no less significance. Again, it mattered not that the majority of houses were simple structures, or that they were scorned by outsiders. What mattered was that they belonged to the occupants, and not to anyone else. In any case the simplicity of these houses yielded its own lessons; they were perfectly adequate, serving their purpose without superfluous trappings. This was one of the lessons that Thoreau deduced from living in his own log cabin:

> Most men appear never to have considered what a house really is, and are actually needlessly poor because they think they must have such a one as their neighbours [60].

Likewise the very process of building such places with one's own hands was no less a source of satisfaction. It had been many generations since people built their own homes; this was one of the skills that had disappeared with the increasing specialisation of society. In peasant societies, building skills and use of local materials would be part and parcel of socialisation, and by no means necessarily a purely functional process. J.M. Synge wrote of a conscious concern for aesthetics in building amongst the Kerry peasantry, who

> 'would discuss for hours the proportions of a new building — how high a house should be if it was a certain length, with so many rafters in order that it might look well...' [61].

The makeshift homes of the plotlands may have compared unfavourably with a finely-developed peasant architecture, but the process of coming to grips with the problem and of helping each other was undoubtedly an enriching experience. And there was the example of Henry Thoreau, whose own log cabin might well have merged within a plotland landscape; of William Morris, explaining in simple terms that a decentralised society could only result from the abolition of capitalism; and Peter Kropotkin, arguing that dispersal was not only ethically desirable but also highly practicable.

Dreams of a higher estate have been a persistent force in English social history, the precise images and their chances of realisation changing over time, but their underlying adherence to the possibility of a better world for common people enduring unchanged. The prelude to plotland development was that of a century or more of industrial capitalism which, in its vigorous growth, had a dual effect on popular aspirations.

On the one hand, it had the effect of rendering their realisation more distant than ever yet, at the same time, the very success of capitalism germinated the seeds of a new popular consciousness. In a dialectic with the mainstream of capitalism, popular imagination developed an antithesis to alienation. The more individuals were divorced from the product of their own labour, the more social relationships were shaped by commercial considerations, the sharper the divisions between town and country, and the greater the distance from nature; so in turn, the ideal unfolded of gaining (or, as popular imagination would have it, of 're-gaining') wholeness.

Another aspect of plotland life which supports the view that it was a liberating process, relates to an absence of external restrictions. Often born of necessity — perhaps because local authorities refused to provide these areas with essential services — plotland communities devised their own solutions. And the more they asserted their independence, the less they needed outside interference. At a price of makeshift services, the plotlands won an enviable degree of local autonomy.

And, finally, a plot of land in the country was a means of achieving a simple but fulfilling life, the elusive goal of townsfolk then and since. It was Arcadia, a healthy outdoor life enjoying nature and perhaps even growing some of one's own food. Workers from the towns used their labour in ways unknown for generations. It was not that fulfilling labour could only be achieved in the country, so much as that the country provided the easiest opportunities for its practice.

As an expression of libertarian ideals, there is much to be found in the plotlands. In their way they embraced powerful elements of a persisting popular dream: property of one's own, a house built with one's own hands, mutual aid in place of external controls, and a rustic setting with all that could mean. All this was of course limited in extent and perhaps a pale image of how utopians envisaged Arcadia but, arguably, for many people the best that was available at the time.

NOTES

1. Pimlott, J.A.R. (1947) *The Englishman's Holiday: A Social History.* London: Faber and Faber.
2. *Final Report of the Departmental Committee appointed by the President of the Board of Agriculture and Fisheries to Consider the Settlement or Employment on the Land in England and Wales of Discharged Sailors and Soldiers,* Cd. 8182 and Cd. 8127. London: HMSO, 1916.
3. In tracing the extent of plotlands, the assistance of County Planning Officers throughout England is gratefully acknowledged. Evidence of the distribution of plotlands has also been gleaned from a wide variety of sources, referenced below and in relation to particular cases in the following chapters.
4. Mais, S.B. (1938) The plain man looks at England, in Williams-Ellis, Clough (ed.) *Britain and the Beast*. London: J.M. Dent and Sons.
5. *Ibid.*

29

6. Steers, J.A. (1944) Coastal preservation and planning. *Geographical Journal*, No. 104.
7. *Ibid.*
8. Public Record Office file H.L.G./92/81.
9. Steers *op cit.* (see note 6).
10. The rationale for designating the land for a new town was frequently couched in these terms, for instance in 'Basildon's special problems' *Town and Country Planning*, October, 1953, in which Brigadier W.G.D. Knapton said that the task confronting the local authorities 'almost amounted to a rural slum clearance scheme'.
11. *Peterlee Artist Project Report.* Sunderland: Northern Arts, 1976.
12. Sidney, Sir Philip (1585) *Arcadia.* Reprinted 1926, Cambridge: Cambridge University Press.
13. Definition of 'Arcadia' in *Webster's Third New International Dictionary.* London: G. Bell & Sons Ltd, 1961.
14. The literary tradition of pastoralism is traced in Williams, Raymond (1973) *The Country and the City.* London: Chatto and Windus.
15. Howlitt, William (1838) *The Rural Life of England.* London: Longman, Orme, Brown, Green and Longmans.
16. *Ibid.*
17. Rix, H. (1889) The return to nature. *Seed Time*, October.
18. For a fuller account of the rural origins of squatting see Ward, Colin (1980) The early squatters, in Wates, N. and Wolmar, C. (eds.) *Squatting.* London: Bay Leaf Books.
19. Hoskins, W.G. and Stamp, L. Dudley, (1963) *The Common Lands of England and Wales.* London: Collins.
20. George, M. Dorothy (1931) *England in Transition.* Reprinted 1953, Harmondsworth: Penguin.
21. *Ibid.*
22. Hill, Christopher (1973) *Winstanley: The Law of Freedom and Other Writings.* Harmondsworth: Pelican Books, Introduction.
23. Thomas, K.V. Another Digger broadside. *Past and Present* No. 42, quoted in Hill, *op cit.* (see note 22).
24. Burnett, J. (1978) *A Social History of Housing, 1815-1970.* Newton Abbot: David and Charles.
25. Dixon, William Hepworth (1879) *Royal Windsor*, Vol. 4. London: Hurst and Blackett.
26. Askew, H. (1932) *Notes and Queries*, 30 July.
27. Lloyd, Katherine (1973) Poachers' pockets in her skirts. *Country Life*, 11 October.
28. *Illustrated Guide to the New Forest.* London: Ward Lock, 1925.
29. *Ibid.*
30. Branson, N. and Heinemann, M. (1971) *Britain in the 1930s.* London: Weidenfeld and Nicolson.
31. Eliot, T.S. 'The Rock', quoted in Barker, Theo (1978) *The Long March of Everyman, 1750-1960.* Harmondsworth: Penguin.
32. Roberts, M. (c.1939) 'In Our Time', quoted in Skelton, Robin (1964) *Poetry of the Thirties.* Harmondsworth: Penguin.
33. In addition to general social histories of the period, helpful sources on inter-war housing include Becker, A.P. (1950) Housing in England and Wales during the Business Depression of the 1930s. *Economic History Review* **3**(3); Burnett, *op. cit.* (see note 24); Jackson, Alan A. (1973)

Semi-Detached London. London: Allen and Unwin; Pawley, Martin (1978) *Home Ownership.* London: Architectural Press; Richardson, H.W. and Aldcroft, D.H. (1968) *Building in the British Economy between the Wars.* London: Allen and Unwin; Swenarton, Mark (1981) *Homes for Heroes.* London: Heinemann; and Thorns, David (1972) *Suburbia.* London: Paladin.
34. Cited in Barker, *op. cit.* (see note 31).
35. Graves, R. and Hodge, A. (1940) *The Long Weekend: A Social History of Great Britain, 1918-39.* London: Faber and Faber.
36. Branson and Heinemann, *op. cit.* (see note 30).
37. Glynn, S. and Oxborrow, J. (1976) *Interwar Britain: A Social and Economic History* London: Allen and Unwin.
38. Helpful sources on changes in land ownership from the 1870s onwards include Douglas, Roy (1976) *Land, People and Politics, 1878-1952.* London: Allison and Busby; Liberal Land Committees (1925) *Land and the Nation.* London: Hodder and Stoughton; Sutherland, D. (1968) *The Landowners.* London: Anthony Blond; and Thompson, F. M. L. (1963) *English Landed Society in the Nineteenth Century* London: Routledge and Kegan Paul.
39. Thompson, F.M.L. (1981) Free trade and the land, in Mingay, G. E. (ed.) (1981) *The Victorian Countryside.* London: Routledge and Kegan Paul.
40. Newby, Howard, (1979) *Green and Pleasant Land?* London: Hutchinson.
41. *Ibid.*
42. Chamberlain, Joseph (1885) *The Radical Programme.* London: Chapman and Hall.
43. Mumford, Lewis (1946) Introductory essay to the postwar reprint of Howard, Ebenezer, *Garden Cities of Tomorrow.* London: Faber and Faber.
44. MacCarthy, Fiona (1981) *The Simple Life.* London: Lund Humphries.
45. Memo from the Board of Agriculture to County Councils, 26 February 1919, in *Journal of the Board of Agriculture*, XXV, April 1918 to March 1919. London: HMSO.
46. Sharp, Thomas (1932) *Town and Countryside.* London: Oxford University Press.
47. *Ibid.*
48. More generally, helpful sources on outdoor recreation in this period include, Brunner, Elizabeth (1914) *Holiday Making and the Holiday Trades.* Oxford; Childs, W.M. (1921) *Holidays in Tents.* London; Ministry of Labour (1938) *Report of the Committee on Holidays with Pay* Cmnd. 5724. London: HMSO; Pimlott, J.A.R. (1947) *The Englishman's Holiday: A Social History* London: Faber and Faber; and Walvin, J. (1978) *Beside the Seaside.* London: Allen Lane.
49. Advertisement for a Standard car in the *Daily Mail*, cited in Branson, N. (1975) *Britain in the Nineteen Twenties.* London: Weidenfeld and Nicolson.
50. From Lewis, C. Day 'The Magnetic Mountain', in Skelton, *op. cit.* (see note 32).
51. *The Long Weekend* is the title of the excellent account of life in interwar Britain, Graves and Hodge, *op. cit.* (see note 35).
52. Graves and Hodge, *op. cit.* (see note 35).

31

53. From Macniece, L. 'Autumn Journal', in Skelton, *op. cit.* (see note 32).
54. Pimlott, *op. cit.* (see note 1).
55. From Edgeworth, Maria 'The Absentee', in *The Oxford Dictionary of Quotations*. London: Oxford University Press, 1980.
56. It is interesting that the term itself was apparently coined in this period by a Conservative politician, A.N. Skelton, and promoted in his book, Skelton, A.N. (1924) *Constructive Conservatism*. Edinburgh: Blackwood.
57. Locke, John (1690) *Two Treatises of Civil Government*, Book II. Reprinted 1970 in Everyman's Library, London: Dent.
58. *Ibid.*
59. Smiles, Samuel (1859) *Self Help*.
60. Thoreau, Henry (1852) *Walden, or Life in the Woods*. Reprinted 1960, New York: New American Library.
61. Synge, J.M. (1909) *In Wicklow and West Kerry*. London: J.M. Dent.

Chapter 2

Property and Control

The time has come when we must definitely choose between the
end of *laissez-faire* or the end of rural England.

(Lady Cynthia Mosley, House of Commons, 1930)

Particularly during the 1920s and 1930s conflict and debate
surrounding plotland development exemplified and even magnified the
wider issue of whether to plan or not. The historic tussle between, on
the one hand, individual rights of property and freedom of action and,
on the other hand, growing State involvement to act in the public
interest, was fought afresh on the unlikely battlegrounds of makeshift
landscapes.

Against a wider background of property and control, nowhere were
the issues more polarised than in the plotlands. Here, on the one side,
were people of modest means defending pathetic homes on land that
none had previously wanted in any case; and, on the other side, a
bureaucratic machine without compassion, growing with every new
bye-law and Parliamentary clause. The point was not lost at the time.
In the courts where disputes were heard and in the popular press,
portrayals were of the 'small man' pitted against the State, of David
and Goliath. Invariably, of course, the contenders themselves were
unaware of their historic roles. Plotlanders did not know that they
were in the front line of a battle that had little to do with their
immediate needs, while conscientious local authority officials in
pursuit of modest improvements in public health were frequently
perplexed by the weight of an opposition which seemed far removed
from reason and fact.

Midway between abstract property rights at one extreme and
practical local disputes at the other, a system of general controls over
land use and development emerged. In catching the public eye,
makeshift landscapes along the coast and in the countryside
contributed to the emergence of these controls and are, in turn, at least
partially ensnared by the new system. It is the interaction between

plotlands and an emergent system of environmental planning that is traced in this chapter. We start by illustrating the preservationists' view of plotlands, as part of a more general concern for the destruction of coast and countryside. This is followed by a review of the environmental controls which take shape and bear upon the plotlands story before the 1940s. We then conclude with an appraisal of how extensive the restrictions really were by the end of this period, and whether or not this spelt the end of popular Arcadias.

PRESERVATIONISTS AND PLOTLANDS

Overnight it seemed, as the cities burst their boundaries, that England was transformed. Town-dwellers, hitherto contained, now came in search of space. Their claim on land was compelling, and no corner of an historic landscape could any longer be regarded as sacrosanct. Yet it was more than a physical transformation; those who now laid claim on the landscape were people for whom, only a generation previously, the possibility of owning a plot of English soil would have been unthinkable. It was a social no less than a physical transformation, challenging traditional assumptions about class as well as place. Inevitably, though, the exaltation of a generation enjoying its newly-found access to coast and countryside was not to be shared by all. Tumbledown weekend shacks, converted coaches and self-built bungalows created Arcadia for some, yet threatened to destroy it for others. Each new encampment, with the promise of a measure of freedom for its proud owners, was at the same time a spur to action amongst an emergent body of preservationists. The very disorder and personal freedom which newcomers sought was anathema to the self-appointed guardians of a more traditional landscape.

To an emergent preservationist lobby, the occupation of every new plot was further evidence, not only of landscape deterioration, but sometimes of social decline too. The old order was changing and, especially from the 1920s, preservationists gather strength as a vocal and influential lobby in defence of traditional ways. Plotlands are opposed, not in isolation but as an exemplar of the very worst in a process of desecration that is seen to result from the relentless spread of an urban way of life. The lobby was, in essence, a fundamental defence of the countryside (its landscape, its class structure and its general way of life) against the ravages of the expanding town.

To the cause of preservation came defenders from all political quarters [1]. A diminishing class of large landowners closed ranks to salvage what they could from this new assault on their territory. Likewise, support for preservation came from a whole spectrum of liberal-minded politicians, for a variety of reasons from a genuine love of the landscape to a continuing faith in rationality to find a better way of organising things. For all its conservative overtones, the preservation movement was also fired by a growing body of parliamentary socialists who saw increased state involvement as the only way to protect a worthy heritage yet, at the same time, ensure that its enjoyment was available to all.

Rallying points for preservationists were frequently to be found within an increasingly influential network of voluntary bodies. It was the voluntary sector that was often foremost in pressing for new and stricter legislation, for planning schemes to be prepared and, generally, in promoting 'a public opinion of decency and amenity' [2]. Beyond that they were also themselves sometimes involved in direct acquisition and management. It is tempting to compare their role, in many ways ahead of the State in getting things done, with that of their mid-nineteenth-century counterparts in the field of housing.

Prominent amongst the voluntary bodies were the National Trust and Council for the Preservation of Rural England (CPRE) [3]. The former, dating back to 1895, concentrated on holding property of beauty or historic interest for the benefit of the public. With land constantly under threat of development, and with planning powers inadequate in many cases to deal with it, the Trust often proved to be the only effective source of preservation. By the end of the 1930s it held no less than 50,000 acres in England and Wales, and these included many areas (especially along the coast) that would otherwise have been developed. In turn, the Council for the Preservation of Rural England operated from 1926 as a pressure group rather than holding land itself. It sought to protect the rural heritage in particular instances when under threat and, more generally, to arouse public opinion on the question of beauty in the countryside. Amongst its various activities was the sponsorship of a number of surveys. of areas at risk (including the Thames Valley, with its weekend cabins).

The National Trust and CPRE were not alone in their struggle to preserve the landscape. Support was forthcoming from other organisations; for instance the Scapa Society (formed to fight against the disfigurement of the countryside by advertisement), the Society for the Preservation of Ancient Buildings, the Commons and Footpaths Preservation Society, the Men of the Trees, and the Pure Rivers Society. Moreover, as well as these national bodies, townsfolk venturing into the countryside would frequently encounter local amenity groups (like the Society of Sussex Downsmen) with interests diametrically opposed to their own. If Arcadia was to survive then it could not, argued the preservationist, be for all.

VOICES FOR PRESERVATION

Even before the main thrust of inter-war development in the countryside, Edwardian children were being warned of what was afoot:

'Perhaps you do not know what a speculative builder is... They bought all the pretty woods and fields they could get and cut them up into squares, and grubbed up the trees and the grass and put streets there and lamp-posts and ugly little yellow brick houses, in the hopes that people would want to live in them. And curiously enough people did... It is curious that nearly all the great fortunes are made by turning beautiful things into ugly ones. Making beauty out of ugliness is very ill-paid work [4].'

By the 1920s astute observers could see that the threat to the countryside was not simply one of 'ugly little yellow brick' suburbs but also one of more scattered development. In 1926, Patrick Abercrombie spoke of the 'week-end habit' and its associated bungalows and huts:

Since the war innumerable wooden shanties have sprung up better sociologically but artistically deplorable. Many of these are on wheels (though unmoved for years) in order to avoid rates; and whole fields have become so packed with them that they are extremely insanitary... the preserver of rural amenities cannot allow any sort of old junk cabin to deform the choicest spots [5].

A major assault on their insanitary condition came from public health officials like the Medical Officer of Health for the Wirral Rural District Council, who described the coastal 'bungalow town' of Moreton in terms reminiscent of a nineteenth-century slum:

The worst field almost beggared description. It contained some 150 bungalows in all stages of disrepair, bounded on one side by a foul-smelling stream and on another by a ditch of stagnant water which was almost pure sewage. This is a comparatively mild denunciation, for the actual state is indescribable and attempted description must leave much to the imagination. The chaotic ugliness is something unimaginable [6].

Ten years later W. Dougill, in writing about the English coastline, noted that this type of situation had not improved. He found:

...congeries of discordant huts and caravans laid out without any consideration for the amenities, without any thought given to the question of access, design, water supply, sanitation, litter disposal and so on. Their cumulative effect is to produce a shoddy, unplanned and unsightly blight, entirely opposed to the natural character and beauty of the seaside... The worst cases are those where the huts and caravans are used for permanent or semi-permanent occupation. Often they are old railway coaches and motor buses, or indeed anything which can afford at least some shelter from the weather. Not infrequently they are abandoned at the end of the holiday season to become ugly heaps of debris [7].

All this amounted to a string of 'seaside slums' around the coastline, which were seen to present 'an almost insoluble sanitary problem to the Local Authorities, depreciate the value of neighbouring lands, and do untold damage to the natural scenery' [8].

Inland the situation was no better, with various commentators finding similar evidence of cheaply-built homes. Darby and Hamilton, for instance, referred the observer to Kent:

> the Garden of England turned back-yard. There he will find in typical growth the straggly patches of bungalows, villas and shacks which are killing the English countryside. He need not go beyond the South Downs, where he will find Peacehaven. [9].

No part of England seemed immune from this new invasion and many of the preservationists took their stand when specific beauty spots or notable features of heritage came under threat. In this way, the South Downs won its defenders, as did the Lake District, the Cornish coastline and Stonehenge.

The process of eating away the beauty of the countryside was likened to a 'corrosive acid' [10]. Everywhere were signs of deterioration:

> Where there was a lovely view he has built houses, and so spoiled the thing he wished to admire. He has used modern transport facilities in order to enable the crowd to visit beauty-spots, and so tarnish their beauty beyond the crowd's power to restore. In his desire to get away from his hideous town and live in more pleasant surroundings he has let loose a swarm of red brick and drab concrete locusts, which have spread over thousands of acres of God's own England and destroyed all the beauty and charm which once graced them [11].

For some, it all took on a deeper meaning. Changes in the landscape symbolised changes in society itself, with new urban values usurping traditions in a decaying countryside. The First World War was a watershed between the old order and a brash new age that everyday became more apparent. G.M. Trevelyan summed up the difference:

> Today the old is almost identified in our thought and speech with the beautiful, and the new with the ugly... A hundred years hence there will be very little beauty left, unless by taking thought in time we provide otherwise [12].

Defenders of the old order could even see themselves engaged in nothing less than 'a form of civil war', championing the cause of the countryside against a new army of invaders intent only on financial profit:

> On the one side are those who realise that in the countryside, wisely cared for and planned, we have a national possession of inestimable value. Ranged against them, militant and greedily active, are the speculative builders, the advertising agents, a whole class who see in the countryside nothing but a source of

profit to themselves. These men, whether they are local authorities intent on 'development' at all costs, or private individuals running their own particular racket, are actuated by no other motive than financial gain. Their sole concern is with balance sheets and profits. The countryside is just another commodity to be exploited to the best advantage [13].

Poets in the 1930s returned frequently to the theme of conflicting values, picking out features such as pylons and arterial roads as symbols of the new order. The contrast between old and new can be illustrated in two verses from Stephen Spender's 'The Pylons':

> The secret of these hills was stone, and cottages
> Of that stone made.
> And crumbling roads
> That turned on sudden hidden villages.
> Now over these small hills they have built the concrete
> That trails black wire:
> Pylons, those pillars
> Bare like nude, giant girls that have no secret [14].

And where would it all stop? The pace of change was quickening all the time, with no end in sight. Would all that was known and cherished in the English landscape be swept away as part of a greater upheaval? The prophets at the time were gloomy.

Thomas Sharp, for instance, could foresee the suburbanisation of the whole of England, an unhappy hybrid that contained the virtues of neither town nor country. With a growing use of the car:

> *all* the land in the country can be regarded as building land and consequently *all* the land in the country is being laid out as a gigantic building estate to be developed at a density not more than 12 houses per acre. On paper London already covers the whole of Kent, Surrey, Sussex, Middlesex, Buckinghamshire, Hertforshire and Essex, and it is only a matter of time before, on the same paper, it will be linked up to Newcastle and Plymouth, with a beauty-spot preserved here and there, and here and there a hundred or two acres reserved as an agricultural area [15].

Others shared this image of an England submerged beneath cheap villas while, for George Orwell, the horror of it all might one day even be exported. What was to stop that very same process of suburbanisation, already desecrating the English landscape, from reaching out to distant corners of the Empire? Thinking particularly of Burma, Orwell contemplated whether:

> in two hundred years all this... will be gone — forests, villages, monasteries, pagodas all vanished. And instead, pink villas fifty yards apart; all over those hills, as far as you can see, villa after

villa, with all the gramophones playing the same tune. And all the forests shaved flat — chewed into wood-pulp for the *News of the World*, or sawn up into gramophone cases [16].

Commentators were as one in condemning the physical desecration of the landscape, but some, at least, tried to understand the social reasons for what was happening. J.B. Priestley made a journey round England in the mid-1930s and spoke of a new scene:

> of arterial and by-pass roads, of filling stations and factories that look like exhibition buildings, of giant cinemas and dance-halls and cafes, bungalows with tiny garages, cocktail bars, Woolworths, motorcoaches, wireless, hiking, factory girls looking like actresses, greyhound racing and dirt tracks, swimming pools, and everything given away for cigarette coupons [17].

But for Priestley, with all its brashness the new England was 'essentially democratic' and he hoped that there would be more not less of it. In Priestley's eyes, England was fast becoming a land without privilege, where suddenly everything was becoming accessible to all people. 'The young people of this new England do not play chorus in an opera in which their social superiors are the principals... they get on with their own lives' [18]. And, true enough, as thousands drove along the newly-built Southend Arterial to spend a weekend at Canvey Island or, further afield, to Jaywick Sands, they were doing things which, only a generation previously, would have been well out of their reach.

Even Clough Williams-Ellis, who championed the cause of the preservationists and deplored the dispersal of refugees from the towns in the countryside, 'destroying and dishonouring it with shoddy but all-too-permanent encampments', could later sympathise with the origins of the process. The people themselves were not to be condemned for choosing to leave towns where environmental conditions were intolerable:

> It was easy to do nothing but revile those who thus spoiled the country with nauseous little buildings, or merely to laugh darkly at their tragic failure to achieve an imagined rusticity. But it was unjust, cynical, and lazy like cursing a stricken family because in escaping from its burning home it trespassed over lawns and flower-beds [19].

In bitter contrast, the influential Thomas Sharp was one who could spare nothing in the way of compassion and understanding, above all despising the aspirations of individuals with their newly-gained access to the countryside:

> For what hope in the modern world can spring from a chaos of individualism?... a romantic universal individualism in which every man glories, and is encouraged to glory, in his self-sufficiency and separateness [20].

39

Tradition was collapsing all around him, and the popular tendencies which Priestley welcomed were anathema for Sharp. The very process of democracy was itself blamed for reducing the beauty of the English countryside from that which it had attained under autocracy. The people who found their way into the countryside were scorned no less than the process of which they were a part:

> Every little owner of every little bungalow in every roadside ribbon thinks he is living in Merrie England because he has those 'roses round the door' and because he has Sweet-william and Michaelmas daisies in his front garden. An amazing conception, but one that exists everywhere [21].

Likewise C.E.M. Joad made no attempt to conceal his distaste for the popular use of the countryside, with:

> the hordes of hikers cackling insanely in the woods, or singing raucous songs as they walk arm in arm at midnight down the quiet village street. There are people, wherever there is water, upon sea-shores or upon river banks, lying in every attitude of undressed and inelegant squalor, grilling themselves, for all the world as if they were steaks, in the sun. There are tents in meadows and girls in pyjamas dancing beside them to the strains of the gramophone, while stinking disorderly dumps of tins, bags, and cartons bear witness to the tide of invasion for weeks after it has ebbed; there are fat girls in shorts, youths in gaudy ties and plus-fours, and a roadhouse round every corner and a cafe on top of every hill for their accommodation [22].

For some, a stake in the countryside was the fulfilment of an Arcadian dream; for others in this period, it was clearly nothing less than a hideous nightmare.

ARCADIA AND THE LAW

The voices for preservation grew louder, though few were deluded that voluntary action would be enough on its own. Appreciation of the work of voluntary bodies was tempered with an awareness of their limitations. The National Trust owned an impressive acreage of cherished land, but to some it did so 'in the doleful guise of England's executor, the pious curator of rare little remnants of loveliness, ticketed specimens of what we have already lost or wantonly thrown away' [23]. Likewise, the work of the CPRE was widely commended, though 'the blessings of the just cannot alone give it the power it needs increasingly and which indeed can only come from a more general support by its direct beneficiaries — the whole people of England' [24].

Increasingly, preservationists called for greater governmental control over the use of land, with proposals ranging from a simple extension of local bye-laws to complete land nationalisation. When Clough Williams-Ellis wrote his campaigning book *England and the Octopus* in 1928 he noted that, in the defence of freehold property rights, the countryside had been left virtually unprotected against any manner of development [25]. But in challenging existing rights of property the preservationists were, sometimes unwittingly, to open a Pandora's box of contention. It was, as Darby and Hamilton said at the time, an issue which went to the very roots of political theory, 'a question of rights is a question for the State' [26].

To some extent, the principle of the State involving itself in land use had, of course, already been won some fifty years previously in the context of growing efforts to improve conditions in the towns. From around the middle of the nineteenth century the focus of attention was very much that of cleaning up the crowded living quarters of the major cities. It was, above all, a concern for public health that first led to State involvement, most notably in housing but also in urban parks and open spaces. A continuing threat of epidemics, together with the sheer economic inefficiency of unplanned cities, lured the State across the traditional threshold of inviolate private property. But, until some years into the twentieth century, State involvement remained an urban issue that left untouched the landscapes beyond.

Only gradually was the hand of the State extended beyond the city limits, and this was largely achieved through the new governmental process of town and country planning. A timorous first step was taken in 1909 — in the Housing, Town Planning, etc. Act — when local authorities were given powers to prepare schemes to guide new building in their area. It provided a basis for planning the suburbs, but left the countryside beyond unprotected; what this really amounted to was a mandate for planning new suburbs.

Limited changes followed in new legislation, all of which (including the first measure in 1909) were subsequently consolidated in the 1925 Town Planning Act. The focus was still on controlling suburban extensions though, by this time, two features pointed the way towards a more positive involvement in coast and country.

For a start, although not compelled to do so, rural districts were authorised to prepare planning schemes if they so wished. Areas to which these would apply were defined as being any land which was in the course of development or appeared likely to be used for building purposes. And if a rural district did go ahead with a scheme it was expected to take account of amenity and the preservation of natural beauty, as well as basic public health and safety considerations.

A second feature of planning legislation at the time was the provision made for local authorities to join in preparing regional plans, as a framework for their individual schemes. The significance of regional plans is that they enabled authorities to look at areas vulnerable to possible future development as well as at those where development was already under way. As such, they encompassed a variety of aims,

41

including policies of land-use zoning, of reserving land for recreation, and of protecting amenities and objects of historic interest.

It was common practice to assign the task of preparing a regional plan to one of the few acknowledged town planning experts of the day. As a result, in the second half of the 1920s a series of advisory plans and reports were prepared (understandably similar in format if not in content) for areas such as the South Coast and Thames Valley which were subject to the greatest pressures. [27]. A proliferation of weekend huts and cabins was frequently noted, though this was not yet generally seen to have become too serious a problem. There was still optimism that a rational approach by local authorities would succeed in keeping this and other problems at bay.

Reviewing the situation in the mid-1920s, Abercrombie believed that there were already extensive powers available to protect the countryside [28]. The problem, as he saw it, was that there were still many authorities not convinced of the need to intervene. To some extent this problem was overcome in 1929, when the Local Government Act opened the way for county council involvement, often at the expense of some of the smaller and less active rural authorities. The new county planning committees, often composed largely of farmers and landowners, proved generally to take a more determined stand against the continued erosion of the countryside.

For all the steady increase in powers to control development, their effect in checking the pace and form of landscape change in the late 1920s was still minimal. Great hopes, then, were pinned on the promise of new legislation to protect the countryside, following the return to office of a Labour government in 1929. In that same year, Ramsay McDonald appointed the Addison Committee to look into the case for a series of national parks. Encouraged by a more favourable political climate, representatives of the various amenity organisations were quick to lobby for a purpose-built Act to promote their interests and, in 1930, a Private Members' Bill to do just this was duly discussed in Parliament [29].

Termed the Rural Amenities Bill, it amounted to an ambitious proposal to roll forward the scope of legislation to protect the countryside. Town planning powers would be extended to embrace country planning, with county councils assuming a major role. Fired by the example of the Council for the Preservation of Rural England in the Thames Valley, local authorities were to be encouraged to undertake systematic surveys. And many of the familiar *bêtes-noires* of the day, like advertisement hoardings, ribbon development and poorly-designed buildings, were the focus of special clauses. Under the banner of 'temporary buildings' shacks and shanties were also a subject of separate treatment, the need for which was taken to be implicit:

> There is no-one who does not know that much of what is most ugly and to be deprecated in the hideous excrescences that we see around our great towns is due to the erection of temporary

buildings, which cannot be controlled by the present authorities [30].

Introducing the Bill to the House, its promoter Sir Hilton Young referred to it as a measure 'to assist those needs of the country which are not purely material but which are rather spiritual...' [31]. The future of the English countryside could always be relied on to arouse deep emotions, as the Council for the Preservation of Rural England well knew when it mounted a photographic exhibition of 'outrages' in the Great Hall at Westminster for the attention of politicians. Opposition to the Bill was centred not on dissent from the idea of preservation, but on the contention that it did not go far enough. The view, repeated again and again in the 1930s, that unless far-reaching measures were enacted the traditional countryside would disappear altogether, was clearly in the minds of various politicians at the start of the decade.

Though an important measure of informed opinion, the Bill itself failed to reach the statute books. It was withdrawn later in 1930, initially to be replaced and strengthened by a much broader Town and Country Planning Bill in 1931. This, in turn, fell with the Labour government in the same year, and though it was reintroduced in the following year the political climate was by then very much cooler. In the hands of a Conservative majority many of the strengths and ideals of the Bill were systematically reduced, and the document which reached the statute book in 1932 was a pale reflection of its original form.

Even with its shortcomings, however, the new legislation did offer some consolation to the preservationists and was generally recognised as an advance on the 1925 Act. Thus, the very title of the Town and Country Planning Act reflected a shift away from a traditional urban and suburban bias and an overdue recognition of the need for countryside planning. Schemes were empowered in rural as well as urban areas:

> with the general object of controlling the development of the land comprised in the area to which the scheme applies, of securing proper sanitary conditions, amenity and convenience, and of preserving existing buildings or other objects of architectural, historic or artistic interest and places of natural interest or beauty, and generally of protecting existing amenities whether in urban or rural portions of the area [32].

And with an eye on a plotland type of development, there was even provision to safeguard local authorities from compensation where schemes sought to prevent development that would be a threat to health or which would lead to 'excessive expenditure of public money in the provision of roads, sewers, water supply and other public services' [33].

As a result of the 1932 Act, rural schemes increased in number and scope. An example, recognised at the time as a pioneering scheme, is that of the Hailsham Rural District Council which sought to protect the complete area of the South Downs within its boundaries. The scheme included a proposal to remove 'a collection of unsightly shacks' in the Cradle Valley, and to prohibit moveable dwellings in one prominent area behind West Dean [34].

Another notable outcome of the 1932 Act was the scope for agreements to be negotiated between local authorities and landowners to restrict development in specific areas. For instance, concerned at the spread of development across the South Downs this was a measure to which both the East and West Sussex County Councils resorted in the 1930s. In that part of the Downs within East Sussex, for instance, agreements were secured with private landowners to protect no less than 24,700 acres [35].

The only other major piece of planning legislation in the 1930s came with the measure in 1935 designed to control ribbon development. Public opinion was united in its opposition to yet another sign of the assault on a vulnerable countryside, the thin necklaces of housing strung out along most of the important urban approach roads. There was also the view that ribbon development was especially prevalent along a coastline that was becoming rapidly urbanised, and that more controls were urgently needed. In response to the weight of this opinion a new measure came onto the statute books, the Restriction of Ribbon Development Act, which really added little and in some ways detracted from powers already available under the 1932 Act.

Although the new Town Planning Acts attracted considerable interest, the emphasis remained primarily that of preventing fresh outbreaks of undesirable development. Those local authorities that were faced, for instance, with colonies of shacks that were already well-entrenched or with particularly concentrated pressures for development, frequently turned to other sources of legislation (like public health and housing, or their own local Acts). For all its changes, legislation in any field in this period still bore the hallmarks of its nineteenth-century predecessors. The State moved in the direction of greater control over the rights of individual property-owners, but it moved uneasily and without an overriding conviction. New laws were passed, but characteristically with loop-holes that reflected compromises in getting them passed, with prohibitive compensation clauses, and still with an unmistakeably permissive flavour.

Little wonder, in this context, that public acquisition of land remained the best means of protection throughout this period. As such, local authorities won acclaim from preservationists when buying well-known beauty spots — as was the case, for instance, when Beachy Head was safeguarded by the Eastbourne Urban District Council.

By far the most ambitious programme of acquisition was that of the London County Council, concerned at the rapid erosion of countryside around the metropolis. Although permanent suburban development was the main problem, weekend huts in beauty spots close to the continuous built-up area were also cause for concern, the North Downs and river banks being especially vulnerable. In consequence, the

'Green Belt Scheme' was launched in 1935, with the object of retaining an accessible reserve of open countryside for Londoners. A sum of £2 million was set aside for its first three years towards the cost of acquiring land in conjunction with neighbouring authorities. Spending rateable income outside their own boundaries proved to be a problem, and existing powers had to be supplemented with a new law in 1938, the Green Belt (London and Home Counties) Act. Although this approach was, to a large extent, outdated by the subsequent 1947 Planning Act, about forty square miles were permanently safeguarded in this way [36].

But there were obvious limits as to how much a local authority could buy and, inevitably, it was to legislation designed to control development that they turned for support. In this respect, public health and housing measures were an important source of authority, not least of all for enabling local authorities to pass their own bye-laws [37].

Most local authorities had bye-laws to regulate new development (though, even by 1930, as many as 110 had not). These were primarily concerned with basic public health and nuisance issues, like the width and construction of roads, drainage and space around buildings. Some of the bye-laws even dealt specifically with the issue of 'tents, vans, sheds or similar structures used for human habitation', and in the 1930s the Ministry of Health issued circulars to encourage their widespread application [38]. The problem with bye-laws, though, was that they varied enormously from one authority to another and, very often, had not kept pace with changing patterns of development as areas became rapidly more urban in character.

Yet even without the bye-laws there was plenty in the main body of health and housing statutes to which zealous enforcement officers could turn in their ceaseless quest to keep one step ahead of the plotlanders. Monthly reports of the Council for the Preservation of Rural England returned repeatedly to the subject, seeking as much to clarify the legal situation as to extend it [39]. Though some authorities were managing quite well, others clearly had failed to piece together the various provisions available to them in a long series of statutes.

Help was at hand for the Council when, in 1933, the Ministry of Health responded with a summary statement of powers to which the local authorities could resort [40]. It was conceded that a problem existed, but whose fault was it? Partly, difficulties encountered by the local authorities lay in the nature of the development itself, with structures varying widely:

> from dwellings that may be practically houses and are undoubtedly buildings of a permanent character, through structures which are buildings not practically moveable without damage but the life of which is a few years only, down to tents and sheds, caravans and railway carriages [41].

At the same time, the local authorities themselves were reproached for frequently letting matters go too far before taking action. It was asserted that the authorities had failed to make full use of the powers available to them, which the Ministry maintained were adequate to deal with the problem.

So the situation was clarified and in subsequent legislation, notably the 1936 Public Health Act, new powers were added. Yet the fact was that throughout the 1930s the means by which plotlands could be regulated remained both complex and cumbersome. The law was generally no match for the speed and ingenuity of plotlanders in staking their claim to a piece of England. And, once installed, the whole aura of a 'property-holder', reinforced by generations of common law and custom, made them very difficult to move. It was correct to claim that public opinion was outraged by the desecration of the landscape, but there was still some reluctance in the 1930s to see bureaucratic bodies step in to usurp traditional rights of property and occupation.

Against this background, those authorities which made most progress were those which, often in the face of unusually pressing problems, obtained their own local Acts of Parliament. Arguably the most interesting piece of legislation in this context is the Lindsey County Council (Sandhills) Act of 1932, admirably researched by John Sheail [42].

In brief, the setting was that of a 25-mile stretch of sandhills along the Lincolnshire coastline which became increasingly popular for cheap holidays in the 1920s. Railway carriages, makeshift bungalows, tents and old army huts all found a place on the dunes. At one point, known as *Bohemia*, the characteristic architecture took the form of circular, corrugated iron huts described locally as 'rusty pork pies'.

And with the haphazard development came the familiar problems of plotlands. On medical grounds, the earth closets and poor drainage in places posed an acute hazard to health while, on economic grounds, local authorities feared they would at some stage become liable for providing main services. A loose scatter of development seemed to be neither one thing nor the other — it was sufficient to jeopardise the natural character of the dunes yet, at the same time, effectively prevented a more intensive use of the coast. Moreover, there was a growing concern that squatters were illegally closing access to the beaches for the general public.

The district councils had shown themselves unable to get control over the worsening situation so, in 1930, the County Council resolved to go ahead with a Parliamentary Bill. Essentially, the idea was to give the Council powers to prohibit all unlicenced enclosures and buildings, and to follow this up in places with compulsory acquisition if necessary. Special legislation was requested because existing measures were seen to be inadequate for the job in hand. County councils were not empowered to initiate a town planning scheme independently of the district councils and, in any case, planning schemes would take too long to enact in a situation where squatters were rapidly claiming more and more land.

Those who doubted the Council's motives were assured that there was no intention to remove all the huts and caravans, only to control their numbers and location. Indeed, it was asserted that a large part of the charm of a holiday on the Lincolnshire coast would be lost to many people if they were unable to secure a hut on or near the beach. Fears persisted, with the passing of the Act, that building regulations might make the huts so costly as 'to prevent the poorer people who need the bracing seaside air the most from indulging in a hut by the sea'. Whether or not these fears were justified there is certainly evidence in the mid-1930s that the Council had prevented 'a lot of very undesirable development', and was imposing its own brand of order on the anarchic landscape; at Chapel St Leonards, for instance, all huts were to be painted white, with panels picked out in green and the roofs in red or green.

The Lindsey Act was something of a landmark, but it was by no means isolated. In Surrey, for instance, a County Council Act of 1931 included specific provision to strengthen that County's powers in dealing with 'moveable dwellings and camping grounds' [43]. Although gypsies had for many years been the object of the County's attention, it was clear that the 1931 Act also had in mind the problem of the weekend visitor. Evidence was cited of 'a miscellaneous collection of shanties' — converted railway carriages, buses and caravans — within a stone's throw of Hampton Court Palace. Frustrated officials claimed they could do little about them unless it could be proved that the structures were a threat to public health. The new legislation was called for, then, not to deal with the sanitary implications of this type of settlement (for which provisions already existed) but to protect the general amenities of an area and to prevent nuisance to local residents.

Elsewhere, too, local authorities resorted to their own measures, sometimes easing localised problems yet adding to the patchwork complexity of legislation at the time [44]. It was not until 1947, with a comprehensive town planning measure, that local authorities everywhere could share a clear and effective brief for controlling the use of land. From that date onwards, the day of an unrestricted spread of plotlands was effectively over.

LIMITS OF CONTROL

Looking back, one can see that even by the end of the 1930s the 'plotlands problem' remained generally unresolved. There were certainly many areas in which a new Jaywick or Shoreham Beach would no longer have been possible. But existing plotlands remained more or less immune from the many-fronted assault of officials and, for all the checks on further development, new shacks continued to slip through the net until the outbreak of war in 1939 and the imposition of new laws in the 1940s.

Why was this paraphernalia of laws and public endeavour so ineffective? In part, contemporary observers thought it was because the effort to control development had come too late. Looking at Kent and Sussex in 1938, for instance, Sheila Kaye-Smith noted that the application of the 1932 Act had 'checked the crop of shacks and "portables", though not before a number of these were already in position' [45]. The new legislation had been a response rather than an anticipation of a landscape of disorder. Even had it been more effective there was no quick means by which it could have got to grips with the veritable tide of development that had taken place in the 1920s and 1930s.

Some like Thomas Sharp blamed the new breed of town planners for making a bad situation very much worse. Above all, Sharp contended that planners were guilty of encouraging the fusion of town and country which others strenuously opposed. Sporadic development in the countryside was seen to be nothing less than an unfortunate by-product of the 'urban decentralisation' which emanated from Ebenezer Howard's garden city ideal. The nation now paid penance for the policies of misguided planners — and Peacehaven, 'which has rightly become a national laughing-stock... now arises to pay them back in their own coin' [46]. In their various efforts, planners had debased rather than enhanced the cause of amenity and beauty.

Others blamed town planners less than the system in which they were working. Both the 1932 Act and the 1935 measure to control ribbon development were widely condemned as weak legislation — the latter especially creating compensation claims which local authorities were unable to meet. And local authorities were normally not only lacking in funds, but also in other ways were not well-equipped to take on the new tasks of preserving amenities. Very often it was the rural districts and coastal authorities with a low rateable income, where pressures were intense and landscapes especially vulnerable, that were least able to offer high standards of planning. Sometimes it was the larger authorities that were taken to task, with even the London County Council meeting the reproach of preservationists. In a letter from the Secretary of the Camping Club of Great Britain and Ireland to the Editor of *The Star*, the authorities were rebuked for dispersing their obsolete trams around the southern coastline:

> I see that the L.C.C. anticipate a good demand for old tramcars to be used as 'ideal bungalows for families' at the seaside. 'Ideal'! Ye Gods! The L.C.C. should be ashamed of itself for encouraging the multiplicity of these eyesores, which are more often than not dumped down in beauty spots with no thought of the destruction of amenities. The L.C.C. itself has no power to prohibit the erection of tents, huts and other moveable buildings in its own area. So why should the L.C.C. encourage the practice of converting old tramcars into 'bungalows'? [47].

A system had been constructed piecemeal, and vital components were found to be lacking. Government controls had increased, but it was still a 'velvet glove' approach. In any case, there were persisting doubts as to how effective land-use controls could ever be. Voicing these doubts, Abercrombie, who was as aware as anyone of the process of rural development, warned against expecting too much from a system of legal controls:

To fit the English countryside to a statutory pattern appears to be a wilful attempt at procrustean bed-making; how can its infinite variety be registered in a legal scheme and the delicate adjustments required by changes to meet modern needs be covered by a set of clauses which must conform to the *intra vires* of an Act of Parliament? [48].

But the weight of opinion was generally to do more, and to remedy the situation there was no shortage of ideas [49]. For all their variety, more rather than less public intervention was gradually accepted as a prerequisite. Increasingly, a notion of the 'common good' was equated with the State, in opposition to selfish acts of individualism. In political terms this formula proved to be unworkable until after 1945, but the seeds were carefully sown for what was later to become a new consensus.

In the late-1930s there was widespread support for something akin to a 'Ministry of Amenities' — 'a new Government department charged with the duty not only of holding a watching brief for our visual background in general, but also of restraining and advising the other Departments of State...' [50]. Centralised ministerial control was generally considered to be preferable to the divided planning responsibilities that prevailed, in which the Ministry of Health held the main brief for amenity.

There was also a growing call for land nationalisation as the only way to secure development in the common good. In turn, though, this was sometimes tempered by doubts as to whether administration by public officials would necessarily be any better than that of private landowners. At the very least, it was suggested that everyone would benefit from a good dose of environmental education. One writer even went so far as to say that the public at large should not be allowed into the countryside until they were properly educated in its ways. But if there were doubts as to unbridled nationalisation, there was almost total support for a network of national parks, where large areas of valuable landscape (including the Sussex Downs in southern England) could be protected for all time.

Others looked at the rash of obnoxious development and simply wished for the impossible. Why not reinstitute the city wall to keep cities within bounds, permitting them to build either upwards or downwards, but forbidding them to spread beyond a defined limit? Or, for R.M. Lockley:

nothing but a dictatorship will save the English coast in our time... when the millennium arrives, when battleships are turned into floating world-cruising universities, perhaps their guns, as a last act before being spiked, will be allowed to blow to dust the hideous, continuous and disfiguring chain of hotels, houses and huts which by then will have completely encircled these islands [51].

49

Many of these ideas were conceived in a period when the imminence of war was widely-sensed. Few, however, can have anticipated that the very process of war would itself achieve what they had themselves desired by more peaceful methods. The fact remains that along miles of coastline, where plotlands proliferated, innumerable seaside retreats were literally swept away by the defending army as part of their coastal strategy. Moreover, the years between 1939 and 1945 also proved to be a period of making plans for peace, anticipating a substantial increase in State involvement over a wide range of activities including land-use planning. Reports were commissioned which laid the foundations for a new pattern of town and country; amongst these a committee to investigate rural development, and a survey of the coastline had a direct bearing on the widespread legacy of makeshift landscapes [52].

The former of these two investigations, its findings known as the Scott Report, had a wide brief to review physical, social and economic development in the countryside. Plotland landscapes were noted in passing in a review of the impact of towns on the countryside — 'the nameless messes, the assemblages of caravans and converted buses and encampments which have littered and spoilt many a once-charming stretch of coastline, lake-side and river-side, and a hundred other attractive scenes...' [53] — but were not regarded as a priority issue in the wide-ranging work of the investigating committee.

A more important consideration of these 'nameless messes' came in the wartime survey of the coastline of England and Wales conducted, at the request of the Ministry of Works and Planning, by the Cambridge geographer J.A. Steers. In what was essentially a physiographical survey, Steers was greatly impressed by the extent to which the natural landscape had been recently lost, not simply to conventional urban development but also to a wide scatter of makeshift structures. His General Report included a chapter specifically devoted to 'Shacks, Huts and Camps', and this interest is reinforced in the supplementary regional reports where Steers returns frequently to this theme. There is no doubt that by the early 1940s this type of development had made a major impact along the coastline, and the survey drew attention to where it existed and went on to make proposals for its containment or removal.

The development in question was categorised into one of three types. There was, firstly, what Steers referred to as the 'unplanned or haphazard holiday camp', where

> certain fields are set aside for the reception of caravans, huts, old buses, and shacks of every description. The result is a humble and unsightly mess of heterogeneous structures. There is no plan, no order, and usually no adequate sanitation. Privacy in the ordinary sense of the word does not exist. There is no common standard of upkeep and an air of unkemptness prevails. The structures are often far too close together, and too often the camp itself is in a conspicuous position and ruins not only itself but also a far greater horizon [54].

For this type of place drastic measures were proposed, with a preference for complete demolition and a new start on many of the sites.

A second category was that of the 'shack towns', notably Canvey Island, Jaywick and Peacehaven. 'Aesthetically and in other ways all these places are abominable, yet they appear to fulfil an urge on the part of a large number of people' [55].

In the case of Canvey Island and Jaywick, Steers noted that they had the saving grace of being largely out of view, and that the best thing might be to consolidate and improve what was there already. But Peacehaven was altogether a different matter, 'on the cliff top and not shut off from the neighbourhood' [56], and its future development was clearly not to be encouraged.

Another category was that of the 'isolated hut, or huts in small groups', the main problem with these being that they were often 'eyesores and they undoubtedly spoil the countryside out of all proportion to their number' [57]. Steers thought it might be possible to get the agreement of owners to relocate them in less obtrusive spots, or at least to repaint them in more subtle colours. Only occasionally did he think that complete removal would be the answer.

Many of these developments which so offended Steers and others were, in fact, soon to be removed not through planning measures but through the effects of war — more often the result of home forces clearing the beaches than of enemy bombardment. But with the ending of hostilities planners were quick to note that a great deal still remained, and that urgent action was needed to prevent a revival of pre-war rates of activity. Ministry officials turning their thoughts to new legislation mapped out the extent of surviving 'shacks and other sub-standard development', condemning it in familiar terms as 'a national menace and... a local and national disgrace' [58]. One civil servant drew attention to the wastefulness of covering this 'good earth' with 'shack blight' when it could be used for much-needed food production.

Local authorities and central government were united in wanting to take positive action, but the official view was still that 'we have very little power of removing development of this nature' [59]. What had changed though was the context in which planning policies were framed. The immediate post-war period was one of hope and optimism; internal memos referred to 'these enlightened days' and the achievement of 'a more beautiful Britain' through planned development. There was a determination now 'to get rid of much unplanned, uncontrolled, selfish development of the past', recognising that this would necessitate tough new legislation and financial assistance for local authorities. Though costs would be high in pure money terms, they were regarded as 'comparatively insignificant in terms of national benefit gained by the return of cleared shack areas to their old unspoilt open natural state for the benefit of all' [60].

Embracing a new spirit of optimism, comprehensive planning legislation was passed in the form of the 1947 Town and Country Planning Act. Yet, effective though it was in a variety of ways, the main impact of the 1947 Act proved to be more in controlling new development than in removing what was already there. Certainly, the day of new 'shack towns' and scattered huts was over. But for many years more, local authorities continued to grapple with a not inconsiderable and remarkably stubborn legacy of makeshift landscapes. This type of development had been quick to take root, but its distinctive features were to remain in evidence until well into the twentieth century.

NOTES

1. Contrasting political sources are succinctly illustrated in parliamentary debates, e.g. the debate which surrounded the 1930 Rural Amenities Bill, promoted by a Conservative, Sir Hilton Young; and supported by politicians from other parties. See *Parl. Debates*, 235 H.C., Deb. 5s, pp. 1747-832.
2. Dougill, W. (1936) *The English Coast: Its Development and Preservation*. London: CPRE.
3. Helpful accounts of the voluntary movement in the 1930s are included in Williams-Ellis, Clough (ed.) (1938) *Britain and the Beast*. London: J.M. Dent and Sons.
4. Nesbit, E.H. (1977) Fortunatus, Rex and Co, in *Fairy Stories*. London: Knight Books.
5. Abercrombie, Patrick (1926) *The Preservation of Rural England*. London: Hodder and Stoughton.
6. Cited in Abercrombie, *op. cit.* (see note 5).
7. Dougill, *op. cit.* (see note 2).
8. *Ibid.*
9. Darby, A. and Hamilton, G.C. (1930) *England, Ugliness and Noise*. London: P. S. King and Sons Ltd.
10. Marshall, Howard (1938) The rake's progress, in Williams-Ellis *op. cit.* (see note 3).
11. Street, A. G. (1938) The countryman's view, in Williams-Ellis, *op. cit.* (see note 3).
12. Trevelyan, G. M. (1929) *Must England's Beauty Perish?* London: Faber and Gwyer.
13. Marshall, *op. cit.* (see note 10).
14. Spender, Stephen 'The Pylons', in Skelton, Robin (1964) *Poetry of the Thirties*. Harmondsworth: Penguin.
15. Sharp, Thomas (1932) *Town and Countryside*. London: Oxford University Press.
16. Orwell, George (1976) *Burmese Days*. London: Secker and Warburg.
17. Priestley, J. B. (1934) *English Journey*. Reprinted London: Heinemann.
18. *Ibid.*
19. Williams-Ellis, Clough (1951) *Town and Country Planning*. London: Longmans Green.

20. Sharp, Thomas (1936) *English Panorama*. London: J. M. Dent and,Sons.
21. Sharp (1932), *op. cit.* (see note 15).
22. Joad, C. E. M. (1938) The people's claim, in Williams-Ellis (1938), *op. cit.* (see note 3).
23. Williams-Ellis (1938), *op. cit.* (see note 3).
24. *Ibid.*
25. Williams-Ellis, Clough (1928) *England and the Octopus: A Plea for Town Planning*. London: Geoffrey Bles.
26. Darby and Hamilton, *op. cit.* (see note 9).
27. These advisory plans and reports are detailed in the case studies in the following chapters.
28. Abercrombie, *op. cit.* (see note 5).
29. Parl. Debates, *op. cit.* (see note 1).
30. *Ibid.*
31. *Ibid.*
32. Section 1, *Town and Country Planning Act*, 1932.
33. Section 19, *Town and Country Planning Act*, 1932.
34. Cited in McAlister, G. and McAlister, E.G. (1941) *Town and Country Planning*. London: Faber and Faber.
35. Cited in Sheail, John (1981) *Rural Conservation in Inter-War Britain*. Oxford: Clarendon Press.
36. Hardy, Dennis (1967) A Reappraisal of the London Green Belt. Unpublished dissertation, University College London.
37. Dougill, *op. cit.* (see note 2), lists various types of legislation available to local authorities, notably the Town and Country Planning, Public Health and Housing Acts; Private Acts of Parliament; the 1935 Ribbon Development Act; Bye-laws; and Owners' Agreements.
38. See, for instance, the circular *Model By-Laws, XVII: Tents, Vans, Sheds and Similar Structures* produced by the Ministry of Health in 1936.
39. See, for instance, *CPRE Monthly Reports*, August 1933, October 1933, February 1936 and March 1936.
40. Cited in *CPRE Monthly Report*, October 1933.
41. *Ibid.*
42. Sheail, John (1977) The impact of recreation on the coast: the Lindsey County Council (Sandhills) Act, 1932. *Landscape Planning*.
43. See *Surrey County Council Act*, 1931 (Part VII, 'Moveable Dwellings and Camping Grounds') and Parliamentary Proceedings 24 March 1931.
44. Further examples of local measures are cited in Dougill, *op. cit.* (see note 2), and in *CPRE Monthly Reports*, *op. cit.* (see note 39).
45. Kaye-Smith, Sheila (1938) Laughter in the South-East, in Williams-Ellis (1938), *op. cit.* (see note 3).
46. Sharp (1932), *op. cit.* (see note 15).
47. Cited in *CPRE Monthly Report*, March 1933.
48. Abercrombie, Patrick (1938) Country planning, in Williams-Ellis

(1938), *op. cit.* (see note 3).

49. A review of proposals is included in Williams-Ellis (1938), *op. cit.* (see note 3).
50. Williams-Ellis (1938), *op. cit.* (see note 3).
51. Lockley, R. M. (1938) The sea coast, in Williams-Ellis (1938), *op. cit.* (see note 3).
52. The countryside report (known as the Scott Report) was published as the *Report of the Committee on Land Utilisation in Rural Areas,* Cmnd. 6378. London: HMSO, 1942; while that on the coast was presented to the Minister of Works and Planning as a *General Report on Coastal Preservation,* supplemented by regional reports; see Public Record Office file HLG/92/80, and a summary of findings by Steers, J.A. (1944) Coastal preservation and planning, *Geographical Journal.*
53. Scott Report, *op. cit.* (see note 3).
54. J. A. Steers, in Public Record Office file HLG/92/80.
55. *Ibid.*
56. *Ibid.*
57. *Ibid.*
58. Ministry file *Removal of Shacks, etc; Development: General Policy,* Public Record Office file HLG/92/81 (ref. 91647/15/2, 6 April 1946).
59. *Ibid.*
60. *Ibid.*

Chapter 3

Arcadia on the South Coast

All is changed today in the English (and in most of the Welsh and Scottish) sea-villages. As the politicians say, the 'danger of proletarianism is near'.

(R. M. Lockley, 'The Sea Coast', in Clough William-Ellis, *Britain and the Beast*, 1938).

Down to the South Coast came 'cockneys' in charabancs and new motor cars and vans. So, too, did the 'Bohemians' — writers, actors, film stars and artists and wealthy professionals. All were drawn to live, for a weekend or longer, in simple conditions by the sea. In their little huts the rich played at peasants, the poor at landowners, before all returned to their different worlds on Monday morning.

From as early as the 1890s makeshift retreats gained an often precarious foothold along cliff-tops, dunes and shingle ridges, jostling with each other for a sight and smell of the sea. Established resorts like Brighton and Bognor Regis now shared the coastline with growing, clusters of huts, obsolete buses, railway carriages and a colourful assortment of bungalows. Few stretches of the South coast, from Romney Marsh in the east to the Solent in the west, escaped the presence of these new self-made resorts.

In the Romney Marsh area, Ministry officials in 1946 found the stretch between Dymchurch and Littlestone-on-Sea 'a depressing area almost completely smothered in shacks, poor-type holiday camps, bungalows, etc. with a considerable sprinkling of permanent residences' [1]. In contrast, a later observer thought the 'jumble of bungalows... probably quite fun to live in if you like having a marsh behind you and the sea in front of you' [2].

To the west of Dungeness, the whole stretch from Jury's Gap, through Camber Sands, Winchelsea Beach, Pett Level, to Cliff End and Fairlight, was dominated by makeshift development. A brief respite was to be found at Hastings and St Leonards, but beyond Bexhill scattered bungalows lined the coast at Normans Bay and Pevensey

Birling Gap: current view of cliff-top development.

Bay, some of it seen as being amongst 'the most ruthless of all shack-slum development' [3].

The scenery changes to steep cliffs beyond Eastbourne and, though this remained largely undeveloped, here and there (most notably at Birling Gap) hut-owners gained a unique view across the English Channel. Though undoubtedly eyesores on an otherwise unspoiled stretch of coastline, clusters like Birling Gap were modest intrusions compared with developments nearby. Visitors were warned that 'unless you wish to see how ugly a thing man can make of beauty, avoid the cliffs between Newhaven and Brighton' [4]. Here the main object of the warning was Peacehaven, on a prominent stretch of the coastline recalled in the 1930s as not long previously 'a piece of unspoilt downland open to the sea... now a colony of shacks' [5]. In its sheer scale and audacity, the name 'Peacehaven' became synonymous with all that was wrong with a system that allowed people to use land virtually as they wished. Closer to Brighton, two smaller outcrops of shack development on the South Downs also attracted their critics, the saving grace of the former being that its 'old buses, railway coaches, and bungalows are mercifully hidden along the hill-side a mile back from the sea' [6].

Brighton and Hove had a reputation to safeguard, but opportunities for more anarchic ventures were to be found again at Shoreham-by-Sea. Seawards of the historic town a previously-uninhabited shingle ridge across the mouth of the Adur became the scene of one of the most colourful instances of a self-made resort, 'Bungalow Town'.

Little of this type of development attracted the eye of critics along the coast-line until Elmer and Felpham to the east of Bognor Regis and

Pagham Beach to the west. Shacks and railway carriages also made their mark at Bracklesham Bay and East Wittering, only to be held back by protectionists who fought successfully for West Wittering and Chichester Harbour. Protectionists had little to celebrate at Hayling Island, however, which became a mecca for varied holiday developments, including an area of shacks and railway carriages in the south-east of the island termed locally the 'Wild West'.

Inevitably, aesthetes viewed what was happening along the South Coast with dismay. It was a part of the world which was especially close to their heart, enshrined in childhood memories and an image of English culture in a way that other areas in the throes of change — Essex, for instance — could never be. It was a hallowed place, assaulted by an invading force:

> London broke out like a bursting reservoir, flooding all the ways to the sea, swamping our history and our past, so that already we are hardly ourselves. Of a week-end the roads from north to south are like a city street. The new engines climb the Downs; they invade every corner [7].

Local authorities too, themselves reflecting the interests of a powerful protectionist lobby, were no less at odds with plotland development and did what they could to keep it in check. At least until the post-1945 period, when intent was matched with new powers, they were always one step or more behind the plotholders. Advisory reports and planning schemes under the early Town Planning Acts showed a keen awareness of the situation, and public health officers battled on with the bye-laws, but opportunities for action were still limited.

Stepping into the breach of a weak system of environmental planning, voluntary bodies played an important role along the South Coast. For instance, the Society of Sussex Downsmen, founded in 1926, was instrumental in helping to protect remaining stretches of undeveloped coastline. It also sought to prevent the dispersal of settlement inland onto the Downs through encouraging local authorities to buy land where possible, to enter into agreements with private landowners, and to restrict new development above a height of 200 feet above sea level [8].

But it was not enough, and Hilaire Belloc, echoing the concern of others, asked whether Sussex would endure. In 1936 his own answer was pessimistic: 'as things now stand there would seem to be no prospect of survival through the coming years; nor will there be any Sussex any more' [9]. Perhaps time has proved Belloc to be right, though he could not possibly have foreseen the effects that war was to have on the South Coast especially. In a few brief exercises at the start of the war, when acre upon acre of scattered development along the beaches was cleared, the defending forces achieved what planners had sought over more than a decade.

Since 1945 the authorities have generally been able to work out a *modus vivendi* with the plotholders. For a start (in spite of a recent

57

trend in 'leisure plots' which has given rise to a different type of problem) it has been possible to prevent new development of this sort. Of that which survived the war, some has been removed through compulsory purchase or voluntary agreement, while some has simply been allowed to evolve and climb 'upmarket'. Many signs remain of what it was all like before, but now it is more likely to be perceived as nostalgic than problematic.

RYE BAY

HOLIDAYS — Winchelsea Beach. Double-deck, super Bus to let, excellently converted. Lge. verandah. Ckg. cabin. On private grd. Ample rm. for cars. Near Sea, shops. Accommodate 6–8. Ideal opportunity excel. holiday.

(Advertisement in *Dalton's Weekly House and Appartment Advertiser*, 8 May 1937).

Salt marshes, shingle ridges, tidal reaches and sandhills mark the low coastline that fringes Rye Bay, from Pett Level, through Winchelsea Beach and Rye Harbour, to Camber Sands and Jury's Gap. With little in the way of established settlements along the coast to the east of Hastings, and with available flat land on which to build, it proved to be an area vulnerable to a variety of incursions dating back to the start of the century.

Converted railway carriages, motor buses, and weatherboarded shacks and shanties all took their place, usually as close to the sea as the tides would allow (and sometimes, as at Winchelsea Beach, with an unfortunate lack of judgement beyond the limits of safety). Tales are told of 'golden summers' and of the 'charm and romance' of informal holidays in a makeshift landscape. In turn, however, public health inspectors and planners, assisted between 1939 and 1945 by the British army stationed in the area, worked overtime in their endeavour to clear the area of what is characteristically referred to in official documents as that 'unhappy, undesirable and unplanned development' [10]. Inevitably, this clash of interests has produced its own distinctive chapter of plotland history.

'WEATHERBOARDING... AND SHRIMPS FOR TEA'

Holiday-makers gained a foothold before 1914 with the Rye Golf Club installed in 1897 behind the sand dunes between Rye Harbour and Camber, and the odd scattered shack alongside coastguards' cottages and fishermen's huts, but it was not until after 1918 that radical changes took place [11].

Looking back on the area as it used to be, one correspondent recalls a visit in the early years of the century to the 'fascinating stretches of

58

Camber Sands: makeshift buildings in the 1930s. (photos courtesy of Rother District Council)

marsh which lie between Winchelsea and Rye and the sea, but then mostly at Dogs Hill — no talk in 1904 about Winchelsea Beach — where there was nothing but Davis's Farm and the old coastguard cottages, with the dreadful stable-cum-hut where old one-handed Antony Eldrdige lurked, and turned an honest penny in the summer by bringing supplies and water to the inhabitants of the cottages...' [12].

And some twenty years later in 1925, another holiday was spent by the same correspondent at nearby Camber where there was already a weekend car-parking problem, but where the number of bungalows facing the dunes were still said to be very few [13].

What brought the changes were general trends of more people being able to reach the coast at weekends and for holidays, combined with local circumstances of land coming onto the market at this time. In the latter case, as well as the break-up of the Fairlight Hall Estate (which extended from Fairlight to Rye Harbour), farmers with land abutting the shingle and marsh-land were only too willing to sell the odd field for building. Overnight, farmland at Winchelsea Beach with an agricultural value of as little as £20 an acre was transformed into building land, sold off in plots at £25 for each 100-foot frontage. Additional profits could be yielded from cheap speculative bungalows, at between £150 and £200 each. But in the early-1920s even at these prices property was not easy to sell [14].

Cheaper possibilities followed when land was subdivided into still smaller plots, and buyers built their own homes. All styles of vernacular architecture emerged, from the shacks perched on the dunes at Camber to the railway carriages and buses at Winchelsea Beach. One of the more imaginative structures at the latter place was a double-decker London tram sliced into two ground-floor rooms, and combined with a railway van delivered from Ashford for £6 including transport.

Behind it all was a world of farmers with an eye to business, and of local traders and small-time entrepreneurs. Mr Fletcher, for instance, was a retired postman who bought some surplus army huts after 1918, and sold them as holiday homes at Camber. Also at Camber, Johnson's Field was named after the man who sold off plots for summer homes, and who later owned the firm Provident Estates which built Camber's amusement arcade. Or there were the farmers at Winchelsea Beach, Messrs. Crump and Merrick, who each sold off plots for a variety of development.

So, for buyers, it was something of a poor person's paradise, with a choice of everything from a cheap, ready-made seaside bungalow to a bare strip of shingle on which at weekends you could build your own shelter. But that was not all, with others attracted less by the low prices than by its very character as a windswept corner of England. From the early days of the Rye Golf Club, visitors stayed on in the district for house parties. Later, in the inter-war years, businessmen and professionals were attracted by the informality of it all, summed up by the random thoughts of one such visitor recalling her childhood holidays at Winchelsea Beach:

A first holiday in a railway carriage converted into a bungalow; buying a plot of land nearby and the building of our own bungalow which was a rather superior model as I remember it — my father designed it like an 'E' without the middle stroke; my brother and I being kept out of mischief by the inspiration of filling the space under the floor-boards with tiny buckets of shingle (an endless task); of ruberoid on the roof, one section of which made the rainwater taste odd; the cess-pool and the chemical lavatory and the spiders in it; the smell of driftwood burning in the little kitchenette and of shrimps boiling; the catastrophe of having papered the tongue and groove bedroom walls the paper split as the wood moved according to the temperature... the religious maniac who used to call from a wooden shack to try and save us; the cockneys who had the bungalow next door (a railway carriage except for the porch); the rather dashing people with fast cars who owned 'Four Winds' which was *several* railway carriages... I remember the 'Old Ship' going into the sea when the sea-wall burst and the bathing huts floating out to sea and the tidal wave [15].

Rye Bay: use of converted trams in the 1930s at Camber Sands and currently at Winchelsea Beach. (Top photo by courtesy of Rother District Council)

Inevitably, too, plotlands acquired something of a 'Bohemian' flavour, and idols of stage and screen also came to enjoy the atmosphere. In the case of Pett Level it gained a reputation amongst artists. The sculptor Jacob Epstein, returning from Paris in 1912, settled there:

> Coming to England I rented a bungalow on the Sussex Coast at a solitary place called Pett Level near Hastings, where I could look out to sea and carve away to my heart's content without troubling a soul... this was a period of intense activity, and were it not for the war and the impossibility of living in the country and making a living, I would have stayed there for ever [16].

But official suspicion of a man with a foreign name, an 'alleged sculptor' who kept pigeons, led him to leave in 1916, 'and I shipped my sculpture to London with regret, giving up a place where I had been very happy, and where I had had a very fruitful period of work' [17]. The painter Mark Gertler (not a friend of Epstein, whose morals he disapproved of) stayed at the other end of the village during July and August 1914. He rented a room from Mrs Cooke at the Old Coastguard Cottage, Pett Level, and wrote to the painter Carrington:

> I like this place enormously... when I get back, I'm going to spend some days in the country — quite near London — because I want to find a little place where I can have a room, to which I can run some days in the week for peace and landscape work, and I am getting to love trees and fields and cows more and more. So I want to find a second home in some little country village... [18].

There were those, though, who were less enthusiastic about the area. In the South East Sussex Regional Planning Scheme, concern was expressed over the growing scatter of development, attributed 'partly to the break up of some of the large estates, partly to the increasing week-end bungalow habit, and partly to the growing desire of workers in towns to live in more rural surroundings' [19]. The surveyors drew particular attention to:

> the Pett and Fairlight district and the Rye and Winchelsea district. In these localities there is a considerable building activity of a kind that is for the most part to be deplored. If this part of the coast is to retain the charm that is at present attracting people to its shore, something will have to be done immediately to prevent the miscellaneous collection of huts and disused tramcars that are rapidly making their appearance in these places and are beginning to do what may easily become irreparable damage from the point of view both of amenity and of rateable value [20].

Local ratepayers, too, anticipating a fall in property values if standards were allowed to decline, were amongst the first to call for public action. As early as 1930 the County Council was urged to take 'immediate steps to prevent the disfigurement of the countryside, particularly with regard to the coastal area lying between Hastings and Dungeness' [21]. At the time, though, it was conceded that there was little which the County Council could do, no matter how sympathetic it was with the cause.

However, the passing of the 1932 Town and Country Planning Act, and the subsequent General Interim Development Order, created new possibilities. For the rest of the 1930s the County Council and Battle Rural District Council jointly sought to use these powers in order to restrict development to its existing limits, and to clear away 'moveable dwellings' where possible.

Draft Planning Schemes were prepared to delimit areas for development, though the County and District Councils were not always in agreement on the details. The County, for instance, noted that considerable difficulties arose in connection with the development of Pett Level and Camber Sands, and that it may be preferable to exclude them from the main scheme and to take 'special measures' to deal with them. Battle RDC could not agree with this, arguing that the sooner there was some form of control over these areas the better. The case was put that their inclusion would help the local authority to obtain control of moveable dwellings as well as to prevent the erection of 'unsuitable dwellings' or the development of 'unsuitable sites'.

Invariably, the public health inspectors were no less involved in looking for ways to curb this type of development than their planning colleagues. Primitive 'back to nature' conditions which holidaymakers enjoyed were to others, nothing less than a public health risk. Apart from the absence of piped drinking water, the main problem arose from the makeshift sewerage arrangements. In what is, essentially, a marshland area with a high water table, there was always a strong chance of contamination resulting from the percolation of raw sewage and the indiscriminate deposit of the contents of earth and chemical closets. Moreover, little attention was paid to the maintenance of field and subsoil drains so that, over much of the year, local flooding added to the problems.

Reviewing the situation that had arisen in the 1930s the County Medical Officer looked back to his annual reports which showed that 'these coastal strips have been increasingly tainted by temporary or other buildings of low grade for twenty or thirty years' [22]. It was noted, however, that although everyone had been very conscious of the undesirable conditions', existing powers were too limited for radical action. Even some of the most ramshackle developments did not necessarily fall foul of the bye-laws. Moreover, it was held that the buildings in question were not, in the main, residences for the 'working classes' and could not therefore be dealt with through Clearance Orders under the Housing Acts.

Officials searched the statute books for ways of coping with the situation. In the end though, there was little they could do but hope that, if things got no better, at least they might get no worse. Indeed, at a later Public Inquiry, the Medical Officer admitted that every summer which passed without an outbreak of disease was hailed with relief by the health authorities [23].

As in other instances, it was the coming of war in 1939 which proved to be a watershed. Not only was the spread of development curtailed but, in the course of the war, many of those buildings which had only recently gained a foothold on the dunes and shingle ridges were forcibly cleared away. With a short Channel crossing, this whole stretch of coastline was considered to be particularly vulnerable to the possibility of an enemy landing. As a result, not only were the beaches sealed off but, in places, the local population was evacuated and many buildings were demolished by the home forces.

At Camber it was the colony of shacks on the sand dunes which incurred the greatest damage, being cleared to make way for defence artillery and to remove opportunities for concealment in the event of enemy landing. Further damage resulted from the occupation of former holiday homes by the armed forces, and from enemy air attacks. By 1945, this whole stretch of coast was a scene of devastation. Abandoned military installations and damaged equipment, together with the residue of a more peaceful era in the form of neglected holiday shacks and old bus bodies, littered the shoreline. But not everyone lamented what had happened. The County Medical Officer, for instance, noted that there was still 'an appreciable number of casual shacks which defy classification; although fortunately a great number were destroyed during the war' [24].

It was clear that things would never be the same again, and officials were quick to seize their opportunity. In a series of plans and policies every effort was made to erase all signs of 'the unhappy development' which had taken place in the inter-war years.

'FOR THE NATIONAL ADVANTAGE'

The immediate concern of the authorities was to ensure that, with the ending of the war, people should not be allowed to rebuild and restore their properties along previous lines. Their concern was exacerbated by postwar pressures for housing which encouraged people to move in on a permanent basis, to what were formerly holiday homes. Yet, while the authorities wanted to prevent this they were, at the same time, faced with the central issue as to whether they had sufficient powers and the political nerve to interfere so directly with individual rights of property. On what grounds should the shack-owners, who had left the dunes and shingle ridges in a time of national emergency, be denied what most people still regarded as a traditional right to return to their little plot?

Even before the end of the war the County Council had prepared a 'compromise plan' for part of the area [25]. The idea behind that was simply to produce a basis for replanning while causing the least possible disturbance of existing interests. But property-owners returning to the area after 1945, and who found themselves unable to rebuild or restore their shacks and bungalows, were soon to take issue with this approach. They claimed that they were placed in the impossible situation of being prevented from improving their war-damaged properties and, because of that, being unable to obtain compensation from the War Damage Commission.

A hardline policy involving compulsory purchase was always going to be a difficult step to take but, in the 1940s, the tide was now undoubtedly running in favour of the authorities. This change of direction was accountable in terms of three sets of circumstances; the urgency for public intervention to restore the natural landscape, particularly the sand dunes; a changing political climate which weighed the national advantage against individual gain; and new powers to turn political will into practical measures.

On the issue of restoring the natural landscape there was, quite simply, a vast amount of military debris to clear away, and advantage was taken to tackle the problem of old bus bodies and unauthorised huts in the same exercise. In addition, there was now a new and, in many ways, more urgent problem in the form of shifting sand dunes. During the war, the long stretch of sand dunes at Camber had taken their own battering from defence installations and heavy use by the army. The natural balance of the dunes, which had more or less survived encroachment in the form of pre-war shacks, was no longer stable. Reports showed that a growing quantity of sand was blowing inland, and that serious flooding could result if the sea wall (made of clay) became exposed and open to the elements [26].

There was little dissent that, for reasons of amenity and coastal defence, a policy of conservation was required for the dunes. In effect, what this amounted to was a programme of planting new vegetation, combined with restricted public access. Such a policy was impossible to achieve while the dunes remained in the hands of some sixty separate owners. It was essential, then, that the dunes should be in the hands of a single, public authority. The logic was simple and incontrovertible, but what it meant was that on a consensus banner a public authority (in this case, the County Council) had manoeuvred itself into the far-from-consensual area of compulsory acquisition.

Beyond the immediate local circumstances of debris and sand dunes, the authorities in the area were greatly assisted by the changing political climate around them. Throughout the 1930s they had looked in vain for ways to check what was widely seen as the relentless desecration of an historic coastline. In the 1940s a new sense of 'national advantage', where individual rights were to be questioned in relation to public considerations, set the whole question of environmental policy within a different context. It was not that people had failed to think in this way previously, so much as that now such ideas became enshrined in official policy.

As an instance, the County Council attached great store to the views of J.A.S. Steers who, as part of his national survey, reported on the particular problems of this stretch of the Sussex coast. It was noted that some of the best sands in the South-East were near Camber and that it was understandable that it had proved popular to holiday-makers before the war. But, looking to the future, it would be a mistake to allow the return of what had been there before. 'It is surely to the National advantage to have a properly planned holiday town at Camber that will cater adequately for large numbers, rather than to allow the small but painful eyesores that spoil Winchelsea and Pett Level [27].

A policy of protecting this stretch of coast in the national interest was also endorsed in two official reports at the time. The Hobhouse Report on proposed national parks recommended its future designation as a 'conservation area' [28]; while the Huxley Report on nature conservation, taking a special interest in the shingle banks, called for its protection as an area of scientific value [29].

Coupled with political support for intervention there were now, of course, powers to match words with actions. The 1947 Town and Country Planning Act proved to be the main instrument for compulsory purchase and for the clearance of debris, though there were also cases where the Housing Acts were applied to acquire properties. In any case, where possible, acquisition was achieved on the basis of negotiation. A large stretch of sand dunes, for instance, was bought directly from the Rye Golf Club, and a number of individual properties were purchased by agreement. Prices varied from about £550 for holiday homes like 'The Outlook', 'Sandgate', 'Bonnybank' and 'Broomedge', down to a sum of £31.12s.6d. for someone's paradise which went by the name of 'Lotzasand' [30].

So for these various reasons — the urgency of the sand dunes problem, a changing political climate, and new powers available to the authorities — the way was open for public intervention. Recognising the same point the County Council noted that 'there is now an opportunity of controlling redevelopment and of preventing many of the evils which have become evident, for example, at Peacehaven' [31]. To the authorities, what greater incentive for planning could be offered to the public than a chance to avoid the fate of Peacehaven?

Parallels with their infamous neighbour along the coast extended to setting up a similar administrative device, in the form of a special planning sub-committee to deal with the particular problems of the area. Dating from October 1948 the job of the Camber and Winchelsea Beach Sub-Committee was effectively to maintain things roughly as they were while, at the same time, advising the main County Planning Committee on a longer-term strategy for the development plan.

The brief for the Sub-Committee was to colour its subsequent recommendations, it being implicit that development would be prevented where possible in the short term, that a policy of acquisition of the dunes should be pursued, and that debris and abandoned shacks should be cleared. Backed up by the new planning controls in the 1947 Act, the public health inspectors, who had struggled with little effect in the 1930s, were at last to have their day when their advice was taken to restrict further development pending the provision of a fresh water supply and main drainage.

Of greater long-term consequence was the mixed policy of containment and growth that evolved. Along part of the coast at Cliff End, Fairlight and Pett Level the aim was to prevent any more

66

development for all time. At neighbouring Winchelsea Beach it was intended that there should be no extension to the line of development, but that it might be possible to allow a limited amount of infilling after the provision of basic services. In other words, it was accepted that there was little that could be done to clear the area, as many would have preferred.

Further along the coast, at Camber, the opportunity to turn back the clock to its days as a small fishing hamlet were even more remote. With a realistic assessment of the odds the County Council decided to cut its losses and go, instead, for a policy of expansion that would, at least, bring with it an opportunity to rid the area of its plotland background. Plans were envisaged for the emergence of a small town, with a permanent population of at least 5000, doubling to 10,000 during the holiday season.

This policy of expansion at Camber, first recommended by the Planning Sub-Committee, was eventually written into the County Development Plan. It was clear, by then, that Camber had an important role in the overall coastal strategy for East Sussex, in helping to lure development away from the unbuilt stretches. The intention was 'that all the undeveloped natural coast that still remains should be preserved and that proposals for the extension of coastal, recreation and holiday facilities should be limited to Camber and to sea front improvements within existing towns' [32]. So a role of 'protector' was posthumously allocated to an area that had not long previously been regarded as an eyesore and a nuisance.

It was argued that transforming Camber from a plotland to a planned settlement would be of benefit, not only along the South Coast as a whole, but for holidaymakers to Camber in particular. In short, the belief was that shacks and shanties, while expressing a demand for space by the sea, were an unfortunate aberration that had been overtaken by events. Holidaymakers of the future would choose, instead, to visit planned vacation centres:

> The unhappy development at Camber expresses the need to encourage the growth of a new type of holiday settlement, designed to meet modern requirements for recreation and holiday purposes. This is the major physical planning problem. These needs have shown themselves round the coast of Britain in the form of shacks and other buildings at points of easy access, where the coastal attraction has enabled large populations to escape from our larger towns and cities... Since the war and by reason of the control of building labour and materials, this problem has diminished. Nevertheless, the demand is still there and is now tending to take the form of the caravan stationed permanently on land. Provision is made, therefore, for an area to be set aside for holiday bungalows [33].

The day of hauling a railway carriage onto the sands was over. New policies were being forged on a watershed between a pre-war age of

67

simple holidays by the seaside and a future marked by a very much higher expenditure on holidays and leisure generally. In sacrificing the individuality of the shack for estates of standardised holiday bungalows, the planners had foreseen at least some of the changes in the scale and expectations of holiday demands in the future. Increasingly, the pattern of holidays was itself to reflect the contradictions of a society where the search for individuality through private consumption was effectively neutralised by the associated tendency of mass involvement. A handful of people before the war with a shack on Winchelsea Beach or Camber Sands were able to 'escape'; a thousand people trying to do the same thing after the war were not. The era so aptly referred to as 'the long weekend' had now passed into history [34].

'AN INDIVIDUALISTIC CHARACTER'

So planned expansion at Camber, combined with containment elsewhere, was the order of the day from the 1940s onwards. Compared with the 1930s fresh outbreaks of sporadic development could now be prevented. But what about the signs of an earlier age that still remained? It was all very well to contain this development but, in time, people asked whether more could not be done. Battle Rural District Council was particularly active in pressing for a tougher policy that would actually clear away whole areas of 'substandard' building to 'restore lost amenities'. Two areas were singled out for special attention — Winchelsea Beach and Jury's Gap [35].

At Winchelsea Beach it was noted that in the early-1960s along a 1000-yard stretch of shingle ridge, there were thirty-nine separate units of accommodation and several vacant plots. Only one of these had been built since the inception of 1947 planning controls. Some of the buildings were still not connected to mains water and electricity, and all relied on their own means of drainage disposal. Twelve of the units were described as being sub-standard, being either wooden huts or railway carriage conversions. Battle Council now urged the County Council to secure the removal of this whole development through compulsory purchase if necessary.

Following a survey of the area the County concluded that such a measure would not really justify the cost (estimated in 1968 at around £80,000). For all the long-standing rhetoric of despoliation it was now asserted that the beach 'cannot be regarded as unsightly', and even that some of the buildings were 'good examples of the informal seaside dwellings of their period' [36]. Time had apparently mellowed both the shacks and official views of them, with even a suggestion that they might be worth conserving. Improvements in amenity that would result from clearance were regarded as too small, 'having regard to the cost involved and the likely opposition from residents and owners' [37].

Much the same was concluded along the coast at Jury's Gap, where a similar number of buildings (thirty-seven in this case) were sited on

Jury's Gap and Pett Level: current views

either bank of the 'Jury's Gap Sewer'. With no mains water or sewerage the owners made their own arrangements. Water was obtained from rainwater storage tanks and by bulk supplies from the local authority, while drainage was to cesspits or chemical closets. Under pressure to compulsorily purchase, the County reviewed various options.

One option was simply to take no action at all, allowing only minimum changes for buildings to be kept weather-proof and fit for habitation. This policy could be supported by an Article 4 direction to ensure strict control by the local authority over any proposal for development in the area.

An alternative policy was to aim for an improvement in conditions in the area. This would have involved the provision of at least a piped water supply and either proper cesspools or a sewerage system. Another side of 'improvement' was to consider a rigorous policy of serving demolition orders on declaring a Clearance Area under the 1957 Housing Act, to cover those buildings considered to be 'unfit for human habitation'.

A third option was to clear the area gradually, perhaps starting with discontinuance orders on the camping sites and huts, and moving on to the other buildings as and when they became available. Set against the advantage of spreading capital costs over a number of years, it was noted that this approach would maximise uncertainty amongst all parties.

The final option was to remove the settlement over a short period, using compulsory purchase powers, the cost being about £90,000. But was it really worth it? At the end of the day, the parish would lose rateable value, the restored farmland would be only of marginal quality and, in landscape terms, the area would still be regarded as unsightly (largely due to overhead low-tension lines which cross the marshes here). Quite simply, it was stated that the expenditure could not be justified 'in relation to the amenities of other residents, since Jury's Gap is comparatively isolated' [38].

What all this illustrates is that, in spite of a growing armoury of statutes, plotlands have proved to be surprisingly resilient. Moreover, this type of marginal development is often relatively remote and, therefore, of limited impact to a large number of people. In time, too, as the buildings themselves have weathered, perceptions also mellow to reduce the sense of urgency to clear them.

Over the years policy-makers have found the option of encouraging the 'improvement' of these areas more attractive than that of clearance. Following local government reorganisation in 1974, both the County Council and the new Rother District Council reversed earlier policies, the Planning Officer for the latter stating that 'the policy of extinguishment and/or restoration or replacement of existing dwellings is now impractical and needs to be replaced' [39]. A series of development and design briefs have subsequently been prepared to guide future changes in the area [40].

A change in policy is not simply a result of necessity. There is evidence, too, that those very same plotland characteristics which were

70

once dismissed as inappropriate are now more widely recognised as being worthy of preservation. This is the case at Pett Level, for instance, where the scattered layout and simplicity of the settlement is now seen to have its own charm:

> The present character of the area is one where nature dominates, and man-made structures are very individualistic. Only a small proportion of the ground surface is 'man-made' — even the narrow tracks are rough. Large areas of plots are in informal garden use. The area is something of a mini-wildlife sanctuary...' [41].

Enclaves like Pett Level remain, but this is an exception rather than the rule. Earlier policies which took a less sympathetic view of the plotlands, combined with the effects of both war damage and market forces, have transformed the pre-war world that is still remembered with nostalgia and affection. New modern houses have replaced original shacks, infilling has changed layouts, unmade tracks are now surfaced roads, and a large holiday camp has taken the place of bus-bodies and railway carriages. And whereas there were previously only a handful of people living permanently in the area, with most coming down for weekends and holidays, the balance is now reversed.

The character of Rye Bay has changed, though a tradition of plotlands lives on now in the form of modern 'leisure plots'. At a number of places near the coast, developers have bought and subdivided fields into small plots for sale, advertised as 'excellent land with future potential in the heart of historic Sussex'. But unlike the situation in the 1930s aspiring Arcadians are now met by a local planning authority with powers to ensure that the development and use of these plots gets no further than the low concrete markers in each corner. The idea of a place of one's own by the sea persists, but modern landscapes and laws leave little space for new ventures of the type that characterised the inter-war years.

PEACEHAVEN

> Leave all your troubles in those drab old towns,
> And fly, fly, fly.
> There's still a plot or two upon the Downs
> Left for you to buy.
>
> (Lyric to the tune of 'Pack up your Troubles', in *The Peacehaven Post*, 2 January 1922)

When the actor Dirk Bogarde was doing badly at the selection board for a commission in the army, he was asked about his father, who was art editor of *The Times*, and, hoping that it would ingratiate him with the board, explained that his father selected the photographs of 'Beautiful

Britain' that filled half a page on Saturdays: 'Yes, Sir; actually he managed to save a great deal of the South Coast from ribbon development, from things like Peacehaven... you know...' [42].

Peacehaven was indeed the *bête noire* of plotland development. It was not that it was in itself more scattered or undisciplined than other examples. On the contrary, there was at Peacehaven an unusual attempt to impose order and, in its way, planning. The problem with Peacehaven was that it flaunted itself. There was no discretion, no attempt to hide behind hedgerows or in off-the-track copses. Instead, it stretched conspicuously over a vast acreage of some of England's most cherished landscape, the South Downs, at its dramatic meeting with the sea. Peacehaven could not be missed. But as if that was not enough, its arrival was proclaimed long and loud by its entrepreneurial developer, Charles Neville. Using to the full the national press as well as less conventional forms of advertising, Neville ensured that everyone had heard of Peacehaven.

As a result, the place that has been variously referred to in contrasting terms, as a 'second Eden' or as a 'byword for everything which is objectionable', became a national battleground. Opposing forces fought over the issue of landscape amenity and the need for

Charles Neville: founder of Peacehaven. (Photo by courtesy of R. Poplett)

72

Peacehaven: musical invitation to buy "a plot or two upon the Downs". (Photo by courtesy of R. Poplett)

greater public controls in the field of planning. Neville's creation had its defenders, but an influential view gathered that Peacehaven had overstepped its mark. And many who took this latter view saw Peacehaven, not as a localised travesty, but as an exemplar of all that was wrong with an essentially *laissez-faire* model of development.

'A GARDEN CITY BY THE SEA'

Peacehaven's development began in the First World War, a plan for peace conceived only a few miles from the massacres taking place across the Channel. A reminder of the times is to be found in its original name, 'New Anzac-on-Sea', and in road names such as Louvain, Mons, Marne and Ypres [43].

In other respects, the war must have seemed far away. The story is told of Charles Neville with his wife Dorothy, driving in their Hupmobile along the coast road from Newhaven. As the road climbs away from the harbour it gradually reveals an expansive view, with cliffs to the south and open downland to the north. In the summer of 1914, apart from a toll-house the only sign of development was further along at Telscombe Cliffs, in the form of a few houses built by a company that had recently bought land from the previous owner, Lord

Chichester. Neville was quick to see the potential, and wondered why others had not done so before him. To his eyes, the prospect of relatively flat land overlooking the sea came to mean only one thing — a site for a salubrious and, of course, highly profitable resort.

By the time he reached the Downs, his eyes were well-trained in these matters. Neville had travelled widely in Australia and North America indulging in both mineral-prospecting and land speculation. In Canada, the propriety of his land dealings was questioned in the press, an experience that was soon to be repeated in England. He also brought back with him an apparent admiration for the low-flung, grid-iron pattern of building that was evident in the expansionist climate of both continents. In all, Neville arrived in the parish of Piddinghoe with unblemished credentials as a property speculator.

What followed was, in its way, quite predictable. His first move, in 1915, was to buy 415 acres (at £15 per acre) from the Cavendish Land Company; he increased his holdings by the end of the war to a total of 600 acres. A continuing policy of acquisition meant that by 1924 his South Coast Land Company owned a massive belt of cliff-top land, some five miles in length and one mile inland, from 'Harbour Heights' on the outskirts of Newhaven to Rottingdean in the west. It was this coastal strip that was later termed 'Lureland'.

For his original holding, Neville devised a plan to subdivide the land into a myriad of plots, each with a frontage of 25 feet and depth of 100 feet. A survey was undertaken and, in advance of any building, a competition was launched in 1916 to find a name for the new resort.

Advertisements appeared in national newspapers, offering a prize of £100 with fifty consolation prizes in the form of building plots, each valued at £50. About 80,000 entries were received, some going so far as to suggest that Neville's brainchild should be called 'The Garden of Eden'. No doubt the allusion to paradise appealed but, in the event, 'New Anzac-on-Sea' won the day (supposedly a tribute to the Australian and New Zealand Army Corps stationed in the district).

The consolation prizewinners, though, proved to be far from elated. For a start, instead of fifty awards, it transpired that no less than 12,500 entrants were told that they had won a plot. And instead of being free, each was asked to pay three guineas for legal fees to transact the land — a sum that was sufficient to whittle down the original list to 2445. Moreover, those who went on to view their plot found nothing in the way of the preparations that were implied in the competition pamphlet. Sceptics were quick to point out that at a purchase cost of £15 per acre and at a 'conveyancing' charge equivalent to more than £47 per acre, even allowing for minimal expenses, Neville stood to gain a profit in the region of £30 for every acre.

Championing the plot-holders' cause, in 1916 the *Daily Express* sued Neville on grounds of fraudulence [44]. Together with 125 plot-holders named in the action, the newspaper contended that the competition was not bona fide, that far more than fifty consolation prizes had been awarded, and that the plots of land were of little or no value. The charge was upheld, with the judge concluding that the plots were

Peacehaven: advertisement in The Times, *10 January 1916, to find a name for the new resort.*

absolutely worthless, and that the scheme was no more than a clever fraud. As a result, Neville had to pay back the three guinea fees to 114 plot-holders (eleven having withdrawn in the course of the action), together with costs. Some consolation was gained for Neville when he was himself subsequently awarded damages of £300 in a libel case against the *Daily Express*.

Appeals and further actions followed but, while the courts wrangled, changes on the ground made all this seem increasingly irrelevant. For, to further the war effort, the Board of Agriculture took over most of the estate to grow crops. Some land was also used for a fleet of anti-submarine aircraft. Barley and aircraft took priority over houses for the duration of the war, and concrete obelisks erected on the South Coast Road in 1916 to signify the opening of the estate, now looked strangely out-of-place in their newly-ploughed setting. The East Sussex War Agricultural Committee (acting for the Board of Agriculture) failed to release the land until 1920, but Neville persisted with his original plans. He announced in 1917, that the new resort would be renamed 'Peacehaven'. And the original street-names, with their unhappy associations of trench warfare, now took on a less contentious ring; avenues with names such as Piddinghoe, Sunview, Gladys and Dorothy were hardly of the sort to give offence in the years ahead.

Looking back to the early 1920s, and even allowing for its unusual start, Peacehaven might well have followed a conventional path of suburban development. Had Neville's plans materialised as intended yet another seaside resort would have taken its place on the South Coast, no doubt wanting in many ways compared with its well-established neighbours, but perhaps not dramatically different from the general pattern of interwar building.

The original plans, however, were not to be, and from the late 1920s onwards there are two characteristics which distinguish Peacehaven. Firstly, far from filling in the massive grid, plot by plot in a systematic way, the process was distinctly haphazard. In particular, a large number of plot-holders never, in fact, took possession of their land. Servicemen in the First World War staking their small claim in the land for which they were fighting, colonialists with vague thoughts of returning one day to Mother England, and competition prizewinners who became landowners overnight, all hung on to their land deeds though with little or no intention to develop. Over the years, plot-holders died and papers were lost or forgotten. When, for instance, the Ministry of Agriculture came to buy part of the estate in the 1950s, for every plot it bought there were nearly as many whose ownership could not be found — 2924 plots were acquired by 1958, with another 2873 untraced. East Sussex County Council faced an even greater problem in 1962. On buying nineteen acres for new schools, it was able to trace only twelve out of 200 'lost' owners [45].

The result of all this was that Peacehaven soon acquired a classic plotland landscape of scattered development, with vacant plots and waste-land interspersed between completed units. A second plotland characteristic was the visible evidence of what was, perhaps, an understandable reluctance on the part of the local authority to invest in Peacehaven's straggling layout. More than twenty miles of unmade roads, and an absence of main drainage until the 1950s, both testified to the enormous costs which development of that type imposed.

Peacehaven: aerial view of the 1920s. (Photo by courtesy of R. Poplett)

Neville, however, had little sympathy for the local authority
(Newhaven Rural District Council until 1934, and Chailey Rural
District Council after that). He recalled instances in Canada, where
developers and local councils worked hand in hand, and saw no
reason for things to be different in Britain. Throughout Peacehaven's
early history Neville campaigned consistently against officialdom,
arguing that the residents paid out far more in rates than they ever
received. He claimed that until 'Lureland' (as he termed Peacehaven
and its environs) had its own local government it could never prosper
as it should, 'free from the men whose livelihood and objects are
entirely opposed to the development of a seaside resort' [46]. Even in
the 1950s, when East Sussex County Council went ahead with a plan
to restrict access onto the South Coast Road, Neville returned to the
fray, reminding his readers that this was but another chapter in a
saga of persecution [47].

For all the controversy surrounding Neville, the new development
started well enough. When the first bungalow was completed in 1921,
Neville claimed that it was the first to be built anywhere in post-war
Britain. More land was bought, known as the 'Annex', and laid out in
the form of larger plots for use as smallholdings and other
enterprises. And between 1921 and 1926 the population of
Peacehaven grew from twenty-four to 3000.

All this was achieved in the face of a severe shortage of building materials. The national call for 'Home for Heroes' was not matched on the ground by facilities to get the job done, and it took Neville's entrepreneurial flair to make such rapid headway. A nearby former army camp provided a source for readymade huts, water pipes, electric cables and hardcore for roads; while a brickworks, concrete block factory, sawmill and joinery were all built on the site. In the early 1920s the building force numbered as many as 1000, including workers drafted in by Neville from South Wales.

The Land Company offered its own 'model' homes for sale, as many as seventy-five variations being available. A double-walled, concrete bungalow, for instance, was listed in 1922 at £500. Generally, plots were sold at between £25 and £75 each, with higher prices for a sea view.

In selling on a random plot basis, Neville was unable to control which parts of the estate were actually developed, but there was an attempt to regulate standards when building did take place. The Company claimed that Peacehaven would never become a town of 'shacks', a claim that was later to be seriously disputed. Covenants were written into the transaction deeds, with building lines stipulated, and safeguards to ensure that it remained basically a residential area.

The Peacehaven pioneers were a mixed crowd. Envisaged first as a holiday resort, a growing number came to settle permanently. One of the first to make a purchase was Midshipman George Kidston, who paid four guineas for a plot in 1916 [48]. After the war, too, members of the armed forces returned with their small gratuities to start a new life in Peacehaven, along with shopkeepers and retired artisans from London. The open aspect and new bungalow style also appealed to travellers home from the colonies, like Captain Somers of 'Kasauli', Cornwall Avenue, who found that the Downs 'remind us of the hills in India, where the climate is similar after the wet monsoon-clear, breezy and delightful' [49].

Perhaps what bound these people together was a desire for what the County Council later referred to as 'the Simple Life' [50]. A lack of services and frontier-type conditions — later identified as the 'problem' of Peacehaven had its own appeal. Sometimes this appeal was based more on financial than philosophical grounds. A lack of services was at least matched by low rates, and even towards the end of the 1930s doubts were expressed as to whether a substantial rates increase was practicable. It could still be said that the 'average person living in Peacehaven has very little margin of income over expenditure' [51].

As well as a proliferation of bungalows, the Peacehaven Hotel was opened in 1922, and the Pavilion Theatre in the following year. Shops were encouraged along the whole of the South Coast Road, a gross over-provision which resulted in a series of closures that matched the dereliction of the vacant plots beyond.

Where companies were either unwilling to provide essential services, or could not do so at an economic rate, Neville filled the gap himself. The Peacehaven Water Company was formed in 1921, pumping water through the pipes from the army camp, until the Mid-Sussex Water

Company took over in 1950. Likewise, the Peacehaven Electric Light and Power Company saw the development through its early days. There was even, in 1922, a private police force consisting of two local residents; and traders organised their own fire service. It was makeshift, but it worked. Peacehaven continued to grow and, by 1938, plots which only twenty years earlier had been written off in the courts as being worthless, were changing hands at as much as £100 each.

'THE ALLURE OF LURELAND'

Peacehaven has evoked powerful emotions, both for and against. Its protagonists base their case on a variety of grounds: on a simple defence of property values, on the fulfilment of an ideal of property ownership in a healthy location, and on the victory of individual values and collective 'untidiness' in the face of bureaucratic pressures for uniformity. Sometimes the arguments became conflated, and bear little relation to reality. But, in the end, it is the image and not the reality of Peacehaven which secures a hold in people's minds, an image that has more to do with dreams and aspirations than with bye-laws and costs of drainage.

The First Step towards Peace, a Haven and Happiness.

Peacehaven Post *cartoon, extolling the virtues of home ownership*

Of all the image-makers the Land Company's own publication, the *Peacehaven Post*, takes pride of place. Ostensibly to keep subscribers informed on matters of local interest, its true intention — to convince residents of their wise decision in coming to Peacehaven, and to lure new investors to the embryo paradise — was thinly disguised. Its jaunty style, illustrated in the opening edition in September, 1921, owed little to subtlety:

> Land ahoy!
> What Land?
> Why, my land, your land, our land.
> Care free and freehold happy land — LURELAND.

Though widely condemned as reflecting the antithesis of good town planning, Peacehaven's proponents argued the very reverse. Pointing to the new vogue of 'garden cities', and carefully evading reference to such essential differences as common land ownership in the conventional application of the idea, Peacehaven was freely referred to as the 'garden city by the sea'. Thus, in 1923, an article in the *Daily Chronicle* described its rapid progress as a product of town planning:

> Yes, Peacehaven, the garden city by the sea, is one of the most remarkable of places in England... As a piece of town planning I have no hesitation in saying it is the finest thing we have in England, and if I were not afraid of using extravagant language I would say in the world... I found the Peacehaveners a happy, jolly community, very proud of their infant prodigy of a garden city [52].

Critics condemned it as an eyesore — a mere collection of bungalows despoiling the Downs — but even on those grounds Peacehaven could find its defenders:

> There is, of course, a certain 'newness' about the look of the bungalows it could not be otherwise; but the wonderful thing is that there is none of that crude messiness we associate with building a block of houses in a town. It struck me that everything is done to retain the beauty of the Downs. The bungalows are mostly detached, and rest contentedly on the uplands, with their bits of gardens, and in many cases with Cornish rustic slate, so that the colours seem to blend with the landscape [53].

A union of Neville's brand of town planning combined with the spread of private property promised benefits hitherto unattainable. At Peacehaven, indeed, no less than 'twelve component parts of a serene and desirable state of life' could be enjoyed: health, happiness, contentment, recreation, satisfaction, freedom, hope, rejuvenation, home-life, prosperity, peace and a haven [54]. At the heart of all this

THIS IS THE AXE!

PEACEHAVEN HOME OWNERSHIP.

THIS AXE IS WARRANTED TO CUT DOWN EXHORBITANT RATES DOCTORS' BILLS AND HOLIDAY EXPENSES. IT MAY ALSO BE USED TO REDUCE YOUR GREENGROCERY & POULTRY BILLS, AND IT GIVES THE DEATH BLOW TO RENT!

Peacehaven Post
*cartoon likening home-
ownership to an axe.*

was the simple act of buying land and a home of one's own. While politicians worked towards the idea of a 'property-owning democracy' Neville was amongst the first to show what it could mean on the ground.

Private property could offer various benefits. For a start, it was consistently represented as a sound financial proposition, available to thousands of small investors. Neville claimed, with some justification, that plots of land bought at Peacehaven for as little as £25 would double or even treble in value before long. Capital invested in a growing locality would be sure to yield high returns. Buying land was only the first stage, and owning a home would subsequently bring its own varied benefits. Making the point in cartoon form, Peacehaven home ownership was likened to an axe — an axe that was warranted 'to cut down exorbitant rates, doctors' bills and holiday expenses. It may also be used to reduce your greengrocery and poultry bills, and it gives the DEATH BLOW TO RENT! [55].

Home ownership had political connotations, and Neville was sufficient of a populist to know what would appeal to his 'petty bourgeois' market. In Peacehaven, he could proclaim that there was nothing in the way of a traditional aristocracy. Instead, all 'residents start off the same mark as it were, striving in co-operation for the advancement, well-being and good of *their* Garden City...' If a leadership emerged it would be 'an aristocracy

81

of merit chosen of the people, by the people, as a mark of distinction for devolution to the public interest and service rendered to the community' [56].

Financial gain and political advancement were important enough, but the theme which was most explored to lure buyers to Peacehaven as opposed to inland sites was that of 'health':

> From the North to the South, from the East to the West,
> Are health-zones of fame and renown,
> And Peacehaven, though small, proudly vies with them all
> By her breath of the sea and the down [57].

In linking Peacehaven with a healthier life, Neville was on firm ground. For more than fifty years a 'back to the land' movement had laid the foundations for him. By the 1920s, whether they agreed with them or not, everyone had heard the familiar arguments in favour of moving from the overcrowded towns, especially London, and into the countryside. It was the same rhetoric which had argued for new agricultural communities at the end of the nineteenth century, which had underpinned the attractions of Ebenezer Howard's garden city idea, and which was already being used to extol the virtues of semi-detached villas in suburbia.

The sea breezes which swept inland across the open Downs, and the southern climate which earnt the new resort 'the sunshine record of England' were, for Neville, pure gifts from Heaven. Discerning property-owners were exhorted to choose their air with all the care they would give to buying any other commodity. At Peacehaven the brand was 'Best Downland Air, healthy and invigorating' — far superior to competing products like 'Town Smoke' and 'Inland Air'.

For those who still needed to be convinced, medical opinion could always be called upon. In an article by Dr. Thomas Dutton (an authority on sea-sickness and health resorts), Peacehaven was described as the place where one discovers health and *joie de vivre*. Convalescents, habitual sufferers from nerves, chest troubles and similar complaints were all encouraged to make their way to Peacehaven. Sun, wind and sea would combine to cure many an ill:

> The glorious expanse of downland and the delightfully invigorating ozone, which are Peacehaven's inheritance, give to all, visitors and residents, alike, a radiant vitality which can seldom, if ever, be excelled elsewhere. I am glad to note that in the laying out and planning of this wonder city of rapid growth every consideration has been given to the promotion of health... Peacehaven is what I term 'an extra lung for Londoners', as it is within easy reach of the Metropolis and can give everything necessary for the enhancement of clean living and good health [58].

What the *Peacehaven Post* did best, though, was to present the 'health argument' in the form of anecdotes telling of rejuvenated residents.

Walks around the estate invariably included 'chance meetings' with plot-holders. In Glynn Road, for instance, 'there's Mr Sanderson visibly rejuvenating', while, across the way is Mr White, partially disabled in the War, and advised to leave his former City business for some healthy spot. Nearby, Mr and Mrs Radcliffe, having spent most of their lives in Poplar, marvel at the effect of their new surroundings on their health, appetites and outlook on life. All 'cheery hearts and happy faces in a new and wonderful world!' [59].

There were tangible rewards in coming to Peacehaven but, more than that, Neville sought to surround it all in an aura of romance. Nothing illustrates this better than his exploitation of its downland setting. Combined with the proximity of the sea, plot-holders were undoubtedly offered a unique location. As if that were not enough, though, the Sussex Downs could provide something more — a mark of cultural respectability and pedigree for the upstart community. The Downs, which others lamented had suffered irretrievable loss from this alien development, were now claimed as Peacehaven's 'birthplace and homeland'. Even the estate newspaper changed over the years to become the magazine *Downland*, designed for a readership with a general interest and love of the Downs. The lure of Peacehaven slipped easily away from a world of measurable gains and losses towards one of pure illusion. What the plot-holders bought was not just a few square feet of real estate but a stake in what was openly referred to as the 'Land of Romance'. The marriage of reality and illusion was a wilful act but, perhaps, one in which both buyers and sellers were willing partners.

'THE POISON BEGINS HERE'

Neville waxed eloquent about his infant prodigy but, from further afield, views were strikingly opposed. In looking at contemporary reports it is as if the two sides were describing totally different places — and, in part, they were. For Neville's sights are invariably cast forward, beyond the minutiae of immediate problems, and towards the vision of a completed mecca. Railway links to London, promenades by the sea with bands playing on the cliff-top, flourishing shops along the South Coast Road, and a cultural life to match the older centres, none of these were to materialise, save in Neville's mind.

For others, though, views were more solidly forged in reality. What they saw was mile upon mile of unmade roads, building plots more often derelict than not, half-finished bungalows and 'temporary' caravans and sheds, a two-mile frontage of shops (many of which had closed) and mixed development along the main road, and a 'prestigious' sea-front that was really no more than an untended belt of crumbling cliff-top. The reality of what was there spurred a dual response — from those who lamented the waste of cherished Downland and decried the ugliness of what was taking place, and those primarily concerned with the public costs imposed by the development.

Preservationists and aesthetes had a field-day at Peacehaven. As their movement gathered strength nationally in favour of a more controlled environment, so the half-finished Sussex estate became something of a byword. Those who continued to uphold an unmodified market system of development, were simply invited to visit Peacehaven. There they would find all that was offensive to civilised taste.

In presenting the case on behalf of East Sussex County Council for legislation to help in preserving the South Downs, the advocate referred repeatedly to Peacehaven to illustrate the urgency of the problem:

> One has only got to mention the word Peacehaven to suggest to everybody's mind something which ought to be avoided. Peacehaven is a post-war development of a portion of the Downs which has become a by-word for everything which is objectionable [60].

Photographs were produced in the House of Lords Committee considering the Bill, to reveal 'the dreadful blot which Peacehaven has created' [61]. A member of the House who went to see things for himself returned in a similar state of shock. 'No nightmare could present the achievements of the jerry-builder in such ghastly guise as they have assumed in the crude and stark reality of Peacehaven' [62].

For some, though, it was not so much that Peacehaven was unplanned as that it purported to follow Garden City principles. This was the view of Thomas Sharp who, while championing the cause of an ordered environment, did not believe that the garden city idea was the way forward:

> The 'reductio ad absurdum' of the garden-city is its extension to absurdity, and of this, unfortunately, innumerable examples exist. The worst in England is Peacehaven, which has rightly become a national laughing-stock... It is indeed a disgusting blot on the landscape [63].

Throughout the 1930s, opprobrium continued to be assigned to Peacehaven — 'a monstrous blot on the national conscience' [64]. It stood out in a long ribbon of unsightly development along the South Coast. 'The poison begins at Peacehaven, which until thirteen or fourteen years ago was a piece of unspoilt downland open to the sea. It is now a colony of shacks, a long ungainly street of houses that all seem ashamed of themselves' [65].

As early as 1925, it had been dismissed as a mere collection of bungalows, and forty years later the accusation still held:

> What is one to say? Peacehaven has been called a rash on the countryside. It is that, and there is no worse in England. Peacehaven derives its name from the end of the First World War. Whose haven was it? Whose haven is it?... Every man his own house, even if only a few feet from the neighbours! [66].

No less telling than the preservationist and aesthetic arguments was the mounting concern that this type of development left the public authorities with enormous bills to service it. Proponents of town planning had long argued that while the grid-iron layout was often presented as the developer's dream, the real costs to the community were of a different order. Early town planning reports demonstrated what this meant.

Thus, in the 1932 Brighton, Hove and District *'Report on the Regional Planning Scheme'* a contrast was made between 'grouped' as opposed to 'scattered' development [67]. It was the latter which was said to be responsible for unmade roads, irregular refuse collection and postal services, lack of public services and, generally, for excessive rates. Peacehaven was cited to illustrate the costliness and inconvenience of scattered development.

Given that there were, at the time, something like 650 houses scattered over 650 acres, it was shown that six postmen would have to be employed full-time; and that to provide sewers, gas and electricity to each house, nearly twenty-six miles of sewer pipes, of gas mains and of electricity cables would be required for each service. Compared with this, had development been grouped at a density of six or seven houses per acre in an area of 100 acres, only one postman would be needed, while the length of services would be reduced to four miles in each case.

Commercial development along the South Coast Road frontage was also called into question. Not only was the location of shops and business premises on what was the main South Coast route incompatible with a free flow of traffic, but the grid-iron layout imposed additional hazards. Over a two and a half mile stretch of road, there were no less than twenty-nine cross-roads. In his haste to create short-term gain, Neville had endowed the local authority with a problem that would take many years and considerable expense to alleviate.

Making similar arguments to those in the 1932 Report, a more recent commentator questioned how people could still dispute the case for planning:

one would have thought that the consequences of not planning which lie all around us would provide sufficient answer — the ribbon of dwellings along the by-pass, the traffic jam in nearly every town centre, Peacehaven and many similar anarchic messes [68].

'BUREAUCRATIC TANGLES'

During the 1930s it became increasingly apparent that something had to be done about Peacehaven. Public outcry was one thing, but, in the end, it fell upon the local authorities (Chailey Rural District Council and East Sussex County Council) to take action [69]. The issue which finally provoked this was that of a main drainage system.

In tracing the official responses, Peacehaven exemplifies the dilemma faced by local authorities before the arrival of comprehensive planning legislation after the Second World War. On the one hand, the authorities were duty-bound to intervene for public health reasons yet, on the other hand, they were unable to match powers in that area with a general control of development to prevent matters getting still worse.

There had been little to stop Peacehaven developing in the way that it did. Neville had been obliged to submit his original layout plans to what was then the Newhaven Rural District Council, but since they complied with local bye-laws the Council had no option but to approve them. Repeated applications to the Ministry of Health for a new urban code of bye-laws to bring the area under their control were rejected, on the grounds that the policy of 'Homes for Heroes' would be upheld at all costs. The only concessions made in the way of controls were, firstly, owing to the use of cesspool drainage the Rural District Council was in due course able to insist that plots were increased from a 25-foot to a 50-foot frontage; and, secondly, from 1924 discretionary powers were granted to deal with the use of army huts and asbestos dwellings. But, by then, the character of Peacehaven had already been forged.

Selling plots without services yielded immediate profits to the developer, while deferring mounting costs to the local authorities which, at some stage, would have to pick up the bill. Though well aware of their impending responsibilities, the local authorities sought to evade these for as long as possible — a strategy which proved possible during the 1920s with a relatively small population in the area, and unusually low rates for Peacehaven which many of the plotholders were prepared to accept in exchange for a low level of services. But it was clearly a situation which could not last indefinitely.

For one thing, Neville's own makeshift services may have been more than adequate in the pioneering days but were less equipped to cater for a large population. In the case of water, for instance, the Peacehaven Water Company had been formed to provide the community with a fresh water supply. However, their source was on the gathering ground of the Brighton Corporation water supply, and it became apparent that if the Corporation was itself to sink deeper adits, the Peacehaven Company's well would dry up immediately.

Roads, too, presented a potential call on public funds. At the end of the 1930s, all roads except one (Roderick Avenue) were still unmade. As there was no legal liability for the local authority to remedy this, the issue could be deferred, at least until 'their condition will become so bad that a strong demand for some action will arise and the County Council may be put under an apparent moral obligation to carry out enough works to prevent danger to health or safety...' [70].

On the issue of main drainage, however, the margin for delay had finally disappeared. With a steadily-growing population in the 1930s and, in the absence of a drainage or sewerage system, reports came in to show that much of the land was 'sewage sick'. Under the 1936 Public Health Act the local authority (now Chailey Rural District Council) was obliged to provide an adequate system, and duly prepared a scheme for trunk sewers with an outfall works at Piddinghoe. The main problem was that, for the scheme to work, branch sewers also had to be provided from the many streets on the estate. And, because of the peculiar layout of Peacehaven, the costs were enormous. So the County Council, asked to contribute to its construction, joined with the District Council in looking for a more economical way of meeting their legal obligations. The answer was to distinguish between that part of Peacehaven already quite intensively developed (immediately to the north and south of the main coast road) and areas where development was still essentially scattered.

In the former area, it was considered that some, if not all, costs could be recovered from existing 'frontages', and that town planning powers were generally sufficient to regulate new development. If the County and District Councils were to provide sewers for this area alone, it would be possible to charge for them either on a frontage basis or, alternatively, by increasing the general rate in the Parish of Peacehaven. As regards the first approach, with the frontages barely one-third developed, a substantial loss would inevitably be incurred by the local authorities. It was also noted that it could be an unfortunate precedent for areas similar to Peacehaven, where developers could say that it did not matter how they developed or what services were lacking since these were certain to be provided at public expense. The alternative was to put the whole cost on to the parish, which would result in a rates increase of fifty per cent. It was an unusual proposal, as charges would normally be spread over the whole of the Rural District, but one that was legally possible. Either way, however, the problem of what to do with the outlying areas remained. Additional plans were therefore considered to prevent or, at least, to bring under control any further building on this marginal land. A policy of inaction was ruled out. 'If nothing is done development will spread, putting further financial burdens on the Authorities, if they are to take measures to prevent the outbreak of disease and the other consequences of neglected and ill-planned development' [71]. All were agreed that further development needed to be checked, but the question was how to do it.

The main obstacle to intervention in the outlying areas was that of compensation and, in the case of Peacehaven (and, indeed, other areas of plotlands) land values presented a particular problem, Quite simply, land could not be assessed at use value, much of which was derelict. Instead, it was valued on the basis of prices paid for individual plots, which was equivalent to between £300 and £600 per acre, something like three times the normal value of the land in compensation. An added twist was that if mains drainage was introduced to the most developed part of Peacehaven, higher rates in that area could actually encourage more development in the cheaper outlying zone which, in turn, could raise land values still more. Against this background, various ways were considered to gain control of the outlying area illustrating, as they do, the range of legal and financial powers available at the time.

One possibility was to promote a Private Bill with special measures for the Peacehaven area, but this was quickly discounted. Not least of the problems with this was that publicity surrounding the Bill itself would be expected to increase demands for compensation. Other possibilities lay within the scope of existing town planning legislation. A wholesale demolition of buildings was ruled out on grounds of costs, which left three options to be considered.

The first option was to draw up a Planning Scheme for the outlying area, and to ensure that future development was of a higher quality than would otherwise be the case. Even if the land was laid out by one of the councils concerned, the viability of achieving good development was seriously questioned. In short, who would want to invest in a higher class of property on the edge of a development with Peacehaven's reputation?

A second option was to sterilise the land permanently against development, either by acquisition or by reserving the land under the Planning Scheme for agricultural purposes. The necessity to sterilise the land in one form or another was generally acknowledged, but the inevitability of compensation at 'excessive values' precluded action on these lines.

The final option was to put a temporary restriction on the land, pending the coming into operation of a General Development Order. This was an attractive option that did not, in itself, involve compensation and which could stabilise values in the area prior to later acquisition. However, if a plot-holder successfully appealed against the temporary restriction, then compensation would be payable not only to him but to all other plot-holders in the area.

It was a complex situation which, given the attitudes and limited resources of the local authorities concerned, presented no obvious solution. In the event, before anything could be done, the outbreak of the Second World War shelved the issue for a further period. Significantly, though, unused land was once again requisitioned for agricultural purposes, the War Agricultural Executive Committee enjoying special powers to do what the County Council had wanted for much of the 1930s.

Aware that the problem had only been postponed and by no means solved, Chailey Rural District Council appointed a planning consultant to recommend a strategy for Peacehaven in the postwar years. Reporting in 1945 he called for a zoning scheme to distinguish areas for development, and for improvements along the coast road [72]. The County Council agreed on a priority of selecting areas for development with, next in importance, a reconsideration of sewerage and highway proposals, the making-up of the private streets, and the general question of coast erosion. At last, the Peacehaven issue ceased to hinge on its sewers alone and, with the passing of the 1947 Town and Country Planning Act, the opportunity to put this broad-based strategy into practice became a reality.

'ERASING DISORDER'

Peacehaven had passed the point of no return. There was no longer any question of either returning the land to its pre-1914 condition or of forcing the developers to meet the costs of providing services. But at least a judicious use of the new planning powers opened up fresh possibilities. In the post-war years a variety of measures were used to transform Peacehaven from its plotland origins to simply another residential community on the South Coast [73].

Because of its special problems, in 1948 the County Council set up a Peacehaven Sub-Committee which reported directly to the full Planning Committee. Its brief was largely that which had taxed the pre-war authorities: the perennial issue of main drainage and the constraint that this imposed on further development, the task of making-up the private roads, difficulties of land acquisition with a multiplicity of small ownerships, and pollution of the foreshore.

The Sub-Committee also pursued the question of what to do with land which had been taken over for agriculture in the war years. This land included the area of prize plots awarded in the 1916 competition, the majority of which had never been taken up. It was considered to be of good quality for farming and, to prevent it reverting to a semi-derelict condition, the Ministry of Agriculture was exhorted to compulsorily acquire it. This it subsequently did (though it was unable to trace the original owners in half the cases, and often paid no more than £3 per plot when it did).

That land apart, the strategy embodied in the County Development Plan has been one of 'phased consolidation'. The idea has been to restrict development to one area at a time, filling in vacant plots and providing services on an economic basis. This started with the release of land on each side of the South Coast Road, followed by the progressive release of other areas to the north. The ultimate objective. has been 'to complete the growth of a small compact residential town with proper services and amenities'.

To complement this general approach, a more detailed Town Map was promised for Peacehaven. What this eventually showed (the plan was not approved until 1965) was an expected population increase from about 10,500 in 1969 to 17,550 in 1981. In turn, two further plans were earmarked for the areas of greatest redevelopment [74].

The first of these additional plans envisaged a new 'inland' town centre, away from the ribbon of commercial properties along the South Coast Road. As well as easing the long-standing problem of through traffic it was also seen to offer 'the urban focus that is now lacking' [75]. Approval was given to the Town Centre Map and Action Plan in 1974, and a new development of shops, a library and community facilities duly materialised as the Meridian Centre in 1979. It was all a far cry from Neville's 'parish of shopkeepers' along the South Coast Road fifty years before.

The second Action Plan was for new housing in Peacehaven North, including the area originally termed the 'Annex'. Here the idea was to get away from the grid layout which had dominated development elsewhere, and towards a more 'organic' layout with a maximum possible segregation of pedestrians and vehicles. What made this possible was the continued existence of large, low-density plots, designed and in many cases still used as smallholdings, which opened the way for its radical transformation. There was no place in the 1970s for an area that could still be described as one of 'scattered dwellings occupying large plots', with 'small tracts of agricultural and derelict land' and roads that 'are no more than rough, frequently waterlogged, tracks' [76]. Characteristics which were precisely those to attract the early plot-holders were now deemed to be grounds for redevelopment. The new plans were approved in 1974, and 'to the advantage of the whole town, a safer and more attractive layout' has subsequently emerged [77].

RETROSPECT

So eventually officialdom won the day, and Peacehaven is now largely indistinguishable from other South Coast settlements. Against a backcloth of open downland, long rows of brick-built bungalows and trim gardens have filled the gaps in Neville's chequer-board. There is still the odd bungalow with its wooden verandah that once caught the eye of colonial travellers; and other quaint reminders of the past, like the concrete obelisks on the South Coast Road, and the clifftop construction to mark the Greenwich Meridian and distances from Peacehaven to outposts of a now-defunct Empire.

And the memory of its stormy background can still invoke opposing reactions from contemporary observers. The invective continues:

It usually leaves most people speechless. It is a two-mile strip of bungaloid horror, perched on a cliff-top between the Channel and the Sussex Downs. It should have been a home for heroes and it became a monument for rapacity [78].

In contrast, John Seymour looks back on Peacehaven in a more sympathetic vein:

Peacehaven is the place most people love to hate. I try my best, but really I cannot find anything so terrible about a township knocked up by ex-soldiers after 1918, with their pathetic little gratuities, in order to have somewhere to live away from noise and violence, of which they had presumably had enough [79].

Or take, for example, Mrs Sayers, who has lived at Peacehaven since 1923 Her husband had been severely wounded in the First World War, and their doctor in London advised a more bracing, upland climate. Consequently they applied to estate agents in the Surrey uplands for houses there, but found prices far beyond their reach. At this time, thanks to the saturation publicity campaign of Charles Neville, every

London tram ticket had on its obverse an advertisement for Peacehaven as 'The Garden City by the Sea'. Mr and Mrs Sayers enquired and, as a result, bought three adjoining plots at £50 apiece. They got title to the land in 1921, they built on it in 1922, and in 1923 they opened their branch post office and grocery store. They never looked back. 'To me', Mrs Sayers recollects, 'it seemed as though we had emigrated'. It was indeed a raw new settlement, and she and her husband were among those who found there opportunities which were denied elsewhere [80].

It is what happened to people like these that one thinks of most. Even the County Council recognised in the 1930s that Peacehaven had its own attractions, that it 'appealed to persons wishing to live the Simple Life untrammeled by restrictions as to the type of house, the making up of roads and the disposal of sewage' [81]. So the question remains where do they find the 'Simple Life' now?

SHOREHAM BEACH

It appears to be, I agree, a not conventional town development, but are we going to plan all our seaside resorts on conventional lines?

(Counsel at Public Local Inquiry, February 1949)

A mile-long shingle spit extends across the mouth of the River Adur, with Shoreham Harbour to one side and the open sea to the other. Unusual in itself as a physical feature, the spit also proved to be the scene of one of the most colourful examples of spontaneous development in the pre-1939 era. 'Bungalow Town', as it was known at the time, exhibited its own distinctive range of holiday homes, from railway carriages in various stages of conversion to motley designs of timber and brick-built bungalows. By the outbreak of the Second World War as many as 700 such buildings had found a place on the shingle.

But primitive conditions in the settlement, no less a part of its character than the free-flowing style of architecture, were from the outset an obvious target for official concern. Subsequent war manoeuvres went a long way towards clearing what local authorities had previously been unable to, but after the war surviving development and individual rights to the land proved to be an important test-case for the efficacy of new planning powers. Well-publicised disputes at Shoreham Beach in the immediate postwar years between plotholders and officialdom serve well to illustrate some of the wider issues and principles at stake at that time.

'COMING OF BUNGALOW TOWN'

The origins of Bungalow Town go back to the last century. It is said that it all started one summer when a camper put up his tent on the lonely expanse of shingle, returning in the next year with a railway

91

carriage. In the 1880s and 1890s others followed, with railway carriages hauled over the mud flats of the Adur at low tide.

Individual initiatives apart, local circumstances favoured development at this time. A long-standing industry of making wooden ships at Shoreham ceased in about 1880 and periodic recessions until the turn of the century encouraged local entrepreneurs to look for new activities. Building bungalows proved to be a timely opportunity for unemployed joiners, just as a growing, holiday trade brought additional income to Shoreham traders. The opening of a fast and direct railway line to London in 1897 enhanced the attraction of the area. From the Edwardian period onwards the pattern of Bungalow Town was set [82].

In its early days most of the land was in the hands of the 'Shoreham and Lancing Land Company' but in 1913 the company sold up to a private owner. Though there was already a substantial community before the First World War, most development took place in the 1920s and 1930s. Railway carriages and timber bungalows jostled for a sea frontage and, increasingly, filled in the spaces on the shingle facing inland.

The Urban District Council added a touch of 'respectability and order' in 1938 with a prestigious beach bathing centre known as the Lido. But Shoreham Beach remained essentially a place for cheap and simple holidays. As one correspondent recalls:

> We rented 'Titwillow' for one experimental August, and in 1908 my father signed a 35-year lease of 'Rosemary' with the Shoreham and Lancing Land Company at a yearly rental of £17.4s. That was another of Bungalow Town's attractions — it was easy on the pocket; and once you'd settled in, there was little to make the holiday money fly; there wasn't even a tavern in the town. And no shop until the Bungalow Stores eventually opened up... [83].

But in common with other developments of this type, it was not simply a place for cheap family holidays. From the 1890s, intermingled with conventionality, there are strong associations too with a Bohemian set. It was the fast train which first opened the way for West End theatre people to spend what days they could at Shoreham Beach, bringing to a quiet seaside town the whiff of another world. Fast cars, weekend parties, extravagant clothes and celebrities of the day brought colour and excitement to what was still, essentially, a humble collection of holiday bungalows.

One of the celebrities to visit Shoreham Beach was the music hall star, Will Evans, who named a number of bungalows after pantomimes in which he had appeared like — 'Cinderella' and 'Sleeping Beauty'. It was also the scene of early film-making, with its own studio and personalities who stayed on in the district.

The architecture of Bungalow Town was a fair reflection of this strange mixture of ways. Some of the earliest buildings, though picturesque to later observers, were quite unpretentious in origin, a simple and economic response to the needs of their owners. Railway carriages

92

Shoreham Beach: railway carriage on its way to Bungalow Town (c. 1911) and internal view of conversion. (Bottom photo by courtesy of D.J. Bull and L.K. Oliver)

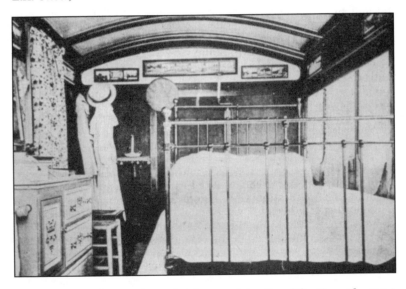

provided a popular starting point for a variety of modifications, the most common being to win more space by siting a second one alongside, with a connecting room in the middle like a letter 'H', and a verandah at either end.

Purpose-built bungalows became popular in the Edwardian era. A variety of styles were introduced by P. T. Harrison, at a selling-price of between £250 and £500. One of his models was 'Homelands', which he

Shoreham Beach: view of Bungalow Town before 1914.

described as being a holiday and weekend home that was 'Bohemian in character'. It was built entirely of wood, with the boarding painted white and ornamentation picked out in green [84]. By 1921 an observer at Shoreham Beach could describe 'an endless variety of styles. Some are fantastic, some grotesque, many are beautiful, and some are — not' [85].

Andrew Rice recalls what it was like from the view of someone who spent holidays there:

> Their wooden walls white-painted, with roofs of red or green, and verandahs open to the sea, the bungalows were not lacking in attraction or variety of design. Some were gabled, or had castellated tops, or towers to give them height, and other such elaborations. After dark, the soft glow of oil lamps filtered through chintzy curtains, while oil-heaters kept the evening chills at bay [86].

Names given to these retreats from city life were no less evocative than their appearance. Associations with the sea were always popular, like 'Gull's Nest', 'Ocean Wave' and 'Sea Spray'; or links with the stage and cinema as in 'Rose Marie', 'Lullaby' and 'Sunshine Suzie'. Other names like 'Daydream', 'The Doll's House' and 'Arcadia' tell their own story.

Conditions were rudimentary (at least until the 1930s) but never, apparently, a problem for those who stayed there; on the contrary, this very simplicity was its attraction. In the early days, planks laid end-to-end across the shingle served as pavements, there was no gas or electricity, no running water and no main drainage. Individual storage tanks provided drinking water, supplemented by buckets of fresh water brought across from the mainland at 2d. each.

Somehow, the whole scene was itself like a film set the flimsy bungalows like props for a make-believe world. For fifty years Bungalow Town was cocooned in an alluring web of fantasy and romance until, in 1939, as if the film had been shot the scene changed dramatically. The actors were moved on to be replaced by defending troops preoccupied now with new dimensions of the beach. Its seaward location made it a prime spot for enemy invasion and this time it was defence artillery rather than the odd railway carriage that was hauled onto the shingle. In the course of the next six years most of the 700 bungalows were demolished (mainly by the defending forces), an exception being a block of the sturdier homes retained as an officer's mess.

With the end of the war, the local authorities were determined to prevent a resurrection of Bungalow Town and promoted various measures to achieve this objective. In turn, the plot-holders were equally determined to thwart this policy. As a result, over a period of two or three years, arguments were polarised into a sharp conflict between those who believed that the common interest would be better served by public planning and those who sought to defend their rights of property.

'THIS APPALLING MESS'

Undoubtedly, Shoreham Beach in 1945 was a scene of devastation; 75 per cent of the buildings had been demolished, the little estate roads were torn apart, and a paraphernalia of abandoned installations and barbed wire littered the beaches. In spite of all this, the plot-holders were quick to return, repainting their former holiday homes where they still stood or, in the majority of cases, looking for ways to rebuild. The local authorities were equally determined that this should not happen and that there would be no repeat of pre-war conditions.

Most of Bungalow Town had been demolished in 1940 and West Sussex County Council immediately saw what it described as a 'unique opportunity' to reshape the area in the years to come [87]. From as early as 1941 an unsuccessful attempt was made to persuade the War Office to purchase the plots and to compensate for the buildings, with a view to selling the land to the County when the war ended. When that failed the County Council collaborated with the Worthing RDC and Shoreham UDC, 'searching for the best means of securing the proper and orderly redevelopment of the Beach area' [88].

Consultations took place between the local authorities and the Ministry of Town and Country Planning which, in the war years, was already preparing itself for a role in promoting reconstruction in the country generally. There little doubt that Shoreham Beach, though limited in scale was, in procedural terms, an interesting test-case with wider implications.

In the opinion of Whitehall, existing laws (including the 1944 Town and Country Planning Act) were inadequate to deal with the problem. Normally, where there had been such extensive war damage existing legislation would open the way to comprehensive redevelopment, but matters were complicated in this case by the fact that the destruction was caused by the defending army as opposed to enemy action. Yet all were agreed, including the Minister, that compulsory powers were required for a public body to buy the whole of the freehold on the Beach. The way forward that emerged was for the County Council to promote a Private Bill, to enable the whole area to be bought and redeveloped [89].

The official view of how Shoreham Beach would look in the future was of a very different place to that which had evolved spontaneously over the previous half century. It was to be totally replanned and redeveloped, no longer primarily as a holiday or weekend resort, but now first and foremost as a permanent residential estate. Property values would be very much higher than in the pre-war years (the presumption being that these went hand-in-hand with 'quality'), a minimum figure of £1200 per house being set for the first phase of development compared with a general value of about £600 in 1939. Moreover, tenure would no longer be in the form of freehold but through 99-year leases. The idea was that the County Council should buy the land in the first place, and then lease it for 999 years to a specially-constituted development company which would, in turn, sub-lease to individual plot-holders.

A Bill was duly promoted to the House of Lords in 1946 and its hearing was a predictable conflict between aggrieved plot-holders fighting for their assumed rights, and agents of local and central government together trying to define new limits of public intervention. In the event, that part of the Bill relating to Shoreham Beach was rejected. Official reasons were not given, but there was clearly disquiet about the role of a private development company (coupled with the Ministry's unwillingness to entertain the idea of a public development corporation).

Victory for the plot-holders was shortlived, however, as in the following year the 1947 Town and Country Planning Act opened new possibilities for the local authorities. It was now possible to obtain permission for compulsory purchase under normal development plan procedures, and this is precisely what happened. Not wishing to delay things longer than necessary — pressures from the plot-holders to redevelop on an individual basis were increasing all the time — the County Council resorted to a 'Part Development Plan'. This enabled them to go ahead with a plan for this area, in advance of the plan for the county as a whole [90].

The Part Development Plan envisaged the same pattern of development as that which lay behind the West Sussex Bill, only this time the County Council assumed the role of ground landlord in preference to a private development company. At the Public Inquiry many of those who had spoken in the House of Lords in 1946 were present again, and the old arguments between plot-holders and bureaucrats were repeated with little variation. This time, though the outcome was different, with the County Council winning approval to go ahead and replan Shoreham Beach.

For all the variety of procedures, the whole purpose of public intervention was, quite simply, 'to clean up this appalling mess' [91]. What was never entirely clear was whether this was purely a reference to the legacy of war, or whether it also embraced a memory of Bungalow Town as it had been before.

Few officials tried to disguise their low opinion of the place in its pre-war years. Through a series of public pronouncements an image took shape of a shanty town by the sea that should not be allowed to arise from the rubble. One of the advisers to the Ministry of Town and Country Planning, for instance, recalled how the Beach 'in the main consisted of a most wretched collection of weekend shacks' [92]. Similarly, in opening the case for a Private Bill, Counsel for West Sussex dismissed the buildings as 'of the very poorest possible type, including... converted railway carriages and what I should describe, if I may do so without offence, as wooden shacks' [93].

The Ministry's own description of the place was that of 'an unplanned collection of bungalows, railway carriages, shacks and other types of buildings' [94]. This view was reinforced under cross-examination, in that Bungalow Town was recalled as 'a very untidy and unsightly piece of development' [95]. Moreover, it was not simply a question of aesthetics: 'As we should see it in the Department, it was an eyesore, and rather more important in those days, it did not really make an economical use of that stretch of coast' [96].

In other words, the view that was fostered was that no one would want to see a return to the type of development that had prevailed up to 1939. Once that was accepted the question remained as to how the area could be replanned. On this, too, an official consensus emerged along the lines that, whatever the details, a measure of compulsory purchase would be required in the years to come. This was the really big step and the one which, understandably, proved to be the most contentious.

Compulsory purchase was advocated on two grounds. The first was that large-scale public intervention was necessary to clear up the substantial war damage — a task which no individual could be expected to take on. The second, and more contentious, reason for compulsory purchase was to overcome the likelihood of piecemeal development if it was left to individual plot-holders.

Thus, the multiplicity of tiny plots of land which permit 'perhaps a single odd railway carriage or a little tiny wooden building, made it quite obvious to anybody who considered the problem that future development on proper lines would be quite impossible unless the whole area came under one ownership' [97]. For town planners the recurring problem of plotlands is not only that it 'is impossible to secure a new layout, but also that one cannot even ensure development of existing plots. So the unwholesome prospect is that of 'development like a row of teeth, or rather a row of broken teeth. You might have houses here and there, but in between you might have a series of little plots, not one of which could be developed' [98].

'A SMALL MAN'S HAVEN'

Undaunted by the weight of argument against rebuilding Bungalow Town on the lines of its former layout, the plot-holders responded in kind. Their case, in turn, presented in various debates over a number of years, explored three themes. It was argued, firstly, that a development such as this provided somewhere for what was repeatedly referred to as 'the small man'; secondly, that the imagery of its opponents was all wrong and that it was by no means the terrible place it was made out to be; and, finally, that the whole idea of the State taking over private land was both repugnant and unnecessary.

On the first point, the plight of the small man was an emotive issue which also contained within it real substance. It was the kind of catchphrase to appeal to the media, and the *Daily Express* (which had some thirty years earlier championed the cause of aggrieved plot-holders at Peacehaven) was quick to take the initiative on this. In an article entitled 'Bungalow Town has Vanished' coverage was given to the plight of plot-holders, who returned to their land to find not only that their properties were devastated but that they were forbidden to rebuild [99].

In a less emotive setting, it was Lord Mersey (as chairman of the House of Lords committee examining the West Sussex Bill) who did his best to ensure that individual rights were not overlooked in the general rush towards public planning. He requested that 'there must be adequate protection given to the small man who is being dispossessed... I am talking about the little man who has been content perhaps to live in a railway carriage. I should not care to live in a railway carriage myself, but there are people who are quite content with that' [100].

The attraction of Shoreham Beach was so often seen to be as a place for cheap and healthy holidays; eulogised by the Shoreham Urban District Council in the 1930s as 'the poor man's and the moderate means man's haven' [101]. Anticipating a problem that became increasingly evident as postwar development progressed, the situation had to be avoided where, in the process of 'improving' an area, the original residents would be driven out by the higher property values resulting from the scheme. A figure of £1,200 was cited as being the sort of price that would be required to rebuild a house to the new specifications, whereas many would be perfectly satisfied with something which cost only half that sum. Again, Lord Mersey recognised the problem in concluding that 'the principle that affects the minds of the Committee is that a man should not be compelled to go and live in a better class of home than he wants if his own house is a reasonable one' [102].

The plot-holders at Shoreham Beach were also indignant at the way their world had been portrayed as an 'appalling mess' of shacks. Certainly there was widespread devastation resulting from the war — 'like a battlefield, or worse, covered with caissons and with gaping holes filled with cement, and all sorts of metal work left by the Army' [103]. But that was not to say that it had been anything like that previously.

To rebut this impression, evidence was supplied to show how Bungalow Town, for all its humble origins, was by 1939 commanding a high rateable value:

> It was, to 70 per cent of it, a well-developed residential seaside resort, and all this talk about railway trucks and shacks and all that sort of thing is nonsense as applied to the position here at the outbreak of war. When I tell you that the rateable value of the properties here, large and small, averaged over £34 approximately... a description of 'shacks and railway trucks' is wholly unreliable and untrue [104].

Lord Mersey took time off from his committee proceedings to see things for himself, and was also favourably impressed:

> I thought there were quite a number of houses which were quite habitable, and which, personally, I should very much dislike being turned out of. I might not select that sort of house to live in, but there are houses which are in quite good condition which have been painted up and people are living in them [105].

More strikingly, the senior civil servant who had advised the Minister of Town and Country Planning that he was dealing with 'an unplanned collection of bungalows, railway carriages, shacks and other buildings', revised his own views following a visit to Shoreham. It transpired that he had in fact drafted his report partly on the basis of 'visiting the place 20-25 years ago when it left a very bad impression on me' [106].

A modified image emerged of Shoreham Beach that was neither of one extreme nor the other. It was neither an up-market resort, nor was it a shanty settlement. Over the years many of the plot-holders had improved and rebuilt their properties and basic services had been brought to the beach. At the same time, as one observer noted, there was still a touch of 'unconventionality' about the place and, at least until 1939, a chance to live simply in a railway carriage or shack for those who so wished [107].

In the last resort the issue which really counted for the plot-holders was not what others thought of the place, but whether or not it was proper for the State to take away their freehold rights. This had both financial and moral implications. For those who were to be compensated simply for the value of their original property it was by no means certain that they could afford to rebuild to the new standards. It was also argued that a right of freehold offered a degree of 'moral satisfaction' to the owner. A typical view of a plot-holder was that 'our house represents not only money but also a great deal of work inside, and the fruition of our hopes and ambitions, and I cannot believe that it is intended to take that away' [108].

Inevitably, the rhetoric of debate at the time was polarised in terms of small plot-holders fighting for their independence in the face of threatened State acquisition. Their plight was compounded in the eyes of sympathisers at the time of the Private Bill when it was intended that the County Council would acquire land, only to hand it over, in turn, to a development company set up specifically for the purpose. Safeguards were written into the arrangement, but that was not enough to allay a deep-felt suspicion and resentment. It was also shown that rates of compensation for individual properties were far from adequate to enable rebuilding.

The ideological stance of the plot-holders was further strengthened by the practical arguments they used to show that there was no reason why the beach could not be rebuilt, plot by plot, as opposed to comprehensively by a central corporation. The overall layout was shown to be by no means as disorderly as was popularly imagined, and the plot-holders were willing to accept planning guidelines within which they could individually work. It was argued that 'once a development plan and layout plan was prescribed, difficulties of plot sizes would be ironed out in course of time by agreement and adjustment between the neighbouring owners' [109]. Evidence was cited of plot-holders returning as soon as they were allowed back after the war, and industriously putting what remained into good order again — the glistening new paint catching the eye not only of Lord Mersey but also of the repentant civil servant who had earlier condemned the whole of Bungalow Town.

Great faith was put in the common sense and self-interest of the plot-holder, while town planners (even before they had really made a mark in the nation's affairs) were already distrusted. In the words of a builder who had a working knowledge of the beach, extending back over thirty-five years, the plan for compulsory acquisition was totally unsuitable:

> I wish to register my protest against the County Council's claim to have a royal prerogative over our livelihood, our destiny and our social life... The town planner dreams his way through life. There is no realism anywhere. I met town planners 40 years ago. They took a holiday in Germany and came home fanatics... the fantasy of the playboy town planner is no good to us [110].

RETROSPECT

The aims of the planning authority have, in large measure, been fulfilled. Gone is Bungalow Town and in its place has come a modern housing estate by the sea. Order and geometry has replaced the spontaneity and 'haphazard development' which so offended the ideals of planners in the 1940s. As an acid test of the planners' achievement, property values now compare favourably with those of any other sought-after location along the South Coast. The odd railway carriage remains today as a curiosity, but 'Bohemians' no longer come to Shoreham Beach.

But the strange thing about the area is that it has never been entirely clear why the authorities were so totally determined to transform it. One

Shoreham Beach: incorporation of railway carriage in modern conversion

official spoke of it as being an 'uneconomic' use of the coast, though, unlike Peacehaven or even Winchelsea Beach, it was not a question of salvaging for the nation a shoreline of exceptional scenic or scientific value. Nor, as in the case of Camber, was it by the late-1930s (when most houses at Shoreham Beach were connected to mains services) really a question of it being a public health hazard.

In retrospect, the impression emerges that Shoreham Beach lent itself as a convenient test-bed for new, postwar town planning procedures. It was a 'unique opportunity', not simply to clear away the rubble, but to pioneer untried procedures that would, in time, become standard in application. How best to introduce powers of compulsory purchase was an issue that was of special interest to the authorities. Though Shoreham Beach was, in one sense, of no more than local importance, as a nursery for new procedures its significance was national.

With the full support of the Ministry of Town and Country Planning, the county and district councils used just about every method available to them. First, they looked back to the well-worn 1932 Act, then to the 1944 Act with its special provisions for war damage and, when these proved to be not enough, onto a Private Bill. This, too, failed to fill the gap so it was, in the end, the new 1947 Act which was put to early use. Even before the Act reached the statute book, plans were being drawn up for a 'Part Development Plan'. It is surely no coincidence that the eventual plan for Shoreham Beach proved to be the first to be approved anywhere under the new system.

PAGHAM BEACH

He came, at last, to the beach... Where it had been bordered on the shoreward side by a great broad strip of open land, rough with tussocks of grass, sea poppies, and a hedge of tamarisk separating it from cornfields, stood, in a medley of confusion, two score or more of dwelling places. Old railway carriages converted into 'bungalows', wooden erections of all shapes and sizes, refreshment huts and a row of bathing cabins. While, on the beach itself, so lonely in those old days, were groups of holiday makers...

(Canon Victor Whitechurch, *First and Last*, 1929).

Further along the coast, to the west of Shoreham Beach, similar developments made their mark. At Elmer, Felpham and Pagham Beach shacks and railway carriages fronted the sea, while further along at Selsey Bill it was old caravans and bus bodies which caught the eye of preservationists. Though condemned as an 'appalling spectacle' in the 1930s [111], the spirit of this type of development equally had its own admirers. In a *Daily Mail* article on Selsey in 1907 reference was made to the 'smartly-painted railway carriages and other amusing oddments in the way of dwellings. Each of them pays a nominal rent of a guinea a year, and their lucky owners have a glorious time, amphibious and happy in their beach-dwellings' [112]. Shacks and railway carriages continued at Bracklesham and East Wittering, only to be held back, in turn, by preservationists at West Wittering and Chichester Harbour. Each of these makeshift settlements has its own story, but a look a just one, Pagham Beach, will be illustrative.

The Selsey peninsula, south of Chichester in West Sussex, has continually changed its shape through the effect of tidal cycles, gales and variations of barometric pressure [113]. In the early nineteenth century Sea Lane at Pagham used to end at the then mouth of Pagham Harbour, with a shingle spit offshore. Then the mouth moved westward and the old channel became a hollow of dry land, merging with the shingle, which extended across the harbour mouth to Church Norton. In the 1870s as the mud flats were slowly drained, a local journalist wrote:

A few years ago the waves swept up to the wall of the churchyard and all beyond was waste. Now there is a green field and beyond that arable land in which men are ploughing... and the sea is now a full half-a-mile off and there is a high bank of beach between it and the land which is overflowed at every tide [114].

Subsequent tides restored the harbour and a lagoon behind it [115]. A High Court action in 1908, concerned with the ownership of land where the sea had receded, determined that the Crown had given over its rights to the Pagham Harbour Company.

The colonisation of Pagham Beach began that year. The young men of the Congregational Church in Guildford were enthusiasts for 'cycle camping' and held an annual camp. Mr Gammon, who had a 'cheap drapery' business in the town, told Mr and Mrs Salsbury that it was a good site and had a well' [116]. The Salsbury's had a jewellery shop in High Street, Guildford, and five children, Jack, Dorothy, Hubert, Bob and Peggy [117]. For their first camp in 1908 they pitched their tents almost on top of the well, in the hollow which was once the watercourse of Selsey Harbour. The only buildings were a fisherman's hut and a 'gypsy' caravan, used for storing nets and eel spears by William Bailey of Nyetimber and another fisherman, Mr Morris. William Bailey explained to young Hubert Salsbury about the well. 'Yes', he said, 'I dugged it years ago, and I'll come along and clean it out for you' [118]. He covered the well with a new wooden top and solved the problem of water supply for the early settlers. It also served as a cold store for butter, kept in an aluminium flask.

The next campers in the Hollow were Charles Thorpe, a widower with a taxidermist business in George Street, Croydon, and his five children, Hettie, Charles, Jessie, Lucy and Janet [119]. With them came Edward and Clarence Crump, who explains:

Originally Charlie Thorpe and me went down to prospect and I reported with enthusiasm that the beach was ideal as a camping site. Later I went ahead by 2s 6d return excursion from Croydon with tents and other luggage. The Thorpes followed on antique

103

cycles. Courtesy prompted us to ask the Salsbury's whether we should disturb their privacy if we camped some hundred yards from their own camp near the well. Mrs Salsbury pointed out that considering the vastness of the beach there seemed little risk of overcrowding. Later Charlie married Dorothy Salsbury and I clicked with Lucy Thorpe and my brother Edward married Nellie Thorpe, so the beach had its romances... The girls slept at the Bear Inn, Pagham and in other cottages, we boys in the tent with shingle under our rugs. In the camping days we each contributed 10s per week for catering and what was over was blued on a tea in Bognor. Cheap but carefree holiday [120].

In the summer of 1910 the caravan was bought by Miss Carre, and the campers dubbed her and her party the 'Caravanites'. She was 'a court dressmaker with a considerable establishment in Bond Street' [121]. There also appeared two bathing huts, one belonging to a Mr Edgell and the other to Arthur Davis who owned the house next to Pagham Vicarage and used it as a summer residence [122].

The first shanty or bungalow was built by Arnold French who had a business in Bognor. His son, C.B. French, recalls the isolation of Pagham Beach at that time:

It is difficult in these days to think of a spot some four miles away by road and about two-and-a-half along the shore, as something quite remote, far away from a town like Bognor. No public transport, very few private cars. Not even so many people with bicycles. You could hire a horse-drawn cab, or walk. The whole way of life was so different... Holidays for those who could take them were usually conventional... I think it is probable that the vast majority of people in Bognor had never been to Pagham... It would be quite true to say that you could stay for many weeks on Pagham Beach and never see anyone from Bognor. In fact you hardly ever saw anyone from Pagham Village or Nyetimber on the beach except Morris and Bailey. It might have been a hundred miles from anywhere... I think perhaps there could not have been very many people at that time who could have enjoyed the very unconventional, perhaps almost primitive life we had there [123].

His father decided to build a holiday bungalow after discovering the caravan while going for a walk in the autumn of 1909, and failing to persuade Miss Carre to sell it. 'She afterwards tried and failed to buy our bungalow, so it was natural we should all become firm friends' [124]. Arnold French ('he always called himself a wood butcher but he was too modest' [125]) built his bungalow in small sections in a shed in the garden of the Norfolk Hotel, Bognor, in the winter of 1909, and in the early spring of 1910 the sections were loaded onto a farm waggon and drawn to Pagham. On the site he made a small shelter in which to sleep and put up the bungalow without help, with nuts and bolts.

104

Called 'The Outpost', it stayed on the beach until 1936 when his son moved it to his market garden. He remembers that a nominal ground rent, 'certainly not more than 30s a year', was paid to the Pagham Harbour Company. 'As the beach population increased after the (first world) war, it went up. The most we paid was £10', in about 1930 [126].

On the night of the 15th December 1910, the sea broke through and flooded the Hollow. After the floods had subsided and the entrance from the harbour into the lagoon had been closed, Arnold French and another local trader, Fred Ball, dismantled the bungalow and moved it on to the high shingle, with the aid of a donkey. The other settlers also built higher up. In 1911, Charlie Thorpe built 'The Shack', which later became 12 Lagoon Road and still belonged to the family, as 'the oldest bungalow on the beach' in the 1970s [127]. The Salsburys bought a garage from a firm of portable building makers, and Hubert and his brother erected it in 1912 [128]. Fred Ball built one for himself, Miss Carre had one built for her, and the Bateman, Chown and Gammon families, all from Guildford, built their own [129]. Dorothy Thorpe remembers that the Gammons built theirs high on a ridge, 'and we were all very indignant and called it 'The Limit' and I believe it is still called that. It broke the skyline. I hasten to add, that in spite of our indignation we remained good friends' [130].

The same magnanimity was not extended to an author called *L'Estrange* who had built a 'rather ugly black timbered building on stilts towards Siddlesham' [131]. The pioneer settlers, showing little respect for the fact that it was the only building in the area to be designed by an architect, called it 'The Jam Factory'. It was not simply the design, though, which aroused animosity, as Mr French recalls:

The whole thing got off on the wrong foot when we found a notice board nailed to a post close to where we launched our boats — stating that the lagoon was 'private' and that rent must be paid by anyone having a boat on it. The owner of the Jam Factory had rented the whole lagoon and clearly wanted to hog it all for himself. I think we resented this because we felt that the whole area should be free and available. We did not like a private person trying to make a profit so to speak. So someone nailed a tin can to the post with a notice requesting 'money to be placed here'. Needless to say no-one ever paid rent and we used the lagoon for boating and swimming as before... Even after the war something of a feud still carried on. I suppose it was really rather a pity [132].

After the First World War, Pagham Beach developed rapidly. Captain Charles Vale, who had just come back from America, bought two railway carriages from Eastleigh for £15, turned them into a bungalow for £30 on a site which cost him £5, 'and was immediately asked if he would sell it — which he did, for £100' [133]. Mr John Apps who had lived for a long time at Nyetimber where his wife kept a shop, began putting up railway carriage buildings, then built a bungalow for himself, while his wife opened a general store. Later a Major Douglas

Pagham Beach: views in the early 1920s. (Photos by courtesy of Gerard Young Collection, West Sussex Institute of Higher Education)

opened a club. The bungalows nearest the sea, in what is now Front Road, became known as the front row. John Apps and 'Punch' Hazelgrove had a boat with a long drag net and sold whitebait and mackerel to the holiday-makers. Frank Adfield of the Old Bear pub at Nyetimber bought a Model T Ford and ran a taxi service to Bognor at 2s 6d a trip [134], The Gammon family sold their hut first known as 'The Limit' (and now called 'Dixie') and built a larger one, which they called 'The Barn' and is now 'Teazles'. By 1935 the Reverend A.A.

106

Evans of Chichester, in his book *A Saunterer in Sussex*, declared that 'Pagham Beach is another outgrowth... It is a crowded wilderness, a gathering place of wooden shacks, homes of corrugated iron and decayed railway carriages. It is the latest horror which has befallen the Sussex coast' [135].

For of course similar bungalow towns were developing elsewhere, at East Wittering on the other side of the Selsey Peninsula, at Selsey itself, and at Sea Road, Felpham on the other side of Bognor. Not everyone saw them as reprehensible. As early as 1916 the authors of the Bognor guidebook remarked that:

> The extension of Felpham-by-the-Sea is quite modern, but it stands almost wholly apart. The most attractive dwellings here are a group of railway carriage bungalows set on high platforms with verandahs and roof-gardens which in summer are gay with colour. These are astonishingly popular as summer houses by the sea [136].

For the original settlers, everything had changed from the days when the close-knit little group fetched fresh water from the well, and milk and eggs from Church Farm, swam and sailed, and gathered driftwood and mushrooms, heard corncrakes and nightjars by night and watched plovers and redshanks by day. 'We were all there on that fateful August Bank Holiday in 1914, but things were never the same again' [137]. But apart from those who married the friends made on Pagham Beach, Janet Thorpe lived for many years in 'The Shack' and was still there in 1939, while Dorothy French wrote *The Flora of Pagham Harbour*, published in 1962 by the Bognor Natural Science Society.

Gerard Young, the Bognor journalist who painstakingly elicited these recollections from the children of the first colonists, recalled in 1963 the official attitude to Pagham Beach:

> At County Hall they offer prayers that it may be destroyed by a tidal wave. The very thought of it numbs the planners' minds. All they can do, as they did at a public inquiry in 1958, is to stop anyone from making any building last longer. Before the Ministry Inspector had a look at, it, the County Council spokesman prepared him for the shock with a speech charged with foreboding and bewilderment: 'When you have seen this area you cannot fail to agree that what exists there is what has been described as a negation of planning. No-one would possibly dream of allowing that today. Nevertheless,it has happened.' Yes, it just happened, like those seeds that fall haphazardly on the shingle ridge and produce flowers. I think it will be there for years [138].

Years later it *is* still there, rapidly becoming just like anywhere else, though still with reminders of its origins. Little bungalows, carefully-concealed railway carriages and weathered asbestos-clad structures stand in rows parallel to the sea. Those nearest the sea command high prices. Gerard Young's own opinion in 1963 was that:

107

Pagham Beach: aerial view in the 1950s. (Photo courtesy of Aerofilms Ltd)

Pagham Beach: current view.

In view of the dreary suburbs springing up between Pagham and Aldwick, I would say that Pagham Beach is, by contrast, almost raffishly picturesque. It is a last outpost, a survival of the old, careless, pioneering days [139].

NOTES

1. Public Record Office file HLG/92/81.
2. Seymour, John (1975) *The Companion Guide to the South Coast of England*. London: Collins.
3. Public Record Office file HLG/92/81.
4. Mais, S.P.B. (1938) *Britain Calling*. London: Hutchinson.
5. Mais, S.P.B. (1938) The plain man looks at England, in Williams-Ellis, Clough (ed.) *Britain and the Beast*. London: J. M. Dent and Sons.
6. *Ibid.*
7. Belloc, Hilaire (1936) *The County of Sussex*. London: Cassell.
8. For more details, see Sheail, John (1981) *Rural Conservation in Inter-War Britain*. Oxford: Clarendon Press.
9. Belloc, *op. cit.* (see note 7).
10. See, for instance, the East Sussex County Council (1953) *Development Plan, Survey Report 'B'*. April; and Minister's Letter dismissing a planning appeal (A.56.201) in Rother District Council (1976) *The Ridge and Morlais Ridge, Winchelsea Beach*. October.
11. Information on the early development of the Rye Bay area has been gathered from a variety of sources. General references include Burke, J. (1974) *Sussex*. London: Batsford; Butcher, Daisy F. (undated) *Jottings of Camber Village*. J.I. Dibley. 'Camber and the County Council' unattributed article in the *Sussex County Magazine*, 28, 1954; and Metcalfe, R.E. (1971) Settlements and planning of the East Sussex Coast, in Williams R.B.G. (ed.) (1978) *Guide to Summer Excursions*. Brighton: I.B.G. In addition to these general references, important local authority sources are the following East Sussex County Council publications: (a) *Town and Regional Planning Schemes under the Town Planning Act, 1925* (E.S.R.O., C/Cl). (b) *Minutes of the East Sussex County Planning Committee, 1929-1949* (E.S.R.O., C/Cll/63/1W). (c) *Camber and Winchelsea Beach Sub-Committee Minutes* (E.S.R.O., C/Cll/63/44-45). (d) *Development Plan, April 1953: Written Statement, Survey Report 'A' — Part I: Summary and Written Analysis, Survey Report 'B' — Town Map Area No. 5 — Camber, Survey Report 'C' — Comprehensive Development Area No. I Camber*. (e) *Coastal Preservation: Restoration of Amenities* 3 December 1968.
12. 'Camber and the County Council', *op. cit.* (see note 11).
13. *Ibid.*
14. For an invaluable insight of the property market at this time we are indebted to Mr J.H. Daniels, who described his experiences as an estate agent in the district.
15. Part of a colourful impression of Winchelsea Beach, provided to us by Miss Pat Green.
16. Epstein, Jacob (1940) *Let There Be Sculpture: An Autobiography*. London: Michael Joseph.

17. Buckle, Richard (1963) *Jacob Epstein*. London: Faber and Faber.
18. Gertler, Mark (1965) *Selected Letters*. London: Rupert Hart-Davis.
19. Adams, Thompson and Fry (1931) *South East Sussex Regional Planning Scheme* (E.S.R.O., C/C1).
20. *Ibid.*
21. Letter dated 19 June 1930 from the Federation of East Sussex Ratepayers to the East Sussex County Planning Committee (E.S.R.O., C/Cll/63/1).
22. Camber and Winchelsea Beach Sub-Committee, 7 January 1949 (E.S.R.O., C/Cll/63/44).
23. 'Camber and the County Council' *op. cit.* (see note 11).
24. Camber and Winchelsea Beach Sub-Committee, 7 January 1949 (E.S.R.O., C/C11/63/44).
25. County Council interest in this area, and the preparation of a 'compromise plan' is reported in the records of the County Planning Committee (E.S.R.O., C/Cll/63/44).
26. Camber and Winchelsea Beach Sub-Committee Minutes (E.S.R.O., C/C11/63/44).
27. J.A. Steers, quoted in East Sussex County Council: *Development Plan Survey Report 'B'*, *op. cit.* (see note 11).
28. *The Report of the National Parks Committee*, Cmnd 7121, London: HMSO, 1947, known as the Hobhouse Report, proposed that 'the Dungeness coastal area extending along the coast through Camber, Rye Harbour, Winchelsea Beach and Pett to Fairlight' be designated as a Conservation Area.
29. *The Conservation of Nature in England and Wales: Report of the Wild Life Conservation Special Committee*, Cmnd 7122. London: HMSO, 1947, known as the Huxley Report proposed that 'Dungeness, extending along the Sussex coast as far west as Hastings, with special reference to the shingle banks' be designated as an area of scientific value.
30. East Sussex County Planning minutes (E.S.R.O., C/Cll/63/6).
31. *Ibid.*
32. East Sussex County Council (1953) *Development Plan, Written Statement*. April.
33. East Sussex County Council (1953) *Development Plan, Survey Report 'B'. Town Map Area No. 5, Camber*. April.
34. Referring to the inter-war period, *The Long Weekend* is the title of the book by R. Graves and A. Hodge, referred to in Chapter l.
35. A history of post-1947 planning policies for these areas is contained in the East Sussex County Council Planning Department Report (1968) *Coastal Preservation: Restoration of Amenities*, 3 December.
36. *Ibid.*
37. *Ibid.*
38. *Ibid.*
39. Rother District Council (1976) *The Ridge and Morlais Ridge, Winchelsea Beach: Development Policy and Design Brief*. October.
40. Rother District Council: *Camber Planning Brief*, January 1976. *The Ridge and Morlais Ridge, Winchelsea Beach: Development Policy and Design Brief*, October 1976. *Pett Level-Marsham Flatlands: Development Policy*, November 1977. *Winchelsea Beach: Development Brief*, April 1979.
41. *Pett Level-Marsham Flatlands: Development Policy*, *op. cit.* (see note

40).

42. Bogarde, Dirk (1977) *A Postilion Struck by Lightning*. London: Chatto and Windus.

43. Peacehaven's early history has been gleaned from a variety of sources, with specific references listed separately in subsequent notes. An important contemporary source is the estate publication, *The Peacehaven Post* (September 1921 to December 1923), renamed *The Downland Post* (January 1924 to December 1925) and then *Downland* (October 1926 to October 1928). See also *Peacehaven Notes*, a folder in the East Sussex County Record Office, containing early Land Company correspondence. Retrospective summaries include Aldous, Tony (1980) Developments at Peacehaven. *Illustrated London News*, January; The changing face of Peacehaven. *Brighton and Hove Gazette Supplement* 14 and 21 March 1969; Dickens, Peter (1975) A disgusting blot on the landscape. *New Society*, 17 July; Moorhouse, Geoffrey (1969) The sad decline of paradise on sea. *The Guardian*, 3 May.

44. Court Records are to be found in King's Bench Division, *Neville v. London Express Newspapers Limited*, 20 December 1916; and *House of Lords, Neville v. London Express Newspapers Ltd*. October and December 1918. See also A Letter from Mr C.W. Neville to the Plot-Owners at Peacehaven. May 1920, in *Peacehaven Notes, op. cit.* (see note 43).

45. *Brighton and Hove Gazette and Supplement* 14 March 1969, *op. cit.* (see note 44).

46. Charles Neville, quoted in *Brighton and Hove Gazette Supplement*, 14 March 1969.

47. Neville wrote a series of articles recalling the early development of Peacehaven, and his constant battle with the authorities on behalf of the residents, in a revived estate publication in 1959 renamed *The Downland Review*.

48. A copy of George Kidston's conveyance, dated May 1916, is in the East Sussex Record Office (E.S.R.O. Ref MS 697). Another source of property transactions is the *Peacehaven Plot Book* and *Peacehaven Prize Book* (in the Homemakers Ltd company records at Haywards Heath).

49. *The Peacehaven Post*, 1 June 1923.

50. East Sussex County Council (1938) *Report by the Clerk to the Sub-Committee appointed by the Town Planning Committee to consider the suggested acquisition of land at Peacehaven*, 17 February.

51. *Ibid.*

52. Sir John Foster Fraser, in *The Peacehaven Post*, 1 August 1923.

53. *Ibid.*

54. *The Peacehaven Post*, 1 August 1922.

55. *The Peacehaven Post*, 1 April 1922.

56. *The Peacehaven Post*, 1 September 1922.

57. *The Peacehaven Post*, 7 November 1921. L

58. Thomas Dutton (author of Sea-Sickness, Prevention and Treatment Voyaging for Health — Health Resorts') in *The Downland Post*, 1 February 1925.

59. From a series of articles on the Annex by 'The Peacehaven Pedestrian'.

60. Mr Tyldesley Jones, in the *South Downs Preservation Bill Proceedings* (House of Lords 6 June 1934).

61. *Ibid.*

62. Cited by Mr Tyldesley Jones, *op. cit.* (see note 60).

63. Sharp, Thomas (1932) *Town and Countryside*. London: Oxford University Press.
64. Marshall, Howard (1938) The rake's progress, in Williams-Ellis, *op. cit.* (see note 5).
65. Mais, S.P.B. (1938) The plain man looks at England, in Williams-Ellis, *op. cit.* (see note 5).
66. Nairn, I. and Pevsner, N. (1965) *Sussex*. Harmondsworth: Penguin.
67. Brighton, Hove and District Joint Town Planning Advisory Committee (1932) *Report on the Regional Planning Scheme*.
68. Keeble, Lewis (1964) *Principles and Practice of Town and Country Planning*. London: The Estates Gazette Ltd.
69. In tracing the early policies of local authorities, important sources are the Minutes of the East Sussex County Planning Committee, 1929-1949 (E.S.R.O., C/Cll/63/1-6) and the Peacehaven Sub-Committee Minutes, 1948-1963 (E.S.R.O., C/C11/63/26-27).
70. East Sussex County Council (1938) *op. cit.* (see note 50).
71. *Ibid.*
72. In the *Interim Report of Peacehaven Sub-Committee*, 28 June 1949 (E.S.R.O. C/C11/63/26).
73. A helpful summary of planning policies is contained in East Sussex County Council (1979) *Meridian Centre and Peacehaven North*.
74. Important post-1947 development plans for Peacehaven are the *Town Map for Seaford, Nemhaven, Peacehaven and Telscombe Cliffs* (submitted as part of the East Sussex County Council Development Plan in 1965); and the later *Peacehaven and Telscombe Cliffs; Town Centre Map and Action Plan*, and *Peacehaven (North) Action Plan*, both dated December 1971.
75. *Town Centre Map and Action Plan*, *op. cit.* (see note 74).
76. *Peacehaven (North) Action Plan*, *op. cit.* (see note 74).
77. *Ibid.*
78. Moorhouse, *op. cit.* (see note 43).
79. Seymour, *op. cit.* (see note 2).
80. An interview with Mrs Sayers, by Middlesex Polytechnic students, May 1980.
81. East Sussex County Council (1938) *op. cit.* (see note 50).
82. Apart from official documents referenced separately, information on the early development of Shoreham Beach has been gathered from a variety of sources, including Bull, D.J. and Oliver, L.K. (1979) *Shoreham Memories: A Photographic Record*. Shoreham: Nostalgia Publications; Cheal, Henry (1921) *The Story of Shoreham*. Reprinted 1978, Bysh; Clunn, H. P. (1953) *The Capital by the Sea*. Brighton: Southern Publishing Co. Ltd; Rice, A. (1973) The heyday of a Bungalow Town. *Country Life*, 19 April. See also Shoreham U.D.C. (1936) *Brief to counsel, correspondence, etc. relating to the Local Inquiry into a Council scheme for a pleasure beach and lido at Shoreham Beach, 1936* (W.S.C.C. Record Office, UD/SH/23/1); Shoreham U.D.C. *Official Guide* (undated but probably 1946, in W.S.C.C. Record Office, Accession Box 249); West Sussex County Council, Town Planning (later Town and Country, and finally County Planning) Committee Minutes, 1929-1961 (W.S.C.C. Record Office, 46/1/1-6); and West Sussex County Council, Consultative Sub-Committee Minutes, 1938-1939 (W.S.C.C. Record Office, 46/2/1).
We have also made use of the excellent museum on local history in

Shoreham; and we are indebted to Dr Peter Brandon for sharing his own knowledge of the area.

83. Rice, *op. cit.* (see note 82).
84. Harrison, P. T. (1909) *Bungalow Residences*. London: Crosby Lockwood.
85. Cheal, *op. cit.* (see note 82).
86. Rice, *op. cit.* (see note 82).
87. West Sussex County Council (1946) *Shoreham and Lancing Beaches*, Report by Clerk of the County Council. 25 February.
88. *Ibid.*
89. Important sources for the *West Sussex County Council (Shoreham and Lancing Beaches, etc;)* Bill are papers relating to its promotion, and minutes of evidence, in *Shoreham and Lancing Beaches: General Sources* (Accession Box 249, W.S.C.C. Record Office); and *Minutes of Proceedings taken before the Select Committee of the House of Lords* (in the Public Record Office, HLG/79/734). See also *Shoreham U.D.C. Correspondence, etc; concerning the U.D.C.'s opposition to the Bill. Feb-May 1946* (W.S.C.C. Record Office, UD/SH/21/1/8).
90. West Sussex County Council, *Shoreham and Lancing Beaches, Part Development Plan* (W.S.C.C. Record Office, C.C.106 and 107, Box 27/9/CD7). Other sources for this important stage in local authority planning include Shoreham U.D.C., *Brief to counsel, correspondence, etc., relating to the Local Inquiry into the County Council's Shoreham and Lancing Beaches Development Plan, March 1949* (W.S.C.C. Record Office, UD/SH/23/2); West Sussex County Council, *Shoreham and Lancing Beaches Joint Committee Minutes, 1946-1960* (W.S.C.C. Record Office 46/5/1-5); and *West Sussex County Council, Shoreham and Lancing Beaches Development Plan* (approved 21.2.1950).
91. Mr Fox-Andrews, on behalf of West Sussex County Council, promoting the Private Bill in the House of Lords (Public Record Office file HLG/79/734).
92. In a letter (dated 31.5.1946) to the Ministry of Town and Country Planning, from Major Poole, who claimed to know the area well between 1940 and 1942 in the course of his military duties (Public Record Office file HLG/79/734).
93. Fox-Andrews, *op. cit.* (see note 91).
94. *Minutes of Proceedings taken before the Select Committee of the House of Lords, op. cit.* (see note 89).
95. *Ibid.*
96. *Ibid.*
97. *Ibid.*
98. *Ibid.*
99. *Daily Express*, 26 March 1945.
100. *Minutes of Proceedings taken before the Select Committee of the House of Lords, op. cit.*, in the opening session, Thursday 30 May 1946 (see note 89).
101. *Ibid.*
102. *Ibid.*
103. *Ibid*, in the opening session, Monday 3 June 1946.
104. *Minutes of Proceedings of Public Local Inquiry, February 1949: Shoreham and Lancing Beaches Development Plan*, W.S.C.C. Record Office, C.C.563.

105. *Minutes of Proceedings taken before the Selected Committee of the House of Lords, op. cit.*, in the opening session, Monday 3 June 1946 (see note 89).
106. From internal Ministry of Town and Country Planning correspondence relating to Shoreham Beach (Public Record Office file HLG/79/734).
107. *Minutes of Proceedings of Public Local Inquiry, February 1949, op. cit.* (see note 104).
108. *Ibid.*
109. *Ibid.*
110. *Ibid.*
111. A view considered in a Selsey Perish Council meeting, reported in *The Chichester Post*, 14 October 1933.
112. These features will make Selsey famous. *Daily Mail*, 20 July 1907.
113. For an account of the combination of factors causing changes to the coastline in this area see Seale, S.A. (1975) *The Tidal Threat.* West Wittering, Sussex: The Dunes Group.
114. Charles Fleet, quoted in 'Gerard Young's Column', *The Post*, Bognor, 19 January 1963. Mr Young was a journalist whose comments on the colonisation of Pagham Beach led to an extensive correspondence with the families of early settlers which is the basis of this account. This correspondence is among the large accumulation of books and other material on Bognor Regis and West Sussex which forms the Gerard Young Collection in the Bognor Regis College Library of the West Sussex Institute of Higher Education.
115. Fleming Lindsay (1949) *History of Pagham in Sussex.* Privately printed.
116. Hubert Salsbury to Gerard Young, 21 March 1968.
117. C.B. French to Gerard Young, 1966.
118. Hubert Salsbury to Gerard Young, 13 March 1968.
119. C.B. French to Gerard Young, 1966.
120. Hubert Salsbury to Gerard Young, 13 March 1968.
121. C.B. French to Gerard Young, 1966.
122. Leslie S. Davis to Gerard Young, 23 March 1968.
123. C.B. French to Gerard Young, 1966.
124. C.B. French to Gerard Young, 25 April 1966.
125. C.B. French to Gerard Young, 17 February 1968.
126. C.B. French to Gerard Young, 1966.
127. Clarence Crump to Gerard Young, 10 March 1968.
128. Hubert Salsbury to Gerard Young, 21 March 1968.
129. C.B. French to Gerard Young, 25 April 1966.
130. Dorothy Thorpe to Gerard Young, 2 April 1968.
131. Clarence Crump to Gerard Young, 21 March 1968.
132. C.B. French to Gerard Young, 1966.
133. Gerard Young in *The Post*, Bognor, 23 April 1966.
134. C.B. French to Gerard Young, 8 March 1967.
135. Evans, A. A. (1935) *A Saunterer in Sussex.* London: Methuen.
136. Bognor Guidebook 1916, cited by Gerard Young in *The Post*, Bognor 19 January 1963.
137. Letter from Hubert Salsbury to *The Post*, Bognor 13 March 1968.
138. Gerard Young in *The Post*, Bognor 19 January 1963.
139. *Ibid.*

114

Chapter 4

Arcadia on the East Coast

'Where else in the country,' Colonel Fielder asked me with outstretched hands, 'could a poor family get holiday accommodation at ten bob a head?'

(C.H. Rolph: Southend's Little Sister. *New Statesman*, 4 August 1951).

London has always had a special relationship with the coastal and estuarial towns and villages of Essex and Suffolk, and those of the Medway and Isle of Thanet in Kent. Water, once far more significant than road transport, linked London with these seaboard settlements; and until the middle of the last century, Barking was the home port of a large North Sea trawling fleet and Greenwich was a fishing village.

A beautifully-balanced transport economy was based on the flat-bottomed spritsail barges and 'stumpies', peculiar to the South-Eastern ports and the estuaries of the Thames, the Swale and the Medway in Kent, and the Blackwater, the Colne and the Orwell in Essex and Suffolk. Those barges, carrying straw and fodder to a city dependent upon horses, would return with dung and stable litter for the farms and market gardens; while other barges carrying the bricks that built nineteenth-century London returned loaded with refuse from the city's rubbish dumps, which not only fired the kilns of the Kent and Essex brickyards but also raised the level of the marshlands that typified long stretches of the South-East coast. Innumerable daily transactions as well as a vast river traffic linked the riverside parishes of London with the coast. By the end of the eighteenth century sailing vessels known as 'hoys', were taking large numbers of Londoners down the river and round the north Kent coast to Margate on the Isle of Thanet, and in the early nineteenth century the age of the steamer began.

One of the historians of Southend notes that:

In 1823 two steamboats, the Majestic and the Britannia, went up to London one day and down to Southend the succeeding day, besides two coaches every day. The early paddle-steamers of the Thames were first introduced as an alternative to the stage coach, and they linked the coastal towns of Kent, Essex and East Anglia with London. They were, however, small and frail, hardly capable of doing the return journey on the same day, and it was not until the 1880s that the steamboat companies improved their fleets and introduced pleasure excursions, in an attempt to wrest the holiday trade from the railways [1].

But the coming of the railways, with their terminal stations in the heart of the city of London, brought Southend within commuting distance, as well as day-trip and holiday distance, of the vast urban population which was just beginning to enjoy Bank Holidays, half-day working on Saturdays, and the idea of a holiday by the sea. One particular speculator, whose name probably appears on more property conveyances than that of any other individual, was Frederick Francis Ramuz (1855-1946). He was born at Leytonstone in east London, in the days when it was a village, and became a land agent by profession. He was one of the earliest of those 'city gents' who took advantage of the new railway and moved to Southend, commuting to his office in the city. There he operated as *The* Land Company (whose advertisements stressed that it was The Land Company) of 68 Cheapside (the same address as that of the auctioneers Protheroe and Morris, who were responsible for the selling of a vast number of sites on the East Coast, though in 1901, his son George became an auctioneer himself).

During the agricultural depression which began with the bad harvests of the 1870s, Ramuz purchased a large number of bankrupt farms in Essex and Kent, and a few in Sussex, and was content to wait for years for a return on his investment. When we asked the last survivor of his eight sons how his father had managed to finance these long-term purchases, he replied that the first Mr Ramuz had such a reputation for probity that solicitors were anxious to invest their clients' funds in his business, in long-term loans at 4½ per cent. Some of these loans were only paid off in the 1970s, but by that time the estate of Mr Ramuz was still bringing in a quarter of a million pounds. 'Put your money in land' he would urge others, 'it's the safest investment there is' [2].

Many of these purchases were in Southend itself, and at Leigh-on-Sea and at Westcliff, where Ramuz himself settled. He claimed in 1906 that 'Ten years ago, when we commenced to purchase land here, hardly anyone (but ourselves of course) anticipated its possibilities'. It was his company, he declared, which 'inaugurated "Plot Sales on the Estate" over twenty-six years ago'. This was the technique of erecting a marquee on the site, providing food and drink, chartering a 'Belle' steamer to sail from London, issuing cheap return tickets from Liverpool Street or Fenchurch Street, and refunding rail or boat fares to purchasers.

Apart from his enormous holdings in the Essex hinterland, Ramuz had acquired sites at Eastbourne and Pevensey Bay, and at a variety of places on the Kent coast: in the Isle of Thanet, the Isle of Sheppey and the Hoo peninsula, as well as at Maldon, on the Blackwater in Essex and at Walton-on-the Naze north of Clacton. By the turn of the century Ramuz had twice been Mayor of Southend, and in 1901 the local guidebook described him in these terms: '"He owns the earth", said one man admiringly, speaking of the most progressive, go-ahead and handsomest man in Southend... revered by visitors and ratepayers alike' [3].

He sold to a carefully-graded market with 'plots and parcels to suit all classes'. Most of the sites he sold in the Southend area were bought by builders who developed them in the ordinary way, under local authority control, with restrictive covenants stipulating a minimum cost (£250 a dwelling). Similarly, at Walton-on-the-Naze, 'the most select resort on the East Coast' the Land Company's catalogue stressed that 'it is emphatically evident that the town is rapidly improving in public esteem, that a good class of people favour it, and that the superior hotels are much in request'. The new roads were 'substantially made, kerbed and sewered by the Land Company, and no charge whatsoever to purchasers will be made'. But in other areas, with a different market in view, the Company reassured prospective purchasers, 'Cheap Iron or Wood Bungalows allowed!' and made a virtue of the fact that there were no tiresome restrictions. Even at Walton there were 'Breezy Sites for Bijou Bungalows' [4].

The Land Company was not without its rivals. In 1886 the *Essex Telegraph* reported that 'The ruthless hand of the builder is about to invade the peaceful little parish of Frinton', and in the 1890s the Marine and General Land Company issued its prospectus for making Frinton a town with 'Broad terraces, squares, crescents, tree-lined avenues and roads, an eight-acre cricket ground, tennis courts, a tidal basin, pleasure grounds, several hotels, and even a town hall, market and new pier' [5]. On the same stretch of coast:

> In 1902 a Mr Preston proposed the building of a new holiday suburb to be entitled Holland-on-Sea. A grid-iron road pattern was laid out, and the land was divided into plots with forty-foot frontages along the sea-front and twenty-foot frontages along other roads. Many plots were sold, but apart from a hotel, there was no building development until the 1920s [6].

In 1900 the Land Company chartered the steamer 'Cynthia' to take two hundred people from London and another two hundred who boarded at Southend to an auction of plots on the Central Estate, Herne Bay. And in the next few years George Ramuz, who eventually settled there as an estate agent, was engaged in attempting to popularise Minster, on the Isle of Sheppey, as London's newest holiday resort.

The forecast by Frederick Ramuz of the immense growth in popularity of Southend itself had already been realised. The pleasure steamer operators and the two rival railway companies brought tens of thousands of visitors to the Essex coast. This brought the impetus for

117

further East Coast explorations by hopeful developers as well as by individual holiday seekers. In her study of the rise of Southend as the epitome of the English seaside holiday place, Sylvia Everritt writes:

> Every bank holiday the number of day trippers who came to Southend increased, and these were mainly from East End working-class families. The number of boarding houses and bed-and-breakfast establishments east of the High Street, between the gas works and the pier, also increased. Southend like other big resorts, created a satellite area as a reaction to the proletarian invasion. Brighton has Hove, Margate has Broadstairs, Blackpool has St Anne's and Southend has Westcliff. As early as 1908 residents and visitors were in flight, preferring the quiet of Benfleet and Canvey Island to the noise of Southend on a bank holiday. Benfleet and Canvey were both to become day-tripper resorts, and during the twentieth century the pattern has continued. The effect of the proletarian invasion has been to send the lovers of quiet and peaceful enjoyment further afield to Devon, Cornwall and Scotland, while resorts like Frinton and West Wittering have firmly entrenched themselves behind a barrier of byelaws and rules [7].

The Land Company had plenty of sites in its portfolio of holdings to cater for the proletarian invasion. But these were mostly inland, and we discuss them in Chapter 6. Other speculators were to attempt to develop new East Coast holiday places, beginning with grandiose plans, but ending happy to sell plots to anyone with a few pounds to spare. Canvey Island was rejected by Ramuz as being no place to build on. But Frederick Hester, another land agent from Southend, was to buy a large acreage there with the hope of making it 'another lung' for murky London (the existing one being Southend itself). Thirty years later, Frank Stedman had the same ambition at Jaywick, south of Clacton.

Jaywick and Canvey became the best-known of the East Coast plotland districts, but pockets of land all along the coast and the river estuaries were sold by lesser entrepreneurs, or by farmers themselves to cater for the continually increasing demand for chalets and shanties by the sea all the way up to North Norfolk. At Hitcham Harbour there, according to Robert Simper:

> in about 1914 a carpenter from Reading arrived and started building the Harbour Rest bungalow on the shingle island near the mouth. This spot could then only be reached by fording the tidal river and the lonely carpenter lived (they say) on a diet of cocoa, rice pudding and cockles. From such a humble beginning began the modern holiday resort of Heacham [8].

Captain Drew brought the carpenter's timber to the site lashed to his yacht, and then became a developer himself, buying old boats and converting them to houseboats on dry land, propped up by brick piers.

118

There were similar sporadic plotland developments on the Norfolk coast at Hemsby, Sea Palling, Lessingham, Bacton, Hunstanton and Snettisham. In Suffolk they grew up at Felixstowe Ferry, on the spit of land to the south of the harbour at Southwold, and on the opposite side of the Blythe estuary, at Walberswick, which became, after Wilson Steer 'discovered' it, a holiday place for artists, and later, for the close-knit professional world of the psychoanalysts. For, like those on the Sussex coast, the holiday Arcadias of the East Coast developed specialised clienteles.

The estuarial beaches and harbours were especially favoured by the growing number of families attracted by boating and sailing. The landowner of one of these little sailing creeks, Maylandsea, on the south side of the Blackwater in Essex, sought to encourage its growth as an exclusive residential and retirement resort. Its roads have names like The Esplanade and Imperial Avenue. In the mid-1930s he was advertising plots of 50 to 60 feet frontage and a depth of 150 feet for £40-£60, and stressed that the Maylandsea Bay Estate was being developed in accordance with the local Town Planning Scheme and building regulations.

> Here are no rows of standard bungalows and houses of the take-it-or-leave-it sort, and there is no speculative building whatsoever. You choose your site and you choose your house. A large portion of the Estate, one hundred acres, which faces the Estuary has been set aside for development under the Town and Country Planning Act, 1933.

All proposed buildings had first to be approved by the owner, and 'temporary buildings, huts and sheds, etc. are not permitted for habitation' [9].

Jaywick and Canvey were both the creations of individual entrepreneurs who seized upon the growing demand for a holiday by the sea among people with little money to spend, and for whom the hotel, boarding house and the legendary seaside landlady had no attraction. The demand they met was later catered for by the operators of 'holiday camps' who emerged in the inter-war period. Significantly, when Sir Billy Butlin pioneered the 'luxury' holiday camp in the late-1930s, he selected the Jaywick side of Clacton and various other characteristically 'plotland' areas on the East and South Coasts, for his first ventures, while other providers later chose Canvey. Both Jaywick and Canvey suffered terribly from the East Coast floods in 1953, just because they had attracted an 'all-the-year-round' population (an illustration of the contention that 'natural' disasters affect people with few choices of where to live).

Unlike the South Coast plotlands, neither Canvey nor Jaywick attracted undue attention from the 'environmental' lobby, concerned with the protection of places of outstanding natural beauty. You would have to make a special trip to be affronted by either of them. But they both attracted enormous attention from the local authorities, outraged by

119

the deliberate flouting of their building regulations, and by the way in which the public health legislation and the slowly emerging consensus about town planning principles were contravened by these settlements. The response of residents, both temporary and permanent, has been an intense loyalty to the places they have chosen, and a deep suspicion of the public authorities. Whatever policy is applied by outsiders is wrong. The outstanding characteristic of the inhabitants of both these settlements, which, as we were often reminded by local authority officers, 'should never have happened in the first place', is *topophilia*: the capacity for devotion to a place.

CANVEY ISLAND

Certain it is that the hitherto obscure and almost forgotten little Island on the South Eastern Coast of Essex is destined to witness a grand and immediate transformation... The present and future inhabitants will have cause to rejoice on the anniversary of the day when Mr Frederick Hester invaded Canvey Island...

(Augustus A. Daly: *The History of Canvey Island*, 1902)

At the height of the Second World War, J.A. Steers reported to the government on the future of the East Anglian coast. He found Canvey 'an abomination... a town of shacks and rubbish... It caters for a particular class of people, and short of total destruction and a new start, little if anything can be done' [10]. But the attraction of any place, for any particular class of people, is in the eye of the beholder. For the McCave family, who produced the guide book, *Captivating Canvey*, in many editions in the 1930s, 1940s and 1950s, it was 'an Isle of Delight in the Mouth of the Silvery Thames' [11].

'COME TO CAPTIVATING CANVEY'

Canvey is an island, thirty miles from London, on the northern side of the Thames estuary, three miles west of Southend-on-Sea. Its 4000 acres of marshland are mostly below sea level at high tide. In the sixteenth century the landowner employed Dutch engineers to drain the island in return for concessions of land. Their sea wall lasted until 1881 when it was breached in a storm. The commissioners responsible for the wall repaired it, but reduced its length from twenty-two to fifteen miles (later further reduced to thirteen miles after the floods of 1953). For although the soil of Canvey was superior to that of the South Essex mainland, it too was falling out of cultivation during the agricultural depression, and by the end of the 1880s, much of it had reverted to scrubby pasture land.

The island was approached from South Benfleet (where a station on the London, Tilbury and Southend railway opened in 1854) by a ferry and by stepping-stones at low tide. The road bridge from Benfleet was not built

120

until 1931. Frederick Ramuz, at the height of his land-buying enterprise, thought Canvey not worth acquiring. His sons remembered travelling across part of the island in a rowing-boat in the floods of 1897 [12].

But in 1899 a rival Southend land agent, Frederick Hester, bought a large acreage at the eastern end of the island and announced his intention of developing it as a 'health and pleasure resort'. Hester had previously bought farm sites at Pitsea, Laindon, Benfleet and Rayleigh, where he and his family lived while developing land as bungalow sites [13]. Mr Hillman, who went to Canvey to buy plots for himself, was offered a cup of tea and a job, and stayed, working for Hester for several years. He described him as 'tall, well-proportioned with large blue eyes, white hair and a beard, a gentleman of great charm who always wore a frock coat' [14]. Others were equally impressed. They found him a 'tall, powerfully built man with a commanding voice and distinguished appearance' [15] and although Hester started with an initial capital of only £2000 [16], he embarked on grandiose schemes for Canvey-on-Sea, as he renamed the island. His family moved once again to Leigh Beck Farm, where he installed an artesian well, wind pump and water tower, to provide a pumped water supply.

Hester planned a rail link across Benfleet Creek to the mainland, but the prohibitive cost led him instead to develop a 'Mono-Rail Tramway'. The track was laid, and four twenty-five seater red and gilt tramcars ordered. The trams were lettered 'Venice-on-Sea and Canvey', for a drainage lagoon was to become the Venetian canal, and the building of a pier was begun. He commissioned Augustus Daly's history of the island, which was of course loud in its praise of Hester's dream, and of the Winter Garden, intended to be six miles long, 'though at the time of writing, rather more than a mile and a half only has been completed and thrown open to the public'. The Winter Garden 'when completed, will be an elegant glass structure, planted with choice fruit trees, flowering shrubs, and climbers, intersecting the whole island' [17].

Hester's admirer used a similar rhetoric to that of Frederick Ramuz and the Land Company, and described how 'with an alacrity and courage that would have done credit to a very much younger man', Hester set out to develop Canvey 'to meet the requirements of London's teeming and toiling millions'. Like Ramuz, he believed that landownership would bring prosperity to all:

Let the people be self-reliant and independent is evidently his motto; but his perspicacity and hardheaded business-like method in dealing with a great social problem, goes to show how the people can with ease and comfort for themselves, be rendered both self-reliant and independent by a well-conceived scheme, based on the foundations of self-asserted thrift. With this laudable object in view he proclaims, as did the Prophet of old, 'Back to the land, O ye people!' [18].

But how exactly was this splendid aim to be achieved? It was explained that Hester, 'having acquired in perpetuity some thousands of acres of

121

the island' had had them carefully mapped and divided into small plots for building purposes:

> These plots are of such convenient size that brings them within the range of almost every one to purchase on the system of easy payments, extending over a given period on the installment system, whereby it is competent for the thrifty toiler of our great Metropolis to become a freeholder of land and house property, in the easiest possible manner... One great feature of his scheme is, however, that manufacturers of commodities of a noxious character are barred, so that the present healthfulness of the Island shall in no way be jeopardised or prejudiced to the detriment of succeeding generations [19].

The conveniently small plots were in fact fifteen feet wide with a depth of sixty feet, set in a gridiron road layout. They were usually sold in blocks of four, known as a 'Canvey Plot'. In 1901 Hester offered 20,000 plots for sale by auction at daily auctions during the summer, conducted by an auctioneer, J. Brooke Stewart, in the open or in a marquee on the site, and offering intending purchasers free travel, 'a free meal and a square deal'. Posters advertised the sales at every station from Fenchurch Street to Benfleet. In 1901 the plots realised about £5 each [20]. In that year Hester bought more land in the area he called Winter Gardens at a cost of £10,000 through the formation of a limited company called Central Park Estate Ltd [21], and by the following year 'Mr Hester has purchased half the island' and plots are selling at about £7 each [22]. One sale at Whitsun in 1904 brought in £600 [23].

But by November of that year, work stopped on the £14,500 electric tramway, the pier and the completion of the Winter Gardens. Notices began to appear saying that the materials on the sites were the property of the contractors. In April 1905 a meeting of Hester's creditors resolved that he should be declared bankrupt. In 1906 in the London Bankruptcy Court it was found that his liabilities were £85,393. The Winter Gardens, the pier and the tramway were dismantled. Messrs Kynoch and a syndicate of creditors attempted in vain to continue developing the seaside resort, pier and parade, with 'many Indian bungalows' [24]. The land could not be returned to farming as roads had been laid out, and the fields were spattered with plots already sold. Hester's local creditors took over the land and attempted to sell the remaining plots, at prices around £3 a plot. By 1914, the average price of a single plot from the Canvey Development Company was eleven shillings and sixpence [25].

CANVEY BETWEEN THE WARS

Not the least of Frederick Hester's errors was his failure to invest in capital projects which would show an immediate return. The ticket office for the tramway was built to cater for the people who would be

Canvey Island: characteristic views in the early Twentieth century. (Photos by courtesy of F. McCave)

'flocking down to Canvey-on-Sea almost every day', but the people were small spenders, and the actual income from the sale of plots was reduced by the fact that it was usually spread out over sixteen monthly instalments after an initial deposit. But the process he had set in motion continued. Canvey had been discovered by East Londoners from the other end of the railway line. In 1906, the year that the tram rails were taken up, the first bus service across the island was opened, and ran at the same sixpenny fare until the opening of the bridge in 1931. Two traders, Mr Cox and Mr Woods, provided groceries, general stores and a post office. The island had changed:

> Very often people did not even bother to purchase a plot of land; they just pitched a tent and became squatters... It became possible to erect any form of structure, and if you were not a permanent resident it was all the more difficult for you to be traced [26].

At one end of the scale, plotholders would buy a factory-made bungalow and have it erected by a local builder. At the other, they would start with a bell tent, sold off as war surplus, and build an earth closet with three-and-a-half sheets of corrugated iron and a door.

The Canvey Island Supply Company was started at the end of 1919 by Mr E.E.O. Lawrence, supplying building materials, delivered by horses, with carts fitted with runners instead of wheels. The early-1920s saw a growing commuting population:

> People made their own bridges across the many dykes which drained the Island. An enterprising builder was advertising telegraph poles, 26 feet and 28 feet long, 'as new' and 'suitable for bridges'. The prices were £2 and £2.10s each. For bungalows galvanised corrugated iron was available, 'splendid, stout, as new' at 11d (4½p) a foot run. Demand must have been running high, for by the early part of 1921 he had only about 200 feet left [27].

Canvey Island: intensification of development in the interwar period. (Photo by courtesy of F. McCave)

As the residential population increased, pressure grew for higher standards of construction. The Canvey Island Public Interests Committee, formed in May 1921, urged that 'eyesores should be forbidden' [28] and the local authority began to insist that a bungalow should not be erected on a site less than 3,600 square feet, or four Canvey plots. Speculative builders began to exploit the new market:

In 1933 brick-built bungalows at Canvey Village were offered at £385. Another builder offered bungalows 'for an agreed deposit, not exceeding £50, and 10s weekly.' An estate agent offered plot prices: Furtherwick Park (concrete road, water and light) £12; Kloster Park (only twelve now left) £10; Oysterfleet £8.10s; Water Gardens £7; Sixty Acres £6.10s. The island was sewered in 1934-36. Property was freely advertised to let — 'bungalows, all newly decorated and in first class condition with every modern convenience, gas, company's water, electric light, concrete roads, lounge, living room, kitchenette, two bedrooms, 16s (80p) a week...' By the summer of 1938 there were 3,010 buildings with a rateable value of £40,315. In 1939, 2,723 of them were able to enjoy mains water [29].

But it was still as a holiday place that the island was renowned amongst East Londoners, just as Frederick Hester had envisaged. It was known as the cheapest possible place for a seaside holiday. The Holidays with Pay Act of 1938 affected eighteen and a half million employed workers, nearly eleven million of whom were receiving holiday pay for the first time. The breadwinners of many East London families were among these millions, and, since the effect of the Act was delayed by the Second World War, if their families had a holiday at all, it was based on the renting of a plotland bungalow belonging to relations or neighbours, or advertised in the local newsagents or in the columns of 'Dalton's Weekly'. To a sophisticated eye, Canvey had none of the attractions of a seaside holiday. The sea was nowhere visible until you had climbed the surrounding wall. But it did have a beach and vendors of buckets, spades and candy floss, and, when the money lasted, the climax of the holiday could be a trip to Southend, with its pier, Kursaal, amusement arcades and Garron's fish restaurant.

There were also people with a more permanent commitment to the island. One informant says:

My grandfather, who was a wood machinist, came back from the first world war to Dalston. His eldest daughter, my aunt, was diagnosed as having TB and the doctor said that the whole family should move to a place with plenty of fresh air. In those days they used to talk about the 'ozone' and sea breezes that were supposed to be healthy round here. Southend was impossible, but he bought a plot on Canvey for next to nothing, and got somebody else to move his wooden hut from another plot. My uncles and aunts were there every weekend, and slowly the whole family moved in [30].

The centre of gravity for his family had moved from London to Southend, and the migration was completed during the bombing of East London in 1940.

Meanwhile the other end of the island was becoming commercially important. In 1921 a House of Commons select committee unanimously threw out a bill for a deep-water wharf and installations on Canvey, and in 1930 there was opposition to the Ministry of Health's sanction to the building of wharves and oil refineries there [31]. In the debate on this issue, Mr F.G. Pickett declared that:

> Ninety per cent of the residents and small property owners on the island are most emphatic. It is part of the development of the Russian Oil Products — the sacrificing of British ratepayers for the benefit of foreigners who have not paid their way [32].

By 1926 Canvey had become an urban district council and one of the tasks of the new council was that of controlling building development. 'However, this amounted to little more than the eradication of the worst properties, such as old railway carriages and bus bodies' [33]. Moreover 'an increasing number of these properties were becoming permanently occupied' [34], and the local authority's surveyor estimated that in 1939 something between a third and a half of the properties on the island were owned by people who lived elsewhere. The road bridge from South Benfleet had ended the island's relative isolation, and the County Council's Regional Study in 1931 forecast both residential and industrial expansion:

> Canvey, being surrounded by the sea, has exceptional attractions and as a seaside resort being nearest to London, is justified in anticipating a prosperity which will depend almost entirely upon the way in which it is developed in the immediate future [35].

The western part of the island, in spite of local opposition, was being developed by the petro-chemical industry. The eastern part with its 'healthy and invigorating' climate 'offering the visitor ozone which few seaside resorts can equal' was recommended as 'a natural choice for jaded business folk' [36]. In practice, as one old resident recalls, 'We were a happy, scruffy community of transplanted East Enders, sitting out the winters as best we could, and making a bob or two in the summer when people came down here in their thousands' [37].

POSTWAR CANVEY

Like the rest of the coastline, Canvey was a 'restricted area' during the Second World War, but many of the plot-owners, living in those parts of London worst hit by the bombing of the terrible nights of the 7th and 8th September 1940, found their way down to their holiday homes with nothing but the clothes they were wearing:

We had nowhere to go and our little shack seemed like a heavenly haven [38]. We spent six nights in a rest centre in a school at Canning Town, and then the Public Assistance gave us travel warrants to get down here. We were laughing and crying at the same time. Dad (who had just been killed in the Blitz) had worked so hard on our little bungalow, and was never to know how much it would mean to us [39].

The end of the war and the acute housing shortage as servicemen returned to pick up the threads of their family lives, resulted in a doubling of the Canvey population to about 10,000 between 1945 and 1947. The local authority tried to upgrade the holiday use of the island by encouraging caravan sites as an alternative to camping. 'In 1947 the land to the west of Thorney Bay was bought by a newly formed company which intended to build a holiday camp, and in that summer tented camping was allowed' [40]. The Thorney Bay Beach Camp was in fact launched by Lt. Col. Horace Percy Fielder, who had been one of the pre-war developers of the island, and sought in this venture to provide 'a low-priced working man's Riviera' [41]. He was successively chairman of the Finance Committee, the Public Health Committee and the Town Planning Committee of the District Council.

The 1951 Census revealed that more than three-quarters of the permanent dwellings were 'light structures of the bungalow or chalet type' with one to four rooms. One-fifth of the inhabitants were elderly people, and one-sixth of the dwellings were used for summer and week-end occupation [42]. Canvey had changed from a holiday colony to a suburb by the sea. There was a daily trek to Benfleet Station, the link with jobs off the island.

Early in 1953 Canvey, like a thousand miles of the East Coast, was stricken by disaster: the flooding resulting from a storm surge and north-westerly gales. On the night of January 31st and February 1st of that year, 307 people lost their lives, fifty-eight of them on Canvey Island. It was the worst affected of all coastal districts, and almost all the survivors of the initial catastrophe were evacuated from the island. A week after the floods only 607 people were still on Canvey, and 10,800 of the inhabitants were being accommodated elsewhere in Essex [43].

During the next few years, Canvey was quietly recovering from the effects of the floods. The sea defences for the residential part of the island were rebuilt three feet higher than the 1953 level. Then came Canvey's boom years in house-building. The Urban District Council approached the London County Council to enlist its aid under the 1952 Town Development Act in housing 'overspill' population from London. Essex County Council objected to this proposal on the grounds that 'overspill' should come from metropolitan Essex, and the move of several hundred families from Dagenham and Walthamstow was sponsored by those boroughs. Private house-building flourished too, and purchasers found Canvey rather cheaper than other parts of South Essex. The process continued, and by 1980 the population of the island was around 33,000. For anyone who knew the place in its pre-war days,

Canvey has been almost totally transformed.

But not entirely, for pockets of the original plotlands remain. Many of the scattered settlements were upgraded over time in the course of redevelopment. The Council set about providing main drainage and made-up roads for large areas. This involved fifty miles of road, not including the more isolated of the original Hester estates. 'These improvements, which were designed to encourage the break-up of larger plots, higher density development and a better urban environment, often placed an impossible burden on old people' [44]. For even though cheap methods of roadbuilding were used — grass verges instead of pavements — the cost to a householder with a sixty-foot frontage was in 1955 about £165, not including drainage:

> Many were forced also to upgrade their substandard shacks. Some gave up their land to private builders in exchange for one of perhaps three or four houses built on each plot. This was an attractive situation as their home was upgraded considerably with little inconvenience [45].

If the vigorous action of the Council caused hardship for some, the policy adopted elsewhere of waiting for people to die off before undertaking comprehensive redevelopment caused equal resentment among others. The two old and sparsely populated areas called Winter Gardens and Sixty Acres were left out of the original redevelopment plans for more intense consideration. In 1966 the firm of planning consultants, W.R. Davidge and Partners, were commissioned to report on these districts, comprising some 330 acres with 500 inhabitants. On the basis of an external inspection they concluded that the majority of the 260 properties had a life of about ten years or less. 'Much of the housing is substandard and obsolete, yet provides living accommodation for many residents, elderly and of long standing, who, it is the Council's wish, should not be disturbed'. They discussed three alternative planning approaches. The first was to adopt the existing road pattern and permit controlled consolidation, the second was to acquire the sites by compulsory purchase, and the third was to acquire the properties by agreement as they came on the market. The consultants concluded that the third course was the most satisfactory, would call for the minimum disturbance of residents, and would provide a reservoir of housing land over the next fifteen or twenty years [46]. The Council's District Plan, approved in 1969, had a detailed scheme of 'systematic renewal and redevelopment' for the Winter Gardens, while Sixty Acres was to be redeveloped 'in the more distant future' [47].

However clear and logical the Council's intentions seemed to its officers, the residents of both areas were puzzled and apprehensive, and most of them wrote individually to the Clerk to the Council in these terms:

> The accumulation of varied — and frequently conflicting advice, proffered from various quarters... had only served to add to the fears, anxieties and worries which all this entails.

I submit that it is unwarranted, unnecessary and unjust that I should be submitted to such treatment — particularly from local government sources. I am innocent of cause and the victim of effect. Indeed, I now suggest that either a plain proposition be placed before me or the long-procrastinated threat of your Plan be withdrawn in its entirety... [48].

Three years later, the Sixty Acres Residents Association was writing to the constituency MP, Sir Bernard Braine, who has always championed the plotlanders:

Since the early 1950s, Sixty Acres has been a restricted area for development and no planning applications have been allowed by the local authority since that time.

Sixty Acres has remained dormant and became the 'Cinderella' area, with residents living a remote pre-war village type of existence alongside the bustling modern township developing elsewhere in residential areas.

During these years residents became aggrieved over such matters as lack of sewerage and other essential services, the complete absence of roads and the hardship of movement through rivers of mud and potholes every winter... Repeatedly when these grievances were contested, assurances were given by the local authority that amenities would improve in time and in due course widespread benefits would be brought to the community when development occurred... [49]

THE LAND GRABBERS

But districts like Winter Gardens and Sixty Acres, and similar plotland sites in other parts of South Essex, were vulnerable to a new threat: the land grabber. In English law the title to land known colloquially as 'squatters' rights' rests on the concept of 'adverse possession', the adverse possessor having been in peaceful and undisputed possession of the land for twelve years. In the case of unregistered land this 'automatically confers a legal title on the adverse possessor and extinguishes the "owner's" title' [50]. In the case of registered land, the registered proprietor is "deemed to hold the property on trust for the adverse possessor who may, on proving the relevant facts and after the Land Registry has served the necessary notices, be registered in his place' [51].

Undoubtedly in the casual early days of the colonisation of Canvey some of the early plot-holders were squatters who eventually gained title in this way, and there were also plots whose owner was untraceable. Nobody worried about this when the land was literally as cheap as dirt, but by the 1960s, with the prospect of a building boom, a lot of people became interested in gaining title to empty sites. In 1969 it was reported that:

Now claim jumpers are invading the island at week-ends, ripping the fences down and erecting new ones. Many locals fear that violence may break out. Mr Albert Reddish, who has lived in a bungalow on the island for 26 years, witnessed both the original claim staking and the recent outbreak of claim jumping. The empty plot of land beside his home sprouted boundary fence posts some years ago. Yesterday he noticed that these have been replaced by posts linked with strands of wire. 'There is some dirty work going on here', said Mr Reddish [52].

A particular firm was involved in 'claiming title to virtually all vacant land in the area and challenging all and sundry who may be affected by their activities, to take legal action to defend their rights' [53]. The Sixty Acres Residents Association, advised that the firm claimed that it had acquired the interest of a local farmer, challenged this on the grounds that 'since the floods of 1953 all this land has stood abandoned, unfenced, and occupied by the community as a whole for social, domestic and pleasure use and that this 18 years of occupation gives our community the most superior title of all' [54].

Sir Bernard Braine took the matter up with the Law Commission, the Law Society and the Lord Chancellor and after declaring to the Council that 'I am quite prepared to come down with a pair of wire cutters myself' [55], he gained an assurance that the Chief Land Registrar would not in future accept applications for first registration based upon adverse possession relating to land in South-East Essex. The land grabbing abated.

CANVEY'S PLOTLANDS TODAY

The reorganisation of local government in 1974 absorbed Canvey into a new, larger authority, Castle Point District Council. Its policy towards the remaining plotland areas is slightly different from that of its predecessor:

> The current policy is that the common sixty feet deep plot should not be developed unless there are two or more together, and this had led to the growth of 30 foot by 120 foot housing plots. In the past Canvey Council bought up any land on request, but the new council only does so if there is no other beneficial use for it [56].

The old people and the old houses are slowly disappearing. As might be expected, there is now a certain nostalgia for the plotlands. One correspondent to the local magazine writes:

> If one wants to get a glimpse of what Canvey looked like, say fifty years ago, the place is Sixty Acres. I wonder how long it will be before that too is turned into another concrete jungle [57]. And

Canvey Island: current views.

another says, 'I still cycle around looking for the old bungalows with their beautiful gardens which are a joy to behold...' [58].

But as an 'issue' the plotlands are no longer discussed. The issue that is argued about continually is the danger to the residential population from the petro-chemical installations and from liquid gas containers at the industrial end of the island.

In a few years time Canvey's housing will be totally indistinguishable from that of any other outer suburb. Ironically, just as the official mind had pushed the plotlands into history, a Canvey representative on Castle Point Council, came up with a 'revolutionary plan'. Councillor Mrs Dot Shaw explained that:

> It is my idea to let large plots of council land on, say, 99-year lease, for people to build their own houses on. It would drastically reduce the cost of buying a ready-made house, in some cases by half. The council would receive money from ground rents. It would take a weight off the council's present housing list, which is a real problem at the moment. Eventually it could solve it... [59].

Though not taken up, it was an imaginative scheme to apply a plotland approach to current needs.

THE ISLE OF SHEPPEY

> One wonders why no-one has ever thought of converting this semi-circle of grassy cliffs, swept by the breezes of the German Ocean, into a Health Resort. Minster-on-Sea, as the unknown paradise is called will find its way into popular favour in a remarkably short space of time. It is the nearest Kentish resort to London.

> (*Daily Express*, 5 August 1903)

After his successful development of Westcliff and other fringes of Southend as holiday resorts, and his activities in Herne Bay, Frederick Ramuz sought to repeat this enterprise on the southern side of the Thames estuary. The place was the Isle of Sheppey, four miles long and eleven miles wide, but newly accessible from London by train, and in those days also to be reached by the Thames pleasure steamers from Southend.

'SEASIDE IN THE MAKING'

The record has it that Ramuz:

> bought up several decaying agricultural estates, about 1,000 acres, and about seven years later started to develop it, by cutting it up into 'plots for the people'. £30,000 was spent in the formation of

132

Isle of Sheppey: use of free railway tickets to attract plot purchasers.
(Photo courtesy of National Railway Museum, York)

roads, some with granite kerbstones for footpaths, and drainpipes. About 3,000 plots were sold to about 1,000 Londoners [60].

Sheppey was, and in some ways, is, the Kentish equivalent of Canvey Island, but it has, on the seaward side, at least, the protection of cliffs, which, are, however, continually eroded. Some of Minster's seaside cabins have already fallen into the sea. It also had the advantage of the 'flourishing Naval and Military town of Sheerness'. Ramuz renamed the little town of Minster, Minster-on-Sea, and was confident that as 'the nearest point on the Kent coast to London' thanks to the opening of the railway line, it was no longer 'inaccessible and unknown' but would 'quickly develop into a prominent water place', since, as he explained in the Land Company's catalogue, it might 'without exaggeration be said to be one of the finest if not the best marine estate ever acquired by us or any other company for re-sale in plots to the general public' [61].

He set up the Minster Development Corporation, operating from the same address as the Land Company at 68 Cheapside, and put his eldest son, George, newly initiated into the craft of auctioneering and land agency, in charge of the project. But in spite of all efforts at Minster and Eastchurch, land sales were very slow. People did buy plots, as holiday homes, for retirement or for smallholdings, but there were enormous gaps in the estate agents' plans.

After the Second World War, a local guide book looked back on the history of the place, and noted that since the initial effort to popularise the island:

the number of houses has risen from about 100 to about 1,800, and the population from about 250 to 5,500... Although the

133

pleasant landscape and marine views have not been spoiled, the large number of vacant building sites has not improved the general attractive appearance of the locality. Where roads have been made up by the local authority, it begins to bear some resemblance to a seaside resort... As a place of residence for retired persons not requiring much artificial pleasure, Minster has much to recommend it... Water, gas and electric services have been much extended in every direction and much capital laid out by the three companies concerned. Large numbers of the original site purchasers bought only as a speculation and are now desirous of re-selling... [62].

The truth behind these euphemisms is that the development of the Isle of Sheppey did not happen as the land speculators intended. The same postwar guide book remarks that Minster-on-Sea 'is a seaside resort in embryo' and, just to rub the fact in, explains that the word means 'in the making'. Even today it presents this appearance, as the plotland bungalows slowly give way to new houses on the steep unmade roads. The local authority encourages the amalgamation of sites as a prerequisite of permission to redevelop, and the sprawling Sheppey plotlands present the same mixture of new commuter houses, undisturbed small-holders' First World War army huts, and riding stables, greyhound-breeding establishments and contractors yards, as the backlands of South Essex, with many inhabitants ekeing out a living in local small-scale labour markets and in the 'informal' economy.

Even the names of many of the plotland houses reflect the gentle irony of the dwellers in a place which was so long in the making that it never quite made it. One is called 'Raging Calm', another 'Once More' and yet another, 'Chaos'.

In 1961 George Ramuz, at the age of 84, gave a remarkably frank recorded interview to a local journalist, Adrian Waller, who was interested because 'A land-hungry Britain is just about to discover Minster. Hundreds of sites have lately been sold to major developers. More will be snapped up soon'. Twenty years later, even Mr Waller's optimism can be seen to be only partly fulfilled, but his interview with Mr Ramuz provides insights into the motives of the plotland entrepreneurs:

Q. Whose idea was it to establish a residential colony in Minster?

A. My father's. He was one of the first men in this country to get hold of cheap land, when farms were going begging, and cut it up into plots — to sell them on easy terms to anybody.

Q. Did your father pass the land he acquired to you?

A. No. The only inheritance I got was a partly developed estate here, subject to big mortgages. You don't want to think that I have done well here and made a fortune. Nothing of the kind. I have had almost anything a common man — like myself — would desire. All sorts of good things, except piles of money.

Q. Who conceived the idea of laying out the streets and the kerb stones which can be seen in the long grass on the site, even today?

A. My father. Together, we promoted a public water company here in 1902.

Q. What were the circumstances that made a wide-area scheme like this seem to have a better chance than any other? Were other schemes thought of?

A. There had been no land schemes or housing schemes here apart from Sheerness — those streets of small houses. Some of those streets are now over eighty-years old.

Q. The original scheme in Minster was rather a flop, wasn't it?

A. Flop? I could tell you the times that I had trying to sell plots of land to Londoners. It was an absolute flop!

Q. What went wrong?

A. The Londoners didn't like it. I managed over a long period of years to sell the majority of the plots which had been laid out. But the prices of the land, when my father was associated with it, were very small. You couldn't get anything for it.

Q. Had everything gone to plan, would it have been reasonable to expect the building to have been completed in about 1914?

A. It looked as if the Londoners would come and build here prior to the 1914-18 war starting. There was a very cheap rail ticket from London — 3s 6d return.

Q. It is said that had one decent road been laid to the sea from Minster — say in the Baldwin Road area — and shops and houses erected along it, Minster would today have a 50,000 population. Is this right?

A. No. Utterly wrong. There was no industry here. And there were no fast trains. In the summer time there were only a few steamers running.

Q. You don't personally feel guilty of having spoilt the Island's chances of development for half a century?

A. No. It will be proved presently. These things take time. Brighton, you know, took over 200 years. Southend has taken about 120 years. And there are a few other places that have taken many years to develop. No. You don't build a seaside resort in five minutes.

Q. It is also said that before 1914 you could have made about £¼ million out of selling these plots. Would you deny this?

A. If we hadn't induced London shopkeepers, tradesmen and publicans, and a few little builders who had got some money to invest, I don't think development would have taken place at all.

Q. Why was it that only London shopkeepers bought plots here and not other people who had a little cash to invest?

A. I was working in the City at the time. I had been for some years. I

135

had that connection with them. I had been in the City from 1891, when I was 14.

Q. Have there been any other schemes for getting rid of these plots?

A. No. We only had one way of selling them and that was on the 'easy terms' system. We had thousands of handbills printed and auction sales here of course at least once a week for six months in the year.

Q. About what year did it first occur to you that all traces had been lost of so many purchasers, and that the land would eventually fall back to you?

A. Before the Second World War started. Somewhere between 1935 and 1939.

Q. What action would you have taken against anyone who squatted on any of the sites? Obviously you could not have proved title yourself.

A. We did, in one or two cases, have to turn some gypsies off.

Q. Isn't it rather remarkable that with all this area, there have been no cases of people attempting to obtain squatter's rights?

A. We had one case. And I wouldn't want to mention the name because it happened to be a local person — now dead. It was in spite of an agreement she had with us. We used to let her have the right of turning her horses out on to some of the vacant plots. After many years of amiability, co-operation, she thought fit to try and claim a few plots. But she didn't succeed.

Q. Would you say you have made quite a fortune out of this land? About how much?

A. I would put it in quite the reverse. I was a creature of circumstances. And I have mentioned that in your newspaper more than once. A great many young men in this world have become creatures of circumstance — however energetic and clever they have been.

Q. Are you the sole beneficiary of the land?

A. Yes. I have no company. I could never get anybody to associate with me.

Q. Why?

A. Why? Because it was a dead end [63].

It may have been a dead end for the land speculator, but for many purchasers the plots on the Isle of Sheppey provided what they had been looking for — a secluded and isolated place for holidays and ultimate retirement. The attraction of the place extended beyond the Ramuz holdings. At the easternmost point of the Island, for example, is Shellness, where a small holiday colony of little stonefaced houses, like an ancient fishing village, is continually rebuilt by its occupants after the buffetings of the sea.

136

Isle of Sheppey: current views.

JAYWICK SANDS

Lord Justice Greer:	Of course it should never have been made a building estate at all.
Mr Montgomery:	That may be, my lord.
Lord Justice Greer:	I think it is perfectly scandalous.
Mr Montgomery:	It may have been unfortunate. I have not a word to say on behalf of Mr Stedman.
Mr Beyfus:	Somebody has said that the bungalow owners were poor people. In fact they were nothing of the kind. They were people who went there at weekends and took their cars with them.
Lord Justice Greer:	Nobody with ample means would go and live in this marsh!

(Court of Appeal, 17 July 1936)

Jaywick is the most recent of a string of holiday places on the Essex coast between the estuaries of the Stour and the Colne. The first was Walton-on-the-Naze, developed in the 1830s as 'the resort of a considerable number of genteel visitors' [64], followed by Clacton in the early Victorian period, and Frinton, conceived as a very exclusive resort, built on the initiative of the local landowner Sir Richard Powell-Cooper and the Marine and General Land Company in the 1890s. Jaywick, two miles south of Clacton, also owes its origins to one entrepreneurial family, the Stedmans.

'SUN AND FUN AT JAYWICK SANDS'

Frank Christopher Stedman (1874-1963) was a surveyor who worked for several of the large London firms of estate agents. In 1916 he bought for £250 an Elizabethan cottage with ten acres at Meopham, Kent, 'for our old age' as he told his wife. The end of the First World War brought not only the breakup of landed estates on an unprecedented scale, but also large numbers of ex-servicemen, thankful for their survival and resolving not to go back to a nine-to-five routine, but to live in the country and keep chickens. One of them bought the ten acres at Meopham, and Frank Stedman, his small capital released, was launched on his career as a developer. In the 1920s he bought, divided up into building plots and re-sold, various estates including Swakeleys and Ickenham, as well as Elmer Sands on the South Coast, where his purchase made him Lord of the Manor.

By 1928 Stedman had developed thirteen such estates, totalling 3,575 acres and eighty-six miles of roads, at places like Sevenoaks, Rickmansworth, Hastings, Horley, Bognor and Bexley. Unlike many speculative developers of the period he did not get directly involved in building houses, leaving this to local contractors. This was probably because he lacked the capital to put at risk in speculative building. He

138

did, however, impose restrictive covenants as to the size of houses and plots, and his grandchildren are to this day consulted about proposals to subdivide the very large plots he sold in his suburban estates. His daughter remembers him as 'a Fabian, with a sense of humour, a talented water-colour artist. People say he was on the make, but in fact he had a very strong philanthropic streak. As soon as money came his way he dispersed it all over the place' [65].

Early in 1928 Frank Stedman embarked on a purchase which involved him and his family and thousands of other people for the rest of their lives: the acquisition of several hundred acres of reclaimed marshland and grazing land at Jaywick. The local newspaper reported in 1934 that:

> Five years ago wild birds screamed and whirled over the marshlands and meadows between the third and fourth Martello towers to the West of Clacton. Cattle roamed at will, and the only sound on the shingly beach was the murmur of the waves. One cold winter day, Mr F.C. Stedman motored there with his solicitor and bank manager. Sleet was cutting down, and a bleak wind whistled through the grass and reeds. He saw it under its worst conditions but he could imagine it at its best [66].

What, in his optimistic way, he did not imagine, was that the estate would be plagued for decades by the danger of flooding and by problems of sewage disposal, which were not resolved for forty years. He and his sons immediately set about the process of development, his eldest son Jack being installed as resident manager, in an office on the Promenade in Clacton. Their first task, in October 1928, was to build a new concrete road linking the estate with Clacton. They then set about building houses and their difficulties began. Frank Stedman made some notes of the sequence of events (no doubt for use in putting his case to the Clacton Council in 1932). His account reads:

Spring 1929	Built 6 houses, being verbally assured we could get through to Main Drains.
Summer 1929	Difficulties arose about drains. Built Golf Green Road and Beach Road — Clacton rejected disposal works because of 'danger of sea flooding'. That 'danger' is so remote I contended the land being sixteen feet above low water mark it must drain off again and flooding if it did occur would be once in 20 years or so whereas the drainage would be there always and at worse it could only be filled with sea water to be pumped out in an hour or two.
Autumn 1929	I had to put cesspools to the houses.
1929	Being forced to abandon sewers I could not build more houses — put in plans for some beach huts

	— thinking they could be sanctioned under tents, huts, caravans bye laws. They passed them
1930	More beach huts passed but footnotes — must not be used for sleeping in — as the plans showed 4, 5 or 6 rooms it was obvious what was meant.
1930	Town clerk said he had heard they were being slept in and warned me he *might* be compelled to disapprove by pressure from the Town.

Medical officer went down, saw several people and said, I see these are being used for sleeping in — if they are used for that, ventilation must be put in and other things done — these were done.

The Publicity official of Council constantly invited me to send details of Beach huts to people who had written to Council asking for particulars of sleeping huts for 4, 5 or 6 people, this strengthened my opinion that it was merely official... as up to now no official act has been taken against anyone for infringing a bye-law [67].

Thus, from Stedman's own account, his original intention was to develop the estate with permanent houses, and he only turned to beach huts and holiday chalets because of the difficulty of selling houses without main drainage. He sold two in fact, and disposed of the others 'at heavy loss'. His notes indicate that he was familiar with the plotland developments on the South Coast. Family tradition has it that it was Jack Stedman ('always the enterprising one') who having seen the holiday huts at Hayling Island urged his father to move into this side of the market, and that all Stedman's troubles with Clacton Council resulted from its being dominated by hotel and boarding house proprietors who did not want to see a new threat to their trade.

Difficulties behind the scenes were not allowed to cloud the confident public image of the development. The Stedmans took the whole front page of the *Clacton Times* on 18 May 1929, to list the advantages of the place. 'Jaywick Sands Estate', the advertisement ran:

'Desire to Announce to the Public of Clacton their aims in the development of probably the largest Single Scheme yet launched in the district. One of the chief aims will be to employ wherever possible local assistance in professional services, trades and labour. Another aim would be to provide a Development Scheme on more spacious lines than is generally achieved. The Estate is being developed so as to secure very open conditions, and a very large proportion will be allotted to Gardens, Tennis Lawns, Sports Grounds, running right down to the Sea [68].'

140

Jaywick Sands: promoted from 1929 as a place for enjoyment. (Photos courtesy of Clacton Public Library: Stedman Collection)

Among the many attractions listed were houses 'carefully planned to avoid ugly reconstruction' with three to six bedrooms, costing £395 to £1,500 'and even at the lowest price a small residue of beauty is ensured'. Roads and tree-lined avenues would give the Estate 'a rural and peaceful atmosphere and the extension of Gas, Water, Electric Light etc to be arranged. The Estate will put in Main Drainage'. Well-known aviators would provide flights over the sea at Whitsun, and a mile-long sporting lake 'of size and character such as is non-existent in any Seaside Resort in Great Britain, is now in course of construction' and would provide motor boat racing, water polo, aqua-planing and water carnivals.

The announcement also showed the area to the west of Lion Point as a 'fine beach for bathing houses' which 'can be built for £25 but again not of the ugly variety. They will be charmingly designed or can be hired, to be placed on a wonderful stretch of beach about 1¾ miles in length'. This was the area which subsequently became the Brooklands and Grasslands Estates. It was outside the administration of Clacton Council, being part of the then Tendring Rural District Council, which raised no objections to the development of about 800 plots there.

By July 1929, the Stedmans were inviting the public to:

> Come to Jaywick to see the Flooding of the Great Lake a mile long. By a huge pump pumping 600,000 gallons per hour now in progress. Then have Tea at the Jaywick Tea Rooms. Dancing from 4 pm [69].

The huge pump was lifting water over the sea wall at the place where the developer's plan showed a 'proposed sea lock', but alas the water drained away. Frank Stedman put a photograph of the operation in his album, with the caption: 'The "great" lake at Jaywick. Another Blighted Hope — Such is Life'. He, as purchaser of Jaywick Farm, joined forces with Mr J.V. Bond, the owner of Cockett Wick Farm, to form the Clacton Sporting Lakes Company. With the failure of the great lake, this company, as he was later to testify in court, 'sold to him beneficially, through his daughter as nominee, the Tendring and Grassland sections' [70].

That summer too the aviators were prosecuted for unlicensed flying, and Frank Stedman was prosecuted for 'causing an advertisement to be exhibited so as to disfigure the view of rural scenery'. This was Essex County Council's first prosecution under a bye-law made under the Advertisement Regulation Act of 1925. Stedman, with a second similar offence to be taken into consideration, was fined £1 [71].

There was one single success in the operation which had tied up Frank Stedman's capital: the sale of beach plots. *The Daily Chronicle* reported in August that 'for £50 you can acquire the freehold of 1,000 square feet with a hut upon it, coloured so gaudily that you would feel as if you were living in a revue'. Soon to be reviled, Jaywick could still attract praise as a 'Seaside Garden Suburb'.

142

'BYE-LAWS, BYE-LAWS...'

On the Sunday before the August Bank Holiday in 1931, the Jaywick Sands Freeholders Association held its first annual meeting, when over two hundred people crowded the Jaywick Beach Cafe. A dominant theme in the discussion concerned the delivery of letters. At that time letters were left, in alphabetical order, in pigeon-holes outside the estate office. The plot-holders maintained that 'as their huts (or bungalows) are freehold dwellings, each with a number and the name of a road there is no reason at all why the postal authorities should not arrange for the delivery of letters to the individual huts during the summer season'. The sympathetic columnist of the local paper agreed with them 'for after all, the huts are packed closely enough together and all the roads are clearly named'. He also considered that their demands for telephones on the estate were justified, since 'Jaywick plot-holders are, of course, in rather a different position to the ordinary visitor. They are ratepayers of the town and are to an extent "permanent"'. He followed this by a comment on the general issue of plotlands in relation to local authorities:

> There is, however, one serious word that should be said as to this and other developments around Clacton. A local authority while thoroughly safeguarding the health and amenities of the district, can still do a lot to help or hinder the growth of the town and district. Progressive authorities do all they legitimately can to attract new residents and new ideas, but sometimes one is forced to the conclusion that the Clacton Council rather resent enterprise and innovation as unwelcome intrusion. It is for the good of the place that they should be helped, so long as the health and safety of the inhabitants are protected. The strict interpretation of the technicalities of the byelaws which are necessary for the populous busy centre may be irritating pedantry for the care of the outfield. The trend of the times is moving towards smaller compact residences, better fitted with labour-saving devices, but it is the nature of officialdom to frown on anything that does not strictly conform to its brickwork, air-space and other provisos for town life, although they may be concerned with lighter structures only intended for summer residences or holiday camps [72].

These comments must have been inspired by a conversation with Frank Stedman, who, while pursuing a very vigorous campaign to find purchasers for plots, was involved, deeper and deeper in Clacton Council's suspicions. The publisher of the paper was also the printer of Stedman's handbills and promotional literature, and a member of Clacton Urban District Council, and knew that a confrontation was impending.

The disapproval of Clacton's councillors of developments at Jaywick was voiced at a meeting late in 1931 to consider the application from numerous plot-holders and from Frank Stedman for a connection to the Council's electricity supply. Councillor J.E. Ball said he could not understand his colleagues' objections to this feasible business proposition: 'We have allowed these huts to go up; we took no action. We have given them water and gas facilities'. Councillor D.W. Fenton-Jones, opposing the proposal, said that the land on which the huts were built was below high water level. There was no protection at the moment apart from the existing sea defences, and there was unsatisfactory land drainage. 'The Council have already instructed the Public Health Committee to take certain action. If that action is pursued to the end it means that those huts will have to come down' [73].

The question of whether or not the huts in what had become known as the Old Section of Jaywick should be used for sleeping in was discussed again in January 1932 at a meeting between councillors and a sub-committee of four members of the Freeholders' Association, who reported:

> The land was sold to us, and although the erections were described as 'beach huts', we were given to understand both by implication and in some cases in writing that sleeping was permissible. Most of us were told that plans had been deposited with the Clacton Council. This was true in about 50 per cent of the cases, but the plans were for beach huts... During the past two years the Clacton Urban District Council have been trying to obtain satisfaction from Mr Stedman, and had advised him that conditions at Jaywick must be in keeping with their byelaws, but he has continued to sell land and permit huts to be erected...
>
> The Council were very sympathetic towards us, as they held the opinion that we had been misled, by not being made aware of the requirements of the Clacton Urban District Council regarding buildings, etc. They took into consideration that many owners would suffer if the Council exercised their powers and agreed that if those whose huts were already erected applied for a licence for a temporary building, they would grant same, for a period of three years, and renew it at the end of that time provided certain things were carried out...
>
> In the opinion of your committee these requirements were and are reasonable, and (they) considered it their duty to accept the ruling of the Clacton Urban District Council. This opinion was strengthened by the fact that Mr Stedman advised us to do so. He has since changed his mind but your Committee are confident they have acted in the best interest of the members of this Association [74].

The Jaywick Sands Freeholders' Association convened a special general meeting on Easter Monday 1932 to discuss this report. It was held in a large marquee on the site and was attended by Clacton Councillors and by Frank Stedman. Councillor Fenton-Jones said that when the huts were first put up in 1930 no plans were submitted. Then 180 plans were submitted for what were said to be beach huts, and the Council on that representation had passed plans for 128 huts. During the year the huts were not used as beach huts but as domestic

144

dwellings and the Public Health Committee of the Council drew Mr Stedman's attention to the matter. Mr Stedman then tried to negotiate with them to see how far they would be prepared to allow those buildings to remain and to build further buildings to be used on the same basis as dwelling houses. They told him all through exactly what they had told the Association's Committee when they met. 'To put it simply, we think you have been misled'.

Fierce debate followed, much of it on the degree to which the plot-holders could be assured that these temporary licences would be renewed. From the floor, a plot-holder, Ernest Lansbury (a nephew of the well-known and much respected Labour politician George Lansbury) declared, 'I do not really believe that the Clacton Council are of that innocent order they would lead us to believe they are. We are asked to believe that Clacton Council seriously thought that we should come here to stick up huts in order to spend a few hours in them'. It was obviously, he said, a definite acceptance of the position at that particular moment, and by that action the Council had condoned the 'offence', if an 'offence' had been committed.

Frank Stedman insisted that there had been no misrepresentation. The Council knew perfectly well that the huts were being slept in. The Medical Officer of Health and the Committee saw those places that were being slept in. The Medical Officer had even made recommendations to make them suitable for sleeping. These recommendations were carried out.

A voice:	Why did you not fight for us?
Mr Stedman:	I have been doing so.
Another voice:	You put us into this position.
Mr Stedman:	I fought for you and you have not lost a night's rest yet. It is your committee who are fighting now.

Ernest Lansbury moved a resolution which was carried by the meeting. It said:

Having heard the report to our Association, we recommend our committee to inform the Clacton Council that we are desirous of assisting them as far as possible, but cannot agree to the suggested application for a licence, because it is unfair and inequitable, and therefore we regret that we are unable to agree to the suggestion of applying for a licence.

The Committee offered to resign, and Lansbury remarked, 'There is no need to resign because you have a difference of opinion. The obvious way is, you just carry on' [75].

By the time of the Association's Annual General Meeting on August Bank Holiday, 1932:

the difficulties had to a large extent been overcome, and it was now possible for plot-holders to build under certain conditions.

145

The Chairman added that Mr Stedman had given the Association £300 towards the necessary water supplies on the Estate. That, however, was only part of what would be necessary in order to comply with Clacton Council's requirements. There were approximately 2,500 feet of mains to lay, at a cost of about £600.

Ernest Lansbury once more expressed suspicion about the arrangement with Clacton Council:

> I do not think we ought to delude ourselves as to where we are in this matter. The Council have not yet met us in such a way that we can say those who have single plots can build on them. We find a number of us have plots which are no use, and with which nothing can be done.

The meeting was also invited to vote on a drainage scheme which would cost about £12.10s for each hutment. A resolution which was eventually passed, proposed that the Committee should 'make it obligatory on all owners to connect with the sewers and water supply when laid on'. One member commented that:

> The idea of having the Estate was to come down for a seaside holiday at the week-end. They had bricks and mortar in London, and most of them were satisfied with the system of drainage they had.

Once more, Ernest Lansbury remarked that they all knew what local bodies were. There was always a grandmotherly interference with people who did things of their own free will. Had they any guarantee that if they put in some system of drainage the local body would not came and say, 'Scrap the lot; you want a licence for this or that?'

Frank Stedman urged the meeting to note the rapidity of growth of the Estate. He remarked that at the end of the first year there were a hundred people, the second year two thousand, and the third year a five thousand population in the summer. Within two years there would probably be nine thousand people at Jaywick. 'I am going to put in a bathing pool, a dance hall, and a licensed club, and tennis courts are being built' and for the benefit of the place as a whole there must be a main drainage system. 'I am definitely going on with a scheme of my own. You can come into this as and when you decide'. His attitude had been the same over a proposal for providing concrete roads, which, the Executive Committee reported:

> would have been provided if the plot-holders agreed to pay 1s. per foot frontage only, this not to include return frontages. That was considered a very fair offer, and it was twice urged upon plot-holders with very poor results, several not troubling to answer at all. The Committee were so impressed with the importance of the project, however, that it was decided eventually to proceed, and to trust to the sense of fair play of the plot-holders to pay the

146

contribution of 1s.6d per foot after the roads had been done, but Mr Stedman, who had several times urged them to reply, had cancelled his cement contract, packed up his plant, and discharged the men, so that the opportunity was lost [76].

In the marquee that summer, church services were held 'on free and easy lines', and Frank Stedman gave a site for a church and headed a subscription list with a cheque for £50. No doubt the freeholders felt it churlish to point out that the advertising of sites had always stressed that main drainage and 'good concrete roads' would be provided. He was evidently increasingly bitter about the attitude of Clacton Council, and inserted a full-page advertisement on the front page of the local paper, addressed to the Unemployed of Clacton:

The Jaywick Sands Estate offered to employ 100 men on Sewer work during the whole of the Winter, 25 men extra on the Estate, 50 men extra on the Estate next Spring, and, consequent on the development, there would be 900 Bungalows erected employing 500 men for Two Whole Years, but Your 'Wise' Councillors Rejected the Plan. Therefore you must remain on the objectionable Unemployment Benefit, with help from kind people, unless you can Persuade Your 'Wise' Councillors to Reconsider Their Decision. Do Not Lose the Work. Insist Upon the Council's Acceptance [77].

He and his sons continued to publicise the estate through every possible means. The beach huts and plots for £50 freehold, with 'access to every plot by car', were continually advertised in the popular London daily and evening papers and in the weekly local papers of north and east London. The holiday chalets were on display at the Ideal Home Exhibition and at the Model Houses Exhibition at Gidea Park. The Brooklands and Grasslands parts of the estate had their roads named after popular makes of car, and under the headline 'A Motorists' Mecca by the Sea, with Brooklands the Main Thoroughfare' the London *Star* stressed the attractions of Jaywick for car owners: 'It is a place which, while offering petrol and oil, food, electricity, light, telephone and other essentials of civilisation, gives rippling sea and silvery sands, ocean breezes, and absolute freedom from inhibiting restrictions' [78].

The Estate's own brochures stressed Jaywick's accessibility:

'Not many years ago it was impossible to buy *at low cost* a seaside cottage just for week-end and holiday use. Since the arrival of Jaywick this is fortunately no longer the case, for here it has been found possible to provide all the essentials at a cost which families of moderate and even small income can easily afford. There are only two seaside places within easy motoring distance of North and East London. Southend is one of them; the alternative is Clacton; a run of 69 miles easily done between late breakfast and lunch-time [79].'

*Jaywick Sands: a close association with the motor car (including roads
named after popular makes) developed in the 1930s. (Photos courtesy of
Clacton Public Library: Stedman Collection)*

For non-motorists, who could not sport the orange and black Jaywick
car badge, there were frequent buses from the railway station at
Clacton, as well as Eastern National's Express coaches from Victoria
Coach Station, and Sutton's Crossley Coaches direct from the coach
station at King's Cross. Hillman's Air Service provided frequent flights
connecting with Hillman's coaches from all parts of London to
Romford. The day return air fare was 20s. and the period return 25s.

In the summer of 1934, the Jaywick Social Club moved from the original
club house provided by Mr Stedman to a 'spacious modern building', and

the Estate was offering to present a freehold bungalow in aid of the Essex Fund for the Blind. Among the swings, roundabouts and coconut shies of the fair, where 'a huge crowd assembled at the "knock the lady out of bed stall" where 'Mr F.C. Stedman, in a pair of striped pyjamas, had taken the place of the lady', the free bungalow and other prizes were presented by the Rt Hon George Lansbury, leader of the Labour Party in the House of Commons, who had an increasing connection with Jaywick in the years leading up to the Second World War.

Interviewed on the verandah of his own bungalow, Frank Stedman looked back on the first five years, declaring that it was his 'sheer obstinacy' that had got him through:

'The first two dozen pioneers have often said they thought they had found a kind of Robinson Crusoe island, where they could be quiet and peaceful and enjoy the difficulties of going to the farmhouse for the well water. But they did not realise the fact that, once started, so many others would find out themselves the healthful air and the advantages of the district. The importance of Jaywick to Clacton is not often realised as completely as it might be. The estate is to be developed on town planning lines, and not on the casual efforts of 'Jerry builders'. Jaywick contributes a large amount of money to the rates at Clacton and the people pay the same rates in the pound as Clacton people. Without the will of the people I should have been powerless to do what I have done. The public demand for this type of thing cannot be stifled, but it can be controlled and guided as it has been [80].'

At the 'big and enthusiastic' annual meeting for 1934 of the Freeholders' Association, the ominous question of sea defence was discussed at length. At the outset of the meeting Mr Stedman was handed a cheque for £366.10s, 'which was money collected by the Sea Defence Committee from Tendring section plot-holders towards sea defence work. Mr Stedman stressed the importance of the members getting together and helping themselves'. He told them that he had been in touch with the Essex Rivers Catchment Board and was trying to get them to take over Brooklands Road and suggesting that the Board should exercise or acquire the power to rate the people there. He also announced his intention of 'handing to the Association an income of £1,000 a year he would derive from the new section', declaring amid applause that 'I think that is concrete evidence that I have the welfare of your Association at heart'.

The Council of the Association reported that:

following the abnormal tides of the Spring of 1933 a meeting was called of the owners affected and a Sea Defence Committee was set up to go into the matter and collect money from the plot-holders on the Tendring section to reimburse Mr Stedman two-thirds of the £1,000 he had estimated it would cost to carry out the necessary protective work

149

which actually cost £1,500. Only about half the plot-holders had contributed and 'for reasons best known to himself, but owing possibly to the poor response mentioned, Mr Stedman ceased the work in hand'. Their report continued:

'The question of dealing with such matters as this by voluntary effort is not encouraging, so that when a further onslaught by the sea was made upon the Tendring section early this year, the matter had to be tackled, if possible, from a different angle. On this occasion the damage was definitely more serious, the sea coming right over Brooklands, flooding the estate in the rear and doing considerable damage to the road and chalets on the front in passing. Such work as could be immediately done to lighten the damage and to defeat further immediate high tides was put in hand by and at the expense of Mr Stedman. This type of work is expensive and it is obvious that the only remedy is for defence works to be carried out along the whole of the Brooklands front.'

They also reported problems of waterlogging in the old section of the estate, and 'Mr Stedman intimated that as part of the estate work his contractors were cutting an opening at Lion Point and when this work had been completed it was anticipated the surface water drainage would present no difficulty' [81].

The problems of flooding and land drainage came to a head in 1936 with a High Court action of enormous legal complexity. Parts of Jaywick were again seriously flooded in January of that year and this was attributed to the Essex Rivers Catchment Board closing a sluice 'which had existed for many years' and was the only means of draining the Tendring section. The Freeholders' Association, through its Legal and Parliamentary Committee, wrote to the Board and to the Ministry of Health and received no reply. The flooding situation was by now so serious that the Association Chairman, Mr H.T. Hobbs, instructed workmen to release the water. 'Workmen from the Board filled in the opening through which the water was being released, causing the section to flood again'. Jaywick Properties Association Ltd, and a representative plotholder, Mr Symes, then took action in the High Court against the Board. The judge, Mr Justice Atkinson, in a ten-day hearing, decided in favour of the plotholders. The Board then appealed against his injunction in the High Court, pleading that it was their statutory duty to keep the farm land at the rear of the estate and behind the sea wall free from salt water. (This land belonged to the daughters of Frank Stedman). The Court of Appeal decided in favour of the Board, and permission was granted for a further appeal to the House of Lords, though after much deliberation the plot-holders decided not to take the matter further [82].

By the time the Court's decision was announced at the end of the year, the Freeholders had decided not to appeal further but to negotiate with the Catchment Board, who would eventually be taking over the sea wall. In December 1936 the highest tide since 1928 caused flooding of the whole of the Tendring section of the estate, and further temporary defence measures were proposed.

The Stedman family was by now promoting a new development to the north of the holiday area, a 'Tudor Village' of permanent houses, and Clacton Council was preparing a Regional Town Planning Scheme which embraced the whole of Jaywick, including the Tendring section. Ernest Lansbury, now secretary of the Freeholders' Association, saw this scheme as a further threat to the people who had made Jaywick their seasonal home:

'Jaywick, as Jaywick, seems to me the most appropriate piece of land to be used for the purpose for which it is used. These proposals are definitely dangerous from many points of view. Those on the old section are already receiving forms regarding licence renewals, etc. I sometimes wonder whether the powers that be really understand the spirit of the people of Jaywick. Sometimes I think they do not. There is no question of defiance or of doing anything except the normal and reasonable thing. We pay rates and get in return almost nothing and then we have to fight step by step these difficulties. There is no power that can prevent justice prevailing provided we all stand together, however.'

Clacton Council's town planning scheme scheduled the Old Section, the Tendring and Grasslands Sections, as areas where permanent buildings would not be permitted, the reasons given being that parts were too densely built upon, that the land was not suitable for permanent building and that the cost of social services, such as drainage and roadmaking would prove too onerous. The Council officers told the Association that they were prepared to consider alternative proposals, provided the density question could be overcome. The Association argued that it was 'practically an impossibility' to reduce densities to the required ten dwellings to the acre. Actual densities were twenty-nine dwellings to the acre in the Brooklands section, twenty to the acre in the Old Section, as opposed to nine to the acre in Stedman's new development.

Jaywick residents got some amusement from the fact that at this very time the Clacton councillors were faced by Billy Butlin's application under the Town and Country Planning (General Interim Development) Order, 1933, to build a holiday camp on a 28-acre site at West Clacton:

'I am sure', said Councillor Green, 'that if we turned down this scheme and Mr Butlin went to the Ministry he would beat us. The position then would be that we would have antagonised a man who would probably be a good friend to the town... We must take Clacton as it was — catering for the masses; we will never get the elite'.

Other councillors pointed out that the proposal ran contrary to the new town planning scheme just as much as Jaywick did, and was just as much a contravention of the building bye-laws. 'Any easement from

151

byelaws should apply equally to all ratepayers'. After a long and acrimonious discussion the council approved Butlin's scheme.

The first phase of Jaywick's history ended in the summer of 1939. Any recital of its ten years of growth is bound to stress the recurring issues of flooding, lack of sanitation, Clacton Council's hostility and the resentment of the plotholders towards the council which took their rates, but provided so little in return. Was Frank Stedman a public benefactor or a shrewd businessman? It is evident that whenever the feeling of the meetings of the Freeholders' Association implied a criticism of his methods or activities, he silenced opposition with a fresh donation or a new contribution to the estate. The truth is, perhaps, that Jaywick in the 1930s had a kind of permanent carnival atmosphere, induced in rather less sophisticated ways than were developed in Butlin's holiday camp. 'It has been a real joy and pleasure to see the good feeling among you', said George Lansbury, and on the same occasion, Miss Bowman, secretary of the Gala Committee, and a councillor in Finsbury, taking a 'busman's holiday' at Jaywick, said she could describe the place in a few words, 'they were just one big, happy family, with Mr and Mrs Stedman as their parents'.

Most people's recollections of pre-war Jaywick have nothing to do with winter floods or Elsan closets being emptied daily. They are of the sea, the sand, the continual amateur entertainments, the coachloads of singing holidaymakers coming from Kings Cross or Victoria, and the crowded dances in the club. When Frank Stedman described the Freeholders' Association as 'in every way a properly constituted council except for official recognition as such', he was not exaggerating. Its packed meetings on bank holiday mornings, its annual reunions and dances in London, the various limited companies it formed to manage the affairs of the place, as well as its continual rows and resignations, indicate an extraordinary commitment to the bleak and troublesome Essex marsh which the members had made their holiday home.

POSTWAR JAYWICK

Jaywick was a 'restricted area' during the Second World War, and only permanent residents were allowed access. The nation had other things to think of, and the tides and winds worked away at the painted bungalows and fragile roads. But during the war, as part of his national coastal survey, J.A. Steers visited Jaywick as he made his way down the East Anglian coast, from Hunstanton in Norfolk to East Tilbury in South Essex [83]. His findings were a constant source of reference for the officers of the newly-created Ministry of Town and Country Planning struggling with the complexities of the new legislation. One civil servant, Mr P.J.F. Mansfield, provided his impressions of the place in a Ministerial memorandum:

I found this extraordinary piece of holiday shack development surprising and rather interesting in a way, though it does leave one perhaps with a feeling of some nausea about it all. There are many hundreds of wooden shacks erected without proper regard for the right use of materials or proper layout but it is an inescapable fact that the colony does provide for many thousands of holidaymakers each year to enjoy a holiday by the sea, under living conditions of some independence... The Jaywick Estate, though it is emphatically not a piece of development which should ever have been allowed to grow up in its present form, is there, and must be accepted, and it does as I say provide admirable holiday facilities for great numbers of people every year, drawn largely from London... But there must, of course, be proper control of all future development, both in the design of the huts and the layout of the land. Extensive development here would be quite justified and would, incidentally, possibly be the means of saving other areas elsewhere from spoliation, and this is not unimportant as this coast has not so much left unspoilt that the good areas can be encroached upon with impunity [84].

Unaware that they were the subject of governmental scrutiny, the returning plot-holders took up the threads of their holiday lives in an almost derelict Jaywick. They had grown older, some were thinking of retirement, or their children had married and had very little chance of finding a home of their own. Percy Harding, whose relations had two plots in pre-war Jaywick and who in 1980 was one of the area's two councillors on the present Tendring District Council which administers an enormous area of the Essex coast, estimates that before the war 97 per cent of the population of Jaywick were holiday-makers, while by 1980 the proportion had been reversed. Like many other seaside districts, Jaywick had become a retirement area.

In the late 1940s big contracts were let to a Clacton firm 'to use two of the only six power barrows in the country' simply because of the urgency of sea protection work. The protection of Butlin's Clacton Holiday Camp was estimated to cost £50,000 and was done at the expense of the local authority. That at Jaywick was estimated at £30,000, of which £10,000 was met by the Jaywick Sands Freeholders' Association. This work, of brushwood groynes and steel piling, is still a matter of contention, as residents complain that they paid their contribution while others had sea defence free.

After serious flooding of the Brooklands area in 1949, a contentious meeting of the Association in 1950 resulted in the resignation of the chairman, Mr E.J. Headworth, the honorary secretary, Ernest Lansbury, and other old committee members. The chairman of the Sea Defence Committee became chairman of the Association and prepared a new and more vigorous approach to the problem. The local paper commented at the time that:

In North-East Essex there is ample evidence of the terrible inroads of the sea. At Jaywick a small body of people are working hard to secure protection for their homes. At Walton and Holland-on-Sea houses which a few years ago were apparently safe and secure are now slipping in the sea. Areas in the district are threatened with a repetition of the floods of last year which damaged so much land [85].

They were indeed, and in 1950 a new body was formed, Jaywick Ratepayers' Association, which urged Clacton Council to take over the 'town-planned section of Jaywick'. Councillor A.B. Quick pointed out to this new association that there were a number of 'adopted' roads in Clacton which were not made up and, if anything, were worse than those at Jaywick:

> The mere adoption of the resolution, assuming it was passed by Clacton Council, would not convert Jaywick into a garden city overnight. Although you have councillors down here who have been 'falling over backwards' in furthering the interests of Jaywick, I think you should bear in mind the fact that there are 28 members of our council.

He recalled the days when Jaywick had a permanent population of 100; now there were over 400. At this stage the chairman intervened to say that there were really 1,000 permanent residents [86].

The following year saw further claims by the Ratepayers Association that the streets and drainage of the 'town-planned' area of Jaywick should be taken over by the local authority, and the members were told by Councillor Ball that 'You are doing the right thing in seeking the same amenities as are enjoyed by other ratepayers. The whole thing now rests with the Ministry and the ratepayers'. It also saw the Freeholders' Association, which one assumes now represented more and more the part of the estate which did not consist of dwellings officially regarded as permanent, trying to find an equitable basis for the cost of defence against the sea. Ernest Lansbury, speaking now from the floor, declared that 'If it was money they wanted for the sea defence wall and its maintenance, then let the council come into the open and tell the people frankly that they had to pay for it' [87].

Fifteen months later Jaywick was, like Canvey, terribly affected by the great tide that hit the East Coast on the night of 31 January 1953. The loss of life was second only to that on Canvey Island. Thirty-five people were drowned at Jaywick. The historian of the disaster, Hilda Grieve, divides the area on the eve of the floods into three sections. The first was the original Jaywick Sands, with 701 bungalows in the built-up, sewered part and 285 chalets in the unsewered part, protected from the sea by a massive concrete wall maintained by the Essex River Board, as far as Lion Point. Beyond the. Point, on the seaward side, also belonging to the River Board, was Brooklands, with 607 chalets:

> protected from the sea by a concrete wall, privately built by the Jaywick Sands Freeholders' Association, and known locally, after the chairman of the Association, as 'Adrian's Wall'... Counter

154

Jaywick Sands: aerial view at the time of the 1953 floods. (Photo courtesy of Aerofilms Ltd)

walls ran inland from the sea, barricading Jaywick against any water coming across the St Osyth marshes. Grasslands, a small corridor between the Essex river board's wall at the back of Brooklands and one of these counter walls, consisted of 195 chalets and huts like those in Brooklands, and caravans [88].

By 1a.m. on 1 February, water was coming over the sea front and Brooklands was flooded. But the disaster came to Jaywick from an unexpected direction with the turn of the tide. Water which had breached the sea wall at St Osyth swept in a torrent towards Jaywick from the rear:

'When the water reached Jaywick it rose so fast in some places that people were drowned in their beds. The village was entirely inundated apart from one small island of dry ground, and the survivors were stranded on roof-tops, windowsills, even on top of wardrobes, tables and draining-boards, where they had clambered to safety [89].'

In spite of the destruction and loss of life, Jaywick, like other places which seemed to be irremediably devastated by the floods, recovered very rapidly. As well as emergency repairs, the Essex River Board had a scheme, at a cost of £100,000, to raise the sea walls from Jaywick to Point Clear by two to three feet. At St Osyth beach, where the caravans had been smashed to pieces by the floodwater, the surveyor to the Tendring Rural District Council proposed to accompany the new sea defences with a half-million pound scheme for the area immediately beyond Jaywick. He explained:

155

St Osyth beach has during the past few years been used by occupiers of a few huts and chalets remaining from pre-war times, in conjunction with groups of holiday caravan dwellers, especially at the easternmost end. Sections of the land to the north of the sea wall are also becoming littered with caravans and camping of all sorts, which are rapidly beginning to detract from the potential possibilities of more suitable development for summer occupation. The Council's policy is a long-term one, with a start made on the beach area only. The main objective is to avoid a repetition of what occurred in the Jaywick area, not only by structures alone, but by similar development of semi-moveable dwellings [90].

It must have amused Frank Stedman to see that the proposal, as illustrated, was a kind of replica of his ambitions in the early days of Jaywick, with boating lakes and 'summer residential huts' identical with the designs he had been offering in the 1930s.

'JAYWICK COMES OF AGE'

The Jaywick Sands Freeholders' Association celebrated its 21st anniversary in 1955 with a carnival of decorated vehicles illustrating the 'Tooth and Nail Drive for Jaywick Improvements' demanding 'adequate sea defence, just rate expenditure, improvements by local authorities, and road repairs'. The meeting, dinner and dance at the Brooklands Social Club was reminiscent of the 1930s; the chairman, Mr A.A. Wolfe, declared that Jaywick must never have a repetition of the 1953 flood catastrophe. 'We shall fight tooth and nail to see that the people of Jaywick get their rights as citizens'. There was now a plan, he said, for a £250,000 sea defence scheme at Holland-on-Sea. 'What has been provided at Jaywick?' he asked. 'Could not £50,000 be spent here on sea defence?' Jaywick brought £100,000 worth of business to Clacton and was entitled to see itself protected:

Were it not for the sea defences provided by the association Jaywick would have lapsed into decay. Clacton Council balances its budget every year with the rates obtained from Jaywick about £6,000 to £7,000 profit. Yet the only service provided by the council is the dust collection. It had been said, declared Mr Wolfe, that Jaywick was a town of 'shacks and shambles'. Was that true? he asked, and, according to the local newspaper, 'A loud chorused "No" greeted the question' [91].

All through the 1950s and 1960s the same issues divided the Jaywick free-holders and Clacton Council. The growing popularity of seaside areas as retirement places meant that the sites which Frank Stedman found it so difficult to sell in the late-1930s rapidly developed as bungalows of the postwar kind, and many couples whose annual holidays for many years had been spent in Brooklands and Grasslands decided to retire there, and brave the stormy winters behind the new sea defences, with the long walk to the bus stop beyond the crumbling roads.

By 1970, when most of Jaywick had become ordinary suburban housing, Brooklands and Grasslands remained untamed and unserviced. In January 1971 Clacton Council decided to eliminate these two sections of Jaywick by compulsory purchase on the grounds that the whole estate was dilapidated and insanitary'. Some owners of the 20 by 50 foot plots accepted the Council's offer of £150 (later increased to £200) which was based upon the site value, and the Council pulled down the chalets, even though there was no other conceivable use for these tiny plots of land, ninety of which were purchased and remain empty to this day. But it was a timorous minority which accepted the Council's terms. The Freeholders' Association, then led by the late Bob Carroll who had been tipped off about the Council's intentions by a local journalist, organised for one more battle.

A London barrister was briefed to represent them at the public inquiry. The inspector from the Department of the Environment, like Mr Justice Atkinson thirty years earlier, spent several days in Jaywick, and concluded, as he had, that here were worthy citizens, enjoying life on their own terms, with a high degree of community organisation, who should not be pushed around because their housing was substandard. He criticised the local authority for its dilatoriness over water supply and drainage, and recommended that the area should be upgraded rather than cleared. Senior civil servants in the Department supported his view, and in 1974 Brooklands and Grasslands were reprieved. By this time the reorganisation of local government had dissolved Clacton Council and vested authority in the new Tendring District Council, which covers an enormous area of the Essex coast and was based many miles to the north, in Harwich. When, following the decision of the Minister, the substandard parts of Jaywick were saved from compulsory purchases and demolition, Percy Harding organised a trip for fellow councillors to see the place at first hand, but only 22 out of 60 turned up'. In his opinion the 'Council are still sulking over the inquiry decisions and don't want to know about Jaywick' [92].

He believes that it was the old Clacton Council's attempt to eliminate Brooklands and Grasslands through the use of Public Health legislation that obliged them to take steps to provide sewerage once the Minister had decided in favour of the residents. As a result of local government reorganisation, responsibility for main drainage was passed to the Anglian Water Authority, and finally in 1980, the task of providing sewers began. Neil Stedman, the grandson of the original developer, and a former councillor for Jaywick, believes that this final step in the upgrading of Brooklands is simply that after forty years, the authorities had run out of excuses for ignoring Jaywick.

The impetus for improvement has moved from the Freeholders' Association, which had to raise £26,000 to fight Clacton Council's clearance orders, to the Brooklands and Grasslands Residents' Association, founded in the mid-1970s, whose chairman is Mrs

157

Elizabeth Moorcroft. She and her husband kept a garage in Dagenham and, soon after the war, bought a pair of adjacent bungalows in Austin Avenue, which they used for family holidays. In the mid-1960s they decided to move permanently to Brooklands and to rebuild their bungalows as one. They were refused planning permission and appealed to the Minister, who decided in their favour. Then, like all other residents, they were served with clearance orders, and after the success of the residents at the public inquiry, Mrs Moorcroft was told by the new local authority that her successful appeal against the decision of the previous authority was no longer binding. Her battle for the right to rebuild took seven years:

'I have fought for this place because I love it', she says, 'and I want it to be civilised. The atmosphere in the old days was marvellous. Then it began to go downhill and got a certain stigma. People would suggest that Jaywick had a criminal element and there is a truth behind this. A man would come out of Chelmsford jail. On his release he would be told to go to the Social Security and the people there would say "We can't give you any money until you find an address" and they would hint, though they wouldn't actually say, that he should break into an empty chalet, and then he would qualify for cash. Mind you, when I had a shop which was burnt down, the people who helped me most were the so-called criminal element' [93].

Her Association took over the daily emptying of Elsan closets, begun in 1932 by the Freeholders' Association with its 'Bisto Kids'. Every bungalow at Brooklands and Grasslands has a card displayed, indicating that its residents are paid-up members of one of the two organisations. The Residents' Association charges £30 a year for summer occupants and £40 a year for permanent residents for a variety of services including a nightly security patrol of two women with dogs, and street lighting (which it, not the council, provides and maintains). With the coming of main drainage it is happily relinquishing the closet emptying, but it would like to take over refuse collection, through dissatisfaction with the Council's service and believing that the Council's heavy refuse vehicles do the greatest damage to the roads, which themselves are the latest subject for improvement. When it was necessary to contact every plot-owner, a task which the Council estimated would take three years, Mrs Moorcroft traced virtually every one in three weeks.

Elizabeth Moorcroft is convinced that the future of Brooklands and Grasslands is as a residential district. 'The recession has meant that a lot of people, worried about spending £25 to £30 a week on rent, would like to put whatever they get in redundancy pay into a bungalow down here'. Sites like those which the Council bought for £150 or £200 in 1970 were valued at £2,000 in 1980, while chalets on the Brooklands estate were being offered for sale at £4,000 to £5,000.

Tendring District Council inherited an unenviable legacy from Clacton Council, of mutual animosity between the local authority and

Jaywick residents. With increasing pressure for the 'normalisation' of the original part of Jawick Sands, it resolved in 1975 to apply an Article 4 Direction under the Town and Country Planning General Development Order 1973, to the area bounded by Meadow Way, Golf Green Road, Jasmin Way and Broadway (which was the new name adopted after the 1953 floods to Beach Road). In this area, development would normally be permitted, subject to certain conditions, which were:

a) Direct road frontage access available to the site.
b) A minimum width and depth to plots for new development of 26 feet and 60 feet respectively.
c) The whole of the site area in front of the dwelling to be a hardstanding forecourt
d) Minimum 15 feet front building line.
e) Minimum 12 feet deep rear yard/amenity area.
f) Minimum 3 feet space between side boundaries and dwellings [94].

Two years later the Council extended these provisions northwards to Crossways, thus covering the whole of the original Jaywick development except for Brooklands and Grasslands. The had achieved a compromise between the standards they would normally approve and a recognition of existing realities [95].

In 1975 as a result of two successful appeals to the Secretary of State for the Environment against planning refusals in the Brooklands and Grasslands area, the Council resolved that:

pending any comprehensive overall layout plan for Brookland and Grasslands, based on its rehabilitation, the siting and design of new holiday development be based on the following guidelines:

1. Single storey development only.
2. Minimum distance of 5 feet from from front face of chalet to back edge of footpath.
3. Minimum width and depth of plots of 20 feet and 50 feet respectively.
4. Minimum distance of 3 feet between boundaries and side of bungalow.
5. Minimum 12 foot deep rear yard/amenity space.
6. Occupation limited to summer period only (1 March to 31 October in each year).
7. All properties to be connected to mains water and drainage as and when provided [96].

Two years later the Council revised these standards, with such stipulations for the extension of existing properties as that 'Applications for kitchens, toilet or bathroom accommodation of single plots will be considered on their merits within the general principle

159

Jaywick Sands: current views.

that this should be provided wherever practicable within the existing dwelling', and that 'The occupation of rear extensions will not be permitted until after other outbuildings have been demolished and cleared from the site'.

In 1978 the Council's Planning Department prepared basic designs for detached, semi-detached and terraced units suitable for Brooklands and Grasslands, noting that in the case of the detached unit, 'it had been found impossible to conform with the Council's guidelines for the area in that it had only been possible to achieve a three-foot maintenance strip on one side due to the need to provide sufficient width for a kitchen and integral garage' [97].

So, over the years, the local authority has moved from the attitude of 'doggedly trying to ignore Jaywick, hoping that it would disintegrate to the point where it could be painlessly removed and redeveloped' [98] to one which provided specimen designs for redevelopment of the plots. Members of the Residents' Association are still critical of the Council's approach, believing that it is still based on the vain hope that Brooklands and Grasslands can be reserved for holiday use only. They claim that the stipulation restricting occupation to the summer months could not be sustained in law since the local authority has for forty years accepted rates based on continuous residence.

'A VIEW OF JAYWICK'

Jaywick is the largest and most spectacular plotland settlement on the Essex coast. A few miles further south, at Point Clear, plots were advertised in the 1930s as 'the farm by the sea', and have evolved in a similar way. There too the local authority attitude has moved from hostility to a willingness to recognise that such settlements are here to stay. Jaywick, like Peacehaven or Canvey Island, owes its original existence to an individual entrepreneur with grand schemes which were not realised, though it is likely that the sheer demand for holiday sites would have resulted in development there whether or not Frank Stedman had bought the site.

It was the sheer scale of Jaywick that made it one of the archetypal plotland sites just as its scale made it one of the spectacular victims of the 1953 floods. Two things are exceptional about Jaywick. One is the very high degree of community organisation that has existed there for forty years. The expenditure of £50 for a plot and chalet in the 1930s brought for many people a lifetime of commitment to the place and responsibility for it. The second exceptional aspect of this particular plotland site is the way in which, with a changing approach to the aesthetics of architecture, Jaywick especially has been seized upon by architectural writers to illustrate, not the horrors of uncontrolled development, but the charm of an indigenous vernacular of makeshift design. Thus for the teachers of architecture at Oxford Polytechnic, it is an example of 'structuring one's own environment in defiance of external authority' [99] and for the architectural critic Sutherland Lyall, it represents 'not shanty town jerry building but an indigenous British paradigm of the way twentieth-century "bricoleurs" respond directly to their exigent circumstances' [100].

For new residents it is simply one of the few places in Essex where cheap housing can be bought. For old inhabitants it is full of memories of happy, crowded holidays on the sunniest south-facing beach on the East Coast.

161

NOTES

1. Everritt, Sylvia (1980) *Southend Seaside Holiday*. Chichester: Phillimore.
2. Information from Mr L.W. Ramuz.
3. *Darbyshire's Guide to Southend-on-Sea*. Southend, 1901.
4. The Land Company catalogue for 1906.
5. Noyelle, Gillian (1981) Frinton — sifting the sands of time. *Essex Magazine*, August.
6. Gayler, H.J. (1965) The Coastal Resorts of Essex. Their Growth and Present Day Functions. Unpublished MA Thesis, University of London.
7. Everritt: *op. cit.* (see note 1).
8. Simper, Robert (1980) Secret waters: exploring creeks and lost rivers. *Coast and Country*, 9 (1), February.
9. Advertising pamphlet Maylandsea Bay Estate (London: Home Publishing Co. n.d.).
10. Steers, J.A, (1943) Report on the East Anglian Coast: Hunstanton to East Tilbury. Public Record Office ref HLG/92/78.
11. *Captivating Canvey*, the guide book produced successively by B.A. McCave, H.V. McCave and F.B. McCave.
12. L.V. Ramuz, personal communication 1981.
13. Simpson, Marie McD. (1966) The Development of Modern Canvey. Unpublished dissertation, Brentwood College of Education.
14. *Ibid.*
15. Whitnall, F.G. The man who dreamed of making Canvey Island a popular holiday resort. *Essex Countryside*.
16. *Southend on Sea Observer*, 18 May, 1905.
17. Daly, Augustus A. (1902) *The History of Canvey Island: A New Health and Pleasure Resort*. London: Henry Dranc.
18. *Ibid.*
19. *Ibid.*
20. Small Grains Park Estate sales 1901 (The actual name of the estate, then and now was Small Gains).
21. *Essex Chronicle*, 16 May 1905.
22. *Essex Chronicle*, 14 March 1902.
23. McCave, Fred B. Canvey Island venture as a holiday resort ended in bankruptcy. *Essex Countryside*.
24. *Essex Chronicle*, 17 August 1906.
25. Gayler, Hugh J. (1970) Land speculation and urban development: contrasts in South-East Essex, 1880-1940. *Urban Studies* 7(1), February.
26. Gayler, *op. cit.* (see note 6).
27. McCave, Fred B. (1980) Chronicles of an island. *The Bulletin: A District Community Magazine*, 1(12), October.
28. Simpson: *op. cit.* (see note 13).
29. McCave, Fred B. (1981) Chronicles of an island. *The Bulletin: A District Community Magazine*, 2(2 and 3), December and January.
30. Mr H. Wigzell, personal communication.

31. *Essex Chronicle*, 3 June 1921.
32. *Essex Chronicle*, 19 September 1930.
33. Gayler (1965) *op. cit.* (see note 6).
34. *Ibid.*
35. Adshead, S.D. (1931) *South Essex Regional Planning Scheme.* London: University of London Press.
36. *Canvey Island Guide and Chronicle*, 1931.
37. Mr H. Wigzell.
38. Blitz recollections. See also Idle, E. Doreen (1947) *War Over West Ham.* London: Faber and Faber.
39. *Ibid.*
40. Gayler (1965) *op. cit.* (see note 6).
41. Island Pioneers No. 1. *The Bulletin: A District Community Magazine*, 1(1), Winter, 1979.
42. Grieve, Hilda (1959) *The Great Tide.* Chelmsford: Essex County Council.
43. *Ibid.*
44. Gayler (1965) *op. cit.* (see note 6).
45. Ralph, Stephen (1980) Canvey Island: The Most Curious Place in England. Unpublished Thesis, Thames Polytechnic, School of Architecture, Division of Landscape Architecture.
46. W.R. Davidge & Partners (1966) *The Winter Gardens Neighbourhood Unit Report.* Canvey Island Urban District Council.
47. *Winter Gardens/Sixty Acres District Plan.* Canvey Island District Council, 1969.
48. Letter from Winter Gardens and Sixty Acres residents to the Clerk to the Council, February 1969.
49. Letter from T.W. Kemp, Chairman Sixty Acres Residents Association to Sir Bernard Braine MP, 6 June 1972.
50. Hayton, David J. (1977) *Registered Land.* London: Sweet and Maxwell; see also Brahams, Diana (1977) Adverse possession: the squatter's title. *Estates Gazette*, 22 and 29 October.
51. *Ibid.*
52. Land war looms on Canvey Island. *Sunday Times*, 23 March 1969.
53. Letter from T.W. Kemp. *op. cit.* (see note 45).
54. *Ibid.*
55. Bernard Braine MP: letter to Mr Rumble of Canvey Island DC, 15 April 1969.
56. Ralph, *op. cit.* (see note 45).
57. Reader's letter in *The Bulletin*, 1(9), July, 1980.
58. Reader's letter in *The Bulletin*, 1(7), May 1980.
59. DIY houses on Council's Land: Councillor's revolutionary plan. *Benfleet and Canvey Standard*, 18 May 1977.
60. Local guide book n.d. (c. 1950).
61. The Land Company catalogue, 1906.
62. Local guide book, *op. cit.* (see note 60).
63. Interview by Adrian Waller with George Ramuz, *Sheerness Times Guardian*, 16 June 1961.

64. Walton Directory for 1839, cited by Pevsner, N. (1954) *Essex*. Penguin.
65. Interview with Mrs Ivy Robinson 30 September 1980.
66. *Clacton Times and Gazette*, 25 August 1934.
67. Ms notes by Frank Stedman in Clacton County Library.
68. Advertisement in *Clacton Times and Gazette*, 18 May 1929.
69. Advertisement in *Clacton Times and Gazette*, 27 July 1929.
70. *Daily Telegraph*, 1936.
71. *East Anglian Daily Times*, 19 November 1929.
72. *Clacton Times and Gazette*, 8 August 1931.
73. *Clacton Times and Gazette*, 5 December 1931.
74. *Clacton Times and Gazette*, 25 March 1932.
75. *Ibid.*
76. *Clacton Times and Gazette*, 6 August 1932.
77. *Clacton Times and Gazette*, 19 November 1932.
78. *The Star*, 22 June 1932.
79. Jaywick Sands Estate, brochure n.d.
80. *Clacton Times and Gazette*, 25 August 1934.
81. *Clacton Times and Gazette*, 7 April 1934.
82. *Clacton Times and Gazette*, 25 July 1936.
83. Steers, *op. cit.* (see note 10).
84. Minute by P. J. F. Mansfield Ref 91647/15/2. Public Record Office Ref HLG/92/81.
85. *East Essex Gazette*, 28 October 1950.
86. *East Essex Gazette*, 9 February 1950.
87. *East Essex Gazette*, 8 June 1951.
88. Grieve, *op. cit.* (see note 42).
89. *Ibid.*
90. *East Essex Gazette*, 18 September 1953.
91. *East Essex Gazette*, 5 August 1955.
92. Street-Porter, Tim (1975) A chalet by the sea. *Observer Magazine*, 15 June.
93. Mrs Elizabeth Moorcroft, interview, 1980.
94. Tendring District Council, Development and Planning Committee, Minute 156, 10 March 1975.
95. *Ibid.* Minute 124, 7 February 1977.
96. *Ibid.* Minute 186, 21 April 1975.
97. *Ibid.* Minute 129, 4 December 1978.
98. Street-Porter, *op. cit.* (see note 92).
99. Responsive Environments Group (1978) *Responsive Environments*. Oxford: The Polytechnic, November.
100. Lyall, Sutherland (1980) *The State of British Architecture*. London: Architectural Press.

Chapter 5

Arcadia on the River

I know the scorn, and the by-laws too, that are heaped on the man who can afford no more than a shelter from the elements. Shacks and huts are said to deface the countryside, but they are no worse than battlemented villas and portcullised boat-houses.

Robert Gibbings, *Sweet Thames Run Softly* (1940)

TAKING TO THE RIVER

Just as the downstream reaches of the Thames, from the Tower to the Nore, had been one of the arteries for the holiday explorations of East Londoners, by way of the pleasure steamers and subsequently the railway, so a slightly different section of the metropolitan population explored the potential of the upper Thames. Access here was also by pleasure craft, and by the minor branches, opened in the 1870s and 1880s, of the Great Western Railway and its competitors.

Matthew Arnold, poet, critic and Inspector of Schools, in the phrase 'sweetness and light' caught the flavour of the gentle rebellion against the stern imperatives of the high Victorian era. The second generation of the Victorian middle class needed a style of living which was less arduous, more rational and less demanding than that of its parents. Architecturally, a new style crept in, which abandoned both the moral precepts of the Gothic revival and the rule-book of classicism. One of the defenders of the new style, J.J. Stevenson, declared that domestic architecture should be 'homely, like colloquial talk'. The new domestic style, spreading patchily up the Thames from Chiswick to Richmond and beyond, as the feasible commuting distance expanded, was 'fundamentally the same as the common vernacular style, which every workman has been apprenticed to' [1].

The new interest in building was accompanied by an appreciation of the folklore and folksong in sleepy villages newly discovered, of the crafts of river users and the integration of the river with the canal system through locks and navigations, and the sporting calendar of boating and sailing. The University Boat Race took an upward turn in popular interest, and the various regattas, races and boating festivals were either revived or initiated to become instant annual festivals of respectable antiquity.

By the late-1870s it was possible for a local bard, J. Ashby Storey, to evoke the Great Marlow Regatta as a social event, with the words:

When London's getting hot and dry
And half the season's done
To Marlow you should quickly fly
And bask there in the sun.

A decade later Jerome K. Jerome was describing Molesey Lock as the busiest on the river:

I have stood and watched it sometimes, when you could not see any water at all, but only a brilliant tangle of bright blazers, and gay caps, and saucy hats, and many-coloured parasols, and silken rugs, and cloaks, and streaming ribbons, and dainty whites; when looking down into the lock from the quay, you might fancy it was a huge box into which flowers of every hue and shade had been thrown pell-mell, and lay piled up in a rainbow heap, that covered every corner [2].

Wandering cricket teams like 'I Zingari' and the 'Nomads' went the rounds of the local sides, colonising the water-meadows with an activity that brought more income for the tenant farmers than cattle grazing. Fishing too gathered a new, self-conscious clientele, with Isaac Walton's book in their lunch-baskets. The discovery of the river was reflected in several best-selling works of fiction including Jerome's *Three Men in a Boat*, whose whole point was that it encapsulated the funny side of widespread experiences; H.G. Wells's *The History of Mr Polly*, where the idyll of the riverside pub, as opposed to the dreary world of suburban small trading, is the epitome of the Thames Valley dream; while William Morris's *News From Nowhere* is narrated around the slow journey upstream of his story-teller from the future. In his dream of a society which has abolished the difference between work and leisure, there is no distinction between commercial and holiday activities on the river. In fact, by the time of the Thames Preservation Act of 1885, most of the river's commercial traffic had been lost to the railways, and the purpose of the Act was 'the preservation of the River above Teddington lock for purposes of public recreation and for regularising the pleasure traffic therein'.

The Select Committee which preceded this Act heard evidence from aggrieved riverside landowners about the new class of people which was now using the river as a holiday resort:

Sir Gilbert Augustus Clayton East, Bart:
I do not object to the public using the river because that I have no right and no wish to do, and I rather like to see them enjoying

166

themselves. From 1858 to 1862 I was at Eton, and during that time the public practically did not exist; the only boats then seen were Eton boys' and masters', soldiers' and a few residents'... I think it was somewhere about 1866 that the Guards Club was started; and that first brought people down to Maidenhead in any numbers... In 1878 the river had become so unpleasant, not from the number of public, though that had something to do with it, but from the way they treated you, that I gave up making these trips at all. They began to be most abusive and disagreeable... My complaint is not of the public coming to use the river, but of the class who come. It is so totally different. You used never to have any unpleasant remarks.

Chairman:
What proportion of the public do you complain of in this way?

Sir Gilbert:
That is what I have often wanted to know; whether these people were naturally savages; or whether they become savage when they come on the river.

Chairman:
What proportion of the public who use the Thames in this way possess the qualification of savages of which you speak?

Sir Gilbert:
I distinctly say it is not the working class; because if you ever see any of the working class on the river, which you do on Bank Holidays, they are always very well behaved. I cannot tell what class it is. I believe it is a class of savages born on purpose.

Chairman:
Is the proportion one in ten, or one in five, or what proportion are the people who make the river a nuisance?

Sir Gilbert:
I should say that many of the respectable people are giving up using the river; it is getting more every year that these savages use the river. It is difficult to speak of any proportion. I will speak of what I know myself at Hurley. What brought them there was the opening of the Marlow Railway in 1878. They did not find that out for a few years; but after a while they did [3].

All classes had discovered the river, and the demand for riverside accommodation grew. Already in Jerome's novel,' which first appeared in 1889, the three Londoners in a boat had 'difficulty in finding diggings' and asked a local lad 'could he recommend us to an empty pigsty, or a disused limekiln, or anything of that sort', though beyond Hambledon Lock was Greenlands, 'the rather uninteresting-looking river residence of my newsagent — a quiet, unassuming old gentleman, who may often be met with about these regions, during the summer months...' [4]. In Morris's utopian romance, published in 1891, his time traveller recalled 'the hideous vulgarity of the cockney villas of the well-to-do, stockbrokers and other such, which in older time marred the beauty of the bough-hung banks' [5], though Eric de Maré, travelling sixty years later, remarks, 'Once we fumed at these fantasies, then we tolerated them, now we regard them with affection, sometimes even with respect, and always with a certain reactionary nostalgia for the departed Forsytean culture they express' [6].

In the wake of the pleasure boat and the twelve o'clock train from Paddington or Waterloo, the week-enders bought or rented their riverside cottages. The most sought-after sites had a frontage on the river bank itself or to one of the innumerable backwaters, or, failing that, easy and nearby access to the river or to moorings where the steam-launch, cutter or dinghy was ready at hand, or might, like a rowing boat or punt, be immediately rented. The ideal was a house, cottage or bungalow with a 'wet' boathouse where one's own vessel could be kept. The cottages of families engaged in traditional riverside occupations, from the days when the Thames was a working river, were sold (with delight that dying trades could still reap a final harvest) to families in love with the idea of messing about on the river. After the initial demand had been mopped up by those who could afford to buy an existing building or employ a builder to erect a new one, sites were sold or leased to humbler purchasers. Farmers and landowners, as well as ordinary householders who were not actually using the riverside end of their long gardens, were willing to dispose of odd parcels of land which were hard to use for ordinary agriculture or grazing through difficulty of land access. They were, for ordinary purposes, islands, or they were real islands, with the extra romance that the word implied, like Eel Pie Island, Pharoah's Island or Tagg's Island.

The bungalow boom was coming, and in 1909 the author of a popular handbook on bungalows reminded his readers that:

> River sites in particular should only be decided upon after careful investigation, as it is well-known that the Thames and other rivers are capable of the most surprising effects and developments under the influence of heavy rainfall. One is apt to recollect the comedian's facetious remark that, though it may be pleasant to have the river at the bottom of one's garden, there are distinct disadvantages in having the garden at the bottom of the river [7].

The same theme and its serious implications were stressed in the series of planning reports and surveys in the inter-war years which were commissioned both by voluntary bodies and by regional joint planning committees. Reporting on north-west Surrey in 1928, Adams, Thompson and Fry wrote that:

Early use of the river: Shepperton Lock on a Bank Holiday c.1910, and the Thames Camping and Boating Association, Walton on Thames, c.1910. (Photos courtesy of Weybridge Museum)

THAMES CAMPING AND BOATING ASSOC.
WALTON-ON-THAMES.

We are here faced with the demand for inexpensive weekend or summer-time bungalows right to the banks of the river. In the nature of a luxury to their owners, the majority of these bungalows have as little spent on them as possible and the great danger is that, unless carefully controlled, they will completely spoil the charm of the river both for themselves and for the general public. Apart, also, from the question of amenity, there is the serious problem of safeguarding conditions of health, which are gravely imperilled because the majority of these bungalows drain into cesspools, the contents of which, in time of flood, are washed into the river and will undoubtedly cause pollution of the water supply [8].

Lord Mayo and Professors Adshead and Abercrombie, surveying the region in the following year, found new developments springing up, even as they wrote. Worse than the bungalows were the shacks and huts they found springing up everywhere; on the island between Henley Bridge and Marsh Lock, by Hurley Lock, 'within the last few months'. They described the process by which a camping site became a permanent settlement; as 'in the insidious manner' sheds grew into established structures:

At first a simple hut is erected behind the tents for cooking and other purposes; the next stage is for the family to take its meals in the shed in wet weather; a dining room follows; possibly a bedroom is added for a maid or for someone who does not care to sleep under canvas; and so gradually is built up a rambling series of shacks [9].

Their assumption that the maid came along too is probably inaccurate. Anthony King, the historian of the bungalow, notes that one of the attractions of the 'free and easy domestic life' of the weekend retreat was precisely because 'the comforts of urban domesticity — servants, social conformity, material wealth — as well as routine, had begun to pall' [10]. One informant told us that 'we wanted a place which was primitive, where the children could do what they liked. They could play pirates, build rafts, fall in the river and get covered in mud, and nobody minded'.
  Such families were adept at discovering riverside sites:

My uncle bought a freehold plot, 45ft by 200ft, one of several on the river frontage of a farm at Penton Hook near Staines, and with it came an old gypsy caravan and a couple of huts. We inherited this site and had enormous fun and enjoyment there until the war intervened and the site was sold. Wanting to give a similar freedom to my own family after the war, we sought out another plot at a place which had been broken from the bush by three Post Office workers who had persuaded the university farm to sell an odd riverside corner of waste land, virtually an island, together with a right of way. They had divided it into three plots which they shared with a local builder in return for his putting in a culvert and making a hard access.

Our informant bought one of these plots in 1960 and sought to replace his predecessor's shanty, built of split willows from the site itself, with a more elaborate boathouse and weekend cottage. After a series of planning applications he was able to do so, and the result is a handsome building 'which more than fulfils our original hopes for both family and friends' [11].

Larger plotland settlements of this kind can be traced throughout the Thames Valley, at Wraysbury and Horton, Bourne End and Purley Park, with inland plots above Marlow. In most of these places the ordinary process of time, increasing land values and affluence, has brought the replacement of shacks and shanties by 'proper' houses, often very luxurious and opulent, so that few traces of the plotland origins remain.

The inter-war planning reports each had detailed proposals for the control of riverside development using existing legislation. In practice it was not brought under effective planning control until the powers of the Thames Conservancy were strengthened and until the development control provisions of the 1947 Town and Country Planning Act were brought into use. Today the Thames Valley plotlands, and every other aspect of riverside development, are stringently controlled through the planning legislation and through the Thames Conservancy Board, now a division of the Thames Water Authority. This body is always consulted by the planning authorities who almost always act on its advice in matters of water supply, pollution, navigation and the maintenance of an unimpeded flow of water in the 'wash lands' or flood plain of the river.

The result is that there will be no further development of plotland sites, while the occupants of the existing ones continually declare that 'they tried to do away with this place, but we were too tough for them'.

THE LONDON HINTERLAND

As there is bloom upon the peach and grape, so this is the bloom of summer. The air is ripe and rich, full of the emanations, the perfume, from corn and flower and leafy tree. In strictness the term will not, of course, be accurate, yet by what other word can this appearance in the atmosphere be described but as a bloom? Upon a still and sunlit summer afternoon it may be seen over the osier-covered islets in the Thames immediately above Teddington Lock. (Richard Jefferies, *Nature Near London*, 1883)

Eighty-five years after Jefferies discovered the bloom of summer at Teddington another traveller, J.B.H. Peel, set out to explore the Thames, by working up-river from that spot to the source 143 miles away. His impression was of the continuous alternation of leafy landscapes and human settlements:

171

At one moment you might fancy yourself in deep country, at the next even the trees flinch to see so many ugly houses. This rapid change of scene is especially evident at Sunbury, where several pleasant islands appear, and the river becomes suddenly very narrow; above the tree-lined lock, but soon afterwards meets a rash of jerrydom which follows it for much of the way into Walton [12].

The closer to the metropolis itself, the greater was the demand for riverside sites and the more it merged with the ordinary spread of suburban development. Though lovers of the 'unspoiled' river objected to any development, it was the flimsy, seaside or fairground character of many a riverside retreat that gave most offence. As early as 1909 the author of Cassell's *The Thames and its Story* observed that:

> Between Staines and Penton Hall Hotel the Surrey bank gives hospitality to a ragged array of those wooden shanties which are dignified by the name of 'bungalows', and which, with their fluttering flags and enamelled trellises, impart a tawdry flippancy to the banks of the river [13].

In 1930, the interim regional planning report on 'The Thames from Putney to Staines' declared that:

> Pettiness of design and the haphazard arrangement of small units close to the river bank are responsible for the greatest amount of damage. This type of development has been called the 'bungaloid growth', and as in the country at large, so too on the river, it is the disturbing and disintegrating element. When it is remembered that the river is a broad, uninterrupted flow of water associated with large open prospects, or with fine panoramas of trees and banks, it will be realised how destructive to this essentially calm and simple statement a row of tiny, fussy little bungalows will be. Like a series of gabled boxes set along the very margin of the bank, the bungalows by the exercise of every possible eccentricity and mark of individuality, break up the line of the river. Each house has its gable, its weathervane; each plot its fence, and railing, its flagstaff, its nameboard and its crazy paving. And in spite of so much striving to be different, they are pervaded by a feeling of sameness. No river can withstand such onslaught as this [14].

The authors of this report found that 'Generally speaking it may be said that wherever land on the banks is unprotected by public or crown ownership or by wise private or public control the bungalow springs to life'. They were anxious to stress that they did appreciate the point of view of the bungalow occupier, remarking, for example, that:

> Thames Ditton Island is occupied along the entire river front and portions of the backwater with small bungalows of a better

172

class than are met with in less fortunate parts of the river. These bungalows are well maintained, freshly painted in season, and the lawns and flowers are evidence of continuous occupation by owners who appreciate their life on the river and are at pains to make it as pleasant and enjoyable as possible. In saying this we wish to show the bungalow habit at its best, and to present the view of the owners of bungalows, for it must be admitted by even those who are the strongest opponents of bungalow development that life on the brink of the river has obvious and legitimate advantages, especially for those whose limited means deny them the luxury of a well-built house or the privacy of lawns. It is the ceaseless multiplication of the small bungalow that turns a simple building into a real offence [15].

Another of the planning reports of this period stresses that there should be a particular riverside architecture:

The character of the riverside bungalow ought not to be that of its prototype that we find at, say, Banstead or Barnet. It should have a riverside character that is its own, and whilst everyone will deplore the general flimsiness of most of these little buildings and the poor materials of which they are constructed, at the same time it is right that they be gay with verandahs and pergolas, and in every way suggestive of an outdoor existence by the inclusion of loggias, balconies and overhanging eaves [16].

Finally, just as the demand for public control of Thames-side building had become effective, other voices were heard asserting, such are the vagaries of architectural taste, that the shanties and sub-standard bungalows did have a certain charm and appropriateness. Barbara Jones, writing about 'The Unsophisticated Arts' in 1948, described the plotland bungalows as 'practical and snug, shipshape dolls' houses' [17], and in the same journal, *The Architectural Review*, two years later, Eric de Maré took a long-term and magnanimous view of riverside development:

steam-plus-petrol brought the bungalow suburbia of the Little Man and this most affected the reaches below Staines. But this is far more pleasing than suburbia proper, partly because water, with its moving reflections, mitigates all ugliness and partly because many of these bungalows have a certain homemade charm. Far too many, of course, are merely squalid shacks, but many, with their jumble of small gables, long verandahs with white, fretted railings, oriental, Art Nouveau, baroque and curly, plenty of fresh white paint, small sloping gardens, ending in a drooping willow, whitened steps and verges, and landing stages of infinite variety. All add to the pleasure and interest of a river journey. We should not scorn these amateur pieces of architecture for they are a kind of modern folk art, the crude

173

and unselfconscious origins of a culture which limited spare time has nurtured and which only more and more spare time together with greater affluence can encourage and develop [18].

De Maré was, at the same time, an enthusiastic exponent of the idea of a Thames Linear Park, an expansion of the idea of a continuous riverside walk, proposed by the Thames River Preservation Committee of 1884, and supported in the pre-war planning reports. All the public bodies involved welcomed the National Parks and Access to the Countryside Act which became law in 1949. In 1950 the Thames River Walk Committee, representing the riparian authorities, and the Thames Conservancy Board agreed that the walk should run from Teddington, the tidal limit of the river, to Cricklade in Gloucestershire, and asked that 'a 25-feet wide strip of land should be set aside as a public open space along the towpath to prevent development which might interfere with the walk'. This proposal was rejected by the National Parks Commission in 1963, but the riparian authorities both before and after the war had a major aim: the extension of public access to the river banks.

Apart from their concern with the river as a visual amenity and as 'one of London's playgrounds', the authors of the inter-war planning reports had to consider it as a commercial waterway, as a provider of water for urban populations, and as a channel to carry away surplus water from the catchment area.

Several of these aims were directly threatened by continuous development of the suburban kind as well as by the subdividing of riverside land into plots, and the public authorities' only pre-war option was public acquisition, though they lacked the funds to embark on such a policy. The authors of the 1930 report commented on the bungalows upstream and downstream from Shepperton that they 'burgeon forth into the semblance of a small squatters' town, occupying every bank, both of river and island', and they added that:

> The profits made by selling river frontage at £2 per foot must be very small when compared with the amount of damage done, for although for the purposes of agriculture the value of low-lying land adjoining the bank may be low, it is now realised that the beauty of the river, which rests almost entirely on the nature of the banks, has a distinct monetary value to the towns that lie near the river. It is, therefore, to the authorities of these towns that the preservation of the banks is a matter of first importance — worth more than the expenditure of £2 a foot [19].

All the local authorities, and the Thames Conservancy, were agreed that there should be a prohibition of building on land liable to flood. The Staines Rural District Council sought such a prohibition. The landowner objected that as there were people who were willing to build on such land it was therefore suitable for building purposes:

It was held by the Minister of Health that it was competent for the local authority to impose the restriction but that the owner would be entitled to claim compensation and the final result has been that as the Staines RDC felt unable to undertake this liability the Ministry allowed the appeal for the owner to have the right to build on the land [20].

The 1932 Town and Country Planning Act disappointed those who had hoped that a truly effective form of development control would ensue, but postwar planning legislation brought such powers. The Spring of 1947, the year of the major Planning Act, brought flooding to low-lying riverside areas, and the Thames Conservancy reported that since, quite apart from the cost, protection against flooding would destroy 'most of the 'well-known river amenities', the only practical approach to the problem of flooding would be to define the flood zones on either side of the river and to undertake the gradual removal of residential buildings from these areas [21].

In its Development Plan of 1951, Middlesex County Council listed its twenty-six built areas liable to flood, mostly in Sunbury and Staines, and including several plotland sites like those in Shepperton, on and opposite Pharoah's Island, and at Penton Hook Road, Staines. These dwellings, the Council reported, were bungalows, mostly permanently occupied, 'nearly all of them deficient in services and adding little to the beauty of the river', and it categorised them as those which conformed to the building bye-laws, those in good condition but constructed of timber and corrugated or galvanised iron, etc, and the various shacks and caravans in poor condition. The Council's policy was that:

It is not considered practicable to propose extensive works of removal, but it is nevertheless felt desirable that steps should be taken to restrict such further development... as would add to the extent and value of the residential property already there. This is considered to be a special case where the rights to alter and extend buildings without having to apply for permission, should be curtailed.

The Development Plan stressed that:

Mobile caravanning mainly for holiday purposes is quite an admissible use of suitable riverside sites. Indeed the legislation itself affords it a large measure of freedom from control. But when caravans congregate in large numbers and settle down in the pretence that they are houses, various abuses often follow, and the colonies are usually unsightly. Such colonies should have no place in the riverside scene [22].

After another decade Middlesex County Council re-affirmed these policies, and its intention 'to obtain the removal of temporary bungalows and shacks whenever possible'. Reorganisation of local

175

government brought the disappearance of Middlesex as a county, and the plotlands on the Middlesex bank became the responsibility of Surrey County Council, which for similar sites on the Surrey side of the river had defined fourteen 'Restricted Areas', with a similar 'particularly strict policy of development control aimed at the purchase and clearance from the bank of existing "temporary structures"' [23].

In the 1960s Surrey County Council also acquired properties from the Thames Conservancy on condition that it would ultimately use them for public open spaces, and it also purchased other riverside properties, with the aim of 'demolishing those at the end of their useful life, or letting more substantial properties for a specified length of time', spending about £90,000 over the decade on such acquisitions.

By 1969 the County Council's Planning Committee concluded that there were loopholes in its policy towards these areas, which did not preclude permission being given for the rebuilding of existing dwellings in these areas, provided that this was consistent with the flood policy and the greenbelt policy, and that 'without any specific policy for open space, rebuilding could mean the loss for ever of opportunities to make new stretches of riverside open to the public'. It therefore adopted a policy in 1971 of 'Windows on the River' areas where land should, where necessary:

> be acquired and cleared both in the interests of amenity and to add to the public open space along the riverside... These were selected where they adjoined land which was already open to the public; at focal points to which the public were attracted; or where a number of riverside facilities already existed and where it was felt that valuable additions to open space might be obtained.

The sites selected were three areas at Windsor Road, Egham, Truss's Island, parts of Penton Hook in Egham and Chertsey, Dumsey Eyot, Dockett Eddy, Shepperton Lock and Thames Meadow. Costs were estimated and it was felt that the last of these sites and one of the areas of Windsor Road should be excluded, so that expenditure could be concentrated on the phased acquisition of the other eight sites. In 1980 the County Council reviewed its progress and its problems in implementing this policy. Its officers reported on the possible modes of site acquisition:

a) by compulsory purchase. This method has not yet been used because of expense and because many residents would undoubtedly resist strongly and a public inquiry would probably be necessary,

b) by purchasing the sites and allowing the existing occupiers to continue to stay on as life tenants. This method has been adopted on several sites, including those acquired from the Thames Conservancy. It avoids hardship to residents but makes the achievement of the open space use a very long-term objective.

176

c) by purchasing properties when they come onto the market. This is the method which has been adopted for most sites recently, and works well in these instances. It is again a very long-term method and it fails when properties do not come onto the open market. Many opportunities to purchase have undoubtedly been lost in recent years.

The Council's officers also reported on the need on many sites to re-affirm the open space intentions, when owners wished to rebuild, extend or improve properties, and the Planning Committee approved two methods. One was pre-emption:

The right of pre-emption can be negotiated in agreement with the owner. This would ensure that, for a period not exceeding 21 years, the County Council would be offered the first opportunity to buy the property at the full market value. The right of pre-emption would be unlikely to be granted by the owner, except in return for a capital payment.

The second was by means of an Article 4 Direction (the withdrawal of permitted development rights):

The imposition of an Article 4 Direction would help to restrict the possibility of temporary riverside buildings being rebuilt or enlarged. The owner may, of course, seek planning permission for such work and compensation might be payable if his application was refused.

When the County Council came to review its policy on the eight remaining 'Windows on the River', it found that in most of them the designated area had been reduced over the years. It recommended the abandonment of the policy in two cases, because as in the case of one of the Penton Hook sites 'the area itself is of no real potential use for recreation, there is no open space close to the site, no towpath access from other areas, and the road approach is unsuitable'. In most cases it re-affirmed its policy, for the reduced areas at least, and thought that the immediate use of Article 4 directions was the appropriate policy. One 'window', Dumsey Eyot, was found to be outstandingly successful [24].

The residents, of course, have a different perspective from that of the County Council. 'They talk about windows on the river', said one, 'but all they want is to take *our* windows away'. He pointed out the ranks of parked cars on the opposite bank. 'Windscreens on the river is all they want'. What they see as a threat to their continued presence has led them to unite their local associations into the Thameside Residents Association, in opposing County policies.

In practice, so far as individual dwellings are concerned, they deal not with the County, but with the officers of the district councils. One claimed that the building inspector remarked to him 'I'll get you off here if it's the last thing I do'. Others feel bemused by what they see as vacillations in local authority policy:

They changed our rates from hutments to bungalows. Then they said there were to be no more wooden bungalows. So I tried in vain for seven years to get permission to rebuild the outside walls in brick or Cotswold stone [25].

On a smaller scale, comparable developments and policies can be seen along some of the tributaries of the Thames, the main example being that of the River Lea. On the east side of the City, the Lea joins the Thames between Bromley-by-Bow and Stratford at Bow Creek. Further up the river, as it meanders between Hertfordshire and Essex, there are little colonies of weekend plots similar to those on the Thames. At Broxbourne on the Hertfordshire side, between the tow-path and the string of greenhouses and smallholdings that line the river valley is a group of caravans, shacks made from railway waggons, and rebuilt pre-fabricated houses from the immediate postwar period, which have become weekend retreats used for fishing, sailing and gardening. Many of the gardens are meticulously kept with lawns, rose-beds and vegetable plots. Of all plotland sites, this one is closest to the continental 'leisure-garden' ideal, though the sheds and shanties are haphazardly disposed, rather than regimented.

On the Essex side, where the navigable source separates from the original path of the river, the tow-path is lined with plotland houses of a more permanent kind, including 'regular' buildings from the early-1920s, and there is much evidence of rebuilding and improvement. A little further north, near the caravan site now operated by the Lea Valley Regional Park Authority, is a series of five short cul-de-sac roads of plotland homes, rapidly giving place to new suburban houses, ranging from 'neo-Georgian' with bow-windows and pedimented doors, to 'ranch-style' houses and 'neo-vernacular' designs, following the precepts of Essex County Council's 'design guide'. Soon all traces of the plotland origins of this little estate will have disappeared.

Thames Valley Plotlands

THAMES MEADOW

Just to the north-west of Walton Bridge is a tongue of low-lying land following one of the meanderings of the river. On its western flank it lies opposite a new channel, cut by the Thames Conservancy on the Surrey side to accommodate the increased flow of water expected from the River Wey drainage scheme of the 1920s and 1930s. The improvement of the Wey was the subject of controversy in the late 1920s, the Earl of Mayo, one of the surveyors of the Thames, declaring it to be an extravagant and unnecessary scheme for the Wey 'to have all its bends cut through' and 'to become nothing more or less than a canal'. The Wey joins the Thames at Weybridge, and the new channel, by-passing the bends in the Thames itself, was completed in 1935. The gravel from the excavation was piled on the opposite bank, and the settlement there began with a former showman's caravan belonging to an insurance clerk. It evolved into a string of riverside plots with a 40-foot frontage, between the meadow and the river, with, to the north, a similar curve of riverside plots known as Sandhills Meadow.

Some of the first bungalows on these sites were old single-decker Midland buses, and the owner of an immaculate and leafy little house invited us to kneel down and look between the brick piers to see, under the centre of the house, the solid-tyred wheels of the bus body it was built around. The sites at Thames Meadow were originally rented at five shillings a week. In the 1950s they cost £52 a year, and more recently, £6 a week. Eleven of them are freehold and the other forty-nine leasehold, on 21-year leases with (in 1984) five years to run.

Today about a third of them are used at week-ends only while the other two-thirds are retirement homes for the owners. 'It's not a convenient place to live' said one, 'but I can't imagine a lovelier place to retire to.' There is a closely-knit community of residents who are all old friends. The bungalows are well-maintained, with lawns leading down to the river. To the traveller by boat or the tow-path walker on the Surrey side, they present a prospect of smooth grass, foliage, bushes and trees, with low-pitched roofs beyond. If unobtrusiveness is the criterion for judging the acceptability of Thameside dwellings, they are far more acceptable and much more interesting than the ordinary suburban houses or grander villas that line the river bank. Sandhills Meadow, in its leafy seclusion, is a nest of do-it-yourself enterprise. One resident was rebuilding his house around the little cabin his parents had erected before the war. Another, with his children, was building a sailing dinghy. 'I've known this place all my life', he said. 'It's Paradise' [26].

MARLOW BOTTOM AND MUNDAY DEAN

Unlike several of the coastal plotland areas which owed their existence to entrepreneurs intending to sub-divide and sell very large sites, the Thames Valley plots evolved as a result of many hundreds of small-scale transactions, where the initiative was often in the hands of individual would-be purchasers. The exception to this is the hillside area above Marlow, the terminus of one of the Thameside branch lines which brought visitors in their thousands to the Regatta. Munday Dean and Marlow Bottom were long, dry chalk-hill valleys with a farm in each, which were parcelled up in plots offered for sale in 1920. The seller of Munday Dean was Homesteads Ltd, a London firm seeking to attract ex-servicemen who wanted to spend their service gratuities in setting-up as chicken farmers or smallholders, or hoped to commute from a rural arcadia. They also had sites at Chelsfield in Kent, at Brentwood and Wickford in Essex, and other parts of the Home Counties referred to separately. Brake Estates Ltd, sellers of Marlow Bottom, similarly had sites in Kent.

The Canadian writer George Woodcock spent his boyhood at Marlow and remembers the failing farms with their few arid barley fields and rough grazing higher up:

As in all the Chilterns, the hilltops were clothed with beech woods, and here the gypsies who had a winter camp at the top of Dean Street in Marlow, near the entrance to Munday Dean, would gather moss for wreaths, which they would sell to merchants in Covent Garden, and also wild belladonna sold to pharmacological firms. The beech trees fed the furniture factories in High Wycombe.

He recalls the people who settled there as retired artisans and foremen, with, on the larger plots higher up the valleys, ex-army officers attempting to run chicken farms on the dry chalky soil:

It was goat, rather than cattle land. All the people I knew who lived up the Bottom and the Dean relied on rainwater gathered from every scrap of roof and stores in underground concrete cisterns. Some time in the 1930s piped water was taken up the two valleys.

Some of the new inhabitants were commuters. 'From early in the 1930s a group of men and women would cycle down out of the Bottom and an even larger group out of the Dean, to catch the 7.25 or the 7.58 up to Paddington, leaving their bikes at the station.' A surprisingly high proportion 'were either socialists or new lifers or both'. Jack David, for example, was an East Londoner who had an office job in the city, was secretary of Marlow Labour Party and was one of the group that published the *Socialist Clarion* in High Wycombe.

As George Woodcock remembers them:

In terms of class, the people varied from the lower upper-middle-class ex-officers on the chicken farms, through the middle-class and lower-middle-class office workers to the upper-working-class retired foremen and engineers and fitters. There were a few strict eccentrics whose class was hard to place and who lived as hermits in tiny shacks.

Some of these were squatters:

There was a nest of two or three of them around the chalk-pit near the entrance to Marlow Bottom, and they were very old. One who was 85 used to talk to me of the 'old bugger up the back', his neighbour who lived in a copse at the top of the chalkpit and was 90. Apart from the squatters, I think everyone bought his land, though they may have done so on installments [27].

The war and the bombing of London brought more permanent residents to Marlow Bottom and Munday Dean. Many families which had used their bungalows on 20-foot wide plots up unmade roads for weekends and holidays, moved there permanently, during and after the war. Postwar planning policy had two aims. The first was to forbid further development in both the Bottom and the Dean, and to refuse applications to rebuild or improve existing dwellings, since the area was designated as part of the London Green Belt. The second was to restrict development to the lower parts of the two sites, and at the same time to maintain an unbuilt area between Marlow itself and its two unwanted suburbs.

In the early postwar years it was thought that what was perceived as the 'problem' of these two sites could be solved by compulsory purchase. This led the residents to organise themselves and to hold protest meetings, but in any case there was neither the money nor the political will to put such a policy into effect. In the 1950s the planning authority kept losing appeals against its refusal of planning permission for improvements and extensions. Many residents, with or without permission, built brick skins around asbestos bungalows, and the whole area has slowly upgraded itself in the affluent postwar decades. There are now about 600 houses, and the narrow roads, mostly now made up, cause traffic problems, so that some planning applications are now refused on the grounds that the roads cannot cope with the traffic they would generate.

To the east of Marlow the pre-war plotland areas of Bourne End have similarly evolved into permanent settlements. Between Marlow and Bourne End there is a sprinkling of riverside plots owned by sailing enthusiasts. At Spade Oak, between the river and the railway, the planning authority refused the application of the would-be builder of 'Arcadia', an addition to the existing row of bungalows. She appealed, and the Minister upheld the appeal, though restricting the use of the new building to the months of April to October. The opposing interests of determined individuals and planners conscious of the public benefit usually result in this kind of compromise.

PURLEY PARK

The Purley Park River Estate lies between the railway and the river Thames, on the south side, almost opposite Mapledurham. It is a low-lying site, severely flooded in 1947 and under threat of flood in most winters. Purley Park itself is a great eighteenth-century house, now in institutional use. In 1934 the then owner put thirty-four acres of land by the river on sale as plots, 'ostensibly for use as camp sites' as the County Planner observes:

> Several purchasers asked the County Council if there were any restrictions on building on the land and were informed that the land would in due course be 'restricted from development owing to its being low-lying and liable to flood' and that any buildings that they might erect would then be removed without compensation; but this did not deter many plotholders.

The cheapest sites were sold for £5, with opportunities for repayment at one shilling a week. As one old lady explained:

181

My husband bought this plot from someone else in the building trade who didn't want to keep up the payments. Our kitchen was the site hut from one of the jobs he worked on. He tipped a friend to bring it down on a lorry, and one summer we put up the front room. The bay window was left over from a building job in New Malden. When the children were small, we used to come down every other week-end. The boys had a tent in the garden and we would sleep in the hut. It was marvellous in those days. In the end we retired down here because we liked it so much.

In 1936 the Purley Park Property Owners' Association was started, to organise social and road maintenance activities, and by the outbreak of the Second World War the population had grown to 800, and the caravans and camping coaches were giving way to more permanent, but substandard, dwellings. A 'guidance plan' prepared by the Berkshire County Planning Department in 1970 reports that:

> in 1947 the local planning authority were faced with a considerable problem, on account of the uncontrolled growth of the Estate, and the County Planning Committee agreed that the only satisfactory procedure would be for the County District Councils to acquire the whole area, clean it up and install water and sewerage services, though this idea was dropped when it was learnt that the cost of sewerage alone would be £40,000.

In spite of this, by the time of the report water had been laid on to most plots and main sewers were installed in 1967.

The local authority's approach in the postwar period has been to approve rebuilding or extensions in the form of additional bedrooms or of bathrooms, where it seemed reasonable, according to the size of the plot:

> In 1952 the County Council refused permission for the erection of a small asbestos bungalow on a site only twenty feet wide, one of the reasons for refusal being that 'the erection of further development is likely to lead to a demand for essential services and the provision of these will involve the Local Authority in an uneconomical expenditure of public money'. The Minister allowed the appeal against this refusal to the extent of permitting the erection of the bungalow for a limited period of five years, but he commented that 'in general your Council are right to discourage the growth and expansion of this estate' and he agreed that 'the permanent retention on the site of substandard housing development of the type proposed by the appellant would be most undesirable'.

By 1966, in the view of the County Planning Department, the estate 'presented an unhappy picture'. The frontage to the River Thames:

> while having one palatial brick house with beautifully tended lawns, presented an intrusion of assorted huts and caravans...

182

Plots were of irregular shape and widths of plot were often well under 50 feet. Some of the buildings were in poor repair and on several plots there were caravans as well as chalets, a problem which seemed to be on the increase.

The then Rural District Council's Public Health Committee wondered if the 'problem' could be approached under the public health legislation, but a survey revealed that few dwellings could be deemed 'unfit'; so to the County Council was approached to see what could be done under planning legislation.

The County Planning Officer responded with three alternative solutions. The first was drastic action in the form of the designation of a Comprehensive Development Area accompanied by an extensive programme of purchase by the Rural District Council, and he listed several disadvantages. Among them were the unlikelihood of getting Ministerial agreement, the extremely heavy cost of such a procedure, the fact that the threat of compulsory purchase 'would tend to antagonise residents', and an overriding disadvantage: that the council would experience difficulty in rehousing people from the estate. His second suggestion was that a Guidance Plan should be drawn up, identifying unfit premises and those where the plot size was considered inadequate, and indicating how, over time, improvements could be made by the amalgamation of plots and purchase by the council as opportunity arose. A key task in such a plan would be the making up of roads as soon as possible. His third alternative was to maintain the *status quo* by using the usual development control procedures, working towards gradual improvement at the rate dictated by applications for rebuilding. This he thought would have the advantage of calling for the least effort and expenditure, and the disadvantage that it 'would prove difficult to arrest the increasing congestion of the estate'.

The Rural District Council favoured the second of these alternatives, that of a non-statutory guidance plan, and in 1966 and 1967 circulated questionnaires among residents, asking them about the ownership of their plots, whether they were occupied temporarily or permanently, whether they were prepared to sell to the council, and whether they were prepared to pay towards the making-up of roads. Inevitably the questionnaire alarmed the residents. There was a 47 per cent response, and of those who replied, 80 per cent were prepared to pay a contribution towards the cost of roads. After much discussion as to whether the District or County Council should contribute to the road building costs, the County agreed to put the four main estate roads on its 'Priority List of Private Street Works', and in 1969 both authorities formally adopted the Guidance Plan [28].

By the 1980s, the visitor to the estate certainly does not see the 'unhappy picture' which the planners saw in the 1960s. Spreading 'ranch-style' houses, of the kind you see in estate agents' adverts anywhere, are cheek-by-jowl with tiny improvised cottages on narrow plots from the pre-war days, usually lovingly painted and gardened. There are still retired people living there who have not connected with

183

the sewer because they cannot afford to.

Inevitably (or is it just that our perception has changed?) these are more interesting to the eye than the everywhere-type houses. And if our criterion is to be the degree of obtrusiveness on the riverside scene, they are, just because of their tiny scale, less noticeable than their newer, larger neighbours.

BABLOCK HYTHE

For those who cherished the upper Thames of their childhood and youth, one of the symbols of the creeping degradation of the whole riverside landscape was the spread of old railway carriages as holiday homes. This was encouraged by the railway companies themselves: the Great Western Railway advertised them on station hoardings and itself operated 'camping coaches' which could be rented for holidays in 'beauty spots'. In the mid-1920s this invasion even affected one of the holy places of romantic Oxford, Bablock Hythe, 'that remote and classic ferry' across 'the stripling Thames' as it has been called by most writers since Matthew Arnold celebrated the place in 'The Scholar-Gypsy'. The landlord of the Chequers Inn erected ten old railway coaches on brick piers along the side of a hedge [29].

The report prepared for the Council for the Protection of Rural England in 1929 on the Thames Valley remarked that 'the field itself at a pleasant bend of the river is eminently suitable for summer camps of tents, but anything in the nature of a railway carriage community is not only grotesque, but extremely undesirable' [30]. A decade later, when the colony had grown, Robert Gibbings found these humble incursions less objectionable than the 'architectural disfigurements' of the riverside. 'If those mansions are the result of man growing wealthy it would have been far better for their owners to have remained poor and to live in converted railway carriages'. After another decade the cycle of taste had gone full circle. No other observer, before or since, has written of the apotheosis of Bablock Hythe with such sympathy as Eric de Maré:

> In the meadow nearby a row of railway carriages are laid out to form a miniature holiday camp, but thanks to bright paintwork, some bunting and a screen of trees, the effect does not insult the landscape... Ahead on the opposite bank lie other strange dwellings in the shape of double-decker buses. This kind of thing usually brings outbursts of abuse from all except the owners of such extemporary housing, but usually for the wrong reasons. They are associated in our minds with poverty and squalor, but there is, after all, no intrinsic reason why tramcars, buses or railway carriages should not be made into attractive structures if treated with gaiety, feeling and an Emmett-like fantasy. Let us adopt a tolerant, hopeful attitude, then, to the individuals who enjoy the river at Bablock Hythe [31].

PRIVATE FACES IN PUBLIC PLACES

More than any other plotland area (with the possible exception of Peacehaven), the private arcadias of the Thames Valley attracted the full weight of Establishment criticism. The class issue is never far below the surface. The Thames — with Eton, Windsor and Henley on its banks — must have seemed the undisputed sanctuary of a privileged caste. So, suddenly to find greengrocers from Acton and printers from Fulham, making free with their 'squalid little huts' must have raised blood pressures to dangerous levels. The impotent rage of Sir Gilbert Augustus Clayton East at the Select Committee of 1884 illustrates this hidden agenda. As much as anything else it must have been a futile cry of despair at seeing such rapid changes in English society — the stark signs of 'democratisation' and the ascendance of vulgar, popular culture. But at the same time the Thames Valley presents genuine dilemmas of public versus personal amenity. You would have to make a special journey to be affronted by the plotland landscapes of other areas, but since the Thames is a national asset, used by vast numbers of visitors, and since it provides every variety of water and waterside sport, the existence of private niches of personal enjoyment creates a problem in the public mind. The idea that the river bank should be accessible to everybody, and consequently to nobody in particular, runs through the vast literature of the Thames. When the Thames River Preservation Committee reported in 1884 on the desirability of a continuous riverside walk, they found that the same notion had been advanced in 1793. Any reader of the pre-war planning reports of official and unofficial authorities will be impressed by their consistency and their insistence on some basic priorities. One was that the riverside landscape should be taken into public control. Their view was expressed with particular urgency in the 1930 report on 'The Thames from Putney to Staines':

> There are bungalows above the lock at Shepperton, but more unfortunately there are further bungalows and more land for sale at £2 a foot along the fringes of the beautiful Chertsey Mead. At Dockett Eddy low-lying and beautifully wooded land is being cut up for bungalows and it will soon be too late to save the banks if no action is taken. Anything that is built either on the bank or upon the flat meadow land is clearly to be seen. The whole and particular virtue of the place resides in the open view across the meads towards Chertsey and St Ann's Hill upstream, or backwards towards Weybridge and its church steeple which rises above the trees. If there is room to build two hundred and fifty bungalows in a line from Shepperton Weir to Chertsey Bridge, and two hundred and fifty families might find space to enjoy their little view across the river to the unspoilt bank opposite, it might be assumed that the countless thousands who will come from near and far to enjoy this beauty that now is here will be cruelly disappointed. It is from this point of view that bungalow development is not only, broadly speaking, selfish but also uneconomical... [32].

Thames Valley: riverside plots highlight conflicts between private and public access to amenity.

This was a sensible and praiseworthy view. All through the 1930s, officials complained that they had neither the powers nor the money for large-scale public acquisition of land. Some measures (for example the 1938 Green Belt Act) provided powers and limited funds, and in the postwar years it was assumed that the powers of development control (which enabled 'undesirable' building to be prevented without the actual acquisition of land, and without liability for compensation) could be accompanied by a policy of land purchase to make riverside land available to the public at large. In practice, since the cost of establishing the Thames Riverside Walk and similar schemes would be so enormous, it has been shunted between the districts and the counties, with the hope that some supra-local body like the National Parks Commission or the Countryside Commission would pick it up.

But the planning authorities cannot be blamed for seeking to make the riverside accessible to the public, nor for enforcing the greenbelt policy. They have a duty to do so. Similarly the Thames Conservancy, in reconciling the conflicting demands made on the river, has to be conscious that it provides more than half of London's water supply. The conservators' nightmare for generations has been that the existence of a multitude of permanent buildings in the flood plain would lead to the demand that the river should be made capable of carrying all conceivable water thus preventing flooding. Lord Desborough, chairman of the Conservancy Board for many years, saw this threat in 1930:

> Those who have built houses which are liable to be flooded, where they never ought to have been built, that is, on osier beds which have been flooded every year that I know of, are now to have their houses and lands absolutely preserved from all danger of flood [33].

It could be done, at enormous expense, but as Lord Mayo said on the same occasion:

> if the Thames itself is going to be treated in this manner, all its beautiful bends, all its picturesque islands, all its peaceful backwaters, all its beautiful bridges will be swept away. And what will you have left? Nothing but a straight, huge and hideous canal [34].

It did not happen of course, but every measure to eliminate buildings from the flood plain or to improve public access to the river, has inevitably been directed to the elimination of the humble plotland dwellings, which were regarded as substandard and consequently cheaper to acquire. Just as poor people in poor property were invariably the victims of plans for urban motorways or comprehensive redevelopment, when both of these were in fashion among the planners, so 'better-class' riverside property is never threatened. In this sense, Jon Gower Davies was demonstrably correct in describing planning as 'a highly regressive form of indirect taxation' [35].

187

The common sense of site valuation, and the calculation of the strength of the potential opposition, dictated such a policy, as did the accepted perception of what was, or was not, the approved standard of riverside development. Very few public voices were raised to suggest that the plotlander's bungalow had a place in the riverside landscape [36]. Yet by the 1980s, when the remaining ones have merged into the landscape, with grass, trees and foliage, they have become the least obtrusive, and for many, the most interesting, of all the Thameside buildings.

One distinguished town planner told us:

> I feel that officialdom and preservation societies batten on the few thousand feet of unconventional development and make it sound as though all the 143 miles, times two, of the Thames are lined with dreadful shanty towns. There must be room for many forms of enjoyment and much variety in such a space. It is quite absurd for authorities and others to seek to reduce everything to a uniform Thameside image when its very variety is its great attraction.

What kind of 'felicitas calculus' can we devise to measure the private happiness of the plot-holding families against the pleasure of the visitors whose parked cars are the riverside landscape of public access? The astronomical cost of maintaining public spaces today may well have made the local authorities glad that they did not succeed in totally eliminating what Eric de Maré calls 'the ten square yards of lawn and pergola at "Beggar's Roost" or "Wyworrie" which dip to the water at Penton Hook', or to pull down 'Paradise' and make it a parking lot. Only the wealthy can afford to build by the riverside nowadays, but in considering the evolution of the Thameside plotlands, we can conclude that to tolerate some private faces in public places might have been the most sustainable policy all along.

NOTES

1. Stevenson, J.J. (1875) in *Building News*, 26 February, quoted in Girouard, Mark (1977) *Sweetness and Light*. London: Oxford University Press.
2. Jerome, Jerome K. (1889) *Three Men in a Boat*. London.
3. *Minutes of Evidence to the Thames River Preservation Committee, 1884,* quoted in de Maré, Eric (1952) Time on the Thames. London: Architectural Press; 2nd edition Hassocks, Sussex: Flare Books, 1975.
4. Jerome: *op. cit.* (see note 2).
5. Morris, William (1891) *News from Nowhere*. London: Reeves and Turner. Morris's account of two journeys up-stream in 1880 and 1881 is included in Henderson, Philip (ed.) (1950) *The Letters of William Morris to his Family and Friends*. London: Longmans.

6. de Maré, Eric (1950) The Thames as a Linear National Park. *Architectural Review* special number, July; expanded as *Time on the Thames*. London: Architectural Press, 1952; 2nd edition Hassocks, Sussex: Flare Books, 1975.
7. Harrison, P.T. (1909) *Bungalow Residences*. London: Crosby Lockwood.
8. Adams, Thompson and Fry (1928) *North West Surrey Regional Planning Scheme*. London.
9. Mayo, Adshead and Abercrombie (1929) *The Thames Valley From Cricklade to Staines: A Survey of its Existing State and Some Suggestions for its Future*. London.
10. King, Anthony D. (1980) A time for space and a space for time: the social production of the vacation house, in King, Anthony D. (ed.) *Buildings and Society*. London: Routledge and Kegan Paul. See also his *The Bungalow: a Cultural History and Sociology*. London: Routledge and Kegan Paul, forthcoming.
11. Personal communication.
12. Peel, J.B.H. (1967) *Portrait of the Thames: From Teddington to the Source*. London: Robert Hale.
13. *The Thames and Its Story*. London: Cassell and Company, 1909.
14. Adams, Thompson and Fry (1930) *The Thames from Putney to Staines: A Survey of the River, with Suggestions for the Preservation of its Amenities*, prepared for a Joint Committee of the Middlesex and Surrey County Council. Hassocks, Sussex.
15. *Ibid.*
16. Mayo, Adshead and Abercrombie, *op. cit.* (see note 9).
17. Jones, Barbara (1948) in *The Architectural Review*, December, subsequently reprinted in Jones, Barbara (1951) *The Unsophisticated Arts*. London: Architectural Press.
18. de Maré *op. cit.* (see note 6).
19. Adams, Thompson and Fry, *op. cit.* (see note 14).
20. *Ibid.*
21. Thames Conservancy: Chief Engineer's Report of May 1947.
22. Middlesex County Council (1951) *Development Plan: Report of the Survey*. London.
23. Middlesex County Council (1962) *First Review of the Development Plan: Report of the Survey*, Vol 1. London.
24. County Planning Department, Surrey County Council (1980) *'Windows on the River' A Policy Review, Consultative Report*.
25. Site interviews 1980.
26. Site interviews 1980.
27. George Woodcock: Personal communication January 1981.
28. Berkshire County Council Planning Department (1969) *Purley Park River Estate: Guidance Plan*. Reading: Berks County Council.
29. Mayo, Adshead and Abercrombie (1931) *Regional Planning Report on Oxfordshire*. Oxford: Oxford University Press.
30. Mayo, Adshead and Abercrombie (1929) *op. cit.* (see note 9).
31. de Maré, *op. cit.* (see note 6).
32. Adams, Thompson and Fry, *op. cit.* (see note 14).

33. Discussion on Professor Abercrombie's paper on 'The Thames Valley Preservation Scheme'. *Journal of the Royal Institute of British Architects*, 37(9), 1930.
34. *Ibid.*
35. Davies, Jon Gower (1972) *The Evangelistic Bureaucrat*. London: Tavistock Publications.
36. Among the few defenders of the plotland landscape have been Eric de Maré, Barbara Jones and Robert Gibbings, whose opinions have been quoted, and John Noble of the Housing Development Directorate, Department of the Environment, in his paper 'Contingency Housing'. *Architects Journal*, 24, October, 1973.

Chapter 6

Arcadia in the Countryside

I am always haunted by the awfulness of London: by the great appalling fact of these millions cast down, as it would appear by hazard, on the banks of this noble stream, working each in their own groove and their own cell, without regard or knowledge of each other, without heeding each other, without having the slightest idea how the other lives — the heedless casualty of unnumbered thousands of men. Sixty years ago a great Englishman, Cobbett, called it a wen. If it was a wen then, what is it now? A tumour, an elephantiasis sucking into its gorged system half the life and the blood and the bone of rural districts.

(Lord Rosebery, Chairman of the London County Council, March 1891)

Ninety years after the chairman of the L.C.C. deplored the overcrowding of London, the 1981 census revealed the loss of 18 per cent of its population in the previous ten years. But the drift from the British city has been a characteristic of the entire twentieth century. Its prophet was Ebenezer Howard, who declared in 1904:

I venture to suggest that while the age in which we live is the age of the great closely-compacted, overcrowded city, there are already signs, for those who can read them, of a coming change so great and so momentous that the twentieth century will be known as the period of the great exodus, the return to the land... [1].

His solution was the planned dispersal of both population and industry to a ring of garden cities, separated by a green belt from the metropolis. But only a small proportion of the great exodus has taken this form. Its characteristic manifestation has been the 'suburb spreading beyond suburb' which he deplored. Nevertheless, speculative developers in the suburban belt, as well as the entrepreneurs of plotland sites far beyond, used the rhetoric of the Garden City movement for their own

191

purposes. It was as natural for every speculative builder in the urban fringe to call his new housing estate a garden suburb as it was for the developer of Peacehaven to call it 'a garden city by the sea'.

The call of Arcadia in fresh air beyond the city, was appealing. With the advent of modern drugs and the elimination of the fogs which were a feature of London life for over a century, we forget how recently tuberculosis and bronchial illness were the scourge of urban life, and how the most usually recommended palliative was for the sufferer to move to a bracing climate and purer air. After the First World War, many a survivor suffering from the effects of gas was urged to get out of London, while there were others, terribly disfigured, who wanted to avoid the daily encounters of city living. And there were yet more who, counting themselves fortunate to have survived, resolved not to go back to the life of the urban toiler, but to invest the gratuity paid to demobilised soldiers in a new life in the country. (Often, like the contemporary equivalent in redundancy compensation, these payments represented the only lump sum of cash they had ever been able to accumulate.) Dreams of chicken-farming or market-gardening may have been easily shattered, but the patch of land and the owner-built house on it remained as some kind of security.

Catering for all these aspirations were a variety of land dealers and estate agents as well as innumerable small-scale private sellers. South and south-west of Greater London, the sites run from the hinterland of the Medway Towns and of Ashford in Kent and across the North Downs from Walderslade, Kits Coty, Culverstone and Knatts Valley in Kent to Tatsfield and Effingham in Surrey. Another belt of plotland areas stretches further south from Ifold Wood at the extreme north of West Sussex, westwards all along the high chalklands of Hampshire from Headley Down near Bramshott and Griggs Green, near Liphook, through Beech and Four Marks, south of Alton, to South Wonston, north of Winchester, and Picket Piece, Grateley and Palestine in the hinterland of Andover. The strip of coastal plotland sites in West Sussex continues with inland areas on the Isle of Wight.

But these are scattered settlements, spread through rolling country or beyond the suburban hinterland of country towns and railway junctions. North of the Thames, apart from the riverside areas of the Thames Valley, the pre-eminent county for plotland Arcadias is Essex. Easy access by train from the densely-populated inner districts of east and north-east London, traditional links as an area providing food and fodder (similar to those which tied riverside London to the coastal areas), and the collapse of agriculture, made South Essex available as a destination for every kind of aspiration for a place in the country.

It also exhibits the greatest variety of official responses to the plotland phenomenon. These range from elimination to provide a country park at Havering, absorption and replacement in a New Town at Basildon, elimination to make room for superior private housing at South Woodham Ferrers, to 'benign neglect' in other parts of the county. Outside those areas where draconic special measures were taken, the hope of the planning authorities that the refusal of permission for extension, improvement or infilling, would cause the plotlands to disappear and somehow go back to nature, gave way to a willingness to come to terms with them and to allow the ordinary processes of upgrading and alteration over time, to absorb them into the twentieth-century pattern of the exodus from the nineteenth-century city.

SOUTH ESSEX: PITSEA AND LAINDON

Essex is becoming the dustbin of London.

(James Wentworth Day. *The Book of Essex*)

In the mid-1930s, a well-known broadcaster of the period, Filson Young, took a trip by aeroplane to look at the expansion of London into the surrounding counties:

> Turning south-east from Hatfield, we crossed the end of Epping Forest and the North Circular Road, and what I think is called the Eastern Avenue. We looked down upon a world that crowded along even these great arteries; they had been established so that men could escape from crowded populations, but the arteries were themselves becoming choked. Over places like Wanstead and Leytonstone, over Stratford and West Ham, one was flying over a world of houses so dense that it was no case of ribbon roads, but roads so choked that it was almost impossible to follow them or mark their direction [2].

This was the ordinary suburban expansion, following first the railway network and later that of the new arterial roads. It was deplored for aesthetic, social or merely snobbish reasons, but it had, for the local authorities concerned, at least the advantages that came from increasing rateable values, thus financing the urban services for which its existence had created a need. But in the plotland settlements further out, just as in any sparsely settled rural district, there was very little rate income to finance public services, and very little potential income to encourage gas and electricity undertakings to install power lines.

The town planner Sir Colin Buchanan characterises the Essex plotland belt as one of 'sporadic eruption' pock-marking the Brentwood-Southend-Tilbury triangle, and he recalls that:

> It was the author's misfortune in the early nineteen-thirties to have the task of recording much of this development for insertion on the ordnance maps. It was queer, lonely work, tramping up and down deserted drives and over derelict fields... A half-finished building estate is a depressing place, but infinitely worse is the estate that obviously will never get

193

finished, will never have the shopping centres, cinemas, churches and schools so optimistically marked on the plan [3].

The principal entrepreneur behind the settlements that Colin Buchanan dolefully surveyed in the 1930s was Frederick Francis Ramuz, Mayor of Southend, whose activities are described in Chapter 4. In Southend itself, his developments overcame original doubts to become the most desirable parts of the town, though in the corridor of depressed farmland between suburban Essex and the sea they took much longer to mature.

The decline in the fortunes of agriculture, already discernible in the 1870s, and hastened by a series of wet summers and poor harvests, became the belated subject of a Royal Commission in 1893. An Assistant Commissioner was appointed to enquire into the desperate situation of South-East Essex, the area bounded by the Blackwater to the north, the Thames to the south and a line drawn through Billericay and Stanford-le-Hope in the west. He reported that 13 per cent of the farmland in this area had gone out of cultivation between 1880 and 1893 and that much more was bound to follow [4]. The heavy clay, known to farmers as 'three-horse land', was hard to work even in good times, and while more suited to wheat than to any other crop, was no longer suited to this purpose since it was wheat which had been most affected by cheap overseas imports. 'In the 1890s the technical knowledge of most farmers was limited, and attempts to make the land suitable for agriculture again were mostly unsuccessful' [5]. The land rapidly reverted to rough pasture and then to self-sown scrubland.

At the same time the whole area had been brought within easy reach of the metropolis by railway building. The London, Tilbury and Southend railway from Fenchurch Street had been opened in the 1850s, and in the 1880s the company had obtained authority to run a shorter, direct line to Southend, avoiding Tilbury and passing through Laindon and Pitsea. At the same time the Great Eastern Railway Company constructed a branch line from its East Anglian service from Liverpool Street, to reach Southend via Rayleigh. The rival companies undercut each other's fares, and in both cases these were about half the national average per mile.

Landowners along the new railway routes were often shareholders or board members of the railway companies, and could expect to profit not only from their diminishing asset of farmland recovering some value as building land, but also from the expectation of increasing railway traffic that any development would bring.

From the late-1870s onward there were continual farm sales in South Essex, often by orders of the liquidators in bankruptcy or 'under distress for rent'. The only incoming tenants that landlords could find were immigrant Scots hoping to convert to dairy-farming, though as Lord Petre's agent reported to the Royal Commission in 1893:

My own opinion, and that of practical men, based on experience, is that a very large portion of the arable land of Essex is unsuitable for the purpose [6].

194

Purchasers, when they were to be found, bought at knock-down prices. They were speculators who, either on their own account or as investment agents for others, were content to exploit whatever market could be developed over time for subdivided portions of this land. The dominant individual was Frederick Francis Ramuz, whose firm The Land Company, in addition to its coastal sites, acquired land at Rayleigh, Rochford, Pitsea, Basildon, Vange, Laindon, Wickford, Langdon Hills and Stanford-le-Hope. Its many thousands of acres represented at least a third of several of the South Essex parishes. Having acquired all this land, Ramuz and other purchasers had to find a market for it and had to avoid flooding the potential market with too much land. Speculative builders were already buying land for development in suburban Essex at one end of the railway line and at Southend at the other. While this was the most advantageous market, disposing of large lots at one time to people willing to take on the risks of development was not easy. When, for example, in October 1893 the Laindon Estate, consisting of 365 acres of land at Laindon, Langdon Hills, Dunton and Little Burstead, was offered for sale in five lots, not one of them was sold [7].

But if land could not be sold en bloc, some of it could at least be sold as individual plots, typically with a frontage of 20 feet and a depth of, say 100 feet, on a notional gridiron of roads pegged out among the thistles and scrub — and some customers could be persuaded to buy several adjacent plots.

Two firms of auctioneers, Protheroe and Morris, operating from the same addresses in London and Southend as The Land Company, and Henry W. Iles, also of London and Southend, whose firm still exists as estate agents in South Essex, developed techniques of wooing potential buyers with free railway tickets or cheap fares refunded to purchasers, with food and drink served in a marquee, as the plots were auctioned. 'Plot sales on the Estate' was the technique which Ramuz claimed to have pioneered at his seaside estates, and the festive atmosphere of these 'champagne auctions' was vividly remembered by many East London families who went for a cheap outing to the country and came back as property owners.

Ramuz had an interest in the large station hotels built outside the small stations along the railway to Southend, and it was the land closest to these stations which was first put on the market in several series of auction sales. At three sales in the summer of 1891, 859 plots were offered at the Station Estate, Pitsea. In the following summer, 1881 plots were offered at the Laindon Station Estate, and in the same year more plots were auctioned north of Billericay Station. Ten years later the Rayleigh Station estate was similarly put on sale by auction at the Golden Lion Hotel, Mr Iles drawing attention to the fact that there were 'fast trains communicating with the City in sixty minutes at only 10d. per day, season ticket rate, affording a good opportunity for City gentlemen to make this their home' [8].

The technique of plot sales continued well into the present century and is part of the folklore of South Essex and the East End of London, rather than that of the City gentlemen. Flushed and weary, the family would return to Stepney, Poplar, Bromley-by-Bow, East Ham, West Ham and Barking. The title deeds to the plot were put behind the clock on the mantlepiece or in a drawer, and quite often forgotten. To this day, the local authorities, the Basildon Development Corporation, and indeed, the present writers, receive enquiries from solicitors acting for clients who have ultimately inherited sites on roads which, if they ever existed, have long since disappeared, asking what had become of their inheritance.

What were the motives of the purchasers? They ranged from people who intended to settle and commute to London by rail; people who wanted a weekend retreat and who could finance the purchase by renting to others; people with back-to-the-land and simple-life ambitions; and would-be smallholders who were attracted by the larger sites offered very cheaply in the areas more than two miles from the railway stations. The advocates of alternative ways of living, just like anyone else, were attracted by the lure of inexpensive land reasonably accessible by rail.

George Lansbury, a much-loved Labour politician from Poplar, was, like so many other East-Enders at the turn of the century, a rural immigrant who completely understood and respected his fellow citizens' aspirations for a taste of country life, and forty years after his death is referred to by plotlanders as 'Mr Lansbury'. We have noted his connection with Jaywick Sands. He also had a continual interest in the efforts of Londoners to make a more ample life for themselves in the abandoned farmlands of South Essex, and when leader of the Labour Party in 1934 declared, 'I just long to see a start made on this job of reclaiming, recreating rural England' [9].

The advertising campaigns of The Land Company sought to attract every kind of back-to-the-land aspirant:

> Toiling, rejoicing, onward he goes,
> He has land of his own and fears no foes

says the Company's 1906 Catalogue. And it also persuades its readers that 'Land is the basis for all wealth. Even an acre leads to independence'. Anxious not to dismay those who only aspired to a plot for weekends, and holidays, it includes an article on 'The Ideal Summer Holiday' urging readers that there were preferable alternatives to seaside resorts, and that 'a piece of land with a small bungalow on it would be the ideal solution'. The family man was encouraged to think of the pleasure of seeing his 'wife and little ones enjoying themselves revelling in the fresh air, feeding on healthy country produce. It would be without doubt a home from home' [10].

At about the same time, another entrepreneur, Mr H. Foulger of Laindon, issued his brochure called *A Guide to Lovely Laindon*, in which he envisaged the decline of the great metropolis, declaring that:

Thousands are taking up residence in the country and sooner or later you will do so too. The question for you to decide is will you pay Laindon a visit and do so now, or will you wait until land values are so enhanced that the benefits to be derived are merely physical, and not financial as well? [11].

Land values were slowly enhanced on the more desirable sites, though on others, where little demand could be stimulated, they actually declined for years. There were a few instances where Ramuz could realise more for a plot than he originally paid per acre. He had bought Highlands Farm at Pitsea for £2,900, just over £21 per acre [12]. In May 1890 an excursion train brought 250 people to Pitsea Junction, from where they were driven for a mile to the auctioneers' marquee. 'Here a sumptuous repast was spread, at which the health of Mr George Ramuz was drunk with much enthusiasm, congratulations pouring in upon him on this, his first appearance as an auctioneer' [13]. Villa plots realised from £5 to £9 and shop sites from £11 to £14. However, at a later auction on the Highland Estate in March 1899, 'some of the plots offered fetched as much as £30 and £22 apiece, and probably in better weather these prices would improve' [14]. That sale realised about £700. The same sum was reached at another auction that year on the Wooton Park Estate, where a large number of plots, 20 feet by 150 feet, were sold for £4 each [15].

In 1899 the Board of Trade held an enquiry into the application of the Laindon Gas and Water Co Ltd to extend the limits of its water supply area and to supply gas. Giving evidence at the inquiry, Mr G.W. Usill said that the population of Laindon had risen to 700. Some 2,700 plots of land had been purchased, but the owners would not erect buildings until they could see that they were in a fair way to obtain water. When the power was granted, he estimated that the population would soon rise to 14,000. The Rev. H. Carpenter said that people were having to drink pond water [16]. That summer the plot-holders on the Station Estate at Laindon decided to form a Plot Owners' Protection Society, with the intention of summonsing people who grazed cattle on their land and to prosecute gypsies. It was agreed that the grass on unfenced plots would be sold to raise funds for the Association. Mr E. Collings, who was elected secretary, declared that 'All that is wanted to make this charming estate go ahead is water and the tithe redemption' [17].

They, like Mr Ramuz, were confident that:

A real garden city without the aid of philanthropists and on a perfectly sound basis, is likely to be created [18].

By 1896 Great Gubbins Farm was acquired for the Laindon Racecourse, to be built by the Croydon Race Company, with provision for cricket, football, archery and golf. In 1907 the Vange Golf Club was actually opened: 'the greens are not bad for the first year and hard clay...' [19].

The plotland settlements that emerged all over South Essex, but particularly in the areas of the Rochford and Billericay Rural Districts, were of three kinds. The first, on those estates near the railway stations, had the familiar gridiron of grass or mud tracks and the beginnings of basic services. The second was a single unmade road with plots on either side, and the third comprised isolated plots in twos or threes, where a farmer had simply sold or leased the corner of a field to raise a little money. In the backlands many estates were pegged out but never sold and reverted to agricultural use during the two world wars, when national need overrode the ordinary economics of farming.

The dwellings ranged from ordinary suburban villas, meeting the requirements of the Public Health Acts, to the familiar range of sheds, shanties or old railway coaches, used only for weekends and holidays. There was very little supervision by the local authorities for obvious reasons:

> Each authority had only one building inspector to encompass a wide rural area, and there were the added disadvantages of bad communications and wilderness areas of scrub which hid so many of the shacks. Large areas never saw a building inspector, and building permits, or refusals were easily ignored. Where building inspections were made it was then difficult to trace the often temporary occupants. The hundreds of substandard shacks offered little in the way of a tax base for the local authorities to provide basic utilities. Furthermore, with so many temporary occupants and squatters it is clear that over whole areas of 'plotland' rates were never paid [20].

The occasional instances of plot-owners being summonsed for not submitting building notices to the local authorities, illustrate this and also show their places of origin. 'In September 1914 at Vange, a woman was allowed to build and occupy a hut on land she had been sold, an "empty shell of boxes" estimated to be worth thirty shillings; she was always excused rates' [21]. In 1907 William Wrene of Barking was brought to court by the surveyor to the Rural District Council for not depositing plans of a timber-built dwelling house on the Barstable Hall Estate, Basildon. A fine of £1 was imposed, with 5s. costs. 'Several of the defendants pleaded that they were unaware that it was necessary to submit plans and that they understood there were no restrictions whatever as to the building of houses there' [22]. In 1922 William Lawrie of Poplar was summonsed for not giving notice of the building of 'Dundonald Drum' on Pitsea Marshes. It consisted of two rooms, each eight feet square, lined with boards from old packing cases [23]. In 1924 the Billericay magistrates heard several charges of the same kind, of erecting temporary buildings which were used as dwellings. The people concerned came from Stratford, Canning Town and Custom House, and were each fined £1. 'These cases were brought as a warning' [24].

Planning controls were, of course, non-existent. The first perception of the Essex plotlands as a planning problem, calling for planning measures to control them, came in 1931 in Professor Stanley Adshead's South Essex Regional Planning Scheme [25]. He remarked that, as the most easily reached county with a coastline, Essex had become the inevitable outlet for London's overcrowded population. Its urbanisation and expansion during the first thirty years of this century had been as dramatic as that of Lancashire throughout the whole of the nineteenth century. Starting as a virgin county, it had been *colonised*, rather than developed.

For the colonists themselves, he, like many a planner since, could not withhold a grudging admiration. 'These enterprising people', he called them. Who were these enterprising colonisers whose new-found land was one which had ceased to be viable for agriculture, who made their homes without capital, mortgages or loans?

PLOTLAND PEOPLE

Mr Syrett of Worthing Road, Laindon, was 85 when we interviewed him in 1972. He was a leather worker from Kennington who had bought the place in 1929 to use at weekends and subsequently retired there. He was not the first occupier of the site, the original occupant being a carpenter from Canning Town who bought three 20-foot plots for £18 in 1916, giving a site 60 feet by 140 feet. In the post-1918 period, when the London banks were changing the decor of their interiors from mahogany to oak, the carpenter brought down bits and pieces of abandoned bank joinery from Fenchurch Street and built his dream bungalow. After Mr Syrett had bought it, the bungalow was burnt down in a fire, except for that part of the structure which was the kitchen and Mr Syrett had built onto it a timber-framed house. Later he had it rendered and had been making improvements ever since. For example, he had recently cut out the mullions of his 1930-type windows to make them more like those of the Development Corporation houses opposite.

We showed him a description of the area as a former 'vast pastoral slum'. He denied this of course, remarking that most people had come down to South Essex precisely to get away from the slums. But what was it like before the road was made up? Well, you had to order your coal in the summer as the lorry could never get down the road in wintertime. But there was a pavement. 'People used to get together with their neighbours to buy cement and sand to make the pavement all the way down along the road'. Street lighting? No, there was none. 'Old Granny Chapple used to take a hurricane lamp when she went to the Radiant Cinema in Laindon'. Transport? 'Well a character called Old Tom used to run a bus from Laindon Station to the Fortune of War public house. And there were still horses and carts down here in those days. They used to hold steeplechases on the hill where the caravan site is now'. Down the same road had lived Mr Budd who died in 1971 aged 97. He was a bricklayer by trade, and every time he had a new grandchild, would add a room to his house.

Mr and Mrs Syrett's house was immaculate — large rooms with all the attributes of suburban comfort. The house had been connected to the sewer and gas and electricity mains in the 1940s and 1950s. The Urban District Council had made up the road under the Private Street Works Act, charging £60 in road charges. More recently when Basildon Development Corporation began building on vacant plots in the road, they made it up again to a higher standard. The rates at that time were £12 a half year, and as old age pensioners they got a rate rebate.

They lived happily within their pension, they assured me. No rent to pay, some fruit and vegetables from their garden and greenhouse. It was a matter of pride for them that they were not obliged to apply for supplementary benefits. It was quite obvious that Mr Syrett's investment for his old age was this one-time substandard bungalow which in the end had all the same amenities and conveniences as the homes of his neighbours [26]. The truth of this could be seen by looking in estate agents' windows, where houses with the same kind of origin were advertised at prices similar to those asked for normal speculative builders' houses of the same period.

The significant thing is that their original owners and builders would never have qualified as building society mortgagees in the inter-war years, any more than people with equivalent incomes would today.

Mr Fred Nichols of Bowers Gifford is in his seventies. He had a poverty-stricken childhood in East London, and a hard and uncertain life as a casual dock worker. His piece of land cost him £10 in 1934. It is 40 feet wide by 100 feet deep. First he put up a tent which his family used at weekends, and he gradually accumulated tools, timber and glass

Bowers Gifford: current view of "Perserverance" (sic), the house built by Mr Fred Nichols.

200

which he brought to the site strapped to his back as he cycled down from London. For water he sank a well in his garden. His house is called 'Perserverance' (sic). In the course of time it was connected for mains water, gas and electricity, though the road is still unmade and unsewered.

Mrs Elizabeth Granger of Hockley was, with her first husband, caretaker in a block of London County Council flats. In 1932 she saw land at Laindon advertised in the evening paper at £5 for a 20 feet by 100 feet plot. She took her unwilling husband on the one-and-twopence return trip to Laindon, and they were advised by the agent to buy two

Laindon: Mrs Granger's house taking shape in the 1930s. (Photos courtesy of Mrs Granger)

plots if they wanted to build a bungalow. She paid the deposit with a borrowed pound. As soon as she could afford it she bought a First World War army bell tent, laboriously got it to the site, and her plotland odyssey had begun. She and her husband would go there on their weekly day off, taking their drinking water with them and straining rainwater for washing through an old stocking. They would rent the tent at weekends to parties of boys from the estate, using the money to buy cement at 2s 6d a bag, three yards of sand for 15s and secondhand bricks at 35s a thousand.

Slowly they built their bungalow and Mrs Granger's husband got a transfer to a job at Dagenham. They reared chickens, geese and goats and bought a pony and trap. Eventually gas was connected. As their family grew they bought a second house in an incomplete state for £180 and, with the bombing of London, relations stayed in their original house which they subsequently sold for £400. Ultimately they moved to a third plotland house which they improved and finally sold to the Basildon Development Corporation for £650. Since then Mrs Granger has lived in several other houses in Essex, enabled to move 'up market' as a result of her borrowed pound. She remarks, 'We never had a mortgage for any of them. I feel so sorry for young couples these days, who don't get the kind of chance we had' [27].

PLOTLAND CHILDHOODS

People who grew up in the Essex plotlands have told us of the wonderfully free, backwoods life they lived as children, wandering at will in the empty scrubland all through the summer. In reminiscence, they make it sound like growing up in the American West or the Australian bush. Mr Cecil Hewett, the authority on wood jointing and timber building, grew up in Laindon:

> His father, a wood machinist, fought on the Somme and must have been an interesting man; he and Cecil used to go for long walks in what was then the countryside where, in the agricultural depression of the 1930s, the old wooden farm machinery, the waggons and the carts were lying about unused and open for examination [28].

There was, however, a less attractive side to plotland childhoods. One informant, a second generation plotlander, who grew up in the 1930s and 1940s in the plotland fringe of a straggling Essex village, paints a picture of a deprived and isolated collection of individual families where 'the moral community spirit of village life had disappeared and the fully fledged urban life had not yet come to pass'. She recalls that:

> One was aware of being a member of an underclass. Educationally we were deprived. We were aware that other children in the school were less peripheral than we were and that they either came from a more elitist area of the street or from a more developed plotland

202

area. At the base of all this was the fact that the adults were indeed economically peripheral and this was paralleled by the material deprivation such as the lack of running water, the lack of sewage disposal, cooking on oil stoves, the perpetual trot to the ironmonger's for a gallon of oil, the bath water being used by the whole family, and the 'junkyard' attitude associated with extreme self-help and of making something out of nothing.

While some plotland children felt they had absorbed independence, self-reliance and the ability to 'make out' in society as well as in 'the network of people and backyard industries that exists in the Essex hinterland' [29], this particular second generation plotlander found the opposite:

> The experience was a narrowing one; there were narrow mental horizons and no helpful relationship between the generations. We were aware that other children said of us that we lived in 'huts'. One grew up to be almost totally inarticulate. We all found, I believe, great difficulty in fitting in socially in work situations. We were emotionally deprived because when we were spoken to it was only to be 'told off'. We did not know what life was about, what work meant, how to find it, and how to behave or use our minds once we had found it. We were unequal to the task of fitting into an urban society [30].

Her story exactly parallels other accounts of childhood in deprived communities, whether among gypsies and travelling people or in the poverty belt of inner cities [31]. But it also reflects the experience, too commonplace to be mentioned, of the same generation of country-born Essex children whose families were not immigrants, but had lived there for centuries. The fluctuations of the rural economy had left them untouched: they were always at the bottom of the pile. Spike Mayes, in the first of his autobiographical volumes, describes the intolerable hardships his family had to endure until his father had the great good luck to emerge with a disability pension from the First World War [32], and the recollections of an Essex country doctor from the 1930s [33] take for granted a world where the 'ordinary farmworkers' tumbledown cottages had neither piped water nor drainage. Naturally they had no gas nor electricity, and their lives were just as isolated from the world of the affluent and successful as those of the plotland dwellers.

THE NEW TOWN SOLUTION

> It is possible to point with horror to the jumble of shacks and bungalows on the Langdon Hills and at Pitsea. This is a narrow-minded appreciation of what was as genuine a desire as created the group of lovely gardens and houses at Frensham and Bramshott.

(Sir Patrick Abercrombie, *The Greater London Plan*, 1944)

The turning point in the history of the plotlands in South Essex as elsewhere, was the Second World War. In the first place it brought an end, finally, to the agricultural depression. Land, which had been parcelled out into plots but never sold, was returned to farming. The activities of the War Agricultural Executive Committees ensured that whoever owned it and whatever the cost, neglected fields and derelict scrubland would be brought back into cereal cultivation.

In the second place, the war brought a mood of public resolution to build a better Britain once it was over. In terms of planning town and country in the South East, Abercrombie's Greater London Plan of 1944 was accepted in principle by the postwar government in 1946, including his proposals for the Metropolitan Green Belt and for a ring of New Towns beyond it. South Essex, with a new town between Laindon and Pitsea, coupled with Green Belt restrictions on new development, was to be profoundly affected by these changes.

A third effect of the Second World War on the plotlands was the very heavy bombing of East London, and especially of the dockland boroughs of Stepney, Poplar, West Ham and East Ham. As at Canvey Island, many families evacuated themselves or were bombed out and moved permanently to whatever foothold they had in the Pitsea, Laindon, Vange or Billericay districts. They were joined after the war by other members of their families returning from war service.

The extreme housing shortage after the war was, in a general sense, more the result of six years of no housebuilding and the result of the lowering of the average age of marriage and the consequent rise in the rate of household formation and in the birthrate, than of the actual number of houses destroyed through bombing and the wartime postponement of maintenance; but the combination of all these factors meant that many people were living in accommodation which had never been conceived as permanent, while some plotland houses, like city houses, were sub-let, room by room.

Until the census of 1951 (the first for twenty years) the local authorities had only a vague idea of the total number of people living in the 'sprawling wilderness of South Essex'. In 1950, Mr (later Sir) Bernard Braine, then Member of Parliament for the Billericay constituency, remarked that:

the previous Minister assumed that there were only some 17,000 people in the area. Goodness knows, that was large enough. I have had a careful check made, and I am satisfied that there are some 27,750 people living in the designated area [34].

The designation he was referring to was that of 7,800 acres as the site for Basildon New Town. When the first round of New Towns was proposed under the 1946 Act, there was in many cases intense opposition, not only from local residents and landowners, but from the local authorities. Basildon was almost unique among the new towns in that the local authorities petitioned the government for the area to be chosen as a new town site. Harlow in North-West Essex had been designated and it was proposed that Ongar should be expanded as the second Essex new town. But Essex County Council and the then Billericay District Council made representations to the Minister of Town and Country Planning that the Pitsea-Laindon area should be selected. They were joined by the County Boroughs of West Ham and East Ham who saw the place as the natural overspill town for their boroughs, many of whose former citizens were already living there. At the first round of designations, the joint application by the various councils was rejected, but after a further delegation to the Minister, the area was accepted. The name Basildon was selected as the village of that name was at the centre of the designated area.

Apart from the fact that transport links were as good as those of any other new town site, and a new urban centre could provide employment and social facilities for the whole South Essex hinterland, the local authorities' case was that the ordinary urban infrastructure was so grossly deficient in the area, that it could not be provided through the usual processes of local government revenue-raising, and could only be met by the direct flow of Treasury funds provided by the new town mechanism. When the newly-formed Development Corporation surveyed the district for which it had been given responsibility, it found that there were some 8,500 existing dwellings, over 6,000 of them unsewered. There were 75 miles of grass track roads; a mains water supply only in the built-up areas, with standpipes in the roads elsewhere; and no surface water drainage apart from ditches and old agricultural drains. Only 50 per cent of the dwellings had mains electricity. There were about 1,300 acres of completely waste land of which about half had no known owner. The average density was six persons to the acre. Of the 8,500 dwellings, 2,000 were of brick and tile construction meeting the standards of the Housing Acts, 1,000 were of light construction also meeting these standards, 5,000 were chalets and shacks, and a further 500 were described as derelict, though probably occupied. The average rateable value of these dwellings was £5 per annum [35].

If the local authority was almost unique (the only other example is Easington, County Durham in the case of Peterlee) in seeking the designation of its area as a new town, the inhabitants were almost united in their opposition. Residents' Protection Associations were formed in Pitsea and Laindon when word got around that the Development Corporation intended to acquire the freehold, by compulsory purchase, of all sites in the designated area. In vain the first chairman of the Development Corporation faced angry meetings of residents, explaining that 'The Corporation will not acquire any property in this area until such time as they want to use it or the land on which it stands' [36].

The passionate feelings evoked by the *idea* of freehold possession were evident at these meetings. The local paper reported that 'One man asked if this was justice after fighting for their stake in the country for six years. Another said "But you don't think we would do it again. We won't fight for rented property" [37]. However, the same

205

paper reported on the same day that 'A young man stood up and said, "I am a property owner, not by choice, but because I needed a home. I bought a bungalow in Laindon and I have no opposition to the New Town. He said that Laindon was going to fall down anyway" [38].

In a few months the local authority, too, changed its attitude:

> Billericay Urban District Council want the New Towns Act amended to allow for an exchange of freeholds for freeholds. During the course of a council debate it was stated that the majority of the houses in the area were worth between £500 and £600 and if people were given that amount for their property they would not be able to buy any other premises for the same price [39].

With great persistence, Bernard Braine raised the issue in Parliament in May 1950, 'in order to ventilate the feeling, which is very widespread in the area and has already resulted in the removal of almost every Labour councillor from the Billericay Council'. He claimed that Basildon was unique in that the area designated was very much larger than that of any other new town and that the existing population was very considerably larger:

> These freeholders I have spent the last four years cultivating their acquaintance; that is one of the reasons why I am here — are, almost without exception people of slender means and owning comparatively small plots of land. In many cases their homes are the result of the labour from their own hands. These people came from the East End of London and from Metropolitan Essex in the 1920s, and they built their own homes during the week-ends. In all cases their property represents a lifetime of abstinence and thrift, qualities which are not exactly encouraged today but without which the State would very quickly fall into decay. Large numbers of these people are pensioners who, if dispossessed, would find it impossible to obtain for themselves another freehold house elsewhere and would find it quite impossible to pay an economic rent. One has only to see the fantastically high rents charged for new houses now being erected in other new towns to see what enormous financial burden would be placed on the community if large numbers of these people were rehoused, as they would have to be if they were dispossessed. The point I want to make at the outset of my remarks is that, whatever their means, these people possess something of infinite value to themselves. They possess their homes, their freeholds, and their pride and self-reliance [40].

Sir Bernard was speaking as a good constituency MP, championing the interests of the plotlanders, as he has frequently done since. But inevitably the debate became a controversy between two opposing conceptions of social and individual rights in land, polarised between the two major political parties. Kenneth Lindgren, as a junior minister of the Ministry of Town and Country Planning, declared:

> If a new town is to be built, the area must be used to the best advantage. Furthermore, which is the proper body to hold the freeholds of land within a town — the individuals, or the community as a whole? There may be a cleavage between the two sides of the House upon this, but I hold the view, as do the Government, that the land belongs to the people, and that the collective owning and use of the land is a matter for the people themselves.

For Enoch Powell, as a member of the Conservative opposition, this was the thin end of the wedge for land nationalisation:

> The Parliamentary Secretary justified the general principle of acquiring freeholds in new towns on the grounds that it was Socialist theory and policy that ownership of the land should be in the hands of the community. If that is so of a new town, then it must be a principle which is applicable to the country at large.

The particular issues which Sir Bernard Braine had raised were almost lost in the debate. They were those of minimum disturbance, adequate compensation, and a further point which he brought into the discussion in answer to Mr Lindgren's claim that:

> in the London area, in particular, it would be absolutely impossible for town planning to take place without disturbing existing development there.

His reply was:

> It would not be; that could well be tackled by infilling and allowing people who wish to build their own homes on their own plots to do so [41].

These were issues which have haunted the discussion of the redevelopment of plotland areas in Basildon and elsewhere ever since. Chastened perhaps by the local opposition and certainly by the slow pace of the development of the new towns through government financial restrictions, the actual policy of the Development Corporation was intended to be more conciliatory than the plotlanders imagined. The town was planned to start from a nucleus in the sparsely populated and dispersed village of Basildon itself, expanding eastwards and westwards to incorporate Laindon and Pitsea. The first General Manager of the Development Corporation, Brigadier W.G. Knapton, set out his policy thus in 1953:

> Any solution which includes the wholesale demolition of substandard dwellings cannot be contemplated. However inadequate,

every shack is somebody's home, probably purchased freehold with hard-earned savings, and as often as not the area of land within the curtilage is sufficient to provide garden produce and to house poultry, rabbits and even pigs. To evict the occupier and to re-accommodate him and his family in a corporation house, even on such favourable terms as the Act may permit, will probably cause not only hardship, but bitter feelings. The old must be absorbed into the new with the least detriment to the former and the greatest advantage to the latter [42].

What the Minister had declared to be impossible, the Brigadier had found to be the only humane policy. His successor for many years, Mr Charles Boniface, adopted the same attitude. He remarked that 'the planners' task here is like a jigsaw puzzle, with the new fitting into the old instead of being superimposed upon and obliterating it' [43]. To prove that this was the Development Corporation's approach, visitors to the new town were shown examples of little bungalows in amongst the new development which had been spared until the old widow died, or accepted a place in a new old people's home.

The policy of starting the development of the new town in the empty centre and spreading slowly over the years into the more populous plotland sites of Pitsea and Laindon, seemed both sensible and humane just because in many cases it allowed the original settlers, with the greatest actual and emotional investment in their homes, to live out their lives without disturbance. It was in any case virtually imposed on the Development Corporation by the Government's Housing Accommodation Direction in the early years, telling public authorities not to demolish unnecessarily.

But this policy also brought a great deal of uncertainty in its trail. 'Basildon was built on heartbreak' is a local saying among old inhabitants, and people still speak bitterly of the lingering death of Laindon as the shops in the High Street gradually closed down, one by one. Imagine the feelings of one of those transplanted East Londoners, on receiving a letter from the Chief Solicitor to the Basildon Development Corporation, saying:

With further reference to your letter... the reason for the Corporation wishing to purchase the above plot of land from yourself is that they have obtained authority from the Ministry of Town and Country Planning to acquire the land to enable them to co-operate with the local planning authority in carrying out a constructive planning policy by offering leases of plots of land in Retention Areas on which disappointed applicants for permission to build elsewhere are prepared to erect their houses...
I shall be glad, therefore, if you will consider this letter and let me know your decision as soon as possible as, otherwise, I am afraid it must be assumed you are an unwilling seller and the Corporation will have to consider whether they should exercise their compulsory powers of purchase [44].

It was possible for plot-owners to operate a kind of compulsory purchase order in reverse: they had the right to serve a 'Purchase Notice' on the Corporation, obliging it to buy the property. In the 1960s many owners did this. Further bitterness was caused by the existence of unscrupulous middlemen who would say to an old resident, 'Look, the Corporation is going to take you over sooner or later. Why not sell to me for £X hundred cash?' Having acquired the property through a nominee, they would then serve a purchase notice on the Corporation, demanding, and sometimes getting a great deal more.

Were the terms of compensation fair? They were, of course, fixed by Act of Parliament, determined by the District Valuer, and differed at various times. Under the 1947 Act, owners would get their house bought at existing use value, and their land, if it was extensive, bought at its agricultural value. After 1951 they were compensated at market value, and there were various concessions like disturbance allowances, rehousing at concessionary rents, or the provision of alternative sites. The Development Corporation had very little discretionary leeway, and whether the procedures were perceived to be fair or not depended upon the circumstances of individual plot-holders. Some have an implacable sense of grievance, while to other old people, after years of struggling to maintain a place of their own, it was marvellous to have a new flat and not to be obliged to trudge to the shops, the post office or the doctor's surgery, up muddy, unmade roads.

Not all the old residents felt aggrieved by their treatment by the Development Corporation. Mr E.C. Charrison, who had been elected to the local council as a Residents Protection Association councillor, sold his smallholding at Pitsea and moved to Nevenden. 'I was astounded by the way I was treated and I now have nothing but the greatest admiration for Basildon Development Corporation' he told the local newspaper, which commented, 'In a matter of hours the very people who he had previously denounced as "legalised robbers" and "snatchers of poor men's freeholds" had proved themselves to be his best friends' [45].

By the 1980s the Basildon Development Corporation is on the verge of extinction, its task completed. It has fulfilled its function in promoting the growth of a vast, populous and industrially successful new town, as effective as any other in the country, and a financial asset to the Treasury which originally provided the funds for its development. There is little visible evidence left of its plotland origins.

It has even provided one of the few examples of plotland sites reverting to 'natural' woodland. In 1950 it was possible for a naturalist to write:

Wander further afield and enjoy scenes of attractive beauty, but avoid Laindon! There was never a town like it! It is interesting, if despairing, to compare lovely One Tree Hill with the hideous scar that man has inflicted on the countryside which, not long since, was equally lovely [46].

But, thirty years later, Oliver Rackham, the authority on ancient woodlands, was able to cite this particular place as an example of the way in which nature re-asserts itself:

> The three-quarters-abandoned town of Langdon Hill demonstrates how secondary woodland has often arisen in the past. The town grew up on what had been farmland divided by mixed hedges with pollard oaks; there were small ancient woods chiefly of hornbeam and hornbeam-ash with some cherry and elm. Hedges and woods survived amid the houses and plots. The town began to 'tumble down to woodland' early in this century; by World War II the woodland was sufficiently advanced to swallow up a crashed Dornier, not seen again until it was recently recovered by aeronautical archaeologists. The houses disappeared remarkably completely, leaving only the telegraph poles still projecting from the trees...
> Plotlands are of value for wildlife because of their varied structure and freedom from agricultural pressures; they are especially noted for badgers. The local authorities have recently included large areas in country parks, and much of Langdon Hills is now a nature reserve [47].

Time changes our perception of the environment, including the plotlands. As the last vestiges of Basildon's origins disappeared, there were voices among the Corporation's board members and its staff arguing that there should be some kind of plotland museum to commemorate the original reasons for the town's existence. Should not one of the original plotland dwellings be preserved for this purpose?

At a meeting of the Development Corporation in 1979, Derek Senior proposed to his fellow board members that an area should be set aside at Dunton, the last corner of the New Town's territory, for do-it-yourself smallholdings, where the building regulations and planning controls could be waived, experimentally, just to see what happened. He was heard in astonished silence, and in the following year the Secretary of State did not reappoint him.

But in 1983, the Corporation, with the assistance of the Countryside Commission, made Dunton an 'informal recreation area', a place for picnics and rambles, *and* a plotland museum. A few of the old bungalows remain in the overgrown gridiron of grassy tracks, and one of them, 'The Haven' in Third Avenue, has been restored to its 1930s state. A waymarked trail takes the visitor on a mile-long plotland walk, while the Corporation has published *A Plotland Album: the story of the Dunton Hills Community*, full of evocative stories and snapshots from the families who lived there, and telling the story of their home-made landscape [48].

Thus in thirty-five years, the Basildon plotlands have shifted in the official perception from the status of a rural slum to that of a distinctive and unique part of our environmental inheritance.

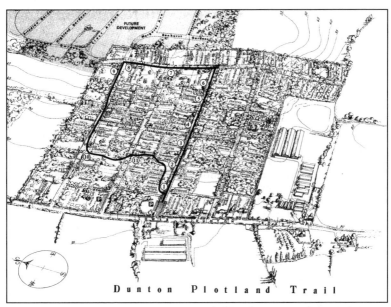

Dunton Hills: plotland trail and house retained as a plotland museum. (Photo courtesy of Basildon Development Corporation)

SOUTH ESSEX: BEYOND THE NEW TOWN

Slowly the anarchic sprawl will be tidied into a new order, and the character of the district will be entirely changed...

(A Land that has Fared Ill, *Manchester Guardian*, 11 November 1950)

The plotland 'problem' was solved in the Pitsea/Laindon area by the designation of Basildon New Town. But there remained 'vast tracts', as the County Council called them, of plotland in the area bounded by Billericay, Wickford and the river Crouch in the north, Dunton and Laindon in the west, and Rochford and Southend in the east. They extended in pockets, even beyond this area. The planner Tom Clarke divides them into three types; the 'pioneer layout' with a gridiron plan, like those on The Land Company's estates close to Pitsea and Laindon stations in what became the new town's territory; the 'cul-de-sac', where one field had been developed with plots on either side of a grass track; and the 'single' type where one or two plots had been carved out of the edge of a field [49].

Abercrombie recommended in 1944 that in each of the existing nuclei Billericay, Laindon, Pitsea and Wickford the attempt should be made 'to concentrate and to a certain extent, to urbanise' the central areas:

This implies the complete cessation of all building outside a tightly drawn line round the central core, the acquisition by the Housing Authority of the vacant plots within this line, and the erection by them of substantially-built houses on a proportion of these sites.

He stressed that it was not desirable to place a total prohibition on the erection of temporary buildings, properly licensed, and thought that there was room for collaboration between the section of the building trade concerned with portable buildings and architects to produce structures which were acceptable to both the dwellers and the planning authorities, and that:

In order to obtain as full a concentration of dwellings as possible within the central core it will be necessary for those dwellings which lie outside the built-up line to be given a limited life, at the end of which time the owners would be offered a vacant plot (or if they preferred it they could buy or rent one of the existing dwellings) within the central area... The land freed from buildings would be returned to agriculture [50].

A year after Abercrombie's plan was published, the journalist Stanley Baron characterised the area as 'The forgotten, unknown city of Britain', with a total population of 40,000 people of whom a quarter left it every day for work. This was, he said, the equivalent of towns like Rugby, Shrewsbury, Dover or Perth, but the forgotten city of South

212

Essex had just one private maternity home with two beds, one bowling green, one recreation ground, one municipal football pitch, no tennis courts, swimming pool or laundry [51]. The local authority officers told him that if they were to make up only 53 miles of the 200 miles of unmade roads and supplied services, it would increase the rates by 7s/6d in the pound; just as a few years later, in presenting to the Minister the case for designation of the Basildon area as a New Town, they estimated that to install basic services would involve doubling the rates and would take up to fifty years.

As required by the 1947 Town and Country Planning Act, Essex County Council submitted its Written Statement for the County Development Plan in 1951, and it was finally approved in 1957. Many plotland areas were designated within the Green Belt in this document, and others outside Basildon became 'Areas without Notation'. The Green Belt policy sought, in effect, to put Abercrombie's recommendations into practice, by putting stringent restrictions on the growth of existing settlements, while in the 'areas without notation' the intention was that no development should be permitted if detrimental to agriculture or to the amenity of the surroundings, or would cause pollution or a high cost in the provision of services [52].

As pressure for new housing in South Essex increased in the late 1950s, the County Council amended its Development Plan to make virtually all the plotland areas subject to Green Belt restrictions. This policy was re-affirmed in 1964 and in 1976 with some minor relaxations on the fringes of some existing settlements, and the County's Structure Plan of 1979 added the Southend Green Belt to the restricted area.

The Minister's approval given to the Development Plan in 1957 was provisional, depending upon the County Council studying the plotlands to see what could be done to meet the housing needs of people moving from metropolitan Essex by making greater use of these areas. The allocation of land for residential development in excess of local needs in the Town Maps prepared for Braintree, Colchester, Chelmsford and Witham was also made provisional until the survey of the plotlands was completed. The Ministry of Agriculture's Land Commissioner for Essex and Hertfordshire also urged the County Council to consider 2,829 acres of land (not all of it plotland) which, because of its poor agricultural quality, was from *his* Ministry's point of view more suitable than the areas earmarked for 'town development' on the fringes of the existing towns.

Accordingly the County Council conducted a survey in 1957-58, which was modified and updated in 1964. The questions for which it sought answers were:

1. Which of the plotland areas in South East Essex are physically capable of economical development? What acreages of land are suitable and how many dwellings could be provided on them?
2. If there are any areas physically capable of economical development (a) What difficulties are there in the way of development of the land? (b) What planning factors are there to

213

support or oppose its development?
3. If any of the plotlands are not suitable for further development, to what beneficial use can they be put? What public agency might be necessary to secure such use?

The Council surveyed 5,222 acres in seven parts of South-East Essex, which included land of poor agricultural quality as well as plotlands. They found 27.5 miles of fully-made roads, mostly ancient roads on the peripheries of the areas surveyed, and 54.5 miles of grass track and partly-made roads. Mains water was provided to almost every dwelling, gas and electricity were fairly common, but main drainage was rare. There were, in the area surveyed, 3,257 permanent houses, 808 substandard dwellings, 706 shacks, and 238 caravans (203 of them on one site) [53].

The County Planning Adviser, Leslie Leaver, stressed two aspects of plotland life in his report, the very low densities and the hardships experienced through the lack of properly made roads:

> The lack of a decent carriageway means that most of the dwellers in these areas are without the normal services taken for granted by other people; coal and coke can be delivered only in the summertime, when the clay soil usually dries hard, and even then it may be deposited at the end of the nearest summer-hard track and has to be carted laboriously in a barrow to his home by the customer himself; refuse vehicles cannot call, so the dwellers have to dispose of their refuse as best they can; the milkman brings his vehicle as near as he can and then either delivers the milk on foot or leaves it at a convenient place from which the customer can fetch it; grocers and butchers do not call so all foodstuffs have to be fetched.
>
> Rubber knee-boots are the invariable footwear in winter and often in summer too. A common sight is an elderly, gum-booted man or woman, trudging a mile or more from the nearest store or bus with heavy paraffin can in one hand, shopping bag in the other. There is standing water and sticky mud everywhere; the old field drainage has been destroyed [54].

As to the return of plots to agriculture, the Adviser concluded that:

> Despite mechanisation, it cannot be expected that these lands will have sufficient agricultural value to repay the cost of buying up existing properties, clearing sites and shacks, and re-draining the land [55].

Apart from the miles of unmade roads, the difficulties of development, as perceived by the County Council for the plotland areas and undeveloped land, were difficulties of providing drainage, difficulty of access and the numerous ownerships of small plots.

The plotland dwellers themselves felt alarmed at the sight of Council surveyors, with clipboards, roaming up the empty lanes, something which they felt could bring nothing but trouble. For daring to live at

Laindon: Old Tom's bus which served plotlanders from 1921 onwards. (Photo courtesy of Mr G. Ward)

uneconomically low densities they saw themselves becoming a land bank, to be drawn upon at will.

One 'self-appointed' spokesman for the plotland interest pointed out that if they lived in more affluent houses, no-one would have questioned their right to live undisturbed:

> If they were worried about our roads and the fact that we couldn't afford road charges, it wouldn't make much of a dent in the council budget, just to put down a concrete strip, and there wouldn't be any reason why it should be built to the usual council standard.

Once a road surface of some kind was there, he was sure that the tradesman would come. 'In the old days there was never a problem about buses. You could buy everything you could possibly want at Wickford or Laindon and bring it back on the bus' [56].

Historically, our informant was right. There *were* better bus services, and in spite of the slow death of the shops which used to serve these plotlanders, even the Basildon Development Corporation's investigation in 1951 had reported that the shopping areas of Pitsea and Laindon had 270 shops, which, however poor their construction and appearance, were 'flourishing and stock a large range of goods for regular needs' [57].

The late-1960s and early-1970s saw changes in the planning system and in the structure of local government, as well as new threats of pressures for redevelopment, all of which affected the plotland dwellers. Central government produced its Strategic Plan for the South East, which identified South Essex as one of five major growth areas which would have a population of about a million people by the end of the century.

215

From the plotlanders' point of view these changes meant a different set of district council officers with whom to negotiate for improvements, extensions or rebuilding, as the local authorities containing plotland areas had been consolidated as Brentwood, Basildon, Thurrock, Castle Point and Rochford.

The County Council, in preparing the new Structure Plan which was to replace its Development Plan in setting out broad policy, embarked in 1975 on a further land-use survey of the plotland areas. The policy that had emerged from the Review of the Development Plan had been that certain plotland areas were allocated for residential development, usually by the 'thickening up' of existing housing areas, while the remainder were included in the extensions to the Metropolitan Green Belt, where it was intended that the land should gradually return to agricultural use.

The 1975 survey showed that the general plotland land-use situation in South Essex was that:

> Overall, the most extensive land use category was 'Agriculture' with 30 per cent, closely followed by 'Smallholdings etc' with 27 per cent of the total. The former category occupied over half the area surveyed within Thurrock, but only 4 per cent in Castle Point... Residential use covered 13 per cent overall, this proportion being quite consistent between the Districts... Overall, dwelling density is about one per hectare (though these are not, of course, evenly distributed). Basildon District contains the largest number of both dwellings and residential caravans, followed by Rochford District. Overall, 86 per cent of dwellings were of 'permanent' construction (i.e. not wooden construction), 15 per cent were judged to be in poor condition, and 90 per cent of dwellings and residential caravans were occupied. Generally, dwellings in the surveyed areas of Thurrock and Castle Point were in better condition than those elsewhere, Rochford District having the highest proportion in poor condition. If it is assumed that the average occupancy rate is three per dwelling, the population of the surveyed areas may be about 6,000; given the small size of most of the dwellings, however, it is likely to be less than this [58].

Surveying the land and buildings of these 6,000 people has been a labour-intensive industry for the public authority staffs, but no social survey has been conducted to ascertain the priorities and aspirations of the plotlanders themselves. One District Council planner, privately and in his own time, has attempted to fill this gap. In 1979, John Whittam conducted sixty-nine interviews, supplemented by postal questionnaires, in representative 'residential' and 'smallholding' plotland areas in several of the South Essex districts [59]. He found that most plotlanders were old (over half were over sixty and nearly two-fifths between thirty and sixty), had low incomes (the majority earned less than £40 a week in 1979 and only one-sixth over £80) and were either retired or unskilled ('90 per cent of those working could be classified in the classic "blue collar" worker mould and only 10 per cent in the white collar worker category. It is also interesting to note that of those retired inhabitants most held "blue collar" jobs during their working lives').

Half of those interviewed in Mr Whittam's sample had plots of less than a quarter acre, and almost three-quarters had less than one acre. Of those who worked full-time away from home, one-quarter worked in their own District and another third outside the District but within South Essex. Nearly half travelled to work by car. Over 90 per cent were owner-occupiers, and about three-quarters of them had lived there for at least seven years or more.

On the question of accommodation standards and basic amenities, Whittam reports that:

> About two-thirds had at least one living room and about a third had two. Of the remainder, three had three living rooms and one had four. Just over half had two separate bedrooms and a quarter had three or more. They all had a separate kitchen and nearly two-thirds had a separate bathroom. Nearly two-thirds had an inside toilet together with one-tenth who had an inside chemical closet... It is possible that the interviewees lacked more rooms, amenities and services than stated. It is probable that they were not prepared to admit the true extent of this for fear of stigmatisation.

Furthermore, the majority:

> stated that they had no intention of making any physical improvements to their dwellings or plots. However, one suspects from such a negative response that this may indicate suspicion and a reluctance to tell for fear of sanctions and reprisals should the local authority get to know. This could be significant, bearing in mind the history of restrictive planning policies in plotland areas.

Of those who did plan or desire improvements, intentions or desires ranged from the provision of basic amenities to complete renovation or rebuilding. In discussing the constraints on their ability to carry out these improvements, the two most common reasons mentioned were lack of finance and personal physical handicap, including age.

By far the most common reason given for moving to their plotland homes that respondents gave to Whittam was a preference for the specific area and the 'frontier' plotland way of life, and by far the most common answers, when asked what they most liked about their way of life and location, related to their feelings for 'the countryside' and 'tranquillity'. However, asked about their perceived disadvantages of plotland life, apart from the 20 per cent who found no disadvantages, 'the major complaint related to the lack of amenities and services including lack of public phone boxes and inadequate post boxes. The next major complaint concerned the unmade roads'. Nevertheless, two-thirds of respondents 'seemed happy with their lot and expressed the wish to stay for the rest of their lives'. The number who would wish to move if the surrounding area were completely redeveloped was 67 per cent, but only 10 per cent would wish to move if the surrounding area was developed at low density.

Whittam sees the main planning issues on which his survey throws light, as those relating to densities. The obvious example is the non-conforming-use aspect of all development in plotlands, and in particular the non-agricultural use of land by the section of the plotland population who work at home in such enterprises as livery stables or car breaking, which are under 'the possible threat of enforcement action'. He notes that:

> Such areas are also used by small entrepreneurs, not necessarily of the indigenous plotland population, who could not otherwise afford to make their livings as they wish. Industrial estate site rents and rates are too expensive for the small profit margins of this type of enterprise... Many provide useful services for nearby urban settlements, such as kennels, catteries and other 'pariah' uses not easily accommodated elsewhere and definitely not wanted in urban locations by the urban population. The planning issue is related to whether this comprises a case for low density mixed uses [60].

He draws a similar conclusion from the plotlander's own evaluation of their way of life:

> The survey reveals that any form of high density development in these areas would destroy their intrinsic value to the incumbents, and, in the long term, their worth to society itself. Anything other than low density development, say two per acre, would crush the plotlanders' way of life and induce them to move. Therefore the final set of issues relates to the unique life style and motivation of the plotlander and whether it should be preserved and expanded for future like-minded people. The plotlander appreciates the low density, tranquillity, privacy and freedom. He sees living on the fringe of urbanity as having the best of both worlds... He does not see his home as semi-rural/semi-urban as planners do. He is therefore happier with his lot than those with different aspirations and expectations. The justification for plotlands may lie in this different, more positive interpretation of urban fringe development [61].

Neither Essex County Council nor the District Councils have taken this view. The County Council, in the Written Statement of its Structure Plan, notes that some of the plotland areas 'have matured into relatively pleasant low density residential areas, or provide opportunities for smallholding-type activities or have nature conservation value' [62], but urges that 'the case for changing policy in a plotland area does not depend

218

on local considerations only, the need must be proved at the County strategic level' [63]. It also declared that 'the remaining plotland areas will be the subject of a detailed study by the County and District Councils which may require substantial alteration to this Plan. In the meantime, it is essential that Green Belt and Rural Area policies are applied to these areas to prevent further sporadic development' [64]. This affirmation was subsequently modified as a result of representations from the District Councils by the addition of the words 'other than within those areas which have been defined in formal local plans where limited exceptions have been agreed' [65].

Behind this chink in the armour of a blanket definition of policy lie not only the inevitable antagonisms which arise from a two-tier planning system, but the experience of the District Councils in trying to enforce a rigid adherence to the Green Belt dogma with a gradually diminishing support from central government in the minority of cases where a plotlander has appealed against a planning decision. The District Councillors and their officers oppose the suggestion of a joint detailed study because they claim that the forging of a policy for plotland areas is a local matter for individual planning authorities. They observe that the County Council's elaborate surveys of the plotlands in 1959 and 1975 have not resulted in new or more flexible policy alternatives for the local councils with the invidious duty of enforcing decisions.

Initially, in matters of development control, all the South Essex districts operated strictly in accordance with the Green Belt policy. Some have been more successful than others in this respect. Brentwood District Council, applying both a strict Green Belt policy and an informal policy of restrictions on extensions to existing houses, claimed that before 1975 only 10 per cent of appeals have been allowed and that since then not one has been lost [66]. Rochford and Castle Point District Councils have also attempted to follow a rigorous adherence to the Green Belt, but in one area of Rochford an appeal was allowed by the Department of the Environment Inspector in 1979 on the grounds that 'the aims of Green Belt policy would not be affected adversely by the rebuilding, but that it should not create a precedent' [67].

But of course, every rebuilding, every extension, every re-roofing and even every re-cladding of an old timber and asbestos army hut with a skin of rustic brickwork, makes it less and less likely that a plotland site will revert to agricultural or 'passive recreation' use. With or without the consent of the local authorities, the improvements that dwellers make to their houses legitimise the plotland settlements. The task of the council Enforcement Officers (usually ex-policemen) is not an enviable one, and is a world away from decisions made in remote offices about the policies which envisage a society where the public interest somehow precludes the slogan which has been repeated to us *ad nauseam* that an Englishman's home is his castle.

In response to pressures from below, which were upheld from above, Thurrock Borough Council has, since 1975, applied a policy in selected areas, of allowing a 'one for one replacement' of plotland houses, and a similar policy has more recently been adopted by Basildon District

Laindon/Pitsea: mixed legacy of plotland development.

Council as a result of the growing number of planning appeals allowed by the Department of the Environment which has shown an increasing tendency to take a benign view of the 'special circumstances' of plotland houses.

Generally, outside Basildon New Town, the South Essex plotlands, apart from being a graveyard for rigid planning policies, represent every stage of plotland evolution. There are places where they have totally disappeared in redevelopment, and their former inhabitants hint at an unholy alliance between the local authorities and speculative housing developers who managed to acquire the sites. There are places on the very fringe of the new town, which have been frozen in the situation of thirty years ago, thanks to refusal of permission to improve. There are places where, behind high walls or barbed wire, business enterprises ignore the Enforcement Officers who do not care to inquire too closely what is going on. And there are places, like Hullbridge, where a relatively benign approach by the local authorities has allowed the unofficial township to evolve into suburban development indistinguishable, except for those who can read the evidence on the ground, from any other settlement in outer metropolitan Essex.

SOUTH WOODHAM FERRERS

It was a strange, remote, dishevelled and haphazard place, or rather non-place — a sort of unplanned shanty arcadia in 1972. Essex decided to pull the whole thing together.

(David Pearce in *Building Design*, 13 January 1978)

South Woodham Ferrers was, when I visited it in 1974, one of the best surviving examples of the owner-built communities of Essex. Nearly all the houses, even the holiday homes, were in excellent condition, and the residents I spoke to were well pleased with their surroundings.

(Patrick Keiller in *Building Design*, 27 January 1978)

In the Southend area, the plotland belt of South Essex extends through Rochford, Ashingdon, Hockley and Hullbridge to the south bank of the estuary of the River Crouch. On the north bank of the Crouch a branch line leaves the London to Southend railway at Wickford and runs parallel with the river through Battlesbridge, Woodham Ferrers, Fambridge and Althorne, to Burnham-on-Crouch and Southminster.
South Woodham Ferrers, a hitherto inaccessible place between Fenn Creek and Clementsgreen Creek, meandering into the river, was a farming and pasture settlement which fell out of agricultural viability at the end of the last century. Its plotland development began in 1893 when the Champions estate was sold at auction by order of the mortgagees for £4,500, which amounted to about £8/10s an acre. It was divided into plots by estate agents whose names occur in the history of other plotland sites: H.J.E. Brake of Farnborough, Hants, and H.W. Brake of Walderslade, Kent. They offered one acre plots as smallholdings at £20, and residential plots, 20 feet by 200 feet at £10, which could be paid on the installment system. Next, in 1898, the land

of Eyotts Farm was auctioned by Protheroe and Morris at prices ranging between £5 and £12/10s for a residential plot. Cheap railway tickets were available and a free luncheon provided. There were further sales in the following three years.

The Champions estate was described as:

admirably adapted for Fruit Growing and Market Gardening... To those with small means who are desirous to live a retired country life this Estate also offers exceptional opportunities, being situated in one of the healthiest and most picturesque parts of Essex, where shooting, fishing, boating and other sport is always obtainable; and the easy terms by which the purchase money may be paid makes it little more than a rent, and in a few years any one is enabled to become his own landlord [68].

In spite of these glowing possibilities, and conditions of sale which imposed a minimum value of £150 for houses and specified that no hut, tent, caravan, or house on wheels was to be erected without consent (conditions which were not in fact enforced) it was not city men and professional growers who bought the sites. John Fisher, a town planner who has traced the early development of Woodham Ferrers, remarks that:

The majority of those people who succeeded in purchasing plots in the area were from the poorer areas of East London; most had been brought up in a climate of social deprivation and all of them had the common desire to break away from it all by any means available... When the handbills for the South Woodham sales appeared in the streets, shops and pubs of the East End, they appeared to offer salvation to the many who had been downtrodden and depressed to their wits' end over many years [69].

He notes that many of the problems of deprivation followed the new owners to their new lives in the country, particularly that of finding work:

Men and their families moving into the area from London found the local employment situation virtually a 'closed shop' and there was sometimes little love lost between the local inhabitants and the 'townie newcomers', over who lived and worked where, and at what. The plot purchasers were forced to make the best they could of their situation, but it is doubtful if many easily adapted themselves to self-employment, an ability more readily found among the country dwellers [70].

In spite of the restrictive clauses, it is not surprising that sheds and shanties sprang up on the estate, and in 1905 the Chelmsford Rural District Council summonsed several occupiers for failing to comply with the building bye-laws and the Public Health Act.

During the First World War, as in the Second, unoccupied land was appropriated and eventually compulsorily purchased by the Ministry of Agriculture, and during the 1920s there was a slight boom in building. Some returning disabled and mutilated ex-servicemen settled in the area, seeking it precisely because of its seclusion and isolation, and the cheapness of sites. There were further cases of building-owners being summonsed by the local authorities for non-compliance with the building bye-laws. In 1924, a London firm, Country Homes Ltd, was summonsed for failing to deposit plans with the Council, failing to obtain a certificate of fitness for habitation and failing to obtain certificates of water supply. The company claimed that the houses were simply for 'weekend Londoners', costing about £150 each.

A South Woodham Smallholders and Social Society was founded in 1923 with 137 members to trade on behalf of growers and to provide a building, opened in 1929, which members 'had patiently built for themselves and which was to serve as a village and parish hall for years to come'.

The years following the Second World War brought new purchasers for some of the original dwellings, new self-builders, and eventually, an interest in the area from speculative builders. In the 1960s a number of planning applications for housebuilding in the area closest to the station were refused, and subsequently allowed on appeal to central government.

Then in 1972 the Department of the Environment issued a circular urging local planning and housing authorities to release more land for private house-building, mainly in the South East, where local authorities were expected to 'orientate their planning policies for growth areas according to the Strategic Plan for the region' [71]. The Department noted that:

A special problem arises in South East Essex where the Secretary of State has already announced his intention to designate, under the New Towns Act, a substantial area of development in connection with the Maplin Project [72].

The government made available £80 million which was allocated to Essex County Council 'and enabled the council to embark upon the first almost entirely owner-occupied new community sponsored by a public authority' [73]. Essex County Council had already 'agreed proposals to undertake the rehabilitation of the area', and after a public inquiry in 1973, the Secretary of State authorised a Comprehensive Development Area and the necessary Compulsory Purchase Order.

The Council set out its objectives as:

1. To provide and service land for building homes for about 13,800 people with all necessary public services.
2. To build an appropriate Town Centre with community buildings.
3. To create employment opportunity for those unable or unwilling to travel, and to relocate existing small industries from the surrounding area.

4. To implement the County Council's Design Guide and establish a high quality of housing environment with well developed recreation space.
5. To cater for the needs of all sectors of the house building industry including large developers, local builders, and those seeking a single plot for house erection [74].

The threat of compulsory purchase, needless to say, alarmed the plotland residents. In the early stages of the new development the then Chairman of Essex County Council's Planning Committee declared that no one would suffer hardship as a result of the County Council's plans. He admitted that hardship could arise but declared that if it did, the Council would 'step in' [75]. 'Alderman Curtis defined hardship as occurring where the terms of the compensation were less than the sums required to buy a comparable property' [76]. But in the event, this was precisely the kind of hardship that was felt:

So many of those involved are elderly. The difficulties and distress of anyone, whatever their age, who are forced to move from their houses, is great, but that distress is compounded and made more heart-rending in that many of these people have lived for years in homes which they may well have built for themselves... [77].

The Chairman of the Planning Committee (by this time Councillor Geoffrey Waterer) replied to protesters that:

I would again reiterate the point which the Council has been obliged to make frequently and that is that financial compensation may only be paid on the basis of the current market value of the property being acquired and not of some alternative property which the vendor may be proposing to purchase. In those cases where problems of re-accommodation arise for example, where the compensation is unlikely to be sufficient to enable the displaced owner to acquire suitable alternative accommodation the duty rests with the Chelmsford Borough Council, as local housing authority, to secure that he is provided with such other accommodation [78].

A local district councillor, John Cox, complained that 'the officers of the county council have succeeded in pulling the wool over the eyes of the councillors who just don't know what is going on here' [79], and a 'Vigilante' group issued leaflets ridiculing the sums offered by the County Council's valuation officers to residents whose houses were to be purchased, and claiming that:

Meanwhile they are being 'encouraged' to leave the homes they have lived in for many years by acts of vandalism the council have been unable to control. Water supply pipes have been

224

smashed. Demolition contractors have called to judge how their homes can best be destroyed. Former neighbours' windows have been smashed as soon as they leave, which encourages further vandalism. Roads which have served Fen residents for many years have become almost impassable overnight. Where are they going? Essex County Council doesn't seem too worried about that. It's not exactly enhancing the quality of life for all residents in the 'Riverside Country Town' of which the County Council boasts. Is the good life being created for some at the expense of others? [80].

This polarity had been expressed five years earlier in local newspaper interviews under the heading ' "Foundations of Heart-break": That's What the New Town Will Be Built On' [81], and the last gasp of local opposition was a complaint in 1978 to the Local Government Ombudsman that 'the Council used unfair methods to persuade the complainants to accept less compensation than they were entitled to and to leave the area quickly'. The Ombudsman reported that 'the four charges of maladministration made against council officers were not proved' [82].

The County Council's officers point out publicly that only four cases of the purchase of sites out of over 200 were the subject of complaint, and privately that the Council's hands were tied by the District Valuer's valuation. 'If we had had the latitude of a private purchaser to pay a few thousand over the valuation, everyone would have been happy and the distress would never have arisen.'

Critics of the new South Woodham Ferrers describe it as a 'seductive architectural vision of fake peasant life' [83], but by the utilitarian test of catering for the greatest happiness of the greatest number, the County Council's intervention can be readily justified. As always, the private visions of the relatively poor were sacrificed for those of the relatively affluent.

HAVERING PARK

I went to school in Forest Gate, and on Monday mornings my teacher asked me to tell the class about the birds and flowers I had seen in the country.

(Childhood recollections of a plotholder, whose parents owned a weekend plot in Clockhouse Lane.)

Makeshift plotland developments on the very fringe of Greater London, abutting more conventional suburban estates, were always likely to be short-lived. Their future was threatened by the emergence of policies, seeking to remove what are commonly regarded as unneighbourly settlements either by the outward extension of London or, alternatively, to tidy up the inner edge of the Green Belt by clearance and restoration of the land to an open use. At Selsdon Vale, near Croydon, where a

225

makeshift colony was well-established in the 1930s it was the former process which prevailed, with its redevelopment as a private housing estate. In contrast, at Havering Park to the north-east of London full-scale clearance has been the order of the day, and the land is now a Country Park [84]. While there have been many cases of plotlands being 'upgraded' to more conventional patterns of housing development, the example of clearance and reversion of the land to an open use is exceptional. There have been few local authorities with plotlands in their area which have not cherished the thought of wholesale clearance, yet experience has shown that this has proved to be a task beyond the ability (or in the end the desire) of most to carry through.

The pattern of early settlement of this area by Londoners in search of a break, usually from the East End, is one that is familiar enough. From the late 1920s onwards, agricultural land in the district (like the Havering Park and Pyrgo estates) was sold off with a view to development. In competition with sites in Romford, Gidea Park and Harold Wood (closer to the railway stations on the Liverpool Street line), some of the ambitions of developers were checked, so that large tracts at Havering Park and nearby Noak Hill and Stapleford Abbotts were subdivided instead into large plots for smallholdings and weekend use. As such, they were immensely popular, being close to the East End and within a couple of miles of a railway station. From stations such as Forest Gate, Seven Kings and Ilford plotlanders made their way to Romford, and then by bus up to Havering Park; and those who were lucky enough came out on their own motor cycles with children and building materials packed into sidecars.

Though only a stone's throw from London, a weekend at Havering Park was another world. Mrs Biggs is one of those who fondly recalls a childhood spent in this way [85]. In 1928 her father, a steel erector by trade, bought an acre and a quarter for £60, repayable in instalments that were taken to an estate agents' shed on the corner of Clockhouse Lane. First, a single-roomed hut was built and then, over a period, it was gradually extended into an attractive three-roomed bungalow — mainly of timber, with a corrugated iron roof. Relatives often came down for weekends and holidays, sleeping in a bell tent that was kept for the purpose. Water had to be fetched from a pump in the nearby village of Havering-atte-Bower, until the family installed a water butt with charcoal filter. Flowers, soft fruits and ornamental trees were grown on the spacious plot, and in school Mrs Biggs was often called upon to stand up and tell her classmates about 'Nature'.

They were above all temporary retreats from life in a smoky, urban environment and there is little evidence of permanent occupation in the early years. Prices remained low throughout the 1930s, and the following advertisement for a plot in nearby Stapleford Abbots is typical:

> Ideal Week-End Holidays — Plot 60ft. by 78 ft., freehold; fenced; Hut 6ft x 5ft., tent (sleep 2); lav.; £30 cash or terms; Beautiful scenery [86].

*Havering Park: the
Biggs family on their
plot in the 1930s.
(Photos courtesy of
Mrs Biggs)*

227

By the end of the Second World War, though, things were changing. As happened in South Essex, many plotholders had sent their families into the country during the war and some stayed on permanently. And in spite of restrictions on rebuilding imposed by the new Green Belt policy, small businesses often managed to gain a foothold. Some claimed existing use rights, while others introduced a further range of urban fringe uses like stables, breeding kennels, scrapyards and storage areas all of which grew over the years. Meanwhile new housing development in Collier Row brought the edge of Greater London to the very boundaries of Havering Park.

Though in the Green Belt the former Arcadian retreat increasingly took on a mixed appearance, with a characteristic lack of services, unmade roads and temporary buildings. In consequence, Essex County Council took a decision in 1961 to clear the area and when the Greater London Council assumed responsibility in 1965 it was agreed to continue this policy. Within four years a survey was initiated to prepare the way for compulsory purchase and, subsequently, in 1971 a Public Inquiry was held to hear the various arguments for and against acquisition [87]. In principle, the proposal was to buy the individual plots and to replan the whole area of Havering Park (some 160 acres) as a regional Country Park. Beyond the immediate details of the case, the Inquiry brought to the surface more general considerations surrounding plotlands; typified in the form of individual rights of property expressed by the plotholders, opposed to the full bureaucratic weight of the Greater London Council.

Supported by the London Borough of Havering, the Greater London Council painted a picture of squalid conditions and, significantly, even resorted to the 1875 Public Health Act to legitimise their desire to clear the area. The Inquiry was told that most of the site was covered by trees and scrub, with a sporadic pattern of building on the long, narrow plots. Much of the land was disused and owners could not be traced, but some of the plots were still in use as smallholdings. Buildings were often of temporary materials and little more than shacks; all lacked main sewerage and most were still lit by oil lamps. In bad weather roads were said to be virtually impassable, and a rash of fly-tipping, scrap yards and abandoned vehicles added to the shoddy appearance of the area. The local authorities argued that permanent improvement would not be permitted because of Green Belt policy, and that the land could be more fully used as public open space rather than for private recreation. It was, in essence, another episode in a continuing saga of public as opposed to private interests.

The plotholders responded in kind. They claimed that, plot by plot, the land was already in recreational use and that the case for more public open space in that part of London was unproven. Because of the use of the 1875 Public Health Act as a source of authority for clearance, it was questioned whether the scheme was really about recreation at all. The Greater London Council had referred to their Arcadia as a 'rural slum', so was it not true that the proposal for a Country Park was just a smokescreen to enable the local authority to remove them?

228

[88]. In any case if the area did have an untidy appearance whose fault was that? Individuals recounted a history of planning refusals to rebuild and of rejected schemes to provide better services, which went back to the 1930s.

Plotholders claimed that the proposal was ill-conceived, and that it would cause personal hardship. It was certainly not true to say that all properties had been allowed to fall into disrepair and decay and, in spite of local authority restrictions, some owners had affectionately maintained and improved their holdings over the years. There were some who had been there since the 1930s, and contested anyone's right to remove them from their land. Reference was even made to a charter granted by King Edward IV, giving special liberties to the citizens of Havering-atte-Bower, with the implication that it was therefore their right and duty to stave off this latest threat to their freedom.

Compulsory purchase also threatened a number of businesses, apparently thriving in the tumbledown sheds and hidden away in copses about the place. Woodcutters, greyhound trainers and horse breeders (including a registered breeder of the Arab Horse Society) emerged from relative seclusion to tell the Inquiry of their claim on the land. One owner who kept a few pigs, along with some rough grazing, argued that it would be against the national interest to end this important agricultural use.

Havering Park in its unkempt state also had an attraction for naturalists, who feared its 'special character' would disappear if its future lay in 'Pop festivals, Battersea-type Fun Fair, ski slopes or a Windsor-type Safari Park' [89]. Likewise the Essex Bee Keepers' Association (Romford Division) had used a plot for years, and pointed to a scarcity of natural pockets like this so close to London.

Perhaps the most illustrative confrontation, though, was that of Mr and Mrs Dean who over the years had accumulated a cluster of sites that, in turn, accommodated a variety of plotland uses. From an initial interest in greyhound breeding and training, Mrs Dean and her daughter had built up (with or without planning permission) a succession of isolation and boarding kennels. In turn, Mr Dean had turned his hand to vehicle breaking for scrap metal, and used land to park a fleet of storage lorries. What especially caught the eye of the Inquiry were the personal circumstances of Mr Dean's life. It transpired that he had once been a wrestler ('Man-Mountain Dean'), but a serious accident in 1963 had since confined him to his bed. In spite of his disability he had a special extension added to his bungalow, overlooking the scrap yard, so that he could continue to play an active part in his business. Mrs Dean came to the Inquiry to advocate his cause, claiming that it was the supervision of his business which sustained his will to live and that if they were forced to move the local authority would bear responsibility for his premature death. 'Stop our trade and my husband will die' were the predictable headlines in the local paper in the week of the Inquiry [90].

In the end, the case of the Greater London Council won the day, though a concession was made to Mr and Mrs Dean, permitting

229

Havering Park: with the occasional exception on the periphery, the former plotland area has been transformed into a Country Park.

continued occupation during the lives of the owners. And a small corner of the woods was set aside to allow the Romford Branch beekeepers to continue to collect their honey. Eight years later, in 1979, the first phase of restoration had been completed and Havering Country Park was formally opened.

Looking back, it is an illustrative and remarkably conclusive chapter in plotland history. For all the obvious signs, though, the dispute in the 1970s seems to evade a simple categorisation of individuals on the side of Good and Right, opposed to bureaucracy on the side of Evil and Wrong. Perhaps it would have looked that way had the confrontation taken place in the 1930s, when families came out for weekends, returning with bunches of flowers and pleasant memories on Sunday evenings to their East End homes. By the 1970s the innocence of Arcadia had been at least partially replaced in this area by opportunistic traders and others with little apparent sympathy for the original sense of the place. It is probable that at Havering Park the Greater London Council was right to claim that Londoners would benefit more from its planned public ownership than from its previous subdivision into private plots.

KENT AND SURREY

After leaving school I worked briefly in the office of the man who bought parcels of land offering promise of profit. He would go out to see them, return to the office, put his feet up on the desk, and think... He bought this particular piece of land, divided it up into plots, and I made the plan tracings. I couldn't know, of course, that I was tracing scenes of bright hopes destined to fade into grey depression and terminate in black despair. Most of the occupants spent their gratuities, exhausted their credit, and learned how quickly a land fit for heroes could become the harsh home of bankrupts.

(Harry Soan, Places I've Lived In, People I've Known, *BBC Radio 4*, 22 September 1981)

The firm that Harry Soan worked for when he was fifteen was Brake and Son of Farnborough, and the land he traced on the site plan in 1916-17 lay between the small village of Normandy and the even smaller hamlet of Wanborough, under the Hog's Back between Guildford and Aldershot on the Surrey/ Hampshire borders [91]. The Brake family was long experienced in parcelling up cheaply bought land into plots. H.J.E. Brake of Farnborough, whose son was Mr Soan's employer, was joined by H.W. Brake from Kent, in selling land at South Woodham Ferrers in the 1890s, and the firm of Brake Estates Ltd was operating similarly at Marlow Bottom in the 1920s.

Walderslade, the base of one branch of the business, was an estate of 415 acres, south of Chatham, which became a characteristic plotland

North Downs: advertisement in Dalton's Weekly, 10 April 1913.

landscape of diverse holdings, divided between the areas of three district councils. On the other side of the Roman road between Rochester and Maidstone, and now on the other side of the M2 motorway, there is a similar, smaller North Downs plotland settlement at Kit's Coty.

Pressure for housing land in the hinterland of the Medway Towns led to proposals for comprehensive redevelopment at Walderslade, firstly under the land assembly powers of the short-lived Land Commission in the late-1960s [92], and then under the Department of the Environment's provision of funds for land acquisition in the 1970s [93]. With the inevitable outraged protests from residents, Kent County Council set about assembling the land from its fragmented ownership and providing for its redevelopment and servicing.

Elsewhere, the Home Counties to the south of London especially along the North Downs were an obvious venue for aspiring Arcadians. Land was generally more expensive and less available than in Essex but, here and there, plotlands gained a distinctive foothold alongside more prestigious development. In Kent, for example, in the early 1930s Brake Estates Ltd bought about 250 acres of the vast estates of the Waterlow family in the north of the county. This is undulating woodland and scrubland a few miles south of Meopham, west of the Medway valley. Brake Estates plotted it out into innumerable small sites and advertised them for sale, on the instalment system, not for would-be smallholders, but for holiday homes. Its evolution has been similar to that of many other plotland enclaves, with a network of unmade tracks, a haphazard electricity supply, part buried and part carried by overhead cables, mains water provided mostly to metered standpipes charged to three residents' associations. Known as Culverstone Chalet Area, by the 1970s it consisted of from 300 to 350 chalets, shacks and caravans of which, the local council believed, some thirty to fifty were in either permanent or semi-permanent occupation.

Culverstone Chalet Area is in the Metropolitan Green Belt and is also within an area of Great Landscape Value, but it was designated too in the Kent Development Plan as 'an area within which weekend

232

chalets and holiday camping would be permitted on approved sites' [94]. Green Belt policy had to bow to necessity and the site has been the subject of 'weighty correspondence over the years' between central government, the County Council, the former Strood Rural District Council, its successor, Gravesham Borough Council, and various local bodies including the organisations of plot-holders.

In 1951 the County and Rural District Councils agreed that 'in an endeavour to control unauthorised development in this area, provision should be made for a holiday chalet and caravan area' in a part of the site, and half the total acreage was designated for this purpose. But in 1954:

> Strood Rural District Council suggested that the designated area be extended to cover the whole of the original estate in view of the difficulties experienced in controlling the spread of unauthorised development. The County Council agreed, but eventually the Minister of Housing and Local Government decided in 1963 not to approve the proposed extension of the area [95].

Efforts were then made to enforce development control in accordance with Green Belt and Great Landscape Value policies, but this resulted in 'numerous appeals against refusals for permanent living accommodation and for commercial purposes and against enforcement action in respect of contraventions'. One appeal to the Minister was allowed for a structure of 355 square feet, subject to conditions which restricted its use to the months between 28 February and 1 November, and the authority subsequently based its chalet policy on this appeal. Another allowed thirteen permanent dwellings and an access road on land within what had become known as the Chalet Area, though a further similar appeal was dismissed. The bewildered planning officers reported that:

> The difficulties of the Local Planning Authority in exercising planning control in the area was acknowledged by the Minister on appeals as long ago as 1963 and in the intervening period control has become increasingly difficult and time-consuming (in the effort) to effectively police the area, particularly where plots are enclosed in high fences and guard dogs are kept [96].

Faced with its inability to enforce Green Belt policy, and with the unpredictability of Ministerial decisions, the new local authority after reorganisation resolved on objectives which interpreted the spirit of these conservation policies as meaning essentially 'restricting all forms of urban-type infrastructure such as urban-type buildings, boundary walls, standard roads and services' [97]. To protect the landscape it applied Tree Preservation Orders and sought to safeguard from further development the 'mainly undeveloped dominant wooded ridges and higher land in the Chalet Area'. Chalets or caravans are now permitted only on plots facing the main track system in the valley bottoms or on infilling plots in the areas already substantially developed. They are restricted to 355 square feet in floor area, are only permitted on plots with an area of at least a quarter acre, and except in an area where a cesspool system is provided, are only allowed a kitchen sink emptying into a soakaway, and a chemical closet. 'There will be a presumption against urban types of materials including brick and block walling' [98]. New chalets or caravans are not to be occupied during the winter months.

Council officers claim unofficially that since the adoption of these policies, the Council has had a virtually 100 per cent success rate in defending its decisions on appeal [99]. People who were permanent residents before the adoption of the current policies are not affected by it, except to the extent that they cannot expect the gradual evolution of a service infrastructure. Anyone who applied to open a general store would not be likely to see his application granted. Families who have been using the place as a holiday retreat for generations claim that it is their resistance that has brought about the current policies.

Another example in Kent is that of Knatts Valley and East Hill. In 1920 a London company, Homesteads Ltd, acquired the 547-acre East Hill Estate, in the parishes of Kingsdown and Shoreham, near Otford, and offered sites at prices from £15 an acre, recommending the land for poultry raising or fruit growing, or for permanent or weekend residence [100]. This firm had a major stake in plotland development, with other sites at Chelsfield, at Marlow Bottom, at Cranmore on the Isle of Wight, and in various parts of Essex. Two years later, however, another firm, Ideal Home Estates, offered 330 acres of the East Hill Estate in the form of 156 plots. In pre-war years, the estate was occupied very patchily, with a scatter of houses and smallholdings isolated in woodland and the former pastures of Knatts Farm up an

Knatts Valley: current view of woodland retreat.

234

undulating grass track. In post-war years, the policy of the former Dartford Rural District Council was to adhere to the guidelines of the County Council's Kent Development Plan which designated the area as one of Great Landscape Value, and as part of the Kent Downs Area of Outstanding Natural Beauty. It is also within the Metropolitan Green Belt. Local planning policy was consequently to refuse development not related to agriculture or forestry, and to confine it to the recognised village nuclei where services were available. Few appeals against planning refusals were upheld by the Ministry's Inspector.

In 1980, Sevenoaks District Council conducted a survey of the area and found that of the original 156 plots, forty-eight were vacant, eight had been amalgamated with other plots, and five were used as caravan sites. The Council drafted a West Kingsdown District Plan, which commented that planning policy in the past had not in fact had the effect of 'returning these areas to a more traditional rural character', that restrictions on public expenditure made future positive action by the local authority unlikely, and that, while new development should be restricted, it would be 'unreasonable to refuse a modest extension to a structurally sound existing dwelling, provided that it is in permanent residential occupation' [101].

Surrey also had its share of plotlands, one example, on the very edge of London, being that of Selsdon Vale. Not all the ex-servicemen returning from the First World War with the ambition to make a new life as smallholders fell into the hands of speculators selling unsuitable land in inaccessible places. Several bodies of unimpeachable moral probity sought to assist the private dreams of rural resettlement. Among them was the Surrey Garden Village Trust which purchased the estate known as Selsdon Vale, a former pheasant shoot, in 1923. This land consisted of 186 acres within the then County Borough of Croydon and a further 114 acres in what was then the Coulsdon and Purley Urban District Council. Both parts of the estate are now within the London Borough of Croydon, but the significance of this accident of administrative geography is that different policies applied to the two sides of a road. One side was zoned as smallholdings, while the other was part of the Metropolitan Green Belt.

The Trust eventually sold the holdings to the occupiers, and many of them have changed hands since. Their subsequent evolution is:

> typical of other plotland areas such as Knatts Valley/East Hill, with a variety of agricultural pursuits such as the cultivation of plants, pig and poultry farming, market garden crops and the grazing of ponies, as well as car breaking and scrap metal collection. A majority of plots had dwellings on them, ranging from substantial houses to what can only be described as temporary shacks [102].

Places like Selsdon Vale, beautifully situated among well-wooded uplands, are an inevitable magnet for people looking for sites for metropolitan expansion. Croydon's Housing Committee sought to acquire 138 acres of the site for housing in 1954, and was vigorously opposed by the Surrey Garden Village Trust, acting for the plotholders, with the result that the Council resolved 'that it is the Council's policy not to use any part of this land for Corporation houses and/or flats and not to grant planning permission to any other person or authority for that purpose' [103]. In 1963 a firm of developers with an unusually good reputation for maintaining the quality of the environment, Wates Built Homes Ltd, applied for planning permission to develop 152 acres of the site for housing. Permission was refused and Messrs Wates appealed to the Minister of Housing and Local Government. At the public inquiry which followed the County Borough claimed that the area had two important functions:

1. It forms a satisfactory link between the built-up area of the Borough and the Green Belt area beyond and in this respect possesses considerable amenity value particularly as the area is heavily wooded and when viewed from Selsdon Park Road on the boundary to the built-up area on the west, the greater part of the appeal site is readily visible and the scattered buildings and open fields backed by woodlands present a pleasing rural aspect.
2. The preservation of this area for smallholdings provides an opportunity for small scale agricultural activity which can be found nowhere else in the Borough and so long as the Surrey Garden Village Trust Ltd has jurisdiction in this area the scope for agricultural activity would seem to be preserved. [104].

In this instance the appellants were not isolated individuals, but were a well-known firm of developers with a good reputation. They went to great lengths to try to prove that the smallholdings were not used for agricultural purposes, due mostly to the lack of economic viability, and indeed this was supported by a majority of the residents themselves who were living on the plots of land. The soil quality was not high and the difficulty for farmers to amalgamate plots to form a viable agricultural holding would not prove to be sound economics either. They commented that 'The agricultural value of that land is nil. The inter-war concept of garden villages of smallholdings died a long time ago and the scheme... has resulted in a wasteful, unproductive, rural slum'. Wates went on to claim that it was 'normal practice to preserve the best existing trees and other landscape features and integrate them in their housing layouts. They would expect to spend up to £100 per dwelling on landscaping on this estate' [105].

The Inspector, on behalf of the Minister of Housing and Local Government, allowed the appeal, having reached the conclusion that very little of the land originally set aside for 'persons who wished to live

Effingham: an example of a plotland development in Surrey — a problem for the local authority, but a place to enjoy for the residents.

237

in semi-rural surroundings and supplement their incomes by agricultural or horticultural pursuits' was now used for that purpose. The site became the Wates Forestdale Estate.

In 1964 the Greater London Council was formed and the new London Borough of Croydon included the part of Selsdon Vale outside the former County Borough. In the following year Ashen Vale Residents Association applied for planning permission to develop a further 22 acres of the small-holdings, adjoining the Wates site. Planning permission was refused, and, following a further inquiry, the Minister's Inspector upheld the refusal, observing that the development would infringe the Green Belt proposals and that the residential density of the proposed development would be excessive for that locality.

A proposal was then made by George Wimpey and Co Ltd to develop another 76 acres also adjoining the Wates site. This proposal was refused and Wimpeys appealed against the decision. The Inspector allowed the appeal, again on the grounds that the smallholdings were no longer viable agricultural units and that the proposal would simply be a 'rounding off' of residential development in the locality and that consequently 'approval would not conflict with green belt policy'.

Most of the original estate has now been redeveloped, and there is every likelihood that the smallholding plots which still exist will become highly desirable and expensive residential sites [106]. The inheriting son of one of the original settlers remarks that 'It just turned out to be our good luck that we were sitting on a goldmine'[107].

Elsewhere in Surrey plotlands gained a foothold on the North Downs wherever they could. Box Hill, in the words of the guide book, 'must be the most famous view-point in England' with its spectacular views across Surrey. But the author warns us that the road leading up to the famous open space 'is not improved by the shacks and holiday camps that have accumulated here' [108]. This square mile is a part of a large estate, broken up and sold in the 1920s. One of these is the Ruskin estate of about ten acres and sixty shacks used mostly at weekends and in the summer by a cross-section of working-class and lower middle-class Londoners. It began as a camp site and grew into something more permanent where the sound of hammering is heard every weekend in a continual renovation and improvement. Sites, with a ground rent in the mid-1970s of £6 a month for about three hundred square yards, are leased from the widow of the original developer and the shacks on them changed hands for between £500 and £1,000. Unlike the guide-book authors, the group of students and teachers of architecture who studied it found it 'an extremely attractive place' partly because the valley landscape of trees, shrubs and gardens had matured and partly because 'you get a feeling as with old towns and villages that it has just "happened"... Ruskin has the feeling of a backwater about it, and in financial terms it is an anomaly, a small remnant of a past age and past attitudes, left behind by the steamroller of commercial progress' [109].

HAMPSHIRE AND THE ISLE OF WIGHT

It is difficult simply to turn a blind eye to an area which, judging by my own experience, an ambulance could never get inside, let alone a hearse...

(Comment on Cranmore by panel member, at the Examination in Public of the Structure Plan of the Isle of Wight, 1976.)

Amidst conifers and rhododendrons, in beech woods and on open chalk downs, a distinctive scatter of smallholdings and makeshift dwellings is to be found in various parts of Hampshire and the Isle of Wight. Dating from the turn of the century, familiar plotland materials — corrugated iron especially, but also timber, brick and asbestos — have been combined in imaginative permutations to meet the simple requirements of an Arcadian ideal. In East Hampshire where even the humblest homes will often include a verandah, estate agents speak in exaggerated terms of 'colonial-type' dwellings.

Invariably, Arcadia is to be found on land which at the time of its development held little attraction to other users. This was certainly the case at Cranmore on the Isle of Wight, a poorly-drained pocket of clay, overgrown with brushwood, gorse and heather. It has never been a productive area for farmers, and has also created difficulties for building. Likewise, on the mainland, St Leonards and St Ives to the west of the New Forest is also an area of low agricultural value better-suited to conifer plantations and general forestry. Elsewhere sites are generally a mixture of dry downland settings on the edge of Salisbury Plain, or sandy, wooded and often steeply-sloping sites in the east of the county.

If the building materials and marginal locations are familiar plotland features, so too is the rhetoric which accompanied their early appearance. 'Back to the land', 'homes for heroes' (reputedly from the South African Wars as well as the First World War) and 'garden villages' were appealing catch-phrases for the ears of would-be purchasers. And when this was not enough, there were always entrepreneurs ready to lay out roads or otherwise ease the transformation to a new life on the land.

At Cranmore, the firm of Homesteads Ltd in 1904 launched an ambitious scheme to subdivide no less than 375 acres into 168 smallholdings and house plots [110]. A peripheral road scheme was laid out, but plans for a 'garden village' were ill-fated from the start. Those who might have been encouraged to go back to the land were either less numerous than Homesteads anticipated, or else they were more discerning in their choice of site. In spite of its beautiful setting, practical buyers might have looked elsewhere than to a site that made neither farming nor building easy. It is also interesting to note that in the year that Cranmore was launched, Isle of Wight readers were being enticed by weekly advertisements for free farms of 160 acres each in Western Canada [111].

Hampshire: contrasting examples of plot development at Four Marks and Beech.

Another scheme which failed to attract sufficient buyers was that at Palestine in north-east Hampshire. In this case it was the Board of Agriculture after 1918 which released some land on the edge of Salisbury Plain to enable soldiers returning from the Palestine campaign to buy a modest-sized plot. A grid pattern of roads was laid out, with names to remind soldiers of their recent experience. Main roads recalled places like Mount Carmel and Mount Hernon, with connecting tracks such as Olive Grove and Peach Grove evoking memories of days spent in a sunnier climate. Gratuities were used to buy one or more strips, and most chose to keep chickens along with pigs and a few crops. But in spite of the popularity of smallholdings at this time most of the land was not taken up in this way, while some who did come soon left in the face of low prices for eggs and a general disillusionment with life on the land. The result has been a very sporadic pattern of settlement around the ambitious road system, with most of the inner area unsettled.

Patterns today on the various sites in this part of the country are mixed, with some developing and changing out of all recognition and others retaining many of their original features. As an example of the former, Headley Down on the Hampshire-Surrey border has seen considerable changes in recent years [112]. From its background as an area of simple retreats in a woodland setting, a planning policy of permitting 'one-for-one' replacements has led to an emerging landscape of high-cost housing and ranch-type bungalows on large plots with mature trees. Unlike some cases where plots are used for a variety of purposes, this remains a low-density, residential area though quite different in character from its humble plotland origins. St Leonards and St Ives is another area where a makeshift scatter of smallholdings and multifarious uses has been largely incorporated within a newer settlement [113]. In other areas — at Grateley and Picket Place, at South Wonston — in the Four Marks region, and to some extent at Griggs Green and Beech incorporation has also taken place, but not to such a marked degree. With odd exceptions, the general scene in these areas is one of rural settlements with the 'colonial-style' dwellings barely distinguishable from neighbouring country cottages and bungalows. Over the years the original homes have been extended and improved, and plots which may once have been smallholdings have evolved into carefully-tended gardens. Here and there, though, signs of a wayward past remain, as at Beech with a number of brightly-painted corrugated-iron dwellings with verandahs, and, in one at least, a typical multiplicity of uses including logs for sale, breeding kennels, goats and chickens.

Cranmore, Palestine and part of St Leonards are settlements where there has been least consolidation, so that a scattered pattern of smallholdings and mixed uses persist. At Cranmore, for instance, development is dotted unevenly along the unmade roads laid out by Homesteads Ltd at the turn of the century. The initial phase of building after 1904 was followed by a second phase with soldiers returning from the First World War, but there has been little building (other than replacements) since the 1930s, partly due to construction

241

difficulties on the unstable sub-soil and partly to planning restrictions. Many of the original plots have since proved popular for holidays and retirement homes, cheap to buy and in attractive scenery. Names pinned to gateposts and porches — 'Pixie's Place', 'Venture', 'Fresh Field', 'Green Acre', 'Homestead' — speak for themselves. Uses are mixed, with everything from the characteristic plotland goats and chickens, boarding and breeding kennels, and livery stables, to a vineyard producing 'high quality estate wines'.

Undoubtedly landscapes have mellowed and makeshift buildings have merged with their surroundings. They are generally quiet, secluded areas, and there is evidence residents will frequently prefer the unmade roads and individual cesspools to modern services at the price of intensified development. There is certainly little in the present scene to suggest the existence of a problem that local authorities in Hampshire and the Isle of Wight have perceived since the 1940s and before.

Though plotlands are universally identified as requiring improvement, it is not always clear in official documents as to what precisely is the problem. Sub-standard dwellings which are a health and fire risk, inadequate or uneconomic services, and a generally untidy appearance are variously cited as reasons for local authority intervention. Thus, at St Leonards for instance:

> the Local Planning Authority since 1948 have been faced with the problems arising from the breaking up of these two estates (Avon Castle and Matchams Park), and the desirability of securing the full development of those parts of the area in which development had been commenced, so that various services could be provided and the existing roads made up in an orderly and economic manner [114].

Elsewhere it is said that 'the development, despite the wooded nature of the sites, has an uncoordinated and, in parts, untidy appearance' [115].

Cranmore is described as 'one of the worst examples of unplanned layouts in Britain' [116], and when Steers visited it on his coastal survey he dismissed the settlement as 'this dreadful mistake' [117]. Though it is on nothing like the same scale, parallels have even been drawn with Peacehaven. In making a case for a new estate on the site, the developers drew a predictably unfavourable impression of Cranmore as:

> a settlement where the amenities of existing residents are considerably affected by bad roads and unsatisfactory cess-pool drainage. Areas of untended waste ground of uncertain ownership, residential shacks, neglected gardens and large patches of wild scrub contribute to an unsatisfactory situation which includes some areas of unsightly dereliction [118].

For all the rhetoric, local authorities in Hampshire and the Isle of Wight have generally responded to the situation through a policy of gradual change rather than compulsory purchase. A policy of 'one-for-

242

one' replacements has in most cases been sufficient to see substantial changes over the years. In places this policy is supplemented with local plans to guide infilling and general consolidation, coupled with the making-up of roads and provision of mains drainage.

Sometimes plotlands are seen as being areas of opportunity, where development can be absorbed to the benefit of other rural settlements regarded as being more worthy of protection. In spite of its very low density and open rural character, Palestine has been suggested as one such area, the development of which would relieve the pressure on neighbouring villages [119].

Likewise, Cranmore has a long history of developers offering to solve the 'plotland problem' at a stroke:

> Further development in this area could easily be absorbed without detriment to the character of the settlement, would improve its appearance and make a contribution to the provision of facilities such as sewage disposal and water supply which are deficient at the present time [120].

The Isle of Wight County Council has itself at various times considered that planned estate development could be used to 'tidy-up' the area, though continuing controversy surrounds the issue. In opposition to development is the alternative view that 'a planner's nightmare the existing scene may be... but an inoffensive one to the passing eye, and no-one has to live there who does not choose to do so' [121]. More than that, those who do choose to live there are not generally the ones to complain most about conditions [122].

But even areas such as Cranmore change over the years, and the irony is that many of those features which have for so long been regarded as offensive are now, as they become scarce, even worthy of conservation. Illustrating the point is the County Council's policy for Headley Down in 1973, where:

> the plan area has a particular character which is largely a result of the relatively low housing density, fairly extensive tree cover and the informality and narrowness of the unmade roads. It is considered to be important to retain as much of this character as practicable and development of the area will be subject to special considerations... [123].

The contradiction is, of course, that as these areas go 'up-market' (in the same way that areas of working-class housing in cities are 'gentrified' and often conserved, to the detriment of the original residents who can no longer live there) the more likely it is that the attractive plotland characteristics that are the very object of conservation will themselves rapidly disappear.

NOTES

1. Ebenezer Howard, opening the discussion of a paper on 'Civics as Applied Sociology', by Patrick Geddes, read at a meeting in the School of Economics and Political Science, 18 July 1904; reprinted in Meller, Helen E. (1979) *The Ideal City*. Leicester: Leicester University Press.
2. Filson Young in *The Listener*, quoted in Marshall, Howard (1938) The Rake's Progress, in Williams-Ellis, Clough (ed.) *Britain and the Beast*. London: J.M. Dent & Sons.
3. Buchanan, C.D. (1958) *Mixed Blessing*. London: Leonard Hill.
4. Royal Commission on Agriculture (1893) *Report of the Assistant Commissioner on The State of Agriculture in Essex*. London: The Commission.
5. Gayler, Hugh J. (1970) Land speculation and urban development: contrasts in South-East Essex, 1880-1940. *Urban Studies*, 7 (1).
6. Evidence of F.J. Coverdale to the Royal Commission, 1893. Essex Record Office Transcript No. 161.
7. Essex Record Office, Southend Branch Acc 2 D/DS/15/2.
8. Sale Catalogue, Rayleigh Station Estate 21 and 28 August, 4 and 18 September, 1901.
9. Cited in Wiener, Martin J. (1981) *English Culture and the Decline of the Industrial Spirit*. Cambridge: Cambridge University Press.
10. The Land Company: Catalogue, 1906.
11. Foulger, H. (n.d.) *A Guide to Lovely Laindon*.
12. Byford, M.S. (Southend High School for Boys) (1979) The effects of the Agricultural Depression upon the heavy clay lands of Essex. Unpublished project. Essex Record Office T/ZB/160.
13. *Essex Chronicle*, 11 May 1890.
14. *Essex Chronicle*, 14 March 1899.
15. *Essex Chronicle*, 7 July 1899.
16. Press cutting of 11 March 1899 in the Cuttle Collection, Essex Record Office TP 181/7/8.
17. *Essex Chronicle*, 7 July 1899
18. Sales Catalogue for the Riverview Estate, Vange, 9 October 1907. Essex Record Office A 143.
19. *Essex Chronicle*, 13 July 1907.
20. Gayler, *op. cit.* (see note 5).
21. Cuttle, George (n.d.) *The Legacy of the Rural Guardians*. Script in Essex Record Office.
22. *Essex Chronicle*, 30 August 1907.
23. *Essex Chronicle*, 13 October 1922.
24. *Essex Chronicle*, 23 September 1924.
25. Adshead, S. D. (1931) *South Essex Regional Planning Scheme* London: University of London Press.
26. Mr Syrett's house has since been demolished.
27. Granger, Elizabeth (1978) A borrowed pound. *Bulletin of Environmental Education* No 64/65, Aug-Sept. Partly reprinted in Ward, C. (1977) Lost freedoms in housing. *New Society*, 12

May, and in *Environment: A New Society Social Studies Reader*, 2nd Edition, 1978.

28. Cutforth, Rene (1979) The detective in the hayloft. *Observer Magazine*, 14 October.
29. Lyall, Sutherland (1980) *The State of British Architecture*. London: The Architectural Press.
30. Private communication 1980.
31. See, for instance Reiss, Christopher (1975) *Education of Travelling Children*, (Schools Council Research Studies). London: Macmillan; and Ward, Colin (1978) *The Child in the City*. London: Architectural Press.
32. Mayes, Spike (1969) *Reuben's Corner*. London: Eyre and Spottiswoode.
33. Baber, Geoffrey (1970) *Country Doctor*. Ipswich: The Boydell Press.
34. *House of Commons Reports*, 15 May 1950.
35. Basildon Development Corporation (1951) *Technical Report*.
36. *Laindon Recorder*, reporting Sir Lancelot Keay, 29 June 1949.
37. *Laindon Recorder*, 29 June 1949.
38. *Laindon Recorder*, 29 June 1949.
39. *Municipal Journal*, 19 August 1949.
40. *House of Commons Reports*, 15 May 1950.
41. *Ibid.*
42. Knapton, W.G. (1953) in *Town and Country Planning*, October.
43. Boniface, Charles (1960) in *Town and Country Planning*, January.
44. Letter in the possession of Sir Bernard Braine.
45. *Laindon Times and Recorder*, 2 May 1951.
46. Morgan, Glyn H. (1951) *Forgotten Thameside*. Hadleigh, Essex: Thames Bank Publishing Co Ltd.
47. Rackham, Oliver (1980) *Ancient Woodland*. London: Edward Arnold.
48. Basildon Development Corporation in association with the Countryside Commission (1983) *A Plotland Album: The Story of the Dunton Hills Community*. Basildon: The Development Corporation.
49. Tom Clarke, interview, May 1980.
50. Abercrombie, Patrick (1944) *The Greater London Plan*. London: HMSO.
51. Baron, Stanley (1945) The forgotten, unknown city of Britain. *News Chronicle, 14 August.*
52. Thomas, David (1970) *London's Green Belt*. London: Faber and Faber.
53. Essex County Council (1964) *Development Plan: Report on the First Review, Part 1*. Chelmsford: Essex County Council.
54. *Ibid.*
55. *Ibid.*
56. Mr J. Peet, interview, September 1980.
57. Basildon Development Corporation (1951) *Technical Report.*

Basildon: The Development Corporation.

58. Essex County Council (1979) *Essex Structure Plan: Report of Survey.* Chelmsford: Essex County Council.

59. Survey results kindly provided by John Whittam.

60. Whittam, John (1980) Plotlands: Low Density Sporadic Development: Anarchists' Opportunity or Utopian Dream? Unpublished postgraduate dissertation, Chelmer Institute of Higher Education.'

61. *Ibid.*

62. Essex County Council (1979) *Essex Structure Plan, Written Statement.* Chelmsford: Essex County Council.

63. Essex County Council (1979) *Essex Structure Plan, Report of Survey.* Chelmsford: Essex County Council.

64. Essex County Council (1979) *Essex Structure Plan, Written Statement.* Chelmsford: Essex County Council.

65. Essex Structure Plan, *Examination in Public*, 15 May 1980.

66. Essex Structure Plan, *Examination in Public*, 25 March 1980.

67. Rochford District Council v. Lind, 18 December 1979.

68. John Fisher, unpublished account of the origins of South Woodham Ferrers.

69. *Ibid.*

70. *Ibid.*

71. Department of the Environment (1972) *Land Availability for Housing* Circular 102/72. London: Department of the Environment.

72. *Ibid.*

73. Philpot, Terry (1977) The making of a new community. *Ideal Home*, September.

74. Essex County Council (1975) *South Woodham Ferrers Development: Objectives.* Chelmsford: Essex County Council Planning Department.

75. *Maldon and Burnham Standard*, 7 June 1973.

76. Letter from Chairman of South Woodham Ferrers Community Association to Chairman of Essex County Council Planning Committee, 21 December 1977.

77. *Ibid.*

78. Letter from Chairman of Essex County Council Planning Committee to Chairman of South Woodham Ferrers Community Association, 7 January 1978.

79. *Essex Chronicle*, 7 July, 1978.

80. Fen Justice Group (1978) handbill 'Justice on the Fen', July.

81. *Maldon and Burnham Standard*, 2 August 1973.

82. *Maldon and Barnham Standard*, 15 February 1979.

83. Sutherland, *op. cit.* (See note 29).

84. For information on sites in Greater London we are indebted to Mrs J. Bellamy and Mr R. Kirk, in the Greater London Council Department of Recreation and the Arts.

85. We are indebted to Mrs Biggs for an interview on her memories of Havering Park, and for access to her collection of family

photographs.
86. *Dalton's Weekly*, 3 July 1937.
87. Inspector's Report on Public Enquiry, 28 September to 1 October 1971, file nos. OF1/4417/13/1, OF1/4417/192/1, OF1/4417/220/1.
88. *Ibid*, pp. 14-15.
89. *Ibid*, p. 26.
90. *Havering and Romford Express* 1 October 1971.
91. Harry Soan, personal communication, 1981.
92. McAuslan, J. (1969) The Land Commission — past, present and future? *Chartered Surveyor*, November.
93. Department of the Environment (1972) *op. cit.* (see note 71).
94. Kent County Council (1967) *Kent Development Plan*, 1967 revision.
95. Gravesend Borough Council (1975) *Culverstone Chalet Area, Meopham, Kent* (updated 1979). Gravesend: The Borough Council.
96. *Ibid*.
97. *Ibid*.
98. *Ibid*.
99. Day, Andrew (1981) *Plotlands — A Comparison of Selected Local Authority Approaches to the Problem*, Unpublished thesis, Polytechnic of the South Bank.
100. Catalogue issued by Homesteads Ltd, 27 Essex Street, Strand, London WC2, n.d. (1920).
101. Sevenoaks District Council (1981) *West Kingsdown Draft District Plan*. Sevenoaks: The District Council.
102. Day, *op. cit.* (see note 100).
103. *Ibid* (citing Ministry of Housing and Local Government, Appeal No. APP/1020/A/76784, 26 June 1964).
104. *Ibid*.
105. *Ibid*.
106. *Ibid*.
107. Interview, 1981.
108. Banks, F. R. (1956) *Surrey*. London: Penguin Books.
109. Arscot, Mary-Lou, Brown, Angus, Dunipace, Robin, Fielden, Richard, Francis, Susan, Gimson, Mark, Piazza, Juan, Salt, Heimer and Stead, Peter (1976) *Alternatives in Housing? A Report on Self Build in Britain*. London: The Architectural Association.
110. Material on Cranmore is derived from a variety of sources including Sprake, R. F. (1967) *Shalfleet, Isle of Wight: some notes on a county parish*. Yelf Bros.; and Isle of Wight County Planning Department publications and files, in particular *A Rural Policy for the Isle of Wight, Part 2*, approved December 1969; Inspector's Report on an appeal by Whitesea Properties Ltd (APP/2496/A/55695), 1973; *Examination in Public of the Structure Plan of the Isle of Wight* (Transcript of Proceedings, November 1976); *Isle of Wight County Structure Plan: Written Statement*, January 1976, and Minister's subsequent approval

letter which makes a specific reference to Cranmore; and Isle of Wight Planning Department Village Plans File Ref. VP/12/1. We are especially indebted to Mr Cadman of the Isle of Wight Planning Department for his assistance in tracing Cranmore's planning history.

111. *Isle of Wight County Press*, 1904.
112. Information on planning policies for Headley Down and other East Hampshire sites has been obtained from the East Hampshire District Planning Department, and we are indebted to Mrs Wood for her assistance in this respect. Particular documents used were Hampshire County Council (1973) *Headley Down Interim Policy*; and East Hampshire District Council (1981) *Alton Area District Plan*.
113. St Leonards and St Ives was in Hampshire until local government reorganisation in 1974, when it was transferred to Dorset. Important documents regarding its planning history are Hampshire County Council (1956) *St Leonards and St Ives Town Map: Written Analysis of Survey*, and Hampshire County Council (1971) *St Leonards and St Ives Local Plan*.
114. Hampshire County Council (1956), *op. cit.* (see note 114).
115. Hampshire County Council (1971), *op. cit.* (see note 114).
116. *A Rural Policy for the Isle of Wight*, *op. cit.* (see note 111).
117. Cited in *A Rural Policy for the Isle of Wight*, *op. cit.* (see note 111).
118. Appeal ref. APP/2496/A/55695, *op. cit.* (see note 111).
119. It should be pointed out that this view is not, at the time of writing, official, but represents the view of a number of councillors and others who are pressing for a policy of development at Palestine to be included in the *Andover Area District Plan*.
120. Appeal ref. APP/2496/A/55695, *op. cit.* (see note] 11).
121. Representative of a conservationist group commenting on proposed development at Cranmore, Village Plans File ref. VP/12/1, *op. cit.* (see note 111).
122. The view of residents as expressed at a public meeting to discuss the proposed Cranmore Village Plan, ref. VP/12/1, *op. cit.* (see note 111).
123. *Headley Down Interim Policy*, *op. cit.*

Chapter 7

Comparative Plotlands

An African villager looking for the first time in his life at a European House does not suspect the travail and anguish that go into building it — the ritual of buying the land with the help or hindrance of agents, lawyers, and local authorities; securing a bank loan or mortgage; preparing plans, estimates, and documents indispensable for the construction of the house; and paying taxes and insurance policies attached to it forever after. To him the result may look elementary. Similarly, a Westerner inspecting an indigenous African dwelling may find it, too, quite plain. For what he perceives is but the tangible substance, endearing in its unpretentiousness, while the all-pervading magic escapes him. He may see it as the container of a life of extreme artlessness — or what strikes him as artlessness and may envy the owner his freedom to build, untroubled by the chicanes of bureaucracy.

(Bernard Rudofsky, The Prodigious Builders, Secker and Warburg, 1977)

In many parts of the world a specific study of plotlands would be impossible because the sale, lease or colonisation of the individual plot for development by the family adopting it, was and is the normal form of residential evolution. Elsewhere, parallels are to be found with plotlands of the type we have already discussed. In this chapter we make a number of comparisons — with plotland-type development that is regarded as 'normal', and with other examples where it is 'deviant'.

UNITED STATES

When observers of the plotland scene compared it with pioneering settlements in the American West or the Australian Bush, they were right. Part of their antipathy to the mushroom growth they witnessed was the 'un-Englishness' of the gridiron layout with its sporadic infilling. The gridiron street system is a characteristic of towns which were laid out in a hurry. John Reps, the historian of frontier urban planning in the American West, writes: 'Easy to design, quick to survey, simple to comprehend, having the appearance of rationality, offering all settlers apparently equal locations for homes and business within its standardised structure, the grid-iron or checker-board plan's appeal is easy to understand' [1]. He goes on to stress the disadvantages of this kind of layout, only too apparent to the inheritors of a settlement like Peacehaven:

'That the plan can also be monotonous, inappropriate for hilly terrain, lacking in focal points for important buildings, monuments, or open spaces, and hazardous because of too-frequent street intersections have become painfully obvious with the passing of years' [2].

But he emphasises that this apparently American plan form has been used in all the great periods of rapid town development in the past. He cites the Mediterranean colonisation by the Greeks and Romans, and mediaeval settlements in south-west France, Poland and eastern Germany, as well as the Spanish subjugation of Latin America and the English occupation of Ireland. He could also have mentioned the ancient gridiron town of Winchelsea (1280), only a few miles from some of the plotlands of East Sussex, or the Victorian bye-law streets of industrial housing from which many plotlanders were seeking an escape.

The same kind of layout, as well as similar materials and styles of house-building are characteristic of the early growth of Australian cities [3], and of course of the military and civilian 'lines' of European settlements in former colonial empires. In several plotland areas Imperial memories are recalled in the house-names of the verandahed bungalows built by returned colonial servants.

The form of development, in which individual plots are sold to individual purchasers, whose houses might be self-built, built to order by a local contractor, or erected from ready-made sections, is characteristically American rather than British, where the pattern of development through speculative building was well-established in the nineteenth century and even earlier [4].

Even the methods by which plots were sold is more typical of the American or Australian real-estate industry than of the practice of English estate agents, and the characteristic 'half-finished' appearance of plotland areas, with a scattering of single-storey timber dwellings over a large area including many vacant plots, was bound to remind the visitor of the fringes of American and Australian cities. Anthony King has reached the conclusion that, although the idea of the bungalow as a house form was brought to this country from India in the 1870s, the inter-war bungalow boom, both in the plotlands and in ordinary suburban and seaside development, was a kind of re-import from America, where the bungalow had become immensely popular in the early years of this century [5].

The instigators of plotland development were certainly influenced by the American and Australian models. John Henderson, who worked for Charles Neville, the Canadian developer of Peacehaven, writes:

He was a colourful figure, typical of the entrepreneurs who were commonplace in the USA and to some extent in England along the south and east coasts between the wars. Some indeed had lesser qualifications such as an ex-farm hand, and an ex-Australian 1914 war veteran, formerly an 'outback' labourer. Both these men built about 1000 houses speculatively... [6].

We were told locally that the original developer of Maylandsea, a riverside plotland in the estuary of the Blackwater in Essex, was an American with grand ideas about the resort this peaceful haven of sailing enthusiasts never became. Similarly, among the papers of Mr Stedman, the developer of Jaywick Sands, is a photograph, torn from a wartime issue of *Life* magazine, of a typical American suburban street, captioned 'This street could be almost anywhere in America, but it happens to be Fair Oaks Avenue in Oak Park, Illinois'. Even though Jaywick looks nothing like Fair Oaks Avenue, Mr Stedman had written on the page, 'This is what I wanted' [7]. Even when there was no individual developer involved in a particular plotland growth, American influences were at work. The first of the railway coach bungalows at Pagham Beach was built by Captain Charles Vale 'who had just come back from America' [8], and the 'show-biz' plotland colony of Shoreham Beach 'was like Hollywood in the days of Mary Pickford and Charlie Chaplin... you know the first all-colour film was made here' [9].

Quite apart from an influence on English plotlands, urban Americans were themselves impelled at that same time to find a place in the country. In 1926, John Erskine wrote that 'he knows little about us who overlooks our buying up of deserted farms and converting them into a refuge from something or other' [10]. This process has been admirably described by Peter Schmitt, who sees it primarily as a movement 'back to Nature' rather than 'back to the land' [11]. By the early twentieth century he concludes that the Jeffersonian ideal of rugged, individual farmers had been replaced by a spiritual search for Nature, conveniently located for town-dwellers as a place somewhere on the urban fringe. For Americans 'the Arcadian myth embodied an urban response to nature that seemed most appropriate for an urban age' [12].

LIBERTARIAN SUBURBS

Whether primarily for Nature or for land, Americans have continued to settle beyond the city limits in low-density, haphazard settlements that the English observer would recognise as plotland development. Unlike England, though, where plotlands have been restricted in extent, evidence of scattered development in the contemporary American landscape is widespread. Attracted by their distinctive character and contribution to the American housing stock, two geographers, Roger Barnett and James Vance have coined the term 'libertarian suburb' [13]. In his research on their incidence in Stockton, California, Barnett contends that the qualities of a housing environment that reflects

Stockton, California: aerial view of libertarian suburb, and ground view of former motel cabins converted for housing. (Top photo courtesy of Roger Barnett)

deliberate choice and a conscious setting of priorities distinct from contemporary suburban norms deserves recognition by a word less pejorative than 'disorderly' [14].

Under current economic and technological conditions, the standard unit of addition to the housing stock is commonly an entire tract, with lots and houses sold as a package, even when prices are in the range where purchasers can select individual house styles and optional features. Before the 1940s, however, the practice was different:

> Under what might be called the 'normal' sequence, lots large enough for their intended purposes were put on the market and as each lot was sold, a house was constructed. Sustained demand resulted in a fully built-up housing area where the pattern of lots was identical with that of the filed subdivision map. Lot sales followed the filing of the plot maps at reasonable speed, going one at a time to individuals who quickly built houses and, in sum, created a stable residential neighbourhood characterised by houses well maintained over time, low turnover, and uniformity of house size and value.
>
> A second, totally different path was followed by other subdivisions. Slow rate of lot sales and construction and a reduction in single-lot sales and a matching increase in multiple lot or even whole-block sales coupled with a tendency to speculative land dealing and tax delinquency forfeitures created a distinct suburban landscape. Four causes of such instability stand out: an oversupply of land at one time, an economic slump, remoteness or poor access and unattractive physical layout. Early residents of such subdivisions created and maintained a particular milieu — one attractive to the libertarian, the non-conformist, the ad hoc builder, the improviser [15].

In the city of Stockton, Barnett shows that freelance subdividing and lot selling in the period up to 1950 have provided a destination for those who find social identity, cultural cohesion, visual uniformity, and attitudes shaped to and by an orderly landscape, unimportant, as well as for the poor or those of modest income who cannot afford the high cost of traditional suburbia.

Several of the characteristics of the places described are paralleled by the English plotlands. One is the diversity of activities:

> The yards of the libertarian householders express their way of life. The land often includes one, some, or all of the following uses: a patio with exotic plants and garden furniture; a vegetable plot; livestock raising, including the rearing of sheep and horses; overflow storage from the house; auto repairing; auto dismantling the list can go on. Some of these activities are forbidden by social pressure in the orderly suburb; others are outlawed as common nuisances. Blatantly visible or discreetly hidden behind an overgrown but thriving hedge, the activities in the yard are a

253

strictly private concern, calling for no external judgement. The land is the property owner's to use or to abandon [16].

This could be any plotland area in South Essex. So, too, could be an observed antipathy to the local authority's attempts to regulate or redevelop:

> Who are the libertarians? How do they profit from the absence of planning and regulation to create an environment that expresses their values? Because we are dealing with a strong element of negative attitudes, the contrary cement that binds a libertarian community together, generalisations are difficult. Many libertarian suburbanities may well be indifferent or apathetic to normative social concerns or values; rarely are they organised into groups. The one issue guaranteed to provoke concerted reaction is the threat of annexation to the city of Stockton; incorporation means submitting to minimum standards and paying for improvements required by municipal regulation. Who needs sewers, wide streets, sidewalks, and a code that renders 'home improvements' subject to visits and approval from building inspectors? Much of the present diversity of the libertarian neighbourhood would disappear under a rigorous enforcement of municipal codes. Sizeable areas of east Stockton have decisively rejected annexation time and time again. Planners think the rejection has cost these individualists the physical upgrading of their neighbourhoods, but residents think that rejection has preserved the very qualities they now enjoy [17].

Barnett concludes that 'The deliberate disorder of the libertarian suburb not only survives, it has even attained a special cachet in an era when alternative lifestyles are widely sought and freely accepted' [18]. This option is again paralleled by English experience. Gerald Young found Pagham Beach 'almost raffishly picturesque' [19] and a planning officer for another English plotland district remarked that it was 'a bit of a mess, but with a certain prestige attached to it' [20].

It would be a mistake to see libertarian suburbs as purely residual, low-income areas, and James Vance is undoubtedly right when he contends that people who have a choice select a suburban location not simply for the space it can offer but also for a sense of freedom and diversity [21]. This is exhibited in terms of plot size, with a characteristically open and irregular form of layout, as well as architectural variety. Take, for example, the high-income suburbs in suburban Berkeley, California.

As the land rises in the east of Berkeley, around the university campus, so a standard grid layout gives way to curving roads and avenues that mark one of the Bay Area's most sought-after suburbs. High above the Bay, on steep slopes (that continue in the adjoining Tilden Regional Park to nearly 2,000 feet), live those who can buy their way out of the fog and decay below.

254

Berkeley, California: current view of high income lot development.

To English eyes what makes it all so unusual is the immense variety of house-types. In England it is common enough to see individual designs in a well-appointed suburb, but more often than not what is seen is a series of modest variations around a familiar, brick-built theme. In suburban Berkeley, the unexpected becomes the norm: a split-level, timber construction with outside stairs and verandahs stands next to a pink-painted, 'traditional' Spanish villa; a modern extravaganza of cuboid steel and glass looks quite at home alongside a white, 1930s liner-style creation on one side and a modest, single-storey timber design (with a less modest double garage) on the other. It offers a kaleidoscope of shapes, styles, colours and textures, yet embraced very comfortably within the rich cover of trees and shrubs on the slopes; with below a spectacular view of the Bay, and the Pacific beyond.

Yet what impresses more than the physical drama of the place is the scope that has been created for individuality. In one sense it is a far cry from the maligned English plotlands, but in another there are interesting parallels. Indeed, in parts of suburban Berkeley, in some of the little *culs-de-sac* the tumbledown arrangement of timber homes on the steep, well-wooded slopes is reminiscent of plotland pockets in Hampshire or on the North Downs. Even the land is, in traditional terms, marginal — spurned by early settlers around the Bay. More than these physical parallels, though, is a common sense of individuals creating their own environment, defying laws of Nature where necessary and challenging the norms of building inspectors and finance companies who would always prefer to see a more conventional, standardised layout. The Bohemians in England who were drawn to

255

places like Shoreham Beach would have found much to enjoy in the spontaneity of suburban Berkeley.

The overwhelming difference is, of course, that whereas the English plotlands were typically the product of people with low incomes, suburban Berkeley is the very reverse. Creating Arcadia here is very much a high-income pursuit. But rather than dismiss the parallels it is interesting to question whether plotlands were maligned in England, not so much because of their physical peculiarities but because too often they represented low-income groups invading high-income territory. Suburban Berkeley shows that there is nothing wrong with the eccentricity of plotland development as such; far from it, as it can be a source of character and attraction in itself. But to be accepted perhaps it has to be a product of people who are themselves accepted in the first place.

CHICKEN RANCHES AND THE NEW AGE

In spite of tighter zoning restrictions since the first waves of development, attempts to create 'deliberate disorder' in suburban and rural settings are enjoying a new lease of life in contemporary America [22]. The frontier has long been conquered, but Americans are once again moving westwards (and now to the South as well) in large numbers. In search of sunshine and work, each year more are leaving the cities of the North and East, to follow the trail taken by the gold-miners of the last century and those driven from the depressed agricultural lands in the 1930s, over the Rockies into the favoured State of California. Many are settling, too, in the booming towns of Arizona and Texas, and along Florida's extensive but rapidly-urbanising coastline.

If what is taking shape is not exactly the frontier townscape of old, around many cities in these areas and in scattered tracts in the countryside, there are at least familiar signs of settlements being thrown together in a hurry and of housing built and located piecemeal. On lots of varying size, served by dirt tracks and often with their own wells and septic tanks, Americans on unincorporated land beyond municipal boundaries in the South and West are relatively free to erect whatever they can afford. Self-build housing is on the increase, producing a variety of shapes and sizes, though many prefer ready-made cabins delivered to their lot. Especially widespread is the 'mobile home' single-storey prefabricated units that normally make only one journey in their life, from factory to site which (like the ubiquitous railway carriage in the English plotlands) lends itself to all manner of extensions and adaptations. As an indication of their extent, there are some counties in south-west Florida where mobile homes constitute more than 30 per cent of all housing units [23].

People are drawn to these peripheral locations for a variety of reasons. Undoubtedly the very fact of owning land continues to exert a strong pull in American culture, and land outside the city will be cheaper. Ownership of lots of an acre or more are not uncommon,

Arcadia, Florida: mobile homes continue to provide opportunities in the search for Arcadia.

enough to keep a horse or a few chickens as many do — 'chicken ranches' as they are often called. There is also the attraction of lower property taxes beyond the municipal boundary, and less in the way of development regulations. An absence of services like street lighting may well be counted as a gain rather than a cost, the whole process itself reflecting a preference for a simpler life than can be found in the cities. The term 'exurbanisation' can be applied not only to the geographical process of population movement, but equally to a social rejection of a high-density, urban culture.

Many Americans have taken this quest for a simple life a stage further, seeing this as the prime gain rather than the mere ownership of land. In these cases the settlement of lots and self-build housing has a distinctive 'new age' feel, in contrast to the more conventional chicken ranches for latter-day settlers. California, with its benign climate and tradition of communes, is an obvious location for continuing experiments. In Mendocino County, for example, beyond the reach of San Francisco, makeshift structures are scattered in the hills, the precious land yielding a sizeable crop of marijuana amongst more socially-acceptable fruit and vegetables. The sense of living with a minimum of regulations is strong, something that is reflected in the seemingly-disordered landscape.

Elsewhere, too, a variety of individual and communal experiments lay stress on the process of building low cost, non-standardised

257

housing, in ways which would not always be possible in a more regulated environment with strictly-enforced land subdivision and zoning procedures. Art Boericke has described his own and other self-build housing ventures, each an attempt to find space for individuality and often at odds with the authorities:

> And if the inspectors come around, call your place a 'potting shed', a 'summer camp', or 'mining claim' — anything that pops into your head. And when they keep on shoving, call it a 'firehouse', a 'briar patch' a 'commune' — whatever riles them most... And remember, too, property is sacred; so if we just keep on building, they're going to step aside see if they don't [24].

Near Tallahassee in Florida an intentional community, the Misty Hills Land Cooperative, has pioneered an imaginative range of house-types. Just as the English plotlanders were adept at recycling building materials so, too, there are homes here that are built with timber from obsolete tobacco farms, materials salvaged from demolition, as well as houses transported in their entirety from construction sites. Land is still, by English standards, cheap and if building inspectors can be kept at bay while improvements are made, the economics of this approach are sound:

> Instead of paying $10,000 for a down payment and owing $60,000 at 14%, Harold and Susan paid $1,000 down for an acre of land and built a home. After spending $5,000 they had an unfinished house they could live in and were able to use the money that had been going for rent to finish their house [25].

Another interesting experiment that has come to terms with building regulations, yet which seeks to innovate and maximise the self-help component, is that of New Village in Pennsylvania. Within a framework of communal planning, the aim is to free the way for individual involvement and variety: 'it will strive to contain shared self-reliance and a spirit of pioneering which is as much a rediscovery of heritage as it is an unfolding of something new' [26].

In a low-income, rural setting, building started in 1980 to provide housing for about 600 people. A local newspaper report catches the mood of the approach:

> By an innocuous room on the second floor of Jan and Jeff"s Hardware Store in this Fayette County town, a humble 'revolution' in thought and deed is taking place. The instigators include some of the notoriously more 'radical' elements of society — secretaries, schoolteachers, real estate agents, lawyers, coal miners and factory workers. Even more radical is what they propose: that a house can be built for half the price of conventional homes and be so energy-efficient that even a person's body heat will help keep it warm. The houses will be heated by solar energy.

258

The key to the low price tag on the homes, scheduled to be built sometime in 1982, is 'sweat equity', or in the words of Ralph Waldo Emerson, self-help and self-reliance [27].

Existing opportunities in the district for acceptable new housing were limited. The cost of private housing was prohibitive for many, while mobile homes (on the increase locally) were cheap but in other ways deficient. In turn, public sector programmes were discounted for a 'top down' approach that blankets independent action while encouraging passivity. The preferred approach is for the future residents of New Village to build it themselves, bringing in skilled labour and expertise only where necessary. Apart from communal gains from the process, there are substantial savings to be made reducing the total cost of building from an estimated $2.9m to $2.1m. Over a three-year period any one person would not be expected to contribute more than fourteen days' labour each year.

Looking overall at the rich variety of settlement patterns in modern America, some wholly unregulated and some making compromises, it is probably more accurate to think in terms of 'lotlands' rather than the English usage of 'plotlands'. The single lot of land has exerted a greater influence on the American landscape than have individual plots in England, and it has over the years permitted a wide variety of building and land use ranging from personalised housing in high-income suburbs to low-income smallholdings further out. This variety, with social and historical dimensions, is reflected everywhere in the present American landscape.

There is evidence, for instance, of frontier-style settlements in the Western States dating back to its original form for little more than a century, where whole townships have inherited the disorder and individuality of its origins. There is evidence, too, of poor farmers forced to leave the impoverished lands of the Dust Bowl in the 1930s, but preferring to resettle on lots of one to five acres on the edges of cities rather than become wholly urbanised. Lotlands are also frequently the home of low-income minorities, in part forced onto the cheaper land around the city and in part seeking an existence with a minimum of regulations to enable a little subsistence farming, dismantling cars or chopping logs for sale. Houses are built by families or with the help of friends, and commonly the lots are enclosed with fences in a way that is less common in middle-income suburbs. Interspersed among the houses are little shops and Fundamentalist chapels. Different minorities tend to settle in their own area; in Stockton, for example, there are three areas of libertarian suburb, one occupied by blacks, one by Hispanics, and one by white farmers primarily from Oklahoma.

More recently, lotlands have developed to meet the needs of people who want space to retire, improving their house over time; or who create fairly primitive settlements in the mountains, on cheap desert lands or by the coast for leisure. Patterns in the past suggest that what start out as temporary leisure retreats very often evolve into

259

South-west Texas and St. George Island, Florida: contrasting examples of modern lot development.

permanent homes; and cabins within reach of New York city where this has been done bear a striking resemblance to examples close to London noted in earlier chapters. Finally, there is the Bohemian tradition, flourishing today but with roots in the past, of those who seek the freedom to experiment, whether just in building or in a total life-style. All this adds up to an immense variety of what English observers would recognise as a plotland landscape and which, in England, has largely disappeared. It is not, in any conventional sense, a beautiful landscape

260

but its untidiness belies an underlying sense of order, in that it has obviously been made to work for those who live there. America is a vast country, and there is a sense of being able to accommodate tracts such as these in a way that may be less acceptable in a smaller country. Above all, libertarian suburbs, lotlands or whatever have undoubtedly filled gaps in America's changing housing needs, and they provide an enviable element of choice that is absent in many European societies.

EUROPE: EAST AND WEST

THE FRENCH CONNECTION

Any visitor to French seaside or riverside resorts will be aware of the wealth of holiday shacks and villas in the plotlands beyond the hotel belt, but it is the hinterland of Paris itself that provides the most striking parallel to the English plotlands. Perhaps, in reaction to the high-density tenement living which has been traditional in Paris, the twentieth century has seen an enormous pressure to get out of the city; easy for the affluent, but needing ingenuity and improvisation for working-class families.

Richard Cobb, a passionate observer of the environmental background of French life, writes of:

the preference shown by the Parisian artisan, ever since the 1900s and the 1920s for the single house, the tiny villa, even a converted railway wagon or an old bus or green tram, pathetic grabs at privacy and individuality that mushroomed along the main lines, often on quite unsuitable terrain, and denied most of the amenities, on the wide steppes north of Paris... Life in the unfinished villa was pretty uncomfortable; but at least one knew one's neighbours living up the muddy, waterlogged lanes; and there was even a wooden cafe that specialised in *bifteck-frites*... the scattered *bicoques*, or shanties of the 1910s, the 1920s, and 1930s, in the valley of the Orge, in the Pays de France, in the valley of the Marne... [28].

His attachment to 'individualism, eccentricity and do-it-yourself' is paralleled by the historian of the buildings of Paris, Norma Evenson, who explains how the *cité jardin* movement provided for only a small part of the outward movement, most of which was in the form of individual purchase in the period of relative prosperity which 'provided many workers with the means and optimism to undertake land purchases' [29]. Her account of the process of development is very similar to recollections of the early days of plotland districts like Pitsea and Laindon:

Facilitating the movement were enterprising speculators, who acquired large tracts of cheap land in outlying areas, parcelled it out into small lots, and sold the lots for modest weekly

261

Paris: suburban settlement in the 1920s.
(Photo courtesy of H. Roger-Viollet)

payments. Systematic advertising campaigns covered Paris with posters lauding the advantages of home ownership, the wholesomeness of open-air life, and the pleasures of hunting and fishing. Promoters often sponsored excursions to their sites, where persuasive salesmen encouraged purchasers to secure their lots with a down payment of as little as ten francs, an average day's wage for a worker. Lot sizes might range from 100 to 450 square metres and be priced at from two to three francs a square metre... The purchasers of these small suburban lots were usually too poor to employ commercial builders to construct their houses, and in most cases they built their own small dwellings from materials at hand. Often they made do with the most minimal temporary shelter, hoping that eventually their resources would permit a permanent house. The new allotments quickly filled up with an assortment of constructions, including shanties of wood, plasterboard, tar paper, and corrugated metal, accompanied by dwellings adapted from old trucks and wagons. Although during the summer months settlement in these suburban tracts may have had some of the charms of camping out, the onset of winter rains dramatised both the inadequacy of the shelters and the lack of drainage... Having no compulsion to do otherwise, land speculators sold the lots without streets, sewers, water supplies, proper drainage, or gas and electrical installations... [30].

Norma Evenson quotes a politician who in 1928 declared 'Let us combat the communists by making property owners of them', but notes that:

It became clear, however, that in the Paris suburbs it was precisely the struggle to own their own homes that was leading many towards socialism. The inhabitants of the new settlements found themselves socially isolated, exploited by the land proprietors, and often unable to obtain assistance and support from local governments. The local communes, in turn, saw themselves as caught between the indifference of the land developers and the overwhelming demands of the hordes of new immigrants for urban services that the communes did not feel financially able to support. The long struggle for improved conditions served to create a new political awareness among the settlers, and they began to organise and consolidate their efforts in such organisations as the *Fédération des Groupements de Défense des Petits Acquéreurs de Terrains* and the *Fédération des Travailleurs Mal-Lotis*. As the Communist party began to gain strength during the 1920s, the consistent support of the suburban voters gave the name 'red belt' to a circle of communities around Paris. The struggle for improvement of the suburban allotments succeeded gradually although in some instances as much as ten years passed before all urban services were provided [31].

Here the parallel with the British experience breaks down. Few of the plotlands of South-East England were so close to the metropolis as those in the Paris region, and when they were within daily commuting distance, the demand for better services seldom led to political militancy. English plot-holders tend to list the absence of made-up roads and main drainage as disadvantages of the places where they live, and some are active in campaigning for these, but at the same time very many fear and resent 'interference' by the local authorities, and so do not want these services, either because their incomes are low or because other priorities are more important for them and they cherish their isolation [32].

CHALET GARDENS IN NORTH-WESTERN EUROPE

Many European countries have the equivalent of English allotment gardens in the form of patches of land, not attached to dwellings, where urban working-class families are able to cultivate vegetables. They are rented individually from landowners on the urban fringe or are provided municipally, philanthropically or by co-operative gardening associations. As the economic necessity to provide food for the family declined, there was a tendency to re-name the allotment garden as the 'leisure garden', as a place where the family could sunbathe rather than dig, a tendency which was reversed by the two world wars and to some extent, much more recently, by a new appreciation of the virtues of supplying one's own fresh fruit and vegetables.

In Britain the only buildings on allotment sites tend to be the characteristic tool shed, and in some areas, a pigeon loft. It is very rare for the hut on the allotment to be used as a habitation (though examples are mentioned in Chapter 1). In many places the local Allotment Society would undoubtedly expel a member who built on his plot. His aspirations would be much more likely to be catered for by the plotlands described in the previous chapters, or, usually deceptively, by the postwar industry in selling 'leisure plots' discussed in Chapter 8.

But in Continental Europe — especially in Scandinavia, northern Germany and the Netherlands — the 'chalet garden', where a flower garden with its lawns and shrubs is augmented by a summer house or chalet, slept in during the summer months, is a fully recognised aspect of the allotment scene. A British governmental committee examining the evolution of allotments reported that:

> The ratio of 'allotment gardens' to 'chalet gardens' varies enormously. In Sweden, the 'allotment garden' has virtually disappeared, possibly because many workers in that country can now qualify for a retirement pension equal to 80 per cent of their former salaries. In Denmark, the 'allotment garden' is today largely confined to rural areas. In West Germany, an edict of 1919 sought to ensure that some vegetables would be grown on every allotment, and although this law is now repeatedly disregarded, we were shown several examples in Hamburg where 'chalet gardens' and 'allotment gardens' flourish on the same site. In Holland, by contrast, the chalet garden represents only a minority of allotment provision... It was emphasised to us in Rotterdam, that the dichotomy between the chalet garden and the 'allotment garden' is by no means as great as one might suppose. Not only does the local authority adopt the same system of administration for both types of allotment, but there has in recent years been an increasing tendency for the occupiers of 'allotment gardens' to graduate to chalet gardens by what is regarded as a natural form of development [33].

The committee was chaired by the late Professor Harry Thorpe, who regretted that so little notice was taken of its findings. (A Dutch advocate of chalet gardens remarked 'I still see him sitting in our drawing-room in Amsterdam, discussing allotment matters till deep in the night, sipping a Dutch Genever and eating a raw herring... Was all the work of my friend Harry done in vain?' [34].) The Thorpe Committee was so impressed by Continental chalet gardens that it asked:

> If the transition from 'allotment garden' to 'chalet garden' has been a natural process, it is pertinent to ask at once why no similar development had occurred in this country.

And it reached the paradoxical conclusion that:

> we are convinced that a major part of the answer lies in the complete absence of mandatory allotments legislation in every

Amsterdam: current view of chalet gardens on the edge of the city.

country which we visited. The fact that every publicly provided allotment site, whether it is composed of vegetable plots or of chalet gardens, exists as a result of voluntary action by a local authority, has generated between the allotments movement and the municipalities a spirit of harmony which has rarely existed in this country and is conspicuously lacking today. Within this atmosphere, there is ample room for experimentation with new ideas, which can be allowed to germinate both in the town hall and on the site without a constant fear that they will offend against some enactment... Throughout our tour, we formed the impression that the planner regards the provision and the effective siting of allotments as an *important* part of his work, not least because he is confident that the sites which he designates will add to the attractiveness of his town... The officials in every town decided voluntarily and as a matter of course that we must talk either to the planning officer or to private planners engaged on the town's development, and some of these planners were themselves chalet gardeners [35].

The committee visited the cities of Rotterdam, Amsterdam, Hamburg, Copenhagen and Malmo, and found that the usual maximum size of the chalet was 10 per cent of the plot area, that its cost in 1966 ranged from £90 to £400, that frequently the local authority provided loans for its cost and that it was constructed by the tenant, either to his own design while sited according to a master plan, or was selected by the tenants from a range of designs or specifications:

265

These systems have one common feature, in that they require the tenant to purchase his chalet. Throughout our tour the view was expressed that only by encouraging pride of ownership could one ensure that the chalet would invariably be well built and properly maintained, and we certainly saw abundant evidence of competition between gardeners to possess the finest chalet [36].

They found that only the most luxurious of chalets had mains services and that, considered as residential units, 'many chalets are somewhat primitive and offer few home comforts'. Nevertheless they were in residential use:

> It is therefore noteworthy that in the whole of our tour we found only one site where the gardeners *and their families* were not permitted to spend the night in their chalets during the summer months and even there the rule is not rigidly enforced. It is today the general practice for the whole family to remain on its chalet garden throughout the summer weekends, and often for the duration of the school holidays. No local authority frowned on this practice which, we were informed, ensured that the tenant would devote more time to his plot and enabled the local association to extend the social life of the site by arranging evening functions [37].

Since the Committee of Inquiry reported on its tour of European chalet gardens, conflicts have arisen with planning authorities in some places. The secretary of the Dutch National Association of Folk Gardens described in 1980 attempts to bring the leisure gardens under the law relating to camping sites, since the chalets were slept in overnight from the 1st April to the 1st October. This was resisted by the plot-holders because they feared 'pressure from government to provide the sites with all kinds of facilities that are required for second homes, a sewerage system, electricity and so on, while the possibility of camping taxes is appearing on the horizon' [38].

HINTS FROM DENMARK

Examples of variations on the plotland theme, both those officially encouraged and those which happen in spite of official disapproval, can be found in all European countries, East and West. The most interesting, because it is the most suggestive of ways in which plotland housing can be legitimised, with its advantages enhanced and its defects minimised, is the recent development of plotlands in Denmark, studied by the architect John Noble, of the Housing Development Directorate in the Department of the Environment [39]. In an earlier paper Noble had made a plea for 'contingency architecture' as oppposed to the mass housing process, believing in the need to broaden the range of housing choices to meet the differing and diverse choices of individuals and their families [40]. His variety of contingencies included the possible steps in a ladder of plot development from mobile homes on a serviced site, to a fully developed family house extending from a hearth unit with cooking, washing and WC facilities.

In Denmark, Noble found that:

> Large scale private speculative development is virtually unknown. Travel outwards from the centre of any town or city and it is apparent that the prevalent tradition at most times in the past has been to make land available to individual households to choose according to their personal circumstances how their houses should be built and by whom; and within limits, what standards 'and cost would be acceptable. Opportunities for self-help are available at all stages in the building process and there is a great deal of competition amongst those who offer assistance to plot purchasers... Over the last 15 years about two-thirds of new housing in Denmark has been in the form of detached houses built individually on single plots, and the relative share of output taken up by plot developments increased steadily during the 1970s... In the past it was fairly common for a plot to be bought in advance of a household's financial ability to build, and to be used in the interim as an allotment or for recreational purposes. Although the need to do this no longer appears to be so great (and the rate of inflation seems to be a positive disincentive to delay) this is said to be an important element of choice for those who must save before building.

In the Danish comparison, then, we have the plotland mode of development as the major form of housing provision. As in the pre-war English plotlands, there is, in John Noble's view, 'considerably greater scope with regard to the timing of building, the method of building, and for economy through using one's own labour than when completed houses are bought from speculative builders in this country'. There the resemblance ends, for the contemporary Danish plotlands are very heavily circumscribed by planning and building regulations. Danish reservations about the plotland form of development are concerned with an apparent extravagance in land use, since plotland houses are free-standing, and with the monotony of overall appearance. John Noble's careful study of Danish plotland housing awakened little response from British architects, but aroused an echo from a New Zealand architect, Clem Green, who found it both interesting and amusing since this kind of individual plot development has been taken for granted in both New Zealand and Australia throughout the century [41]. (New Zealand also scores at the humbler end of the plotland scale. In that country it is usual for a family to acquire a quarter acre beach section and erect a beach house of timber and corrugated iron for holiday and weekend use. These are known as 'baches' and are thought of as a normal and natural aspect of the seaside scene).

YOUR *DACHA*, COMRADE

The chalet garden form of plotland dwelling is not confined to Western Europe. The visitor to Warsaw sees, on the journey from the airport to the city, chalet gardens which have evolved in a similar way to those of Holland, and the same phenomenon occurs on the perimeter of several of the cities of Czechoslovakia, Hungary, Rumania and Yugoslavia. One student of the cities of Eastern Europe explains that:

> The existence of peasant-owned land on the fringes of cities offers opportunities for piecemeal evolution indeed even 'overnight mushrooming' — of 'wild settlements', as in Nowy Dwór and elsewhere outside Warsaw or in Kozarski Bok and Trnje on the margins of Zagreb. Such communities are not encouraged, yet they are tolerated and even provided with utilities and welfare since they relieve some of the pressures on city housing and budgets. Recently, too, increasing demand by city-dwellers for land for second homes has brought uncontrolled building to potential 'green belt' land around larger cities. In this market there is little control over land sale prices between peasants, collective farm workers, and individual buyers. State organisations and industrial enterprises have begun to build 'estates' of second homes for their key workers. Such second homes are cheaper to the employees than those purchased privately, although they may well have to wait longer for them [42].

The evolution of plotland homes in Eastern Europe generally, resembles the characteristic development of the plotlands of southern England, rather than the chalet garden pattern. Deals tend to be struck with individual landowners, rather than with speculative entrepreneurs, though these are by no means unknown in the 'black' or 'grey' economies of the communist State [43]. In Bulgaria, Mount Vitosha has on its lower slopes, the second homes of families from Sofia, which tend to become the permanent residences of their owners on retirement. In Prague, every fifth household has a second home, many second-home owners coming from the old industrial quarters of the city. Indeed, a situation has gradually evolved whereby most Prague citizens live during the week either in new State and co-operative buildings, or poorly maintained dwellings in the city centre. This has led to many inhabitants preferring to concentrate their energy and private initiative, not on the upkeep of their State flats or renovation of their obsolete city apartments, but on privately owned second-home accommodation outside Prague. In time, particularly for the older age groups, these short-term second homes, as in Sofia, become permanent residences on retirement [44].

In the Soviet Union itself, the *dacha*, or wooden house in the country, was, long before the revolution, taken for granted as one of the appurtenances of life among the upper and the middle classes. In its construction, its lack of main services, and its sheet-iron roof, it was no better provided than the typical English plotland house, though the servants lived in a turf shed at the rear. Advances in transportation brought the dacha within reach of a wider range of citizens, and post-revolutionary developments simply changed the occupants. Ownership of a *dacha* is a prerequisite of privilege in modern Soviet society, and is of course a status symbol:

> The *dacha* today falls under official suspicion not only because it constitutes a second home but also because it is an individual recreational form in a society largely given to mass planning. However, the authorities have proceeded cautiously in this matter... and near Moscow and Leningrad in particular there are many *dachas* belonging to private individuals and to organisations. Some extremely large *dachas* are located on the western side of Moscow, for example, and especially on the Moscow River at such places as Serebryanny Bor. These belong primarily to the Soviet government and its officials, to foreign embassies, and to other organisations [45].

Some attempt was made to accommodate the difference between the official reality and people's own housing aspirations, and this resulted in 'the so-called garden co-operative', the equivalent of the leisure gardens of Western Europe:

> Land is frequently allocated in this way to factories whose workers are given their own plots of land. The plots are sometimes rented but are often treated as the workers' own with a right of sale either to another member of the cooperative or sometimes apparently to the general public [46].

Such plots, even though 'vegetable growing on the English model is less widespread', contribute very significantly to local fruit supplies, but more and more, the significant feature of the garden co-operative 'is the so-called "summer garden cottage" or tiny wooden chalet which people are permitted to erect upon it. Soviet laws which restrict the building of further *dachas* do allow these chalets to be built with the proviso that no central heating be installed'. Dennis Shaw notes that 'the whole subject of *dachas* and garden co-operatives is an uncomfortable one for the authorities and information about them is surprisingly hard to come by'. He cites an article by a Soviet writer V. Kherkel, who, under the title *Vasha Dacha* (meaning Your *Dacha*, and implying an everyday familiarity with the topic), observes that gardening has often become only secondary to general leisure on the co-operatives in Estonia, while outside Moscow 'some summer garden chalets constructed in the 1950s already have central heating and an obvious air of permanency' and around Leningrad, 'many *dachas* are uncomfortable, poorly constructed, and situated either in areas which are aesthetically poor or on land that would be better put to other purposes'. They 'continue to play an extremely important role in the hinterland of the larger city, catering for 93 per cent of rest places around the city of Leningrad and 62 per cent around Moscow' [47].

THIRD WORLD SHANTY TOWNS

At first sight a comparison between the English plotlands and the shanty towns of the exploding cities of Latin America, Africa and Asia, appears absurd. The plotlands of South-East England are marginal to the general housing situation, while 'the cities the poor build' in the Third World house millions of people. In some cities the 'unofficial' population of the squatter belt is actually greater than the city's official population. The English plotlands, although they are now very often the permanent homes of the settlers, usually began as holiday homes. It may be insulting to the poor of developing countries to make such a comparison, and English plotland dwellers who resent phrases like 'shanty town' and 'rural slum' would not welcome it either.

But similarities *do* exist. The first is the obvious one that houses in both instances tend to be built by the families that occupy them. The second is that they tend to be improvised through the *ad hoc* use of cheap or recycled materials. A third similarity is in the characteristic gridiron layout and the fact that the dwelling begins unserviced and develops its services over time, often through the initiatives of the inhabitants. That the Jaywick Sands Residents Association should buy and install its own street lights, would be readily understood in Latin America, but would mystify the residents of any ordinary English housing estate.

A fourth similarity is in the evolution of the dwelling over time. The holiday home in Canvey that becomes a permanent dwelling and the shanty in Cuidad Guayana that evolves in the same way, are both examples of people without initial capital turning their own labour into a capital asset over time, an asset that could only be acquired through the normal channels of housing provision at a much greater cost, usually beyond the reach of the owner-builder, since institutional sources of housing finance are not available to such people in either case. A further point of similarity is that such housing, in both instances, is regarded as substandard and undesirable by the public officials concerned with housing and planning. Related to this is the changing public perception of the shanty town. Initially, like the plotlands, the shanty towns were perceived as a regrettable blot on the landscape and a menace to public health and good order. Slowly and partially, a new perception has arisen which salutes the ingenuity of the owner-builder, sees his or her activities as a praiseworthy triumph of self-help and independence, and demands that they should be assisted and encouraged rather than persecuted and frustrated. The improvement grant (ideally) replaces the bulldozer.

The dweller-built settlements on, and often beyond, the periphery of the cities result from the enormous exodus from the rural hinterland, as households decide to move, usually because they calculate, often correctly, that there is a better chance for their children in or around the city. They tend to migrate, first to the inner-city slums, and then, having been introduced to the urban economy, to land on the fringe, where there is space for them to build for themselves. The situation is comparable to the American example, where the poor were faced with the choice of renting within the city or purchasing small lots outside city limits [48] or the Parisian example, where the choice was overcrowding at high rents in the city slums or buying space on the fringe [49]. In the case of the Third World cities the change in perception of the shanty suburbs was the result of the observations of an American anthropologist, William Mangin, and an English Architect, John Turner, following their experience of the shanty towns of Lima, and subsequently in other cities. Citing the then universal stereotype of these places as breeding grounds for crime, disease, social and family disorganisation, they wrote:

> Ten years of work in Peruvian *barriadas* indicates that such a view is grossly innaccurate: although it serves some vested political and bureaucratic interests, it bears litle relation to reality... Instead of chaos and disorganisation, the evidence instead points to highly organised invasions of public land in the face of violent police opposition, internal political organisation with yearly local elections, thousands of people living together in an orderly fashion with no police protection or public services. The original straw houses constructed during the invasions are converted as rapidly as possible into brick and cement structures with an investment totalling millions of dollars. Employment rates, wages, literacy, and educational levels are all higher than in central city slums (from which most *barriada* residents have escaped) and higher than the national average [50].

The Turner/Mangin perception has by now become the official orthodoxy, at least so far as international bodies like the UN and the World Bank are concerned, and 'site-and-service' housing or 'aided self-help' are the recommended policies, though often interpreted in ways about which the original instigators have reservations. Third World housing has generated an enormous literature [51], some of which supports and some of which opposes the Turner/Mangin view. Peter Lloyd, a social anthropologist, remarks that:

> The rival viewpoints proceed from different ways of explaining man's actions in society. One sees him as blindly accepting the fate thrust upon him, responding emotionally to its strains; the other portrays him as rationally calculating the possible outcome of the opportunities offered to him and seeking his own self-interest [52].

They also proceed from different assumptions about the role of the State and of public authorities in people's lives. The plotlanders, whether at Laindon or in Latin America, seem to be people who have concluded that the best way to get anything done is to do it yourself. Turner's experience in various parts of the world can be distilled into three laws of housing [53]. One is that the important thing about

271

Isidro Fabela: squatter settlement on the south side of Mexico City.
(Photo courtesy of Peter Ward)

housing is not what it *is*, but what it *does* in people's lives. In other words that dweller satisfaction is not necessarily related to the imposition of standards.

Another is that deficiencies and imperfections in *your* housing are infinitely more tolerable if they are your responsibility than if they are *somebody else's*. But the most important of Turner's laws is the proposition that:

> When dwellers control the major decisions and are free to make their own contribution to the design, construction or management of their housing, both the process and the environment produced stimulate individual and social well-being. When people have no control over, nor responsibility for key decisions in the housing process, on the other hand, dwelling environments may instead become a barrier to personal fulfilment and a burden on the economy [54].

The truth of these contentions is one of the lessons of the plotland experience. They explain the remark by Mrs Granger, whose first plotland home was started with a borrowed pound (see page 200) 'We never had a mortgage for any of them. I feel so sorry for young couples these days. They don't get the kind of chance we had'.

CONCLUSION

The existence all over the world of analogies and counterparts of the plotlands of Southern England suggests that they were not merely the exploitation of gaps in an incomplete system of development control. They were a reversion to what can be seen as a universal propensity, given access to land, to provide a dwelling, temporary or permanent, through the dweller's own efforts and to improve or extend it over time. The very defects of this form of development were the result of its having been outlawed to the margins of the accepted system of housing provision: to marginal land (because it was cheap), to marginal activities (holiday homes), and for marginal people (those without access to the accepted modes of housing finance, or those whose aspirations were best met by providing what they could for themselves).

NOTES

1. Reps, John W. (1979) *Cities of the American West: A History of Urban Planning*. Princeton, NJ: Princeton University Press.
2. *Ibid.*
3. Barratt, Bernard (1971) *The Inner Suburbs*. Carlton, Victoria: Melbourne , University Press.
4. Simpson, M.A. and Lloyd, T.H. (eds.) (1977) *Middle Class Housing in Britain*. Newton Abbot: David and Charles; Hamden Connecticut: Archon Books.
5. King, Anthony (forthcoming) *The Bungalow*. London: Routledge and Kegan Paul.
6. Letter from John Henderson in *New Society*, 7 August 1975.
7. Stedman papers in Clacton Public Library, Essex.
8. Gerard Young in *The Post*, Bognor, 23 April 1966.
9. Interview with Mrs Cox at Shoreham Beach, 31 May 1980.
10. Erskin, John (1926) A house in the country. Century, CXII, July.
11. Schmitt, Peter J. (1969) *Back to Nature: The Arcadian Myth in Urban America*. New York: Oxford University Press.
12. *Ibid.*
13. We are indebted for personal interviews with Professor Roger Barnett at the University of the Pacific, Stockton and Professor James Vance at the University of California at Berkeley in November 1982. Barnett's Ph.D Thesis: Suburban Subdivision: The Morpho-Genesis of Housing in Stockton, 1850-1950. Berkeley, 1973, has proved to be a valuable source of information for this section.
14. Barnett, Roger (1978) The libertarian suburb: deliberate disorder. *Landscape*. 22(3), Summer.
15. *Ibid.*
16. *Ibid.*
17. *Ibid.*

18. *Ibid.*
19. Gerard Young in *The Post*, Bognor, 19 January 1963.
20. Interview with Planning Officer, Adur District Council, 30 May 1980.
21. The view expressed by Professor James Vance in an interview (see note 13).
22. Our interpretation of current American developments has been assisted by a study tour in November–December 1982. In addition to Professors Roger Barnett at Stockton and James Vance at Berkeley, valuable help was received from colleagues in the Departments of Urban and Regional Planning and of Geography at Florida State University, Tallahassee, and the Department of City and Regional Planning at the University of California, Berkeley.
23. Winsberg, Morton D. (1981) Population, in Fernald, Edward A. (ed.) *Atlas of Florida*. Tallahassee; Florida State University Foundation.
24. Boericke, Art and Shapiro, Barry (1973) *Handmade Houses: A Guide to the Woodbutcher's Art*. San Francisco: Scrimshaw Press.
25. Felder, David W. (1933) *The Best Investment: Land in a Loving Community* Tallahassee: Wellington Press.
26. *The New Village: Concepts and Early Practices*, Uniontown, 1980. In addition to this source we are indebted to Andy Wood of the Open University for his first-hand account of this experiment.
27. From an article in the *Pittsburgh Post Gazette*, 27 December 1979.
28. Cobb, Richard (1980) The assassination of Paris. *The New York Review*, 7 February.
29. Evenson, Norma (1979) *Paris: A Century of Change 1878-1978*. New Haven: Yale University Press.
30. *Ibid.*
31. *Ibid.*
32. This is the way we would interpret the data kindly made available by John Whittam, whose interviews with Essex plotlanders are reported in Chapter 4.
33. Departmental Committee of Inquiry into Allotments (1969) *Report*. London: HMSO.
34. Speech by Mr G. v.d. Pouw Kraan at the 50th anniversary conference of the National Society of Leisure Gardeners, Hastings, 10 June 1980.
35. Departmental Committee of Inquiry, *op. cit.* (see note 33).
36. *Ibid.*
37. *Ibid.*
38. Pouw Kraan, *op. cit.* (see note 34).
39. Noble, John (1981) Housing: plot developments in Denmark; *The Architects Journal*, 4 and 11 March.
40. Noble, John (1973) Contingency housing. *The Architects Journal*, 24 October.
41. Green, Clem L. (1981) Nothing new under the sun, letter in *The Architects Journal*, 12 August 1981.

42. Hamilton, F. E. Ian (1979) Spatial structure in East European cities, in French and Hamilton (eds.) *The Socialist City* Chichester: John Wiley and Sons.
43. Kenedi, Janos (1981) *Do It Yourself: Hungary's Hidden Economy.* London: Pluto Press.
44. Carter, F. W. (1979) Prague and Sofia: An analysis of their changing internal city structure, in French and Hamilton (eds.) *op. cit.* (see note 42).
45. Shaw, Denis J. B. (1979) Recreation and the Soviet city, in French and Hamilton (eds.) *op. cit.* (see note 42).
46. *Ibid.*
47. *Ibid.*
48. Barnett, *op. cit.* (see note 14).
49. Evenson, *op. cit.* (see note 29).
50. Mangin, William P. and Turner, John C. (1969) Benavides and the Barriada movement, in Oliver Paul (ed.), *Shelter and Society.* London: Barrie and Rockcliffe.
51. Studies of Third World squatter settlements are included in, for example, McGee T.G. (1971) *The Urbanisation Process in the Third World.* London: Bell; Payne, Geoffrey (1977) *Urban Housing in the Third World.* London: Leonard Hill; Roberts, Bryan (1978) *Cities of Peasants.* London: Edward Arnold; Turner, Alan (ed.) (1980) *The Cities of the Poor.* London: Croom Helm; Dwyer, D.J. (1975) *People and Housing in Third World Cities.* London: Longman; Wilsher, Peter and Righter, Rosemary (1975) *The Exploding Cities.* London: Andre Deutsch; Ward, Peter (ed.) (1982) *Self-Help Housing: A Critique.* London: Mansell.
52. Lloyd, Peter (1979) *Slums of Hope?* Harmondsworth: Penguin Books.
53. Ward, Colin (1976) Preface to Turner, John F. C., *Housing by People.* London: Marion Boyers; New York: Pantheon Books.
54. Turner, John F.C. and Fichter, Robert (eds.) (1972) *Freedom to Build.* New York: Macmillan.

Chapter Eight

Arcadia in Perspective

Looking back on plotland history certain conclusions can be drawn, as much with an eye to current society as to the past. For a start, we can reflect on what has actually happened, registering the story of plotlands as an interesting and hitherto neglected area of social history — a record of numerous individuals seeking their own place in the sun. And, in the light of this experience, we can return to questions raised in Chapters 1 and 2 about relationships between planning, property and freedom. Secondly, the story can be brought up to date with evidence of modern counterparts in the form of, for example, leisure plots. And, finally, we can take all this one stage further by suggesting ways in which the plotland experience might be seen to be of more than passing interest for current society.

REFLECTIONS

In looking back at what actually happened our first view is less than clear; a haze of nostalgia softens the outlines of plotland history. Recollections of 'the smell of driftwood burning... and of shrimps boiling' [1] or of 'the soft glow of oil lamps filtering through chintzy curtains' [2] contribute to an alluring image of people and places.

Characters are recalled with affection and admiration, the story of their deeds embroidered over the years into a tapestry of pioneering effort and achievement. We have been told of personal endeavour in a variety of situations — there was the man who built his Arcadian retreat, 'Perserverance' (sic), with materials which he carried by bicycle and bus from his East End home to Essex plotland country; or Mr Poplett at Peacehaven whose own success as a local businessman is interlocked with the growth of the new settlement itself. Elsewhere, we talked with Mrs Granger at Laindon who, with 'a borrowed pound', took her family from poor living conditions in Stoke Newington and over the years transformed their own circumstances; and with Mrs Moorcroft at Jaywick Sands who, in campaigning for better services, proved to be every bit a match for uncooperative public authorities.

More often, though, the recollection of plotland people is a simple tale of quiet enjoyment, without personal gain or pretension. Almost without exception our interviews revealed that plotlanders themselves retain fond memories of childhood holidays and a kind of pioneering experience. We met and heard of many people of modest means who bought a little plot of land on which they built their own retreat or ordered a cast-off railway carriage or bus body for holidays and weekend breaks. There is no 'typical' plotland person, but in every location there will be people such as these — remembering the wild fruits picked in summer, the children collecting fresh milk from nearby farms, relations coming to join them for holidays and pitching their own heavy canvas tents, and improvements and changes made to their property from year to year. It is invariably the good things that are recalled most vividly.

Likewise, the plotland landscape, product of a thousand separate decisions and widely reviled by outsiders at the time, has been accorded a status hitherto unknown. Strange 'Emmet-like' structures, defying accepted conventions of architecture and building construction, are now regarded as 'modern folk art'; while surviving timber bungalows are sympathetically compared with pioneering log cabins on the American frontier. And modern commentators, who for years would have had little good to say about such places, make radio and television programmes and write colour supplement articles about the charms of Jaywick Sands, Canvey Island and Peacehaven.

Even local authorities, long-standing adversaries of plotlands, have in some cases softened their approach as the landscapes themselves have mellowed. At Pett Level, Cranmore and Headley Down, for instance, talk of clearance has been replaced by thoughts of conservation — the large plots and varied vegetation in these places providing an informal setting and haven for wild-life that has now acquired something of a scarcity value.

Viewing plotlands through a nostalgic haze is an attractive vantage point. But when the haze lifts, a less exceptionable if not a rather harsher view is revealed. What one can see then is a scene that is neither particularly glamorous nor romantic; folk heroes are reduced to the stature of ordinary mortals, and the qualities of a folk architecture may be far from apparent. Images of plotlands are replaced by what Raymond Williams would term 'real history' [3], in this case a mixed story of personal sacrifice and public conflict as well as harmony and achievement. It is a more complex story but it is where we must now turn if we are to unravel some of the issues of 'property' and 'control' that are wrapped up in plotland history.

On the question of plotlands as a distinctive form of property two issues are especially intriguing — namely, was the whole business of land subdivision and the spread of property ownership a democratising process, and was there anything more in it than personal economic gain?

As a democratising process, it is unquestionable that more land became available, and more people gained access to this land than would have been possible simply through the mainstream transfers of the property market during this period. Large tracts of land — derived, in turn, from the break-up of some of the great estates, from tenant farmers unable to survive the agricultural slump of the 1930s, and from hitherto neglected pockets along the shoreline and river banks — were subdivided into small plots. At this level then, there is the simple fact of more people owning their own land than was previously the case. Whether or not this was a democratising process is more debatable. It is certainly tempting, for instance, to see the transfer of land from aristocratic owners to industrious artisans in this way though it is misleading to the extent that these very sales facilitated fresh investment by the old owners in more lucrative outlets than agricultural land. Equally, it is tempting to envisage a massive, unsolicited surge of land pioneers drawn from the city by thoughts of their own place in the sun and, again, it would be misleading to see things quite in this way. The time was right for this movement, but it was in many cases certainly not unsolicited. The hand of the land company and of the entrepreneur has seldom been far from the initial process of plot disposals, and we have on several occasions drawn attention to a likeness with the subdivision and disposal of land in the pioneering days of North America and Australia. Developers like Charles Neville, Frederick Ramuz and Frank Stedman were each of them in their way manipulative characters who, if they did not create the process of 'freehold land for the people', undoubtedly encouraged it. So too, did companies like Homesteads Ltd., whose activities touched upon a wide range of plotland developments, dating back to the turn of the century.

If all this is to suggest that the process itself was not entirely in the hands of people who simply wanted a plot of their own, this was not always the case. Land companies and entrepreneurs may well have had their way in the early days, but gradually the tempo and form of transactions changed. After the colour and excitement of national advertising, of free railway tickets and sale documents signed in beer tents, the plotlanders themselves took over. We found many instances of rentals and sales staying in the family, or of details being passed on by word of mouth to friends and neighbours. When this was not enough, cards in shop windows and adverts in local newspapers were easy alternatives; or, for a bigger catchment still, weekly publications like *Dalton's Weekly* were popular and widely-known. A regular page in the paper, headed 'Caravans, Camping Sites, Houseboats, Huts, Tents etc — To Be Let, Sold or Wanted' was to all intents and purposes, a gazetteer of plotland places. And the two-and three-line entries, offering 'an ideal holiday in a first-class railway saloon' at Pagham, the lure of a 'long, healthy and happy life' through weekends in a gipsy-type caravan at Althorne, or a 'fur. dble-deck Bus Caravan on Lge., secluded plot, few mins sea' at Selsey Bill come closer to the meaning of plotlands than some of their more colourful precursors [4]. They were, essentially, very modest places offering simple pleasures for generally poor people; what was seen to be important, and the way in which this was brought to the attention of others, may have seemed

279

unusual to outsiders but was meaningful and consistent for those involved in the process.

As to whether there was anything more to plotlands than economic gain, the evidence suggests that this was seldom a prime motive. It is true that plotland advertisements exhorted would-be purchasers to think in terms of the gains to be had. It is equally true that plotlanders (more often than not unexpectedly) later found themselves owning a valuable slice of real estate, and able to sell the dwelling they had improved over the years at prices comparable to more conventional suburban developments. But it is unlikely that many ventured into their first plotland with thoughts of economic gain uppermost in their mind; a few square feet of shingle ridge or waterlogged clay seemed unpromising sources of investment. Invariably, the plotlands comprised a world of small-scale occupants, where the main gains appeared other than economic — if not always to the extent expressed by a plotholder at Pagham Beach, that 'we did not like a private person trying to make a profit so to speak' [5].

Instead, the plotlands offered more immediate attractions than a nebulous promise of long-term gain. One such attraction was that they were cheap enough to be accessible to many people who would otherwise have been denied the opportunity for weekends and holidays in the country or by the sea. With poor quality agricultural land prices as low as £15 per acre, small plots were regularly on sale for just a few pounds; and where even a few pounds presented difficulties, 'easy payments' were available to secure a sale. Constructing a dwelling was also a manageable proposition, and without restrictive byelaws to raise construction costs, plotholders enjoyed more or less a free hand to design what they wanted. Commonly, a permanent structure emerged in stages — perhaps with an ex-army bell tent to start with, progressing on a weekend and holiday basis to a presentable building, extended and improved over time with new additions to the family or thoughts of a comfortable retirement home.

The economics of plotland development were such that cheap summer rentals not only reached out to a further sector of the market who could either not afford to or chose not to buy their own property, but also the additional income helped owners to improve their holdings. As late as 1937 a holiday hut could be rented for as little as fifteen shillings a week, a large houseboat for thirty shillings, or a luxury railway saloon for forty-two shillings.

Apart from the simple attraction of cheapness, plotlands were also widely appreciated for the opportunity they provided for poor people to enjoy a spell away from city smoke. Throughout the heyday of plotlands, respiratory illnesses and smoke pollution in cities were prevalent, and the pursuit of fresh air was soundly-based. Previously available only to a privileged minority, advertisements now lured poorer families to the ozone-impregnated air of the South Coast, to the healthy sea breezes at Canvey and Sheppey in the Thames Estuary, or simply the tranquillity of a riverside haven or woodland setting.

Our experience is that the health-giving qualities of plotland life are frequently recalled. In some instances, the story is a dramatic one — like the ex-soldier who returned from France in 1918, suffering from inhalation of gas, and who subsequently led a long and active life at Peacehaven; or the lady who thanked the Jaywick environment for her survival through an illness for which her doctors held no hope. Other instances are less dramatic though more common — with landowners recalling the enjoyment of good fresh air and local farm produce. It is interesting to contrast these recollections with the fact that Medical Officers of Health were amongst the main adversaries of plotlands, constantly warning (sometimes with good reason) of the threat that rudimentary water supplies and disposal systems posed to health in the locality.

Another attraction of plotlands is to be found in the opportunities provided for informality and a simple way of life. Compared with the regimentation and hierarchical structure of working-class life in towns, plotland life imposed the very minimum in the way of restrictions and social convention. House design was a product of basic needs, available materials and occasional flights of fancy rather than of someone else's standards. Material distractions were few and holidays comprised long days in the open air, working on the plot or enjoying the natural surroundings. Little else was required, and makeshift arrangements were made for supplies of food and fresh water, and for waste disposal; rarely did these meet with the approval of local government officers, but more often than not they worked.

For most people this simplicity and absence of a social hierarchy was an obvious source of freedom, and Charles Neville at Peacehaven was amongst those who reminded plotholders that all were on the same footing. Referring to Shoreham Beach, Lord Mersey urged recognition of what it all offered for 'the small man'; while East Sussex County Council, in similar vein, saw that for all its ills, Peacehaven provided a unique setting for 'the simple life',

This simple life was attractive to working people from shops, offices and factories but it attracted others as well — amongst whom were the 'Bohemians'. Along the South Coast, especially, but also in riverside haunts and other countryside retreats we have been told of artists, actors, film stars and writers lured by the informality and relative freedom of plotland settlements. Though few in number, places like Shoreham Beach, Pett Level and Winchelsea Beach gained colour and something of a raffish reputation.

There is irony in the fact that the simple life and the rural weekend also attracted those members of the liberal intelligentsia who, in other circumstances, deplored the way in which their social inferiors flocked to their own vulgar version of the escape to arcadia. Reginald Bray was a progressive philanthropist who worked among poor children in South London and was a member of the London School Board and the London County Council. In 1919 he left London to look after his father's estates based upon Shere, near Guildford in Surrey [6]. The Bray estates were conscientiously administered and the estate papers have been studied by Peter Brandon, who finds that Bray provided sites for weekend cottages on his estate for many of the good and great of that period, including the majority of the members of the first Labour cabinet [7]. Among the weekend residents on the Bray estates were several crusaders for the protection of the countryside. They included the architect Clough Williams-Ellis, who later built the delightful make-believe holiday village of Portmerrion, and was the author of *England and the Octopus* and the editor of *Britain and the Beast*. He deplored the way in which 'the adventurous bungalow plants its foundations — a pink asbestos roof screaming its challenge — across a whole parish from some pleasant upland that it has light-heartedly defaced' [8].

Another weekend resident was Bray's fellow Harrovian, the historian G.M. Trevelyan, who lamented that 'the State is Socialist enough to destroy by taxation the classes that used to preserve rural amenity, but it is still too Conservative to interfere in the purposes to which land is put by speculators to whom the land is sold' [9]. Many other part-time champions of rural England deplored the desecration of the countryside, and at the same time had their own second home, correctly built to blend with its surroundings, but there is something unattractive about the way they took for granted that they were entitled to have a country retreat while wanting to deny, on aesthetic grounds, the same opportunity for people further down the hierarchy of income and opportunity.

Looking back more generally on plotlands and property, one conclusion is that, on balance, they offered many people opportunities which might not otherwise have been available. But at what cost to the rest of society? It is this question which underlines the debate surrounding continued attempts to control this type of development. Were these attempts justified in terms of a common good?

Although the formation of plotlands dates back to the end of the nineteenth century, it was only from the middle of the 1920s (when the tempo of development increased, and more was clearly on the way) that public concern about its impact on the environment was expressed. It was still not regarded as a major problem, though 'the weekend habit' attracted growing attention in the regional plans that were prepared at that time. By the 1930s public awareness had increased but so, too, had the incidence of plotlands. In spite of an influential preservationist lobby, there was still a resistance to introduce legislation that would seriously interfere with traditional rights of property. Some legislative changes were made (in the form of general and private Acts, and through local byelaws) but public authorities were seldom able to check, let alone turn back, the tide of plotland development throughout the 1930s.

Returning year after year for summer holidays at Camber Sands or Shoreham Beach, in a hut on Box Hill or a cabin by the river, most plotlanders remained blissfully unaware of the 'public nuisance', they were said to be causing. But opinion was hardening against them, with objections based on a variety of grounds. For one thing, preservationists argued that plotlands had already despoiled large areas of attractive coast and countryside, and that remaining areas of

282

natural beauty should be protected from further onslaughts. As well as the amenity argument, local authorities opposed this type of development on account of costs — for uneconomic road layouts, street lighting and other services — that they would be asked to meet in the future. Local authorities also objected to the makeshift water collection and sewage disposal systems, and to what were by usual standards low-quality housing on the grounds of the threat posed to public health. Reference has also been made in the case studies to a class-based resistance to working townspeople usurping a traditional countryside hierarchy and way of life. In short, then, plotlands epitomised brashness and disorder, in sharp contrast to established standards of integration and order.

What turned the tide in the first place was less the weight of rational argument and new legislation, and more the unintended consequences of war. The very outbreak of war in 1939 had the effect of freezing plotland boundaries as they stood and, as it happened, these were never again to increase. More dramatically, especially along the South Coast, military operations cleared away numerous huts and holiday homes that stood between the home artillery and an enemy across the sea. Some years later, in 1953, the great floods did a comparable demolition job along the East Coast, removing plotland properties on Canvey Island and at Jaywick Sands.

In the postwar period, the 1947 Town and Country Planning Act provided what the 1930s officials had so obviously lacked, namely, an effective means of controlling new development and therefore preventing fresh plotlands. This has been reinforced by a substantial battery of byelaws to ensure a much higher level of minimum building standards than had existed before.

Preventing new development is one thing, but what proved to be far less tractable for local authorities was the task of removing or at least bringing under control what was already there — the legacy of a half century of unrestricted plotlands. With very few exceptions a direct confrontation to remove a plotland colony, and then to restore the land to its natural state, has not proved possible. Shoreham Beach was an early test-case, where the local authorities were thwarted in their attempt to win compulsory powers to finish the clearance of the holiday settlement started in the war. In other instances, too, as at Jaywick Sands or in some of the riverside colonies, the plotholders proved to be remarkably effective as political campaigners, resisting time and again the efforts of local authorities to remove them. The sheer cost of compensation and land restoration was also a weighty obstacle to removal; East Sussex County Council, for example, costed the exercise along their stretch of coastline and decided that the public benefits would not be sufficient to justify this expenditure.

The most important exception is, of course, the Laindon-Pitsea network of plotlands where New Town machinery was used to clear the area and, more recently and on a smaller scale, the new development at South Woodham Ferrers has replaced another collection of plots. Planned residential estates have inherited the land in this way elsewhere too, while at Havering Park buildings and individual plots have been replaced by a landscaped park.

More often, though, local authorities have lacked either the political will or finances to engage in protracted conflicts with plotlanders, preferring instead to see a steady transition of such areas from their haphazard past to more orderly settlements. Conciliatory planning policies, allowing 'one-for-one' replacements, have oiled the wheels of a process of improvement that is the natural order of things in plotlands. Over the years, properties have changed out of all recognition, the result very often of an incremental process of enlargement and improvement.

So the days of bitter conflict between individuals and authorities are now generally over. But were they ever justified in the first place? Was the Arcadian quest really the threat to the rest of society that it was made out to be? In one sense, public concern was justified and understandable. In an area of the country with a high density of population and growing demands on a fragile environment, preservationists undoubtedly had a case. And with the tangible and widely-appreciated gains made through public intervention to raise health and housing standards, no one wished to see a reversal on that front.

What is debatable, however, is whether restrictions and standards needed to be applied uniformly and indiscriminately in the way they were. Was it really necessary to protect an out-of-the-way site of no particular scenic charm with the same rigour as a much-visited beauty spot? Were the byelaws drawn up to tackle nineteenth-century urban slum conditions necessarily the most appropriate standards for temporary holiday accommodation in the countryside? And, for local authorities worried about costs they might have to incur, why did they take it upon themselves to provide a full range of urban services for settlements where most people preferred in any case to live 'a simple life'? These are questions which retain their topicality, and which will now be pursued in the context of what is happening today in Arcadia.

THE LEISURE PLOT INDUSTRY

'Cheap land (Freehold). Your own leisure garden. Beat the falling pound and inflation. Invest in land for growing and leisure, from £195 full price. Plot sizes approximately 40 ft by 100 ft. Larger plots, with some future building potential also available on easy terms.'

Advertisement, 1975.

In 1946, the first postwar summer, holiday visitors to the Bournemouth area were lured to the Avon Castle estate, south-west of Ringwood, by the implied promise of the chance of a lifetime, to purchase a site in balmy Hampshire for the home of their dreams for

284

holidays or retirement. The auction particulars were most carefully drawn up with the 'small print' disclaiming almost everything. 'Lot 99 — a beautiful site for a picnic!' As the auctioneer knocked down odd lots and glowingly described the wonderful opportunities that lay ahead of purchasers, many of them visitors from the north of England with army gratuities in their savings banks, the local area planning officer, stationed at the back of the hall, protested that the Town and Country Planning Act of 1943 (a wartime interim precursor of the Act of 1947 which was at that time still in its passage through Parliament) would make it unlikely that purchasers would actually be permitted to build anything. The auctioneer scorned such a ridiculous idea and urged his audience to carry on bidding [10].

In the same summer an officer of the new Ministry of Town and Country Planning was noting with alarm the postwar resurgence of plot development in East Essex.

On Bridge Marsh Creek, Althorne (west of Burnham) there are the beginnings of a piece of shack development which I think is potentially dangerous. At present it consists of about 20 wooden shacks and moveable caravans which are located in a field adjoining this tidal creek. I understand that the structures have been put up without any consent of the local authority the Maldon Rural District Council. The site is in a field in an area very subject to flooding.... I understand that the landowner is selling the land in small plots and I noticed that a few of the plots seem to be roughly laid out and roughly enclosed in wire fencing. It is difficult to understand why anybody should actually mean to install themselves here for holiday making. The land is low, very damp at ordinary times whilst the nearest habitation is miles away... The Council were apparently wholly unaware of this development until it was casually brought to their notice and they have, apparently, no intention of agreeing to development here on the grounds of unsuitability of the site for building and because they do not want to encourage shack development. They are very anxious to take steps to have the unauthorised development removed and they ask for the Department's advice on this matter and how they should best proceed... It is impossible I suppose to stop the landowner from selling plots of land, but the Clerk said that the Council were proposing to erect a notice board adjacent to the area and on neutral ground warning the public that development here would not be sanctioned... I think we might ask the Treasury Solicitor to advise upon the action which the local authority could reasonably take to get rid of the unauthorised development. The Council is quite anxious to do the right thing in this matter and they should receive encouragement from us... [11].

The Town and Country Planning Act of 1947 and subsequent planning Acts (together with the General Development Orders made under these Acts and the use of Article Four Directions, removing permitted development rights) have in theory given local planning authorities power to prevent the formation of new plotland areas. The political consensus that demanded that postwar Britain should have no more Peacehavens or Jaywicks, had won its point. But to legislate on any issue where there is a disparity between private interests and the public good is to invite a conspiracy between buyers and sellers to circumvent the law (as is made clear by the history of laws on prohibition, prostitution or pornography).

While land remains a commodity, the phenomenal rise in site values in the postwar decades ensures that there are plenty of people who see a prospect of gain in subdividing it. Similarly the rise in the standard of living has meant for many families a demand for more private space. For the affluent this aspiration was easily met. Families with less disposable income sought a humbler kind of leisure space just as the pre-war purchasers of plotland sites had done. And just as motoring was only perceived as presenting problems when the motor-car ceased to be a rich man's plaything and a mass market arose, so second homes or 'a place in the country' were only considered a menace when people of modest means sought their version of this widespread aspiration. Of British households by 1980, 2 to 3 per cent owned second homes, and it is interesting to compare this figure with the 10 per cent in Denmark, 18 per cent in France and 20 per cent in Sweden.

Increasingly in the 1960s and 1970s speculators, often as companies difficult to trace or registered overseas, acquired and divided up a few fields or a piece of woodland into small plots of about a tenth of an acre, advertised them alluringly, and succeeded in persuading people that this was the opportunity of a lifetime. When the purchasers came down with their primus stoves and sleeping bags to take possession of their few square yards of England, they found that the local planning authority had read the advertisements too. The enforcement officer (usually a retired policeman) had posted up a notice of the Article Four Direction indicating that the plot-owners could not build, park a caravan or car, pitch a tent, put up a fence, or in theory even take a walk on their plots. Often they found that there was no means of access to it either, except over someone else's land. If they applied for planning permission to do anything with the place, it was refused by the local authority. If they appealed to the Department of the Environment against this decision, the appeal was refused.

The leisure plot phenomenon can be found in many parts of the South East within reach of London, but especially in Kent, Essex and Sussex. For planning authorities, attempting to control it is a labour-intensive and time-consuming activity. Their enforcement officers work overtime in woods, dells and hidden pastures, or sometimes by helicopter, trying to catch up with it. Their lives are punctuated on sunny Saturdays with angry weekenders, claiming that an Englishman's plot is his potential castle.

The district and county councils are concerned about the loss of visual amenity, the loss of what might be economically productive land,

Winchelsea: modern leisure plots in an area of former plotland development.

and the complaints of nuisance and disturbance from local residents, who find a procession of cars choking up the leafy lanes and farm tracks, and the assumption of a right of way where none exists.

Surveyors and land agents are concerned about the slur on their profession. John Heddle, who has been concerned with this issue as a surveyor and as a county councillor in Kent where the leisure plot industry has flourished, and subsequently as a Member of Parliament, tried very hard in all three of these capacities to seek some public control of the leisure plot industry. When we asked him what he found most objectionable about it, he replied, 'I hate to see unscrupulous firms trading on people's aspirations through speculation' [12].

The Incorporated Society of Valuers and Auctioneers keeps a dossier on the companies involved in selling plots, and it is evident that it is a highly profitable and legal business. The advertisements are carefully worded to imply that, in the continuing inflation of the currency, such purchases are bound to be a good investment, and that while some plots *may* have 'future building potential', any agricultural or forestry use is possible, like 'fir trees, fruit or decorative trees, shrubs, vines, market produce, such as your own fresh, chemical-free salads'. There is usually the implied hint that some relaxation of planning policy might turn the purchaser's investment into a little gold mine.

In 1975 Mr Heddle pointed out to his fellow county councillors that 'These land speculators now own at least twenty six sites in Kent alone

£500 price of private picnics for life

By Julia Langdon

The good life goes bad on buyers' little acres

Leisureplots: current developments. (From the Guardian)

— well over 1,000 acres — from Cobham Woods in Gravesham, to Seasalter Marshes in the Canterbury district, from Perry Woods in Faversham to Fordcomb in Tunbridge Wells' [13]. He described the Article Four procedure as 'shutting the Planning Officer's door after the speculator's horse has bolted', and urged that Section 22 of the 1947 Planning Act should be amended to declare that a change of use from agricultural land to 'leisure purposes' constitutes in itself a development for which planning consent is required, and that planning authorities should be enabled to use the powers of Section 86 of the Agriculture Act of 1947 to control the subdivision of agricultural units.

This view was upheld by Mr George Dobry QC in the review he conducted of the development control system, where he recommended that 'Section 22(3) of the 1971 Act should be amended to provide (for the avoidance of doubt) that a change in the use of a separate plot of land from agricultural to a "leisure" purpose would constitute development' [14]. Keith Speed, MP for Ashford, Kent, raised the issue in the House of Commons, but the Minister while expressing sympathy with the view that something should be done about these sales, replied that 'It is however a long-established principle that the Town and Country Planning Acts exist to regulate the development of land, and not changes in its ownership' [15].

Several years elapsed before the opponents of the leisure plot industry were able to bring the matter, once again, before the legislators. The Kent County Council Bill, introduced in 1980, included clauses on the Control of Leisure Plots, but on advice from the government, and in the

288

interests of getting the Bill enacted, withdrew this section. At the same time, John Heddle, after several years of trying, was able to ventilate the issue in the House of Commons. He described how the speculators operate, buying poor quality grazing land, deep in the heart of the country, and usually in the Metropolitan Green Belt.

Depending on the area, they buy land for between £500 and £2,000 an acre. In the guise of £100 companies that are controlled by nominee directors and have £2 shares, the speculators parcel up the land into separate plots. The plots usually measure about 100 feet by 40 feet. In rare cases they may measure half an acre and in still rarer cases, an acre. They then advertise the plots in the 'land for sale' columns of the popular weekly press at anything from £150 per plot to £1,000 a plot. Their profit margins are not difficult to calculate. At the minimum they are usually £3,000 an acre [16].

The solutions he proposed were that the government should invoke the Fair Trading Act and extend to land the provisions of the Trade Descriptions Act, and that it should amend the Town and Country Planning Acts so that the subdivision of land should itself be regarded as a form of development, except possibly where this was for agricultural use, and that the Dobry proposal should be adopted.

Replying to Mr Heddle, Marcus Fox, Under-Secretary of State in the Department of the Environment, agreed that speculators were 'taking advantage of ordinary people who simply wanted to acquire a small plot of land in the countryside where they can spend some of their leisure time' but thought that John Heddle under-estimated the degree of control that could be exercised by vigilant planning authorities. He thought that the provisions in the County of Kent Bill, which included provisions for a licensing system for plots, to be operated by district councils, would produce 'little short of a bureaucratic nightmare' [17]. And he drew attention to the decision made in the previous year by Peter Shore, the then Secretary of State for the Environment, in deciding on appeals against enforcement orders concerning leisure plots on the Blackwater Estuary near Maldon, which ruled that the creation of a leisure plot on former agricultural land was a form of development subject to control [18].

There the matter ended, the publicity given to the disappointment of purchasers has made it more difficult for the plot sellers to find a market. But not all the plotholders thought of themselves merely as victims.

Seasalter Meadow and the adjacent Vikings Estate is an area of about 160 acres of coastal marshland in the Canterbury district of Kent, divided into plots by Messrs A.R. and G.E. Darling of Cheam, Surrey in 1972. The firm's literature said that:

The present council is opposed to building on the site as it stands today. However, the estate is well situated on a coastline

289

which already has a number of existing developments and the possibility of future development permission being obtained can by no means be ruled out [19].

Canterbury City Council, on the other hand, affirmed that 'No planning permission will be granted for any structures on Sea-salter marshes'.

By 1975 more than 200 plots had been sold, for figures between £500 and £2,000. John Heddle claimed that Mr Darling's firm was buying useless land at £30 an acre and selling at more than £1,000 an acre [20], and that there was a danger of a 'Klondyke-like encampment of shanty towns with rural slums developing as purchasers erected sheds, tents, fences, portable conveniences and caravans on their piece of "rural bliss" ' [21].

One of the purchasers, a retired postal worker, Thomas Nihill, responded that:

> A lot of rubbish is being spoken by certain councillors about this land at the moment. And that is why we are sending a letter to Canterbury City Council asking them to come here for a site inspection to see exactly what we have done with the land. It's absolutely mad for people to criticise us when we are producing such large quantities of food on this fertile land [22].

The most bitter of all the disputes about leisure plots has been fought over the saltings, marshes and mud-flats of the Blackwater Estuary in Essex. This area is under heavy pressure for recreational use, being 'within two hours' drive of two-fifths of the population of England and Wales' [23], and at the same time is classified, because of its wildlife, as a Grade I Site of Special Scientific Interest.

The Maldon District Council has introduced a Blackwater Estuary Recreation and Conservation Subject Plan, being in an unusual position of control over the estuary since a Charter of 1171 gave the Borough all rights over the sea bed and foreshore, while outside the town similar rights are leased from the Crown Commissioners. The plan takes note of the existence of long-established plotland sites and leisure plots:

> Apart from the 2,500 caravan and chalet pitches on sites around the estuary there are about a thousand leisure plots spread over a hundred acres of former farmland. The policies attempt not to be prejudiced against these forms of development *per se* but to set down criteria which should be met before an application can be approved. Five locational criteria are set out, specifying that the site should be: well screened, not directly on the riverside but not so far away as to generate traffic at riverside centres, adjacent to an area with capacity for increased boating use, and not disturb either local inhabitants or wildlife [24].

In 1972 the then local authority was granted an Article Four Direction to enable it to control caravans and fences on leisure plots, but in 1975, after an appeal which was regarded as a test case, the then Secretary of State, Anthony Crosland, refused to uphold the Council's attempt to oblige plotowners in the Heybridge and Bradwell areas to remove caravans and fences from their 240-square-feet plots:

> The decision means that plot-owners need not remove fences from their land, provided the plot is being used for agricultural purposes. Other plot-owners have also been allowed to keep sheds while the sites are used for growing vegetables or flowers. Although not allowing the indefinite parking of caravans on leisure plots, Mr Crosland has granted a stay of execution of enforcement notices requiring the removal of caravans... He also adds that it would be unreasonable to require the removal of all trees and plants on existing leisure plots [25].

On what had become known as the Blackwater Estuary Estate a local farmer sold leisure plots in 1971, each of about 30 feet by 80 feet in two fields adjoining the river and one further back. He acquainted the purchasers of the restrictions on the use of the land, which was also subject to flooding. In spite of this there was a ready flow of purchasers, many of them buying two adjacent plots, taking advantage of the permitted development right of caravan parking for up to twenty-eight days a year.

In 1972 the then local authority, Maldon Rural District Council, sought the advice of the Department of the Environment as to how the sale and subdivision of land could be stopped, just as it had sought similar advice for the site at Althorne in 1946 from the one-time Ministry of Town and Country Planning. The Department replied that there was no legislation available and urged the Rural District Council to ask the County Council, as planning authority, to apply for an Article Four Direction.

The County Council did so, and the application was granted by the Secretary of State, in a ruling that the change of use was a development requiring planning permission [26].

The Blackwater Estuary Estate Association fought back, appealing against the enforcement order from what had now become the Maldon District Council. Mr Ernest Fisher, representing himself and other owners, claimed that the application for an Article Four Direction stated that it was needed because agricultural land was being sold for other purposes and that the site was not suitable for caravans, although the real reason — set out in correspondence between the councils — was that they simply wanted to stop the sale and subdivision of land. The direction, Mr Fisher claimed, could not be legally used to stop the sale of land and was thus *ultra vires* — outside statutory powers. 'It is a conspiracy to pervert the text and sense of the law' [27].

Mr Fisher sought a High Court writ for damages against the District Council, the County Council and the former Secretary of State, but his application was struck out by the court as 'frivolous and vexatious' [28].

291

He told the public inquiry into the appeal against enforcement notices that:

> We want to be an asset to the area. We will pay a considerable amount in rates to the council but we will not cost them a penny. We will provide our own sewerage, our own rubbish collection, our own roads — anything the council ask us to — if only they will give us a chance.

He was supported by another plotholder who had been imprisoned rather than pay fines for not removing a caravan from his plot, and the enforcement officer confirmed that the site had been run in an 'exemplary' manner [29].

The motives of the buyers and sellers of leisure plots have been exactly the same as the motives of those concerned with the prewar plotlands. The difference is that in those days people had a reasonable expectation of being able to do what they wanted with their piece of ground. The worries of the local authorities were much the same too. What would happen if everybody did it? Would the whole of the Home Counties become one vast shanty-town? What the leisure plot industry reveals is that there is a vast unfulfilled demand for private leisure space in the country. The experience of other countries suggests that, with different attitudes, it can be met without an undue loss of public amenity. A former senior planning officer from the Department of the Environment remarked to us:

> What is the point of outlawing people's legitimate aspirations? In the absence of a proper outlet, this kind of development still happens, but is driven into the hands of the wrong people. We will be left with a situation where both buyers and sellers don't give a damn for official attitudes, and until we have clear-cut policies so that people know what to expect and an approach that acknowledges the *demand* for a plotland way of life, we will go on having exploiters and exploited, and we will continue to bring the idea of planning into disrepute among enterprising people.

PLOTLAND PROSPECTS

Is housing an object merely for consumption and/or investment, and is owner–building just another means to attain those ends? No-one can give a simple answer to that question; yet our research suggests that a man who builds his house gains something more than shelter and equity. If this is true, it should be encouraged because it represents the basic human desire to exercise control over the making of one's environment which may be especially important both to those who have relatively few economic options in life and to those who wish for greater personal fulfilment.

292

William C. Grindley: Owner-Builders — Survivors with a Future, in Turner and Fichter (eds.): *Freedom to Build.*

The quiet social revolution in housing in Britain all through the twentieth century has been a revolution in tenure. Until the First World War, 90 per cent of families in the country, rich or poor, rented their homes. By the last quarter of the century, well over half became owner-occupiers while another third were tenants of local authorities. Many years ago Lewis Waddilove discovered that 'the range of choice open to the family in Britain seeking a modern house is more limited than is the case almost anywhere in Europe' [30], and until the belated rediscovery of housing associations and housing co-operatives (which suffer from the same limitations as to finance and standards as the two main sectors and the same governmental bureaucracy in providing consent and cash), the individual aspirant to a family home has had to fit into one of two categories.

Either he had to be the kind of person whose occupation, income and prospects qualified him to become the owner of the kind of house in the kind of area which suited the policy of the building societies, as the main providers of mortgage loans, or he had to be the kind of person whose family's needs, assessed on a 'points' system or whose ability to lobby councillors or their officers effectively and persistently, qualified him for a local authority tenancy. The people whose attributes did not fit in the Building Society office on the High Street, or in the Housing Department, at the back of the Town Hall, had to fend for themselves.

The enormous interest of the plotlanders, statistically insignificant (though you have only to open a conversation with Londoners of a certain age to learn that many have spent a holiday at Jaywick, Canvey, Shoreham, Pett Level or the Selsey Peninsula), is that they reverted to the 'timeless way of building', seized the opportunities available to them when marginal land was as cheap as dirt, and built for themselves. They had opened a crack in the crude duopoly of access to housing in Britain, a country where the use of land is more strictly limited and controlled than in almost anywhere else in the world. (In peasant Andalusia, the local phrase for getting married is 'building a house', and the village finds a site and helps with the quarrying of materials.)

The fact that most plotland homes were first intended as merely holiday shanties or caravan sites is of little importance: in the first place, because we have seen everywhere that the plotland hut has grown to be the retirement home of its owners; and secondly, because in the actual lives of families, as so many people have recalled, those country holidays were more significant than their normal round-the-year routine in fully-serviced and sanitarily-approved houses. Jean Metcalfe, for example, remarks that the time spent with her 'radiantly eccentric and go-as-you-please' [31] grandparents in their railway coach home in the New Forest, surrounded by animals, flowers and old motorbikes, were 'the days I remember most vividly' [32].

There is scarcely a plotland area we have visited, in those areas where planning policy has come to terms with reality, where we have

293

not seen some ultimate legatee of the old cabin building a new house around it, thankful for the land, and the existing accommodation around which to do so. This is simply an alternative version of the paradox which has been observable for decades in every British city. On one side of town is expensive municipal housing, built to Parker Morris standards, often despised by its inhabitants and deteriorating at a terrifying rate, so that in a growing number of instances it is obsolete and uninhabitable many decades before the money borrowed to pay for it has been repaid. On the other side of town is the sub-Parker Morris speculatively built estate which is improved and enhanced from the moment it is occupied, is painlessly maintained and improved at the level and the pace which suits the occupier, so that its value increases as the years go by while the notion of its obsolescence never arises. Surely there is *something* to be learned from this?

To our mind we should quietly and humbly re-think our housing policy from first principles, and then consider how the circumstances we have inherited can be re-shaped to fit the principles of housing. Fortunately we have two excellent guides to the discovery of a viable philosophy of housing. One is the work of John Turner, cited in Chapter 7. The other is that of the Dutch architect Nicolas John Habraken.

Habraken's book, *Supports: An Alternative to Mass Housing*, appeared in his own country in 1961, but it was eleven years before we got an authorised English translation [33]. The fact that his outline of an architectural solution is less convincing today than it might have been twenty years ago has obscured the importance of the first part of his book, which is a sustained criticism of the idea of what he calls MH — Mass Housing. Habraken remarks that:

> It is one of the wonders of our existence that the satisfaction of some requirements demands a very positive, personal, almost creative action on our part. Even today no-one would maintain that we can live merely by consumption, no matter how attractively or skillfully consumer goods are presented. But Mass Housing reduces the dwelling to a consumer article and the dweller to a consumer. For only in this way can it be expected that the consumer waits until he is offered a completed product. It need not surprise us if this approach proves wrong because individual human action should form part of the housing brief.

It is time, Habraken declares, 'to break the bonds of Mass Housing, and at least to inquire what the individual can contribute to the housing process' — something which, as he says, policies of Mass Housing deny *a priori*, and consequently leave out of the discussion of housing policy.

> Mass Housing pretends that the involvement of the individual and all that it implies simply ought not to exist. The provision of housing therefore cannot be called a process of man housing himself. Man no longer houses himself: he is housed.

Now you might observe that Habraken has a selective view of history, since, if they were poor, his ancestors and ours in, say, the seventeenth or eighteenth centuries, lived in shanties of mud and straw, not a trace of which remains. The vernacular architecture we have all learned to love, housed the superior artisan class rather than the poor of pre-industrial society, while, as we all know, the industrial poor of the nineteenth century lived in grossly over-crowded slums. They had nothing to contribute except an exorbitant rent. We do not know whether anyone has ever raised this criticism with Habraken. If they do, we can expect him to reply with this remark from another page:

> In fact, Mass Housing in its original conception was never intended to house the entire community. It was merely an emergency measure which was seized upon when the normal process fell short. It was a means which was useful when large numbers of people had to be housed in a short space of time. It was used when for various reasons the natural relationship had already been interrupted, and when certain groups of people for one reason or another could not house themselves — groups which were originally housed in this way were paupers just because they had no place in the normal pattern; because they had become isolated from it; and had to be housed by an external measure, by an artificial effort. Mass Housing has indeed been a blessing in recent times for countless people, and as an emergency measure has contributed to the fact that our civilisation has survived the industrial revolution. *But our problem began when this emergency measure from the turn of the century grew into housing for the entire community, and thus became the norm [34].*

In practice of course it only became the norm for those ideologists in his country or ours who confused society with the State, and assumed that the activities of central or local government were to be equated with socialism. The norm, statistically, is owner-occupation as we have mentioned, in this and in many other countries, East and West, and this is just as well, or the public cost of housing an inert community would absorb the whole national budget. It is only of course in the capitalist West that people who regard their views as progressive have ideological difficulties about owner-occupation. In the countries of Eastern Europe, by the simple device of regarding a home as 'personal' rather than 'real' property, they have avoided this sterile blind alley. Several of the communist countries have a higher proportion of owner-occupation than Britain. In a Chinese commune, we are told the normal way for a young couple to get a house is for them to build it, with the help of their neighbours and with materials bought from the commune, and to own it personally. A combination, in other words, of self-help and mutual aid.

The plotlands, on the very margins of the organised system of housing, whether public or private, exemplify the principles for which

295

Habraken and Turner were looking. Their settlers had no help, and usually a great deal of hindrance, from the public authorities, and had no access to the normal sources of housing finance. In this light, and especially when compared with the much-publicised expensive disasters in public housing, they represent, not a housing ideal, but a striking example of how much was achieved by relatively poor people with few resources beyond their own labour and enthusiasm.

What were seen at one time as overwhelming objections to the plotlands, do not appear so crucial today. Perhaps the most important objection was that they were sub-standard, as though housing standards were immutable. The notion that housing standards are absolute, and that every house must meet them right from the start, has led to the unrealistic assumption that every couple setting up a household should have everything that various governmental committees have seen as desirable, from the very beginning of their life together, and that these desiderata should even follow them on holiday. Apart from the fact that people *do* have a variety of personal priorities, which may not include a ventilated food cupboard or the appropriate square footage of bedspace, this attitude is one reason why many young couples, as an alternative to living with their parents or in rented rooms (which do not meet the standards either), prefer to venture outside the approved housing market into a 'mobile home', a permanent caravan which has notional wheels to meet the legal requirement that it is a temporary dwelling. Their popularity is simply because they evade the requirements of planning, building and housing legislation. It is an unintended compliment to the plotland philosophy.

The administrative objection to the plotlands is simply to do with the fact that local authorities prefer to deal with large housing developers and with large landowners. The 'fragmentation of ownership' is frequently cited in planning reports as a difficulty in coping with the plotlands, as though providence had decreed that in an ideal world, land-ownership should be confined to the affluent. To this the authorities add the problems of servicing plotland areas. But the same difficulty, and the same absence of those services taken for granted in urban areas, is found everywhere in rural England. People who have always lived in sparsely populated districts accept this as the norm. People who move to such places must expect it. The plotland areas of other countries exhibit this assumption. In the Norwegian mountains, there is a *hytta* zone, where people build holiday huts or second homes, which for some become first homes because they have chosen a simple way of life. The normal urban services are neither provided nor expected. Conversely, there are plenty of plotland sites in Southern England, in the hinterland of established residential areas, denied services for years as a result of the pursuit of unattainable planning ideals, where the provision of a simple service like a hard road, however far below the standards of the highway engineer, and however little the residents could contribute to its cost, would have immeasurably upgraded the whole area.

The aesthetic objection to the plotland landscape expressed, no doubt, the received opinion of one particular generation. Time and again the critics complained in the 1920s about the 'cheap and nasty salmon-pink asbestos-cement roofs' of places like Peacehaven. Fifty to sixty years later those cheap and nasty roofs still exist, but have attracted moss and lichen and have the colour and appearance of Cotswold stone. Any new housing is raw and intrusive until it has mellowed into its surroundings. William Morris loathed Gower Street, for its soulless Georgian regularity, and wanted to blow it up. The Victorian bye-law street was despised for almost a century, but already has its champions [35] and we will no doubt soon have a society called Bring Back the Bye-law Street, especially since we have seen system-built tower blocks intended to replace it, built at terrifying cost and destroyed within one generation, long before they have been paid for. The semi-detached suburb, despised for years by the taste-makers, now has its fervent admirers [36]. The plotlands too have already reached the stage, as we noted at Jaywick, where their *ad hoc* aesthetics enchant people who find the work of the artless *bricoleur* more enticing than the calculated and expensive whims of architects.

There remains the land-use objection. It has been claimed for years that low-density housing of any kind, let alone plotlands, is wasteful and anti-social in a country like Britain. Frederic Osborn, as an advocate of low-density housing, argued that the produce of the ordinary garden, even though a small area of garden is devoted to food production, more than equalled in value the produce of the land lost to agriculture in commercial food production. Surveys conducted by government and by university departments in the 1950s proved him right [37]. Considering the smallholding aspirations of many plotlanders, it is as well to consider the argument of John Seymour who remarks:

> There is a man I know who farms ten thousand acres with three men (and the use of some contractors). Of course he can only grow one crop, barley, and of course his production *per acre* is very low and his consumption of imported fertiliser is very high. He burns all his straw, puts no humus on the land and he knows perfectly well his land will suffer in the end. He doesn't care — it will see him out. He is already a millionaire several times over. He is the prime example of that darling of the agricultural economist the successful agri-businessman [38].

The alternative he proposes is the same aspiration that appealed to many of the plotland settlers:

> Cut that land (exhausted as it is) up into a thousand plots of ten acres each, give each plot to a family trained to use it, and within ten years the production coming from it would be enormous... The motorist wouldn't have the satisfaction of looking out over a vast treeless, hedgeless prairie of indifferent barley — but he could get out of his car and wander through a seemingly huge area of diverse countryside, orchards, young tree plantations, a myriad of small plots of land growing a multiplicity of different

297

crops, farm animals galore, and hundreds of happy and healthy children... [39].

He is giving voice to the same dream that appealed to many of the original rural plotland buyers seventy or eighty years ago. But there is also the aspiration to build among people who are shut out of the ready-made housing market and whose yearnings are not met by the municipal housing sector. When an opportunity arises, as it did with the dweller-built houses promoted by the London Borough of Lewisham [40], the interest aroused indicates how widespread this submerged yearning is.

One of us had the opportunity in 1975 to address an audience of New Town officers and board members on the potential for a 'do-it-yourself new town', drawing on the pre-history of Basildon New Town as the plotlands of Pitsea and Laindon and on the Third World experience of site-and-service housing:

> Suppose we applied such a policy to some of the derelict inner city districts, in the man-made wastelands. Provide roads and services and a service core: kitchen sink, bath, WC and ring-main connection, put up some party walls (to overcome the fire risk objection) and you will have long queues of families anxious to build the rest of the house for themselves, or to employ one of our vast number of unemployed building workers to help, or to get their brother-in-law or some moonlighting tradesmen or the Community Industry to help, within the party walls. Such a carnival of construction would have important spin-offs in other branches of the social problems industry: *ad hoc* jobs and training for unemployed teenagers, turning the local vandals into builders, and the children into back-yard horticulturalists. Why, it would be like those golden days at Letchworth! [41].

Such an approach may seem more like the spirit of the mid-1980s than the mid-1970s but it did have echoes, apart from Lewisham, among people looking for dweller-involvement in housing. Don Ritson, when Assistant General Manager of Milton Keynes Development Corporation, won the support of his Board for an odd corner of the new city to be made available for an experiment in making plots available for people to build what they liked for living and working. Planning consent was withheld by the County Council, but the chairman of the Board, Lord Campbell of Eskan, was led to recall his experience many years ago in the sugar plantations of what was formerly British Guiana, where there were over 60,000 people living in 'disgraceful housing conditions which were morally, socially and politically' unacceptable:

> But with the price of sugar and the profitability of the company as low as it then was, by no stretch of the imagination could we afford to build proper houses for everybody. And then an idea struck me: why not lay out building plots on spare land adjacent to each

estate about ten to the acre; put in roads, drainage and water standpipes and let each family have a building plot, the materials of their present abode all (the buildings were in wood) with free paint, a present of £25 and an interest-free loan of £250 to be repaid slowly out of their wages. These modest figures went up later on. The scheme took on like wildfire, and within a few years virtually everyone was rehoused in the new areas. As there were no effective planning or building regulations in the Colony, every sort of house under the sun was built from corrugated iron shacks with the rest of the space on the plot used for cattle and goats, to palatial housing costing £10,000 or more [42].

The remembrance of this activity in the Third World led Campbell to urge the Town and Country Planning Association, as heirs to Ebenezer Howard's 'astonishingly fresh and relevant' principles of the garden city, to sponsor a Third Garden City which took note of intervening experience and current pre-occupations. Among his suggestions was the question:

Harking back to my unplanned but remarkably successful development on the coastlands of British Guiana, can we encourage social change by offering greater freedom for people to build their own homes to establish new communities? Is it possible to combine Howard's principle of a social environment in which the individual can develop his own ideas and manage his own affairs in cooperation with his neighbours: with essential environment planning? [43].

This challenge was taken up by the TCPA. The Association produced an outline prospectus for a Third Garden City, one of whose characteristics was to be that:

A great variety of housing accommodation would be encouraged and would, we believe, be possible. Conventional owner-occupant and local authority housing would not be specifically excluded but there would be a much higher proportion (at least 50 per cent) of housing accommodation provided through self-build, owner-starter homes, shared equity, co-operative owner-designed schemes, and by incorporating homes with workshops and other employment.

The prospectus stressed that:

A conscious effort throughout the planning, development and management of the town will be made to test traditional rules and assumptions, either before adopting them and/or by hypothesis and direct experiment. This will apply to such mundane matters as building and fire regulations, housing standards, road widths, site lines etc., and to basic social matters like education and health care [44].

The idea of a Third Garden City was to have two immediate results. The first was the formation of a cooperative housing and planning venture known as the Greentown Group, with the aim of building a new village on a site on the edge of Milton Keynes [45]. A second result was for the TCPA to establish a 'New Communities' project, designed to investigate whether innovative new settlements were really a practical possibility. When the project's working parties reported in 1982 the mood was one of optimism matched with a sense of realism about the constraints to be overcome [46].

Two institutional constraints invariably crop up when contemplating development initiatives from the 'bottom up' rather than from the 'top down'. One constraint obviously relates to the Planning Acts, devised as they were in part to combat the original self-build settlements of the 1930s. Over the years, high standards of housing design, layout and location have been introduced to prevent a repetition of haphazard landscapes like Laindon-Pitsea or Jaywick Sands that remain to this day a recurring nightmare in the minds of planners. A second constraint is to be found in building regulations and bye-laws. It is interesting to note what one of the TCPA's working parties had to say on this:

> The question of standards is a difficult one. Nowadays they are mainly applied through the building regulations which are set nationally but applied by local authorities with some regional variations. Originally standards were introduced to prevent exploitation of the individual by the housing developer. It is assumed that this reason for their continued existence would not apply in a new community... A community may decide to retain certain standards for the good reason that they are desirable. In the case of insulation, for example, the community may well wish to retain the current standards for insulation in new buildings or, more probably, impose even higher ones in order to reduce individual expenditure on fuel bills and to reduce the community's reliance on external sources of supply... Standards can be set by the community but can be regarded as ideals to be achieved over time rather than, as at present, all embodied in the construction immediately. In this way the community could achieve a lower initial cost and then improve the housing as more money became available. Such an option has obvious implications for the way in which housing is designed, and naturally certain standards would have to be built into dwellings during initial construction [47].

This cautious statement is much to be welcomed, in that it raises a crucial issue for advocates of self-help housing: that the major obstacle is not the planning legislation so much as the building regulations and the way in which they are locally interpreted, and that what begins as a substandard dwelling can evolve over time into a personal and social asset of high quality. In a similar vein, Bob Greenstreet has drawn attention to the incompatibility of centrally-imposed standards and localised initiatives:

300

In order to achieve the objectives of user participation in the housing field, an individualistic, informal approach to the building process would seem appropriate, given the possibility of non-expert administration, small scale construction and the wide range of solutions that could be employed to fulfil user satisfaction. This approach, however, is often restricted or contracted by the publicly imposed legislative requirements determining fixed criteria of acceptable performance and favouring standardised patterns of development [48].

And yet, while planning legislation and building regulations certainly impose serious constraints on experimental new forms of settlement, a consensus of public opinion would undoubtedly not wish to see their total abandonment. Over the years it is widely recognised that these measures have contributed to the protection of a countryside under persistent pressures and that, by and large, new developments have been physically tolerable if no more. These are no mean achievements, but it remains to be questioned whether the full paraphernalia of protective legislation needs to be applied unyieldingly in all places and for all uses. The present generation owes a debt to those who pushed back the frontiers of urban filth and squalor that characterised nineteenth-century cities, and who later worked to protect a diminishing countryside from indiscriminate development. But ways can surely be found to allow room for modern innovation without letting in all the evils of the past.

Without abandoning the general principle of environmental and building standards, a way forward might be to think in terms of localised areas where standards could be relaxed. Obviously these 'pockets of disorder' would not be in landscapes of special environmental quality but, like many of the plotlands of the past, could be in relatively secluded and out-of-the-way parts of the countryside. Likewise there is every reason to think in terms of inner-city wastelands (like the London Docklands) where both land and labour could be made available to create a new environment.

A precedent in relaxing standards in localised areas is to be found in Enterprise Zones, designed for employment rather than housing and for private profit rather than community gain. For all their differences the point is that something along the lines of 'Housing Enterprise Zones' is an idea which would undoubtedly provide scope for a variety of experiments. It is not a totally new idea. In 1969, in an article 'Non-Plan: An Experiment in Freedom', the question was asked: 'Why not have the courage, where practical, to let people shape their own environment?' [49]. It was not calling for an end to all planning, but suggested a few experimental zones in the first instance.

At a more localised level the architect Roger Westman has promoted a scheme called 'Walls' — described as 'a framework for communal anarchy' — where plots are laid out and made available with basic services only, leaving the residents to do their own thing within their own plots. A level of communal organisation is therefore guaranteed, yet with scope for individual variations and for improvements over time. Building regulations are again seen to be a constraint on local initiatives, 'protecting people from making mistakes, but in such a way that they cannot take risks, even when they are accountable only to themselves' [50].

In practical terms there is already evidence of growing support for localised initiatives and, in particular, for self-build housing as both an individual and a collective enterprise [51]. Some local authorities, for instance, make sites available as housing plots [52]. But availability and finance are still generally dependent on producing a fully-finished unit of housing from the moment of occupation. There is still a long way to go. Yet advocates of a 'new' approach take heart from the lesson of history, of the Third World, and of the plotlands that:

> ordinary people use resources and opportunities available to them with imagination and initiative when they have access to the necessary resources, and when they are free to act for themselves. Anyone who can see beyond the surface differences between the many forms of dwelling places people build for themselves is bound to be struck by the often astonishing economy of housing built and managed locally, or from the bottom up, in comparison with top-down, mass housing, supplied by large organisations and central agencies [53].

It is arguable that a society whose industrial base is slipping away, which cannot provide employment for its population, and where house-building, public or private, has reached its lowest ebb for decades, might well seek to encourage rather than deter those who choose to turn their own labour into capital, in housing themselves. Far from relegating the story of plotlands to the annals of history, there are lessons of endeavour that are of more than a passing interest for contemporary housing and planning.

NOTES

1. Miss Pat Green's recollection of her holiday home at Winchelsea Beach (see Chapter 3).
2. Mr A. Rice's recollection of holidays at Shoreham Beach (see Chapter 3).
3. Raymond Williams distinguishes between images and 'real history' in *The Country and the City*. London: Chatto and Windus, 1973.
4. Advertisements in various editions of *Dalton Weekly* 1937.
5. C.B. French to Gerard Young, 1966 (see Chapter 3).
6. Gilbert, Bentley B. (1973) Introduction to reprint of C.F.G. Masterman (ed.) *The Heart of the Empire*. Brighton: The Harvester Press.
7. Brandon, Peter (1980) Sussex and Surrey in the 1920s, Lecture to Rogate Field Course of Middlesex Polytechnic, 30 May.

8. Williams-Ellis, Clough (1930) Introduction to *The Face of the Land: The Year Book of the Design and Industries Association* 1929-1930. London: George Allen and Unwin.
9. Trevelyan G. M. (1938) Amenities and the State, in Williams-Ellis, Clough (ed.) *Britain and the Beast*. London: J. M. Dent.
10. Information from Tom Clarke. It is interesting to note that the sale of picnic sites in Hampshire continues through to the present day: 'One of the few remaining picnic sites where plots are for sale is in Horndean, Hampshire, just outside Portsmouth. The plot is at Stubbins Down in Catherington Lith, a wooded area divided into 170 picnic plots in the days when the tramline from Portsmouth terminated at Horndean, about 10 miles from the town. When the area was designated a picnic site all plots measured about 20ft. by 130ft., but the site was so popular that many owners extended their own plots by buying up their neighbours' land, and today they have substantial holdings.' *The Times*, 29 November 1982.
11. Minute by P.J.F. Mansfield: Ref. 91647/15/2, Public Record Office Ref. HLG/92/81.
12. Interview with John Heddle, 13 May 1980.
13. Motion put by John Heddle, Kent County Council meeting, 4 December 1975.
14. Dobry, George (1975) *Review of the Development Control System*. London: HMSO.
15. House of Commons Report, 19 November 1975.
16. House of Commons Report, 20 May 1980.
17. *Ibid*.
18. Department of the Environment (1979) Planning Decisions on Leisure Plots in Essex Press Notice No. 93, 8 March. London: Department of the Environment.
19. We'll kick them off the marshes: Private caravans anger Council, *Whitstable Times and Observer*, 6 June 1975.
20. Motion put by John Heddle, Kent County Council meeting, 4 December 1975.
21. Plot owners reap record crops, *Whitstable Times and Observer*, 10 October 1975.
22. *Ibid*.
23. Cronin, Anna and White, Andrew (1980) Blackwater fever: conservation and recreation management. *The Planner*, November.
24. *Ibid*.
25. Council fears for future of Essex coastline, *Daily Telegraph*, 23 March 1976.
26. *Maldon and Burnham Standard*, 24 July 1980.
27. *Ibid*.
28. *Maldon and Burnham Standard*, 22 August 1980.
29. *Maldon and Burnham Standard*, 24 July 1980.
30. Waddilove, Lewis (1962) *Housing Associations*. London: Political and Economic Planning.
31. Metcalfe, Jean (1980) *Sunnylea: A 1920s Childhood Remembered*. London: Michael Joseph.
32. Personal communication.

33. Habraken, N. J. (1972) *Supports: An Alternative to Mass Housing*. London: The Architectural Press.
34. *Ibid.*
35. Jones, M. Francis (1968) The aesthetic of the nineteenth-century industrial town, in Dyos H.J. (ed.) *The Study of Urban History*. London: Edward Arnold.
36. Oliver, Paul, Davis, Ian and Bentley, Ian (1981) *Dunromin: The Suburban Semi and its Enemies*. London: Hutchinson.
37. Best, R.H. and Ward, J.T. (1956) *The Garden Controversy*. Department of Agricultural Economics, Wye College, University of London.
38. Seymour, John (1974) *The Fat of the Land*. London: Faber and Faber.
39. *Ibid.*
40. Ellis, Charlotte (1980) Do-it-yourself vernacular building study. *The Architects' Journal*, 17 December.
41. Ward, Colin (1976) The Do-it-Yourself New Town, paper given at the Garden Cities/New Towns Forum, Welwyn Garden City 22 October 1975, partly printed in *Town and Country Planning*, May 1976, *The Municipal Review*, May 1976, and *Undercurrents*, June-July 1976.
42. Lord Campbell of Eskan (1978) The Future of the Town and Country Planning Association. Speech at the TCPA Annual General Meeting, 23 May 1978.
43. *Ibid.*
44. *A Third Garden City: Outline Prospectus*. London: TCPA, October 1979.
45. Cowan, Robert (1980) Greentown at Milton Keynes. *Town and Country Planning*, April.
46. TCPA New Communities Project (1982) Reports of Working Parties (unpublished).
47. TCPA New Communities Project (1982) Housing Working Party, Interim Report. London: TCPA.
48. Greenstreet, Bob (1981) The impact of building controls, in Hamdi and Greenstreet (eds.) *Participation in Housing*. Working Paper No. 58, Oxford Polytechnic, November.
49. Banham, Reyner, Barker, Paul, Hall, Peter and Price, Cedric (1969) Non-plan: an experiment in freedom. *New Society*, 20 March.
50. Roger Westman exhibited his scheme *Walls: A Framework for Communal Anarchy* at an exhibition on New Communities at the Institute of Contemporary Arts, June-July 1981.
51. See, for example Stead, Peter (1979) *Self-Build Housing Groups and Co-operatives*. London: Anglo-German Foundation.
52. Noble, John (1981) Housing plot developments compared, Part 2. *Architects Journal*, 11 March; Lewis, Sian (1981) *Plot Developments: Their Promotion and Control*. MA Dissertation, Oxford Polytechnic.
53. Turner, John F. C. and Roberts, Bryan (1975) The self-help society, in Wilsher and Righter (eds.) *The Exploding Cities*. London: Andre Deutsch.

Index

North Downs, 4
Norway, 296
Nottingham, 9, 10

Orwell, G., 38-39
Osborn, F.J., 297

Pagham Beach, 57, 102-109, 280
Palestine, 192, 241, 243
Paris: plotland suburbs, 261-263
pastoralism, 9-11
Peacehaven, 7, 51, 56, 66, 71-91,
    277
Penton Hook, 170, 172, 175, 176
Pett Level, 55, 62, 66, 69, 71, 278
Pevensey Bay, 56
Pharoah's Island, 168, 175
Picket Piece, 192, 241
Pickmere, 6
Pitsea, 7, 193-221
Planning Schemes, 41, 43, 46, 62,
    63, 67, 88, 198
Point Clear, 155, 161
Poland: plotland housing, 267
prices, plot and dwelling, 3, 22, 60,
    74, 89, 90, 93, 96, 105, 119, 122,
    124, 125, 142, 157, 158, 174, 197,
    200, 201, 221-223, 226, 238, 265,
    282, 287, 288
Priestley J.B., 39, 40
Proudhon, P.J., 27, 28
Public Health Act 1936, 46
Purley Park, 171, 181-184

railway carriages, converted, 3, 7,
    17, 25, 34, 36, 45-47, 60, 61, 67,
    68, 71, 91-93, 97-102, 105, 107,
    108, 126, 184, 251, 261, 278, 279
Ramuz, F.F., 116-118, 121, 132,
    133, 194, 195, 279
Ramuz, G., 116, 117, 133-136
ribbon development, 40, 42, 48, 85,
    89, 193
Romney Marsh, 55
Rottingdean, 74
Rousseau, J.-J., 36
Rural Amenities Bill 1929, 42
Rye Bay, 58-61, 71

Soviet plotlands, 268, 269
Spade Oak, 181
Spender, S., 38
squatting, 2, 4, 12-15, 46, 129, 180
Staines, 170, 172, 174, 175

Stedman, F., 118, 138-152, 161,
    251, 279
Steers, J.S., 6, 7, 50, 65, 66, 120,
    152, 153
Stockton, California, 251-254
Sunbury, 175
Surrey County Council Act 1931, 47
Synge, J.M., 28
Syrett, T., 199, 200
St Leonards, 7, 20, 240, 241
St Osyth, 155
Sandhills Meadow, 178
Scott Report, 50
Sea Palling, 119
Seasalter, 286-288
Selsdon Vale, 224, 234-237
Selsey Bill, 102, 279
Seymour, J., 297, 298
shanty towns, Third World, 270-272
Sharp, T., 21, 22, 38, 40, 48, 84
Sheail, J., 46
Shellness, 136
Shepperton, 176, 185
Sheppey, Isle of, 117, 132-138
Shoreham Beach, 7, 91-102, 281
Shoreham by Sea, 56
smallholdings, 7, 11, 18-22, 24, 28,
    77, 90, 178, 179
Smiles, S., 27
Smith, A., 26
Snettisham, 119
Society of Sussex Downsmen, 35, 57
Southend, 115, 116, 118, 125
South Wonston, 241
South Woodham Ferrers, 192, 221-
    225

Tagg's Island, 168
Tallahassee, Florida, 258
Tatsfield, 192
Teddington, 171 174
Thames Ditton, 172, 173
Thames Meadow, 176, 178, 179
Thames Preservation Act 1885, 166
Third Garden City, 299, 300
Thoreau, H.D., 10, 20, 28
Tolstoy, L., 10
Town and Country Planning Acts
    1932–1947, 43, 47, 48, 51, 63, 66,
    95, 96, 102, 171, 213, 283, 285
Town and Country Planning
    Association, 299-301
Town Development Act 1952, 127
Town Planning Act 1923, 41

tramcars, converted, 3, 7, 48, 60,
62, 184, 261
Trevelyan, G.M., 37, 282
Turner, J., 271, 272, 294

Walberswick, 119
Walderslade, 192, 231-232
Walton on the Naze, 117, 178
Whittam, J., 216-218
Wight, Isle of, 7, 20
Williams-Ellis, C., 39
Winchelsea Beach, 55, 58-61, 66, 68
Winsford Lower Flash, 6
Winstanley, G., 12, 13, 27
Wraysbury, 171
Wye Valley, 6

Young, G., 107-109